YO-CBV-536

THE

School Secretary's

HANDBOOK

JOHN ALLAN SMITH, Ed. D.

And Contributing Authors:

Helena Hilleary, Ed.D.

Russell E. Johnson, Ed.D.

Mary Givan Jones, M.A.

Clarice Olson Wells, M.S.

Pauline Hollis Belcher

Prentice-Hall, Inc. / Englewood Cliffs, N.J.

Sixth Printing.......... June, 1969

© 1962, by Prentice–Hall, Inc.

All rights reserved. No part of this book may be reproduced in any form, by mimeograph or any other means, without permission in writing from the publisher

Library of Congress Catalog Card Number: 62–9583

Printed in the United States of America. 79452—B&P

Property of
Norma Lyght

THE

School Secretary's

HANDBOOK

Preface

THE PURPOSE of this book is to help school secretaries and clerks perform their office work and other duties easily, quickly, and correctly. The book is a guide to those practices and procedures which experienced school secretaries have found useful. The book is intended to serve primarily the secretary who works in a school, whether elementary, high school, or junior college. It also is a reference work to which the secretary can turn when she has a bothersome question or an unfamiliar problem.

School office procedures are constantly emerging, developing, and increasing. The operation of schools, like knowledge itself, is becoming exceedingly complex. Training as a general secretary or office clerk now can only be regarded as a prerequisite. The position of school secretary is becoming a profession, or at least a sub-profession, in its own right. The diversity and multiplicity of services a school secretary is called upon to perform is evidenced in the comprehensive nature of this book itself.

The authors have designed this book to meet the needs of school office workers in all parts of the country, but one word of caution is in order: Every principal and every school has the right to specify how a task shall be done and what the responsibilities of a school secretary shall be. These individual preferences should be respected and observed.

Literally hundreds of successful school secretaries from all parts of the United States, in large schools and in small schools, have contributed their methods and techniques to this volume, and this debt is acknowledged with humility. Special appreciation is expressed to the officers and members of the National Association of Education Secretaries, an affiliate organization of the National Education Association. Finally, it is the desire of the authors to express by this means their gratitude to Mrs. Ella May Street for the countless hours of help she has given so unstintingly toward making this book a reality.

Contents

Figures

THE

School Secretary's

HANDBOOK

1

The Secretary and Her School

1

School Secretaryship as a Career

THE NUMBER of school secretaries is increasing with the growth in school population and the number of teachers. Every time a new school is opened or enlarged, another job as school secretary is created. And today, the school secretary is rapidly nearing professional status. Your opportunities to grow from a routine-type "clerical job" to a secretarial position with many interesting and varied activities are unlimited. However, you must first fully understand the school system and its overall purpose. Then you should become acquainted with the functions of all the service personnel in your school. They include everyone in the school who serves the student. The student is the *raison d'etre* for the school—otherwise the school would not exist.

YOUR RESPONSIBILITIES AS A SCHOOL SECRETARY

Primary responsibility. In essence, your primary concern is to help your boss (principal or superintendent) serve the students better. The school office is the heart of the school and the clearing center for the problems of pupils, teachers, parents, and many others. Your principal cannot be expected to perform efficiently the broader aspects of his position and at the same time have personal contact with everyone who seeks information or help from his office. You are the principal's right arm, the person who attends to the office duties, who conserves the principal's time and energy, and frees his mind from the responsibility of minor details.

Specific responsibilities. A school secretary worth her salt periodically checks her job responsibilities against what she is actually doing. It might be a good idea for you to check on some of your specific responsibilities. Are you living up to the expectation of the job? Are you actually serving a real purpose in the school as the secretary of the top notch leader of the school? Or are you becoming a "goof off"? Such secretaries can easily be replaced when the principal or others in the school catch on.

Mechanical responsibilities. A quick tour of the office will tell you if the clocks are on time, the lights working, the bells set to ring, the custodian on the job, the teachers' keys on hand, the sign-in sheet placed on the counter, the last of yesterday's mail in the teachers' boxes, the counter cleared, the supply shelves in order, fresh flowers arranged attractively. A note left by the night watchman tells you if anything unusual occurred during the night. A glance at the principal's desk and a quick replacement of penholder and telephone guide puts his desk in order. A thoughtful scanning of the principal's and your own daily calendar reminds you of appointments, reports, and special duties for that day.

You should also check your security measures. When you leave the office, whether for coffee, lunch, or at the end of the day, see that your desk is cleared of all readable material. Never leave correspondence, reports, or confidential material lying exposed on your desk. (Develop this habit in your principal, too. Or get him to let you help him.) Always check the office windows and doors (the principal's too) to see that they are locked. Turn off the lights before you leave.

Clerical responsibilities. Your clerical duties include planning the clerical work of the school office, handling the mail, typing the correspondence, organizing the files, handling the telephone or switchboard, serving as receptionist, and keeping the principal's calendar of appointments. You will also be expected to give school information to callers, parents, teachers, and pupils.

In the elementary school you must expect, at times, to be called upon to perform many different duties such as typing lesson materials for use of the teachers, scoring and entering test results in the pupils' Cumulative Guidance Records, acting as cashier in the cafeteria, selling theater or bus tickets, banking school moneys, telephoning the homes of absent pupils, reading children's absence excuses, handling lost-and-found articles, and administering first aid to pupils.

You are almost always the one who prepares attendance reports, issues supplies, and delivers messages to the custodian and others. Typing and duplicating, preparing requisitions and purchase orders, and stenciling notices to be read in the classroom or posted on the bulletin board are also part of your everyday duties.

Stenographic responsibilities. You may be asked to take dictation if you are so skilled and if your principal prefers not to write out his own letters. Most secretaries do possess stenographic skills and such skill should be a perquisite of the job. If you do not have adequate stenographic skills, then you cannot be classified as a top-flight secretary until you acquire them. Go to evening school and re-equip your stenographic skills. Raise your professional status!

Supervisory responsibilities. In high schools and very large elementary schools, you may be asked to supervise the activities of a small group of clerical employees, interpret school policies and procedures when necessary, attend administrative meetings and prepare agendas and minutes, type correspondence and reports of importance requiring a high degree of accuracy, organize and type the school budget, instruct personnel in duties of working in the attendance, counseling, and finance offices— even possibly the library. On the other hand, you may not be asked to supervise special jobs. For example, the work of the counseling office may be so specialized and voluminous that one of the clerks with highest classification will do all the supervising. However, some principals may ask you to supervise such jobs as organizing and editing material for the daily bulletin or the pupils' newspaper.

Another responsibility of this nature is to keep the handbook of the clerical staff up to date. It is your responsibility to keep this guide on hand for new employees and as reminders for other employees. It is your job to check with these people periodically to make sure if the handbook is an adequate guide.

OPPORTUNITIES AND REWARDS

Career opportunities. Boards of education, school superintendents, and principals have established a series of promotional positions each calling for more experience and qualifications and paying increasingly higher salaries. The lowest positions call for few if any office skills, but the employee should be a high school graduate. The school secretary learns her job after she is employed—all, that is, except for perhaps typing, some shorthand, and simple bookkeeping. Until very recently there were no courses, workshops, or institutes a school secretary could attend to learn the specific skills needed on her job. Even today there are only several junior colleges, adult evening schools, and one or two universities in the entire United States offering training to prepare for the profession of school secretary.

School secretaries must learn their duties from their principals and other school secretaries, by reading secretarial magazines, or by attending meetings of school secretaries at which they can exchange ideas and experiences. The National Association of Educational Secretaries, with state and district associations, is an example of an organization for school secretaries. This national organization is affiliated with the National Education Association, the nationwide teachers' organization.

Types of positions. If you are thinking of enhancing your career opportunities in school secretaryship, you should have some knowledge of the three basic types of positions. Figure 1 shows the relative importance of positions in the three branches of educational secretaryship. As you move up the employment ladder in a school system, you will be paid more because your services are worth more. Positions at the top of the chart pay the highest salaries and positions at the bottom pay the lowest. Positions shown on the same horizontal line pay approximately equal salaries. Note, however, that few school districts use exactly the titles listed below nor do they pay exactly the same salary for the same type of service. This chart indicates only relative occupational status and salary.

Figure 1. Career opportunities in school secretaryship.

SECRETARIAL	CLERICAL	"BOOKKEEPING"
Require shorthand and typing	Require typing	Require bookkeeping
1. *Administrative Secretary		
2.	*Principal Clerk	*Auditor
3. Senior Secretary, Secretary-Stenographer		
4. Secretary (High School)		*Senior Financial Clerk *Senior Bookkeeping Operator
5. Intermediate Secretary Elementary School Secretary *Receptionist-Secretary	*Senior Clerk	*Financial Clerk *Bookkeeping Machine Operator
6. Junior Secretary	Clerk	*Junior Bookkeeping Machine Operator *Clerk-Bookkeeper
7. Secretary-Clerk	Intermediate Clerk	
8.	Junior Clerk	

* Indicates jobs not commonly found in individual schools; but rather, in the central administrative offices of a board of education.

Status and prestige. We now need to take a look at some of your other opportunities and rewards. The school secretary enjoys preferred status in the eyes of teachers, custodians, and other school employees. They know that she has the ear of the principal, is the first to know of imminent changes, is the one who controls supplies, is the one who can grant or deny small courtesies, and can even express a good or unfavorable opinion about the quality of another person's work. Some secretaries for these reasons are unjustly—and justly—charged with being the real principal of the school or at least the power behind the throne. The secretary with a power complex in her personality can ride roughshod over teachers and pupils alike. For this very reason, the effective school secretary should always be most careful in her words and actions so that no one will be able to charge her with letting her job go to her head.

Working conditions. A five-day work week is customary. A workday of seven and a half or eight hours is standard in most schools, and the school office provides as pleasant physical surroundings as are likely to be found anywhere.

Overtime work. At times, especially when reports are due, the school secretary may have to work overtime. While overtime pay is possible, many schools prefer to allow time off (compensatory time) on some other day when things are less rushed. This is, however, not considered good personnel practice in many schools. When you wish to utilize compensatory time, always ask for it; never state, "Mr. Principal, I'll not be here tomorrow. I'm taking compensatory time." In other words, don't just take compensatory time; ask for it.

CHARACTERISTICS OF THE OUTSTANDING SCHOOL SECRETARY

What are the characteristics of the outstanding school secretary? This is a question you should ask yourself from time to time. Someone at sometime must have thought you had secretarial potential or thought you would grow into the job. The following checkpoints should help you in your answer. If most of your answers are in conflict, then you should seriously consider whether or not you should remain in the position. The outstanding school secretary would have the following characteristics with regard to her interests, aptitudes, abilities, and temperament.

Interests. She is a person who enjoys the routine of office work and is interested in people, particularly children. In fact, she has high tolerance for children and their behavior. She is the kind of person who likes orderliness without being compulsive about it. She has an interest in adults, too, and has the capacity to accept their foibles, a feeling that she might even be able to help them with their problems. She feels a certain compulsion to get the job done right and yet she does not feel annoyed when she must do checking, re-adding, and retyping that may be necessary. She is more inclined, if in doubt, to look up needed information than to guess. She likes to plan and organize. She enjoys learning new methods and techniques, and she takes satisfaction in her newly acquired information. She has sufficient mechanical interest and aptitude so that she can operate office machines and devices, and feels some assurance in removing a screw or fastening down a bolt.

Aptitudes and abilities. She is a person who is sensitive to the proper use of language, knows when it is used incorrectly, and has an appreciation for expressions which are apropos. She also is able to add long columns of numbers accurately. She develops the ability to recall proper names and directions, and she possesses some aptitude for figuring out answers for herself. She is able to schedule her own work to meet deadlines and has the self-discipline to see that they are met. Being efficient she is able to speed up when necessary and to coast at appropriate times. She has an aesthetic sense and a feeling for symmetry, balance, and proportion. This ability is an asset to her in keeping the office pleasing and in producing work that is attractive.

Temperament. She is a person who likes to have children around, yet she possesses the firmness to tell them to "be on their way" when she has her own work to perform. She does not feel annoyance at repeated and continued interruptions, and she does not experience too severe frustrations if she has to lay aside her work again and again to do jobs for the principal and others.

The outstanding school secretary finds it easy to make the principal's interests her interest. She takes pride in being closemouthed and open-eared, especially when trusted with confidences; she has developed the temperament to be a good, sympathetic listener but not given to making everybody's problems her problems. She has abundant energy, a zest for what the school is doing, a pleasant voice, and no tendency to jump into a task before she has had adequate instruction or has only half thought through what she is to do.

OPPORTUNITIES FOR ADVANCEMENT

There is a real future in educational secretaryship. It need not be a stop-gap job until you marry. School districts know that it is far less expensive to retain you as an employee than to let you go and then hire and train another girl.

Benefits of your position. School districts will go to great lengths to keep you on the payroll. They will give you sick leave, maternity leave, or a personal leave. They will transfer you from one office to another, or from one school to another as openings permit. Salaries are arranged so that you receive annual, automatic increases in pay, up to three or five, in each higher bracket you attain. There are vacation and retirement plans; and if you quit, your retirement money is refunded with interest. There are parties and clubs to take care of your social needs and provide you with a way to voice your opinions, even grievances. Why all this? Because as a good secretary you are a valuable employee—and you become ever more valuable as you gain experience.

Earn and advance as you learn. The beginning school secretary earns while she learns. Every school district provides the basic training, together with conferences, workshops, and institutes for the improvement of their secretarial staff. Your complete training is worth a college education to you. As you increase your skills and knowledge, you will become eligible for advancement and higher pay. These promotional opportunities are open to every school secretary. Each is given an opportunity by examination and interview to demonstrate promotional qualifications. A system equivalent to Civil Service protects you in every promotion you earn, and assures you of equal treatment in moving to the next higher rank. The top positions are executive in status and responsibility and pay salaries comparable to those received by teachers.

Recognition through National Association of Educational Secretaries. The National Association of Educational Secretaries has done much to give recognition to school secretaries and to encourage them to increase their qualifications. The association has developed a "Professional Standards Program" whereby the educational secretary is certified nationally for her achievements and accomplishments. There are nine levels or grades of certificates based on experience, education, and professional activity. Credit is given up to eight years of experience without college training. Education can be evidenced by college courses or by taking tests given by the Association. A point system governs the evaluation of one's participation in professional and association activities.

2

The American Educational System

PERHAPS you went to an elementary school that included kindergarten through the sixth grade and from there you went to a junior high school for three years, followed by senior high school for three more years. It is quite likely, on the other hand, that you went to an elementary school that ran from first through eighth grade, then to a high school for four years. In any event, not counting kindergarten, there were twelve grades or years to your elementary and high school education. Also, many states offer two years of junior college education as part of the public school system.

Schools of yesterday and today. As you entered your secretarial duties, you probably found your own school days coming back in vivid force to your memory. Even now, you'll find yourself recalling how things used to be when you were a pupil, and you'll be making comparisons. Sometimes you'll be wondering if all the changes you see around you are for the best. Many times you'll wonder if all these things really happened when you were going to school. Then there'll be times when you'll have to admit that pupils today get a lot more attention and service than in the "good old days."

EDUCATIONAL LEVELS

As a school secretary, you may be employed in one of the following educational levels: elementary; junior high or senior high school; a junior college; or in the central administrative offices of the board of education. You should be acquainted with the function of all the educational levels so that you can better understand your role in your particular position.

Elementary schools. All elementary schools, whether of six or eight grades, are administered by a principal. Unless the school is very small, there will be only one school secretary or school clerk. Some large elementary schools now employ a second clerk.

Nature of instructional program in elementary schools. Elementary schools offer basic instruction in reading, writing, spelling, penmanship, arithmetic, science, social studies (geography, history, civics), physical education and health, art, music, and sometimes homemaking for girls and industrial arts for boys. Kindergarten and grades one and two (and sometimes three) are often called the "primary" or "lower grades." Grades three and four in a six-year elementary school or grades four, five, and six in an eight-year school are called "intermediate" or "middle grades." Grades five and six in a six-year elementary school and grades seven and eight in an eight-year school are called "upper grades."

Division of the elementary school day. The school day for kindergarten and primary pupils is shorter than for pupils in the middle and upper grades. Pupils in the upper grades may attend school for five hours a day, whereas pupils in kindergarten and the primary grades may only attend three hours. Sometimes crowded elementary schools may have two kindergarten classes, one in the morning and one in the afternoon, both taught by the same teacher. Each school day will have morning and afternoon recess periods. Some schools may have varying dismissal times usually depending upon the weather, transportation, and other conditions.

Regular personnel of the elementary school. On the staff of the medium-sized elementary schools, besides the principal and teachers, are to be found one or more custodians, perhaps a gardener, a cafeteria manager and several cafeteria helpers. The custodian performs the janitorial services for the school, helps unload supplies and equipment, changes lightbulbs, and fuses, and does a host of minor repairs and services. The gardener trims the hedges, mows and waters the lawn, cleans the walks, marks off the playground area, and cares for the fences. The cafeteria manager often arrives on the job earlier than you, and except for a request for some secretarial help and cashiering, you may see little of her except at coffee time and lunch. Somehow she and her assistants seem to manage quite well by themselves.

Other school personnel. Other school personnel make their appearance on more or less fixed schedules. The man who picks up and delivers school mail, the bus driver or drivers, the repairmen, the locksmith, the electrician—all present themselves to the school secretary, sometimes only for the purpose of checking in and out. The school nurse comes one or more days a week, and the school physician less frequently. The attendance officer—you used to know him as the "hooky cop"—calls frequently to check on pupils unduly absent. The school psychologist and psychometrist may call less frequently. They come to confer about children with various problems and to test the intelligence and special capacities of pupils as requested by the principal. The school supervisor or supervisors occasionally call to confer with the principal, meet teachers, or to hold meetings about the curriculum and instruction. These are the employees of the school district you will meet and come to know well. There will be others you will meet less frequently, sometimes only by means of the telephone or memoranda. They all make up your fellow employees in the elementary school. Larger schools may also have an assistant or vice-principal, a librarian, and teachers of music, art, and physical education.

Secondary schools. Whereas elementary schools usually have but one office—the "principal's office"—most junior and senior high schools have several offices with a staff of school clerks and a senior clerk or school secretary to serve as office manager and secretary to the principal. Essentially the same services are performed in the secondary school as in the elementary school except that they are likely to be more complex and numerous.

Nature of instructional program in the high school. High schools generally offer a broad, diversified instructional program to meet the common educational needs and to serve various individual interests and talents. Every student will be in class for at least six periods a day, one of which may be spent in the study hall. In elementary school, pupils are promoted by an entire grade; in secondary school, they are promoted by separate subjects.

Students taking courses designed to prepare for entrance to college may be referred to as "college preparatory" students. Sometimes they may be called "academic" students, though "academic" usually is reserved to describe individual classroom courses such as mathematics, foreign language, and science. All other students may be described as "non-academic," "non-college preps," or even "general." Such designation simply means that such students are not planning to enter a college or university. Though in all fairness to this latter group of students, it should be asserted that most students taking college preparatory courses won't go to college either. A lot of young people know that to be a "college prep" student carries social prestige and insist upon being enrolled in such courses even though they have little ability to do the work or there is small likelihood that they will enter a college or university.

Many high schools classify their pupils, according to the major field of study being taken, as "mathematics," "science," "homemaking," "industrial arts," "business education," or "art" majors.

Division of the school day. One of the major organizational differences between an elementary school and a secondary school is that pupils in an elementary school spend the entire day with the same teacher, whereas the students in a junior or senior high school have different teachers and subjects every hour or period. Schools differ in the length of a period, which is usually from 40 to 55 minutes. The number of periods in a school day is generally six to eight.

Most secondary schools designate one period in the day, often the first or second period, as a home room period. This period is for the purpose of taking attendance and reading the daily bulletin to the students. It is a time for selling tickets and giving information to students. Sometimes this period is incorporated into a regular period which runs five or ten minutes longer than the other periods. On days when assemblies are held, most high schools have shorter class periods. Special schedules may also be arranged for days when faculty meetings and special athletic events are to occur. There also may be a separate schedule for final examination week.

Regular personnel of the high school. Every high school is headed by a principal who may be aided by one or more assistant principals or vice-principals. Assistant principals usually assume responsibility for handling disciplinary problems, guidance, athletics, and the social program of the school. Sometimes a teacher may, in addition to teaching, be designated as "dean of girls" or "dean of boys" for the purpose of handling the respective problems of girls or boys. A counselor or staff of "grade" counselors may be assigned full or part time to interview and counsel pupils about their progress in class, job opportunities, scholarships, college entrance requirements, military obligations, and a host of personal problems. A registrar or attendance adviser may be assigned to record attendance and check upon absences. All of these administrators and teachers, including the school librarian, have files and records to maintain. A major task of any secretary assigned to one of these persons is to learn the problems and special procedures that are to be met in their offices.

Every secondary teacher, it might be added, has some non-teaching responsibility, such as sponsoring a club, doing office work, advising the student newspaper staff, or handling audio-visual aids.

Other personnel of the high school. A high school will have every type of school employee to be found in an elementary school, and more. There will be typewriter repairmen, toolkeepers, finance managers, not to mention several others. Because there are ever so many more subjects taught in a high school than in an elementary school, there will be many more supervisors calling upon the school to work with the teachers and to coordinate what is being taught. There will be someone responsible for every subject area as English, music, science, or social studies. In school districts with but one or two high schools, one supervisor may coordinate a group of subjects.

Junior high schools. Most junior high schools require that all pupils take essentially the same courses. There may be a limited choice of subjects or electives. Senior high schools, particularly for eleventh and twelfth grade students, allow considerably more freedom of choice in the courses that a pupil can elect and those that he is required to take for graduation or university admission.

The guidance program. Most modern high schools, including junior high schools, have a guidance program to supplement the curriculum. The purpose of the guidance program is to help students select the courses they should take to prepare for employment or college, apply for scholarships, and understand their interests and aptitudes. It also serves to counsel them about personal, social, and financial problems.

Junior colleges. The office organization of a junior college is likely to be much like that of a high school. The functions of athletics, social events, guidance, finance, curriculum, and attendance all must be supervised. The same is true of a college or university except that there will be many more offices with their own clerical staffs to do the work.

A public junior college is usually administered by a board of education in the same way as an elementary or high school. Often the same board of education controls the elementary schools, the high schools, and the junior college of a district. Occasionally there are separate boards of education.

Nature of the instructional program. Most junior colleges offer two years of education beyond high school. These two years, if the student chooses his courses with care, are equivalent to the freshman and sophomore years of the university. Frequently such junior college courses are called "transfer" courses because the student can transfer his credit to the university with no loss in time or standing. Other junior college courses may not carry university credit. These are courses usually designed to prepare the student for employment. They often are called "terminal" courses because the student is not expected to continue further study beyond graduation from junior college. Instead of a diploma, as in a high school, the junior college student who completes the prescribed two-year course usually receives an Associate in Arts or an Associate in Science degree. Most states have laws which prescribe the requirements.

Personnel of the college. The administrator of a junior college most often is called a "director" but also may be called "president" or just "principal." He is assisted by assistant directors or deans. Sometimes these titles are equivalent and sometimes they are not. College instructors, other personnel, and personnel guidance programs are very similar to those found in high schools.

ORGANIZATION OF THE SCHOOL DISTRICT

Every public school is part of a school district. A school district is a geographical area in which all the schools are under the direction of a common board of education and administered by a superintendent of schools. A school district may be only one school or many schools; it may include only elementary schools, or only high schools, or only junior colleges. It may combine both elementary and high schools; it may even include the junior colleges. The legal boundaries of a school district are not always the same as those of the city in which the individual schools are located.

The board of education. All public schools in America are headed by a board of education or board of school trustees. These board members are usually elected by the voters living in the school district. It is the job of the board of education to hire a superintendent of schools and to be concerned with the functioning of the schools. The number of members on a school board varies from three to nine or more people. Five is the most common number of elected board members.

Functions and limitations. No board of education is completely free to do as it pleases. First of all, boards of education must please the tax-payers, parents, pupils, teachers and, yes, school secretaries. Second, boards of education are limited by state law in what they can and cannot do. These laws are passed by the state legislature or are approved directly by the voters themselves. Sometimes the state places responsibility upon the state superintendent of public instruction to set up rules, regulations, and procedures for the conduct of schools. If so, then your board of education must also carry out and enforce such regulations.

The major functions of the board of education are to establish policies for running the schools, to establish a curriculum and course of study, to adopt a budget to cover the payment of teachers' salaries and other expenses of operating the schools, and to hear the wishes and problems of taxpayers and others interested in the welfare of the schools.

"Bosses." Sometimes a board of education is responsible, not to the electors directly, but to the city council or other designated civic body. If so, you can be sure such a board of education also will have a whole set of mandatory regulations which they must abide by and uphold. So, even a board of education can and does have its "bosses."

Meetings. Meetings of the board of education are held at regular intervals, sometimes twice a month and sometimes more often. Detailed minutes are kept of the transactions of each meeting and the names of the members present. The recording and typing of these minutes undoubtedly is the responsibility of some secretary in your school district.

The superintendent of schools. The board of education selects a superintendent of schools to administer the schools. Usually the superintendent works under a contract of four years, more or less, which can be renewed. The superintendent must attend all board of education meetings.

The superintendent's cabinet. Most superintendents have a cabinet or council composed of principals, supervisors, and other administrators to advise them on policies and procedures. It is at these cabinet meetings that the superintendent does much of his work. He hears about the problems connected with running the schools, discusses solutions, and arrives at courses of action. He explains to the principals the wishes and sentiments of the board of education. Sometimes minutes are kept of these meetings, and usually "outside" people may attend only upon invitation.

Assistant superintendents. Whenever there are as many as five or more schools in a district, there are generally assistants to the superintendent. These assistants are assigned in various areas of responsibilities such as: personnel, instructional services, educational services, elementary and secondary education, and business services.

The business manager. Frequently the business manager also carries the title of assistant or associate superintendent. The business manager handles a great variety of details such as directing the custodians in the care of the buildings, purchasing supplies and equipment, buying land for new schools, working with architects in the design of new buildings, making out the annual budget, making out the payroll, and running the school cafeteria. The business manager needs the services of several secretaries and clerks to help him with all his work.

The director of instruction. Whenever there are a number of schools in the district—eight or more—there is likely to be a director in charge of instruction or educational services. Frequently his title is that of assistant superintendent in charge of educational services. His work is to plan the course of study, select the textbooks, evaluate the progress of the pupils from one grade to another, prepare publications that will help teachers know what is to be taught in the different grades and classes, provide for the guidance and testing of pupils, and to conduct educational meetings for teachers and principals.

Supervisors of special areas. The assistant superintendent in charge of educational services and the various supervisors will have a group of clerks and school secretaries to assist them. Often the assistant superintendent is assisted by one or more supervisors who will be responsible for such special areas as music, art, health, elementary education, secondary education, and attendance. There also may be psychometrists to give mental tests to individual students and psychologists to advise about the education of pupils having difficulty in school.

Personnel director. Many districts also employ a director of personnel to hire the teachers and other school personnel. Sometimes this director reports to one of the assistant superintendents or, as often is the case, he reports directly to the superintendent himself. The day is fast disappearing when school principals do their own hiring of teachers.

Three major divisions. From what has been said about the administrators of a school district, it may be inferred that there are at least three main divisions in the organization of a school district. This is true of all school districts, whether large or small. The main divisions of a school system are (1) business services, (2) educational services, and (3) instruction. The first two divisions constitute the central administrative offices or staff of a school district. The third division comprises the individual schools and all the principals and teachers.

Growth of school districts. As a district adds schools and becomes ever larger, the business and educational divisions also grow and subdivide into a whole series of branches or offices. This is because more services are demanded, and smaller groups can be more highly specialized in their services. In a large school district, the business and educational divisions can become exceedingly complex, and hundreds of people may be employed in them to keep the school system functioning smoothly. Just like a railroad or radio station, a school district has to run on a clocklike-precision schedule every school day of the term. It takes careful planning with everyone's shoulder close to the wheel to make certain that everything in every school is in readiness when the bell rings each morning. Every school secretary carries her full share of this responsibility.

Function of the central office. Most lay people are only vaguely aware that there is a central office or headquarters for the superintendent and his staff of aides. It is easy for the general public to get this impression. They see school buildings here and there with principals, teachers, and pupils, but the average person has to stop a moment to realize that someone has to make out the payrolls for these teachers and principals, to buy the chalk and paper, to choose the textbooks, to hire the teachers, the custodians, and the clerks. Providing these services is the role of the central office or administrative staff.

Certificated and classified employees. Employees in the schools generally fall into two categories: the certificated, and the classified or non-certificated employees.

Certificated employees. Every teacher and principal, by law, must have a license or certificate to teach. Sometimes this is called a credential. A credential to teach is issued on much the same basis as a lawyer or doctor or accountant is authorized to practice his profession. Every teacher must complete a university education with specified courses in teaching methods and educational psychology. (Although all university courses, properly speaking, are education, professional courses specifically designed to prepare people to teach are called "education" in contrast to "law" or "medicine" or "accounting".) No public board of education is permitted to employ a teacher unless that person holds a valid license or credential to teach. Formerly it was possible for a person to take an examination and if he passed, to receive a credential without regard to how much college work he had done. This is now a thing of the past.

Classified or non-certificated employees. Besides the employment of teachers there are many other employees hired by the board of education. The reader of this book may be one of them. There are secretaries, clerks, bus drivers, custodians, cafeteria workers, gardeners, stationary engineers, plumbers, carpenters, electricians, painters, locksmiths, and a host of other skilled workmen. The state usually does not require credentials for these people to become employees of the board of education. The expression "non-certificated" employee is rapidly disappearing and its place is being taken by the term "classified" employee. Many boards of education have found it necessary to rate or classify the so-called non-certificated employees on the basis of their skills and training in order to have a fair and just basis for paying salaries. Hence, non-certificated employees are more properly being designated "classified" employees. As a secretary, you are a classified employee.

FEDERAL, STATE, AND COUNTY DEPARTMENTS OF EDUCATION

United States Office of Education. In America the United States Office of Education, which is a part of the Federal Department of Health, Education, and Welfare, plays but an indirect role in the operation of local school districts. This is not true of ministries of education in other countries, but in America each state and local district is responsible for its own schools. In some cases, the federal government works through the department of education of each state, which in turn follows the chain of command down to the local school district.

Function of the United States Office of Education. The major functions of the United States Office of Education are to collect national statistics and facts about education, to provide information about education and educational facilities, to serve as a liaison body between American and foreign educators, and to distribute federal funds (particularly for vocational education, national defense, and research) as Congress directs to the several states, who then redistribute the moneys to their own schools.

State departments of education. A state department of education usually is responsible for the operation of the educational program within its state. Its functions are governed by the state constitution and statutes, the state board of education, and the state superintendent or commissioner of public instruction. The state department of education establishes the broad features of the state educational program which local schools and school districts are expected to observe and enforce. The department also distributes funds for operating the schools. The amounts may vary from little to almost the total cost of operation. Authority for operating schools derives from laws adopted by the state legislature and through state referendums. School laws are generally written into book form and are referred to as the "Education Code."

County boards of education. The functions of a county board or office of education differ with each state. In some states the county office operates as a school district, administering the schools, hiring the teachers, and educating the pupils. In other states the county board of education may stand as an intermediate unit between the state department and the local school district. As such it may serve primarily as a channel to distribute state and county funds to the several school districts, to disseminate state policies and regulations, and to receive statistical reports concerning attendance, budgets and building construction. It may or may not have subject supervisors to help write courses of study and to work with teachers in the development of their teaching skills.

County services. By mutual agreement, individual school districts may contract with a county to perform services which might be too expensive for any one of the districts alone. Among such services might be the employment of doctors and nurses, the purchase of library books and motion picture film, the production of educational television programs, and the scoring of tests.

3

Working with the School Principal

THE SCHOOL SECRETARY is the principal's indispensable aide. Your principal will learn to delegate to you his responsibilities as office manager. In this capacity, you will perform for him many official and personal services. You will become, in effect, his eyes, ears, and memory—and often his spokesman.

As you perform your day-to-day functions, you will become more and more aware of what your job entails. This chapter is designed to help you improve your working relationship with your principal. It gives you general guidelines to help you in working with your principal, and more specific information regarding your principal's callers, his calendar, his appointments, his desk, his office and personal details, his faculty meetings, his service club obligations, and his professional and honorary organizations.

GENERAL GUIDELINES IN WORKING WITH YOUR PRINCIPAL

As you start to work with your principal, both of you should have clearly in mind your share of the office routine. You should know the best channels of communications with your principal and the limits of your authority. The following guidelines will help you improve your working relationship with your principal:

1. Find out which duties your principal ranks "top priority." Work out a list of duties for various times of the year: before the opening of school, during holidays, at the close of the year.
2. Determine how far your own initiative should extend. Know which types of problems go to your principal, to the teachers, to the custodians, to the central office.
3. Study the instructional guides and bulletins issued by the central office of the district.
4. Study the files for examples of adopted procedures.
5. Brief the principal on official information that reaches you unofficially even if you think he already knows it. Filter out the trivial information.

6. Accept your principal as the administrative leader of your school. Don't fight him or his ideas.

7. Observe the order your principal follows in doing things and the items on which he spends the most time.

8. Assess your own characteristics and see how they complement those of your principal.

9. Try not to make snap judgments. Think before doing or saying anything concerning the school program or the principal's purposes. When questions are directed to you that you do not wish to answer, you can say pleasantly, "I don't think that has been fully decided yet," "I really don't know all the details," or "Mr. (principal) is handling that situation."

10. Know at all times where your principal can be found. After you have had experience in handling various types of callers when your principal is out, you will become more discreet in following his wishes. "Mr. (principal) is away from his desk" or "Mr. (principal) has just stepped out" will satisfy most callers. If your principal is negligent about this matter or steps out of the office without telling you where he is going, study his habits to discover where you may most likely find him. Never admit to anyone that you do not know where to locate your principal.

11. Design a schedule for ending the day's work according to your principal's schedule and your own. Establish a time for taking dictation, checking reports, signing payrolls, and making appointments with callers.

    Have your own schedule of work, a time for transcribing dictation, doing reports, preparing the school bulletins, counting school moneys, and other items ready for his signature.

12. Ask your principal to list items he wants you to take care of, the times they must be completed, and to whom he wants copies sent. Note these items in the same notebook you use for dictation. Do not use slips of paper, another notebook, or depend on your memory.

Your principal's callers. Your principal will have many callers throughout the day—those with appointments and those who just drop in.

Appointments. If the caller has an appointment, do not let him wait much past the appointment time. If callers have to wait ten or fifteen minutes to see the principal, and when teachers have to make an appointment to see your principal, his appointment schedule is not working properly. Announce to your principal (by note, buzzer system, or orally) "Your 2:30 appointment, Mr. (caller), is waiting to see you."

Drop-ins. Inquire tactfully of drop-in callers how long their business will take. Check with your principal before telling any drop-in caller that the principal is or is not available.

Ushering in a caller. When ushering in a caller, lead him toward your principal's desk, stepping aside so as not to stand between him and the caller. No formal introduction is needed. Merely announce the caller's name to your principal. It also may be advisable to give your principal a slip of paper with the caller's name on it.

Your principal's calendar. Your principal's calendar provides a list of each day's commitments and a record of the day's activities. To keep your principal's calendar functioning properly:

1. Make and check entries on at least three calendars, your principal's desk calendar, his pocket calendar, and your own desk calendar.

2. Check your principal's desk calendar each day for appointments scheduled. It is a good idea to check appointments for the following day and even a week ahead.

3. Watch your principal's calendar closely for appointments he may make without telling you. Encourage him to inform you of appointments he may have arranged on his own.

4. Tell your principal about appointments you have made for him and enter those on his calendar.

5. Make, at the beginning of each school year, calendar entries of recurring and established events for the year. Search the school district's master calendar for dates of concern to your school and principal.

6. Note on important school events, holidays, and important personal days, such as the birthday of your principal's wife and his college class reunion.

7. Enter advance reminders of time-consuming tasks, such as speeches, and reports that the principal must personally prepare.

8. Duplicate on your principal's calendars only those entries that are important to both the principal and you.

9. Turn your principal's desk calendar to the current date each day.

10. List appointments with the hour, including those copied from your principal's pocket calendar. Also include the matters of the appointments.

11. Enter on your own calendar all the items on your principal's calendar plus notations of your own responsibilities and appointments.

Calendar manufacturers produce renewable and permanently bound diaries designed to suit almost every need and preference. At least two manufacturers sell calendars starting on September 1 and running to the end of the academic year. Pocket calendars that start a new page with Sunday are preferable to those that run every day of the month one after the other.

Your principal's appointments. Remind your principal of his appointments for the day. You may wish to type a list of your principal's appointments.

Appointments away from the school. If your principal has an appointment away from the school, be sure to include in his briefcase the appropriate papers for the meeting or conference he is to attend. You may wish to include extra notepaper, sharpened pencils, and if he is leaving town, envelopes stamped and addressed to the school.

Help your principal to leave his office in time for any outside appointment. You may need to get him out of the office past persons who are insistent upon seeing him. When he is on his way to an appointment, never usher in a drop-in visitor unless you are quite certain that the principal is desirous of seeing him. Indicate by gesture (your principal's briefcase or portfolio in your hand) to the detaining visitor that your principal has an outside appointment and must leave immediately.

Buzzer system. You may work out a buzzer or other signal system to help your principal terminate an interview when it runs overtime. One technique is to write a note and take it to him. Another is to telephone your principal or tell him in the visitor's presence that someone is waiting for him. Beware, though, of rudeness.

Your principal's desk. Arrange your principal's desk as he wants it— otherwise, little or nothing on the desk top, except for work trays and perhaps personal reminders.

See that your principal's desk is dusted every day. Check frequently that supplies are replenished. If your principal smokes, check to see that the ashtrays are kept clean.

Your principal's office and personal details. You will soon learn to bring up ticklish details only when things are going well with your principal. You should be very tactful in mentioning these items. Whenever you have a great deal of work to do, tell your principal early in the day. Ask him if there is anything more urgent.

It is a good idea to keep a small can of spot remover and a clothes brush on hand. You will find it worthwhile to install a small mirror in the principal's desk or coat closet. (Occasionally you might compliment your principal when he is dressed particularly well.)

Ask your principal if he wishes you to list his appointments with the dentist, tailor, or barber (or, if the principal is a woman, appointments with her hairdresser).

Your principal's faculty meetings. Most faculty meetings are held on a regular schedule. The faculty meeting is your principal's opportunity to communicate directly with his teachers. Faculty meetings must be well planned. They should be as short as possible, particularly when held at the end of the day. You can contribute toward these objectives by noting the following points.

1. Keep a folder marked "Faculty Meeting" into which you and your principal place items to be brought up at the next faculty meeting.
2. Remind your principal to plan the faculty agenda a day or two in advance.
3. Remind your principal to secure outside speakers sufficiently in advance to insure their presence.
4. Notify all those who are to be present. Place a reminder in the daily bulletin and on the faculty bulletin board.
5. Arrange for the meeting place and check it for ventilation, lighting, seating space, and availability. In emergencies, you might even need to dust off the podium or chairs.

6. Provide for equipment such as charts, easels, and projectors, and, if required, an operator for the projector.
7. Provide forms and assemble other materials that are to be distributed at the meeting.
8. Type and distribute the agenda in advance of the meeting.
9. "Star" on the agenda, at your principal's direction, items of particular importance. Other items can be omitted if time runs short.
10. Take roll at the meeting. Prepare a list of names in advance.
11. Take minutes or notes of the items discussed and prepare a summary of the discussion. Chapter 23 contains suggestions for preparing meeting agendas and writing minutes.

Your principal's service club obligations. Many principals are members of a service club. They also have affiliations with the local Chamber of Commerce and other groups interested in youth activities and public education programs. Here are some suggestions:

1. Keep the principal's calendar clear of appointments when his service club meetings are held.
2. Enter on your telephone list the names and telephone numbers of the officers of the principal's club.
3. Help your principal with notes, jokes, and the like when it is his turn to be master of ceremonies or chairman of the day.
4. Acquaint your self with the charities and major activities of your principal's service club.

If your principal is an officer in one of these clubs, you may be called upon to do extra typing and letter writing. If your principal is treasurer, you may be asked to assist with the bookkeeping of one of these organizations.

Your principal's professional and honorary organizations. Your principal will undoubtedly be a member of numerous professional and honorary organizations—maybe those he joined when he was back in college. He is proud to say he is a member of all of these organizations. You should, with the help of your principal, make a list of all these organizations. (They will be listed on his Biographical Data Sheet.) Determine which organization requires membership dues, and remind your principal at the beginning of each year the status of his membership. Sometimes a principal is so busy that he forgets to pay his membership dues in these organizations. It is embarrassing for him to learn he is not a voting member when important issues arise in one of his active organizations. Then sometimes, he may pay his dues twice in an organization. As his secretary, you will be of great help to him if you keep him informed of his membership status.

4

Working with Teachers and Other School Personnel

A LARGE PART of the school secretary's work involves relationships with fellow workers. The atmosphere created in the school office depends greatly on the secretary. This chapter offers some guidelines in working with school people. It also describes the secretary's duties and responsibilities in (1) working with teaching and non-teaching personnel; (2) instructing and supervising the clerical staff, relief clerks, and student helpers; (3) handling employment applications.

GUIDELINES TO WORKING WITH OTHERS

Your principal guideline for establishing satisfactory working relationships with fellow workers lies in your ability to help others and to have a pleasant disposition. There are a number of ways in which you can improve your working relationship with others.

Develop a helping relationship with fellow workers. A good way to develop a helping relationship with fellow workers is to notify them of changes to be made, help create group feeling, and listen to their requests.

Notify fellow workers of change. You may help others by notifying them in advance of changes that will concern them, by helping them to meet deadlines, and by having supplies or materials ready for them on time.

Help create group feeling. It is probably unwise for you to become a bosom companion to any one teacher or group of employees. As the principal's confidential aide, you must exercise a certain amount of reserve. You should be impartial in your relationships with staff members. However, helping a new teacher or clerk to become acquainted with his associates, inviting a new clerk to lunch with you, posting notices of social events, and informing newcomers about the community are all acceptable ways of helping others that contribute to the high regard of the school and its office staff.

Listen to others' requests. How different are the people in the school who make the following requests of the secretary in the course of a day?

"We wanted 5¢ tickets for the school carnival, but the clerk ordered 10¢ ones. What do we do now?"

"We received a beautiful picture and want to have it framed for our classroom. Can this be done out of student body funds?"

"I lost my bulletin for the Red Cross drive. Where can I get another?"

"I can't get my attendance report to come out right. Will you help me?"

"My baby is sick this morning. Will you call a substitute?"

"Will you call the superintendent's secretary and find out when the textbook committee is to meet?"

"Can you tell us how we can have the P.T.A. popcorn machine moved?"

The secretary needs an answer for requests that range from the trivial to the vital. You should give your answers as promptly as possible, definitely, and in a manner implying that you understand the request is important to the person who made it. You should accompany a "no" answer with an explanation. If you do not know the answer, try to find a satisfactory answer. Perhaps you may find there is a school rule or regulation, or policy which covers it. It might be a good idea to keep in mind the following maxims:

"First things in first place!"

"Don't 'expert' another's job!"

"Words not said will never come back to haunt you."

"Admit your boners! Everyone loves to feel superior."

The members of the National Association of School Secretaries, who call themselves "Nancies," have developed a code of ethics to help all school secretaries make their jobs and their personal relations more effective:

CODE OF ETHICS FOR EDUCATIONAL SECRETARIES

SERVICE

The Educational Secretary should exalt her profession on all occasions and sincerely strive for a finer and more efficient service to the school and the community.

The Educational Secretary should have membership in her local, state, and national professional organizations and should participate in their activities.

INTEGRITY

The Educational Secretary should be courteous, just, and professional in all her relations with administrators, office personnel, pupils, teachers, and other visitors to the school office.

The Educational Secretary should not disclose any information of confidential nature and should do or say nothing that would cause her to lose the confidence and respect of others. She should avoid voicing unfavorable criticism of other school employees unless that criticism is formally presented to a school official for the welfare of the school.

The Educational Secretary should recognize and perform all the duties of citizenship and should be loyal to the school system, the state, and the nation.

The Educational Secretary should refrain from the use of pressure on school officials to secure a promotion or to obtain favors for other people.

SKILL

The Educational Secretary should perform her duties with dispatch and accuracy.

The Educational Secretary should maintain her own efficiency by study, by travel, and by other means which keep her abreast of the trends in educational and business practices.

The Educational Secretary should make the office a congenial and welcome place for all without allowing it to become a social center.

The Educational Secretary should practice the qualities which promote good human relations and good public relations—cheerfulness, honesty, tact, understanding, patience, good judgment.

Develop an atmosphere of friendliness. In order to get along well with fellow workers, the secretary should develop, within the school, an atmosphere of friendliness. This can easily be done by practicing the following: develop a friendly manner; learn people's names; add a positive note to the day; develop a pleasing personality.

Develop a friendly manner. Your ability to get along with school personnel will be enhanced if you are a friendly person. Distinguishing characteristics of a friendly person usually include a pleasing appearance, a real interest in others, and personal qualities that attract others.

Learn names of personnel. You should learn the names and be able to locate the addresses of the people with whom you work. You should know the importance of the work they do and note their accomplishments—particularly their habits and enthusiasms.

Add a positive note to the day. When it would be appropriate, you might compliment a teacher on her new hair style or a beautiful dress; congratulate the members of the winning faculty bowling team; or praise the gardener for the beautiful roses in front of the school.

Develop a pleasing appearance. A friendly smile, unobtrusive make-up, suitable clothes, and an unhurried manner rank high on the list of traits contributing to a pleasing personal appearance. Your appearance and your voice make the first impression on others. Distinctness and low tones create the best impression in an office. Simple words and intelligent questions make you more easily understood by others.

Develop "plus" personal qualities. Personal qualities that others like and expect in a fellow worker include honesty, loyalty, cooperation, patience, tact, discretion, and poise. *Honesty* is more than truthfulness. It includes admission of your errors. It includes integrity—doing and saying what you believe to be right. *Loyalty* involves believing the best about your co-workers, acting in their best interest, standing by them when they are under attack, and accepting their weaknesses. *Cooperation* involves helpfulness, unselfishness, reliability, and tact. It includes the acceptance and appreciation of others' ideas and ways of doing things. *Patience* involves the acceptance of the other person's characteristics. Try to understand his ways and the methods he uses to solve problems. Try to avoid judging and imposing your methods on other people. *Tact* is the ability to sense the other person's feelings and to adopt a course of action that still achieves the desired goal. *Discretion* includes the ability to keep a confidence and know which matters should not be discussed. *Poise* is that assured gracious manner that develops when one knows one's job well, feels secure in doing it, and has no sense of loss when meeting new sets of circumstances.

GUIDELINES TO WORKING WITH TEACHERS

The list of things the school secretary does for teachers is a long one. She not only performs tasks specifically delegated to her by the principal, but she frequently is asked by teachers to do little "extras" that actually may be "beyond the call of duty."

Doing "extras." Doing "extras" for teachers may involve innumerable tasks such as helping them to find lost keys, instructing them in the use of office equipment, typing and duplicating instructional materials, and assisting them with reports. Willing as you may be to do strictly personal services for teachers, you must take certain precautions. You should have an understanding with your principal of the services he expects you to do for the teachers, those he considers "extras," and those which you are not to do without his special permission.

Principals ordinarily regard such work as grading papers and typing college term papers as the personal responsibilities of the teacher. The point at which extra services are beyond your responsibility depends upon the principal's attitudes as well as his instructions.

Limiting the "extras." When your principal has defined the limits of your work, ask him if all the teachers are informed as to the amount of service they may expect. This information would include the periods or hours when such help is available, the amount of advance notice required to request such work, and the form in which such work must be presented. For example, some school offices will do duplicating work only during vacations. Many large schools provide equipment and supplies for teachers to do their own duplicating, usually in a location away from the school office.

Before agreeing to do those "extras," you may well ask yourself questions such as, "Would this 'extra' be done for all teachers?" "Am I setting a precedent I will be unable or unwilling to continue?" "Does my doing this 'extra' help the principal in his job?" If you set a line beyond which your sociability with teachers does not go, you will be less apt to be asked for "extras" and have less need to turn them down.

Helping the substitute teachers. You can help a substitute teacher in many ways. Give her maximum advance notice of the day and time she is to teach, a description of what the assignment entails in terms of subject matter, and an estimate of how long the assignment is apt to last. A little advance planning on your part plus the cooperation of your principal in making sure that the teacher's roll book and keys are available and the lesson plans up to date will help make the substitute's day go smoothly. Of course, you should know the location of these items so that they will be available when the substitute arrives. In a high school or departmentalized elementary school, you may need to notify the absent teacher's chairman of the substitution.

Many schools have a duplicated sheet which is headed "Information for Substitute Teachers." If your school does not have one, you may wish to seek your principal's help in preparing one. The following form is a good example of what might be included.

INFORMATION FOR SUBSTITUTE TEACHERS

1. School Hours
   a. Beginning and ending times
   b. Periods or program
   c. Nutrition
   d. Lunch period
   e. Variations in schedule for assemblies and the like
2. Attendance
   a. Where and how to sign in and out
   b. How and to whom absence should be reported
3. Work Location
   It is advantageous to have a map of the school and grounds with rest rooms clearly marked.
   a. Room number
   b. Building
   c. Keys
4. Duties
   a. Teacher's lesson plans or plan book
   b. Teacher's roll book
   c. Daily reports to be made
   d. Name and location of principal, department head and/or other teachers who may assist with information
   e. What to do in case of fire drill, alert, or the like
   f. Reporting out at end of day and/or assignment
   g. Teacher's extra-curricular duties
5. School Regulations
   a. Discipline
   b. Rules governing grounds

6. Personal
   a. Location of rest rooms, cafeteria, public telephone, and other facilities
   b. Provisions for coat, purse, and other personal belongings
   c. Parking facilities and public transportation available
   d. Smoking regulations

When the substitute teacher arrives, introduce her to the principal, and to the department chairman, if appropriate. Many principals delegate such routine functions to the secretary. If this is the case in helping substitutes, you should go over all necessary information with the substitute, have her sign whatever papers may be necessary, escort her to her room and introduce her to the class. You should also see that roll books, keys, and lesson plans are returned at the end of the day or assignment.

When a substitute is not available. When a substitute is not available or has not arrived on time, your principal will make provision for another teacher to supervise the class of the absent teacher. The principal usually chooses whom he wishes called for this duty. In an elementary school, the principal himself may take the class. Sometimes the class may be sent to another teacher's room, or the class may be divided between two teachers. In a high school, the class may be supervised by teachers who have non-teaching assignments. Your principal will appreciate your help in seeing that all classes of absent teachers are promptly covered. Be sure to keep a record of the times each teacher on the faculty has covered another teacher's class so that assignments can be distributed objectively.

Helping new teachers. When a new teacher is assigned to the school, you will be asked to give her all the help you would give a substitute, and more. Actually, your principal is responsible for inducting and orienting the new teacher, but he will often leave many of the clerical details to you. Your principal will discuss the teacher's assignment with her, provide her with the course of study, and usually introduce her to her co-workers. If your principal is away, you will have to pinch hit for him as best you can. Provide the teacher with the forms that must be filled out and arrange for processing them. Assign her an office box for school mail and bulletins. Give her information on how to secure equipment and supplies. If your school has a handbook or bulletin of special information for new teachers, supply her with a copy. In addition to the information you would supply the substitute, be sure that the new teacher knows how to get information about her hours of work, her pay—including pay days—and other personnel information.

Keeping records of teachers' credentials or licenses. Credentials, certificates, or licenses are names for legal documents that substantiate a teacher's qualifications to teach. Unless these documents are valid and on file or registered with the local county or parish, the school district cannot employ the teacher or continue him in pay status. The teacher may be licensed to teach at certain grade levels only, or to teach specific subjects only. After the teacher has taught for a number of years and complied with specific qualifications, these licenses may become permanent.

Keeping credentials active, in order, and in a safe place is really the responsibility of each individual teacher. However, should you ever be required to keep such credentials in your custody, keep them in a locked compartment of the school safe or in a fireproof cabinet. Also, supply each teacher with a receipt for her documents.

Keep a record of each teacher's current credentials for payroll and assignment purposes. Usually this information is included on the teacher personnel cards supplied by the school district. The type of document and its expiration date should be recorded. Since it usually takes a considerable period of time to secure renewals of these documents, it may be wise for you to review this file at least three months in advance of renewal dates, and notify the teachers as well as the principal of credentials that must be renewed.

GUIDELINES TO WORKING WITH NON-TEACHING PERSONNEL

You will be working with non-teaching personnel by transmitting the principal's orders, by understanding your own and others' shares in the work done, by assigning and instructing personnel, and by supervising office personnel, including relief clerks and student helpers.

In dealing with most of the non-teaching employees in your school, you will often be the principal's spokesman. You will transmit the principal's orders and wishes. You will also be dependent upon these employees, especially in emergencies—when the bells fail to ring or when the sink in the science laboratory overflows.

Making requests for service. Some of the people who do the so-called menial tasks around your school can add a great deal of smoothness, and even pleasure, to your work if you show appreciation for their efforts, recognize their feelings, and do what you can to make their work easier.

When you transmit your principal's orders to custodians, building engineers, gardeners, or maintenance men, it is a good idea to preface the order with a phrase like, "The principal asked me to tell you . . . ," "The principal says," or "The principal wishes." Before giving such orders, be sure that you have clearly in mind what is to be done and that you can express it in words. If an item is to be repaired, you must describe exactly what is wrong with it. Never word a request as if you were issuing an order. And whatever you say, send a smile along with it.

Make the work of the custodian easier by being a good office housekeeper. Often it is impossible for the custodian to give the school office a thorough cleaning. Important materials may not have been put away, and the custodian may fear to move them. Try not to call upon the custodians for every little item. Do some things for yourself, such as opening windows, moving plants, and throwing out old flowers.

GUIDELINES TO INSTRUCTING AND SUPERVISING CLERICAL PERSONNEL

In assigning and orienting office personnel, you should assign them to their work areas or desks and instruct them in their duties. The new employee's work area should be presented to her in the orderliness in which she will be expected to keep it. It should be stocked with the supplies she will need. Provisions should be made for her chair to be adjusted so that it is comfortable for her.

Instructing new clerks. You should put the new clerical employee at ease and find out how much she already knows about what she is to do. An attentive, unhurried manner on your part and an outline of what the job entails will start the new employee off very smoothly. Next, you should tell and show the new employee what to do. Proceed slowly, a step at a time, showing and telling the new worker and giving her an opportunity to ask questions. Check the new clerk's work frequently at first, and encourage her to ask questions. Praise her for what she does well, and show an interest in her progress. It is especially important that you stress the confidential nature of school records and tell her that these are never to be discussed with outsiders. Essentially the same points should be covered in the orientation of a new clerk as in that of a teacher.

An inexperienced office employee may be careless in her personal appearance and care. If you are a model of cleanliness and appropriate dress, she may take the cue and improve. If not, there is probably no other course for you than to talk privately with her, pointing out ways she may improve her appearance.

Supervising clerical personnel. If you have properly oriented the people whose work you supervise, and continue to show an interest in their progress, you will have gone a long way toward establishing good working relationships with them.

In day-to-day relationships with employees, you should be firm in the work standards you set, and fair in assignments. Lend support to the employee, correct her privately and considerately, and listen to her complaints. If you have done all these things and still have an unsatisfactory or disgruntled employee, you should probably seek your principal's help in solving the problem.

Evaluating clerical personnel. Most school districts require an evaluation or performance report of each employee at least twice a year. The purpose of a performance report is to help the employee become more effective. The report usually includes such items as: work habits, dependability, attitudes, quality of work performed, ability to work with others, personal qualities, punctuality. (See page 34.)

Many school districts prefer that a conference be held with the employee so that this report can be discussed when it is marked. In the conference, the items mentioned above are marked by degrees; such as, excellent, average, or improvement needed. The performance report is actually a part of the training program of the district. It should not be viewed as a rating; neither should it be used as a threat. The employee should not be made to feel that if she gets an excellent rating, she has no need to be continually working for improvement. On the other hand, if she gets a poor or weak rating, she should not be made to feel unimportant or that she will be punished (e.g., "fired"). If the rater in any way expresses such feelings to the employee, then the training aspect of the performance rating is lost. No doubt, your principal will ask you to help with the ratings of classified personnel who are under your supervision.

Assigning relief clerks. Temporary clerical workers are sometimes employed and assigned to a school to relieve the school secretary of such tasks as scoring achievement test papers, taking a special inventory, or preparing an evaluation report. If you give the relief employee adequate instruction by providing a thorough introduction to the work and a careful explanation of the work situation, the temporary employee will probably develop a confident attitude, and reach an acceptable level of performance in a short time.

Some relief helpers may be hampered by lack of incentive or a "here today, gone tomorrow" attitude. Your conscious effort to show sincere appreciation of such workers' help and to make them feel that they "belong" while they are assigned to your school will promote their best efforts and feelings toward their work.

Obviously, you should keep records of the days and hours every temporary clerk works as well as the nature of the assignment and the quality of work done. It is a good idea to keep a record of the relief clerk's home address and telephone number even though the district personnel office may have the information.

Using student helpers. In schools of all levels, you will discover that pupils are ready and willing office helpers, but the amount and kind of service they can render depends upon their maturity. Young children lack the capabilities to perform tasks that require judgment or initiative, such as answering the telephone or sorting books in the book room.

You will soon find that some student helpers are more dependable and efficient than others. There is always a temptation to call upon the best of these, but you should not show partiality to a few children. Patience and praise usually secure good work from less able but willing student helpers.

It is a good plan for you to establish a definite spot for picking up and returning things to the office. Helpers can then be taught to wait on themselves without interrupting your work.

On the elementary level. Elementary pupils can be called upon to run

PARAMOUNT UNIFIED SCHOOL DISTRICT
EVALUATION FORM FOR CLASSIFIED EMPLOYEES

NAME OF EMPLOYEE _____ FROM _____ TO _____

UNIT _____ POSITION _____

NOTE: Ratings of OUTSTANDING or UNSATISFACTORY are to be supported by written comment

UNSATISFACTORY	NEEDS TO IMPROVE	DISTRICT STANDARD	ABOVE DISTRICT STANDARD	OUTSTANDING
		RELIABLE – Does routine work well		
		SYSTEMATIC – Is orderly in daily work		
		JUDICIOUS – Makes sound decisions		
		INITIATIVE – Is resourceful and self-reliant		
		DIPLOMATIC – Is tactful in dealing with others		
		ADAPTABLE – Adjusts to existing and new conditions		
		COOPERATIVE – Works well with others		
		LOYAL – Is loyal to district and co-workers		
		SAFETY CONSCIOUS – Is aware of and practices safety measures		
		PUNCTUAL – Reports to work on time; meets deadlines		
		OPEN-MINDED – Willingly accepts suggestions		
		NEAT – Is dressed and groomed appropriately		
		DIRECTIVE – Gives directions clearly		

Other outstanding contributions: _____

_____

Other areas needing improvement: _____

_____

- 1 -

Figure 2. Performance report for permanent classified employees.

PARAMOUNT UNIFIED SCHOOL DISTRICT
EVALUATION FORM FOR CLERICAL EMPLOYEES

NAME OF EMPLOYEE _____ FROM _____ TO _____

UNIT _____ POSITION _____

NOTE: Ratings of OUTSTANDING or UNSATISFACTORY are to be supported by written comment

UNSATISFACTORY	NEEDS TO IMPROVE	DISTRICT STANDARD	ABOVE DISTRICT STANDARD	OUTSTANDING
		RAPPORT — Has a good relationship with contacts		
		STABLE — Works well under stress		
		GRAMMAR — Uses good English; enunciates clearly		
		WORK METHODS — Understands principles		
		PROFESSIONAL — Is a member of and participates in professional organizations		
		JOB SKILLS		
		RECORDS & TRANSCRIPTION — Neat and accurate; types with reasonable speed		
		FILES — Neat and accessible		
		TELEPHONE TECHNIQUES — Tactful and courteous		
		OFFICE EQUIPMENT — Understands use and care of		
		OFFICE MACHINES — Operates accurately and with reasonable speed		
		OFFICE APPEARANCE — Orderly and pleasant		

_____
Signature of Evaluator

This report has been discussed with me. My
signature does not necessarily imply agreement.

_____
Signature of Evaluee

_____
Date

-2-

Figure 2 (*continued*). Courtesy of Paramount Unified School District,
Paramount, California.

errands, take messages, and deliver supplies. They should not be asked to help in any situation that requires them to handle money or use their own handwriting. Upper grade children may be assigned duties in the cafeteria, library, or on lost-and-found.

On the secondary level. In high schools, the helpers may be advanced students from office practice classes, who are granted credit for the work. The teacher always gives the student his mark, but you will probably be asked for an evaluation of a student's work. Often, a high school student service group or club will render service. It is worth noting that honor students are not always the best helpers; others often respond more willingly.

GUIDELINES TO HANDLING APPLICATIONS FOR EMPLOYMENT

Applications for employment may come to the school directly from an applicant, but the vast majority of applications will probably come as referrals from teachers' agencies or college placement offices. In most cases, applications for employment will be accompanied by transcripts of college courses, letters of application, and other credentials that should be returned to the applicant or the agency if the teacher is not employed by the school district. Whenever applications are received, you should make a special note of information that is to be returned to the sender.

Filing applications. If your principal is considering the selection of several teachers, he probably will ask you to arrange applications according to subject or grade level for his consideration. He may also ask that you write or telephone applicants to come to the school for an interview. When applications are not being perused, they should be filed, usually according to the surname of the applicant. There are few embarrassments equal to losing or misplacing a person's application.

Interviewing applicants. In most school districts actual employment is the responsibility of the board of education. However, many districts automatically accept the principal's recommendation. When applicants drop in and the principal is not available, you should limit yourself to telling them the application procedure for and overall requirements of any vacancies.

While the principal is interviewing applicants, you should be within calling distance because he may call on you for courses of study, copies of textbooks, and other items that he may wish the prospective employee to review. Some principals lend these materials incautiously. You must be prepared to tell your principal in the presence of the caller that, "This is the file copy," "This is the last copy available," or even, "We must have a receipt for this copy if it is loaned." Your principal may also wish you to make an appointment for the candidate with other school personnel or call them in for the interview.

5

Working with Pupils, Parents, and the Public

WORKING with pupils, parents, and the public involves the school secretary in establishing and maintaining good public relations for the school, its teachers, and the principal. As the secretary, you will receive office callers, screen their requests, route them to others, make appointments, and furnish information. In order to perform these duties, you must be a true public servant and have the other person's interest at heart. You must learn to accept interruptions, even when you are concentrating on the details of your own work. Your performance reveals your personality —it will make friends or foes for the school, and all of education as well.

WORKING WITH PUPILS

Pupils will come to you seeking help and information. They may be good, naughty, shy, or troubled. Children are not small adults, but they do have the same essential needs. Children acquire the characteristics of the people in their environment. Most of the time, you will treat children as you would adults. However, there are times when you will have to do for them things they are not yet able to do for themselves.

As the principal's representative. When you are dealing with pupils, always remember that you are the principal's representative. Try to understand and follow his instructions and his techniques in dealing with pupils. Your principal stands legally in the place of the parent (*in loco parentis*) with responsibility for and authority over the pupil. He cannot delegate his responsibility and authority to you. So, guide yourself by the fact that you have no legal authority or responsibility for the individual pupil. Your role at most is that of the child's custodian.

Talking with the pupil. When talking to pupils, do not use words they will not understand. Avoid metaphors, such as "on cloud nine," "in seventh heaven," and "in the depths." Never refer to pupils as "monsters," "dopes," or by other impolite words—even to the teachers or other office workers. If you have given a child information, but you are not sure that he understands, ask him to repeat it.

Children pay particular attention to the words you use. Most young children take every statement literally. Few elementary children are sufficiently developed mentally to understand satire, sarcasm, or allusions to things beyond their experience. You will find that even teen-agers often do not grasp such statements.

Supervising pupils sent to the office. Pupils sent to the office for disciplinary action are always the responsibility of your principal, or, in high schools, of the dean or the assistant principal. Regard such pupils as you would any other caller in the office awaiting your principal. If your principal is away, it is not at all improbable that you will be the custodian of a hyperactive, belligerent, or fearful child. Regardless of what the child may do in the office, avoid showing signs of annoyance with him. This may be the very reaction he is seeking.

Keeping the pupil occupied. Undoubtedly your principal will brief you on some of the techniques he wishes you to follow in supervising pupils waiting to be disciplined. Among these techniques will be providing a place to sit, away from the stream of office traffic, where there will be something for him to look at, or something constructive to do. Minor chores like sharpening pencils or counting sheets of paper into 25's may serve to keep the small child occupied. Your principal will probably limit the length of time—usually no more than twenty minutes—that a pupil may be held in the office. By school law, the pupil must be released for recess periods and lunch, and also must be permitted to go to the lavatory if he so requests. Ask your principal what to do if a pupil leaves the office or creates a disturbance in the hallway.

Lending funds and handling lost money. Pupils of all ages will forget or lose money. Most schools provide a petty cash fund from student body or Parent-Teacher Association funds for such situations. Accounting for petty cash is described on page 126. Usually, loans are made only for lunches or transportation.

Accounting for loans. To keep the loan fund functioning properly, you should devise a simple form in duplicate. Give the pupil a copy when making him a loan, and keep the other in the cash box for a follow-up if the money is not returned immediately. Besides giving the borrower a reminder copy, tell the pupil to be sure to tell his mother that he borrowed money. When the money is returned, be sure to destroy the copy of the form. To keep such accounts from becoming delinquent, check them every week or so. If necessary, you might send a reminder note to the child through his teacher, or call his parent by telephone.

Accounting for lost money. Frequently, lost money is turned into the office in amounts from pennies to dollars. You should try to make a note of when and where it was found and the name of the finder, so that when losers come seeking their money, you will have a basis for questioning them. A packet of small end-opening envelopes on which you can write the note and into which you can put the money will help you in this task.

Determining ownership of lost money. You will have to be the judge as to whether a pupil actually lost the money you are holding. Talk to the pupil alone, sending his companions away, since pupils often visit the office in two's or three's. Ask yourself if the pupil would be apt to have money for any purpose. Only by the child's replies can you decide. You might ask him, "Where do you think you lost it?" "When do you last remember having it?" "How much did you lose?" "Why did you bring it?" Try to determine the denominations of the coins he lost. If the sum is more than a dollar and you cannot decide ownership, telephone the pupil's parent to determine if he brought money to school. Whenever you return lost money to him, or lend money to a pupil, try to do so in the absence of other pupils. Be sure to record the name of the pupil to whom you return lost money.

Holding or "safekeeping" money. The holding or safekeeping of money that pupils bring to school is more apt to be a problem for the teacher than for you. However, when young children ask you to hold money for them, you should treat the amount as precious, whether it be a penny, a quarter, or a half dollar. If a pupil asks you to hold his penny, you might be tempted to tell him to put it in his pocket because to you it is a small amount. To him, however, it is of great value. In this service, small end-opening envelopes are useful.

Delivering messages, lunches, and clothing. Your service in delivering messages, lunches, and clothing will depend upon how much help you have from other members of the staff and whether or not you have student help. Messages should be brief. Such statements as, "Your mother will call you at 3:10; come to the office at that time," are most appropriate. It is helpful to use a printed form for messages with spaces for time, date, and the telephone number of the person calling. If there is any doubt in your mind as to the validity of the message, call the telephone number to verify it. Also check to see if the number given is the pupil's own home telephone number. You should never, of course, give any information about a pupil, even to another pupil in his class.

Using the communication system. Most schools have an intercom telephone system to communicate with classrooms. Such a system can usually be utilized to request monitors to pick up items or messages for pupils from the office. Even if you have to take the message, lunch, or forgotten umbrella to the pupil yourself, do so promptly.

Receiving and disposing of lost-and-found articles. The quantity of unclaimed garments and other articles turned in to the office will amaze you. To provide for such items, you will need a simple record-keeping system, storage space, and a means of disposal.

Keeping a record. A simple record of items turned in and requested may be entered in a bound notebook in which finders and losers may record identifying details of what they bring or seek. A rack with hangers in an out-of-sight spot with ventilation is ideal for garments. Labeled boxes or plastic bags are suitable for storing other articles.

Disposal of lost articles. Claims for lost items can be spurred by publicizing them in the school bulletin, or by putting notices on the bulletin board. Some elementary schools put all the clothing and "jewelry" on display and parade the members of each room by the items. Pupils will not usually claim or take articles that do not belong to them.

Disposal of items should be made every month or six weeks. The secretary may arrange to give the clothing to charity and to have the custodian throw away other items unless they are of value. Valuable articles are kept indefinitely.

WORKING WITH PARENTS

Your role in working with parents involves meeting their requests (some of which will be unusual or unreasonable requests), dealing with irate parents, helping with parent-teacher conferences, and performing services for the Parent-Teacher Association.

Answering parents' requests. In your contacts with parents, you will probably feel a great deal of responsibility for representing your principal. To fulfill this responsibility and not overstep your own authority, listen carefully to parents' requests and follow or quote the rule that applies to the situation. If you do not know the rule or guideline, just listen. If listening is not enough, call on your principal for help.

Whenever a parent requests to take his child from school before school is over, he is usually required to sign a release slip provided in the main office. The parent must present such a slip to the child's teacher to secure his release from the classroom.

Conferring with parents. Realize, in talking with parents, that relatively few of them ever come near the school except when their children are small. Some parents never gain more than a vague idea of the school's responsibilities toward children. Therefore, when you talk with parents who seek help or information, your "listening ear" must be larger than usual. Avoid using such pedagogical terms as "curriculum" or "course of study," and avoid giving advice or information beyond what the parent requests.

Arranging appointments. Parents will usually be seeking appointments with your principal or a teacher when they call. They will also come to enroll their children, to see them, or to seek their early dismissal from school. They will ask for such information as graduation requirements, supplies needed, and bus schedules. For many parents, you will be their only contact with the school.

In addition to arranging appointments between parents and teachers, you should also arrange for a place where they may confer. Although it is preferable that a parent see a teacher in the classroom when no children are present, such arrangements may not be practical in crowded schools. The location that you select for a parent-teacher interview should be private—especially when the students are of high school age.

Dealing with irate parents. Parents' complaints do not usually involve you beyond the listening stage. In a junior or senior high school, there are usually deans or assistant principals to whom you can refer parents' complaints. However, in an elementary or small secondary school, neither the principal nor the teacher involved may be available. In such a case, you may have to help the parent tell his story and record it objectively— describing what the parent said and did—in a memo for the principal or the teacher, or both.

There are times when a parent charges into the school office ready to do verbal and in some instances physical battle with a teacher. This situation is perhaps the most taxing that you will meet in your efforts to maintain good public relations.

Helping to calm down the parent. When you are dealing with a person who is angry, it is well to remember that she does not want explanations, excuses, or honeyed words. She wishes to be told three things: (1) that she is right; (2) that the school has been wrong; (3) that the school will do something to correct the situation.

Before introducing the irate parent to the teacher or your principal, it is your task to calm the person down to a point where she is ready to use reason rather than emotion as a means of communication. You will have to be the understanding, sympathetic, and attentive listener while the irate parent is blowing off steam in telling her story. You should not attempt to oppose her words at this time; rather, encourage her to repeat her story. By doing this, you may help the irate parent to feel that she might have been unfair in at least a few of her accusations. Then, study the complaint and see if there is something you can do for the complainant. If you are bound by regulations and other circumstances, as you are sure to be, just explain your position. Your principal can discuss the problem from the school's viewpoint.

Meeting unusual and unreasonable requests. Out-of-the-ordinary requests from parents—and sometimes from others—occur fairly frequently. They involve enrollment of children below school age, requests for use of school facilities, explanations of report cards, requests for addresses —and even occupations—of classmates' parents, requests for the services of school personnel in programs of non-school organizations, and requests to see children by parents forbidden to do so by court order. You will refer many of these requests to the principal; others, you will learn to deal with yourself.

New educational programs, redistricting, testing programs, and the like are sometimes announced prematurely in newspapers, on the radio, or over television before you or your principal may know the details about them. When parents inquire about such developments, inform them frankly that you do not know all the facts yet, but that *all* parents will be notified as soon as the official information is available.

Lending school property and equipment. Your principal will undoubtedly brief you on the school district's policy regarding lending of school district or student body property. Many districts forbid such loans—even to teachers. However, should you be authorized to lend school equipment or property in compliance with regulations, you should always keep a record of the loan. Such a record should include the name of the item, the name, address, and telephone number of the borrower, and the promised date of return. Secure a receipt for the item from the borrower or have him record his receipt of the item on the loan record.

Complying with court orders. When parents are in domestic difficulties, one parent may be under court order not to see a child. If that parent comes to the school in an effort to see his child, he must be refused. The responsibility for showing such a court order to the school authorities generally rests with the one who procured it.

As a general rule, if parents restricted by court order—and any loiterers as well—are seen waiting at the school gate or riding around the school looking in, you should be authorized to call the police.

Helping with parent-teacher conferences. The school may hold group conferences of administrators, parents, and teachers at the beginning of the year and during such periods as Public Schools' Week or American Education Week to acquaint parents with school personnel, objectives, and policies.

Group conferences are usually arranged by committees of teachers with the guidance of administrators. Parent-Teacher Association officers and chairmen also may help provide for the reception of parents and for the serving of simple refreshments.

Your role in group conferences will vary, depending upon the duties delegated to you. You may prepare invitations to parents; type or duplicate programs, parent education materials, and letters of appreciation; introduce or direct parents to teachers; and check fire and safety provisions.

Performing services for the Parent-Teacher Association. Many secretaries regularly join the Parent-Teacher Association and feel that helping this organization is a worthwhile part of their job. Depending upon the level of the school and the activity of the group, you may perform a variety of services for the P.T.A.; e.g., typing the treasurer's report, cutting stencils, mimeographing their monthly news sheet, preparing ballots. During membership drives, you may assist in the collection of dues and find locations in the office or adjacent rooms where the P.T.A. officers may establish headquarters. When the P.T.A. gives membership teas and holds other meetings, you may help locate table cloths, silver, and dishes for the occasion.

Some Parent-Teacher Associations will call upon you for a volume of work that requires more time than you have. Arrive at an understanding with your principal as to how much work this organization should expect you to do. He may help you out by saying "No" to some of their requests.

Some school administrators believe that the more the secretary and the principal can help the Parent-Teacher Association officers to become self-sufficient, the better off the P.T.A. will be. These administrators suggest that the principal and secretary give the association advice on ways to do things rather than assume responsibility for doing clerical work.

WORKING WITH THE PUBLIC

Your role in working with the public starts with your function as receptionist. You receive and identify school callers, give information, and make referrals, look after callers awaiting appointments, protect pupils and school personnel from interference, and maintain good relations with the press.

Receiving school callers. Every caller is a guest in the office of the school, whether parent, taxpayer, salesman, a child, the superintendent himself, or a member of the board of education. A cheerful greeting and a smile can go a long way toward making every caller feel welcome. All callers should receive the same courteous attention, regardless of their importance. It is likely that the more important the caller, the less impressed he will be if he feels you are obviously giving him more attention.

Since many persons feel self-conscious in a school office, you should not allow any caller to wait unnoticed. "I'll be with you in a moment" will serve to recognize their presence if you cannot immediately take care of their needs. A warm "Good morning (afternoon)—may I help you?" covers most situations.

Many schools insist that all callers first present themselves at the school office to register and, perhaps, obtain a visitor's card before attempting to go elsewhere about the school building. Some schools accomplish this requirement by maintaining the central doorway as the only means of entrance or by having student hall monitors stationed near entrances and staircases.

Identifying school callers. It is your responsibility to get the name of the caller, and if possible, the purpose of his visit. "May I have your name, please?" politely asked, suffices. If a caller fumbles in stating his business or gives you any cause to doubt his identity or the purpose of his visit, you should not hesitate to ask him for identification. You may ask him to wait while you verify that identification by telephone, reference to files, or by other means. It is better for you to check out of earshot, but you should not fear that a legitimate caller will be offended by your care in taking adequate precautions.

Giving information and making referrals. Questions to determine the nature of the caller's business will help you decide whom the caller should see. You may refer him directly, or make an appointment. Or, you may give the caller the information he came for, if it is the kind you are authorized to give.

Should callers be visiting a classroom or keeping an appointment elsewhere on the grounds, they may be guided by a student monitor or permitted to go by themselves. You might even give the visitor a map of the school plant and mark the place he wishes to visit.

Should callers wish to see a teacher or pupil, you should make it clear to them that teachers and pupils are not to be disturbed during a class, that they are available only during their free or unassigned time.

Should the caller's business be something forbidden on school property, you should explain to him the regulation that forbids it. When a caller leaves with an explanation of why his request was denied, he will not feel that the denial was from lack of desire to help him.

Should the caller request to see your principal when you think the caller wants only information regarding details or routines, tell him that your principal is busy. Ask him if you can't be of assistance.

Looking after callers awaiting appointments. When callers arrive in the office and must await appointments, you should see that they are comfortable and have reading materials available. To keep them from feeling isolated and forgotten, you should check with them occasionally with a remark such as, "I am sure Mr. (Principal) will be along in a few minutes," or "This seems to be a long conference, but I think they are nearly finished." If a caller's wait is likely to extend indefinitely, you should find out if the caller can continue to wait, if there is someone else he can see, or if you should make another appointment.

Receiving special callers. You should receive the superintendent, supervisors, and even board of education members much as you would anyone else, courteously and graciously. You may expect these visitors to announce themselves first at the school before proceeding anywhere on the school grounds, since this practice is universally considered a professional courtesy. If these visitors are to observe classes or attend school functions, you will gain the appreciation of teachers or others concerned by giving them advance notice. Always remain in the background when these officials are dealing with your principal.

Should one of your principal's superiors start to walk right past you into the principal's office, or should you fail to recognize one of these important people, you should behave as you would if any other caller did the same thing. Your poise and graciousness will come to your rescue. You might say "I am Mr. (Principal's) secretary. May I help you?"

Protecting pupils and school personnel from interference. To protect pupils, teachers, and the principal from interference, and even from harm, you must learn the regulations and laws regarding who may come on school property and what they may do there. You must also learn what to do when these rules are violated. Rules forbid loiterers on or around school property and usually prohibit the distribution of advertising and publications. Rules also limit calls and demonstrations by salesmen unless authorized by the superintendent or by the board of education. Refer to your own district policy for these regulations.

Callers wishing to see pupils. Relatives of pupils, neighbors, and others may come to the school seeking the release of pupils before the school day is over to take them to the doctor or to some other activity. Some callers may wish to see or talk to a pupil at school. Usually, the rule is that no pupil shall be released to anyone or allowed to see or talk to anyone except a parent, or someone having a parent's official and verified authority.

In high schools and large elementary schools, all determinations of whom a pupil may see at school or with whom he may leave the grounds are made by an assistant principal or dean. In a small school, the principal makes such determinations. In the principal's absence, if you are so delegated, you must insist scrupulously on correct identification of anyone wishing to see a pupil. Do not hesitate to call on another administrator or teacher to assist you in this task.

One method of checking an unknown adult who appears to have authorization to see a child is to observe the child's face and behavior when he meets the person. Should any questions arise in your mind when observing such a face-to-face meeting, call the child aside, question him, and prevent his leaving the school until you have rechecked the caller's credentials.

Maintaining relations with the press. Reporters, even commentators and newspaper photographers, may visit the school. To establish and maintain good relations with the press, you should be friendly but reserved in your speech, lest you let a detail about the school slip that might make a story on a day when news is scarce. Never give a reporter information about the school without the sanction of the principal.

You should be alert to the reporter's technique of "fishing." When a reporter knows a few facts or has heard a rumor, he may tell you his facts or hunch. You think he knows more than he does and consequently you may reveal facts you would not tell otherwise.

2

The School Secretary
and Her Office Duties

6

Managing the School Office

THE SPECIAL DOMAIN of the school secretary is the office area and waiting room. It is not only the nerve center of the entire school, it is the personal working area of the secretary. You, as the school secretary, are in charge and responsible for the smooth operation and functioning of the school office. Although the principal's office adjoins yours, you must regard the entire office suite as your immediate responsibility. You should also be aware of some of the routine functions of the office as they relate to clocks, bells, keys, and emergency routines such as fire drills.

The office suite. Most school offices are separated by a counter into a waiting room area and an office work area. Your principal's office, the supply room, and the mimeograph or duplicating room complete the usual office suite. There may also be a school vault or fireproof room for records. Sometimes the health room may adjoin, and when the nurse is not there, you may have charge of it, too. The waiting area often serves also as a teachers' area. It has a series of boxes or large pigeon-holes for teacher mail and communications. Occasionally there is a nearby room for teacher use, for the upkeep of which the school custodian is most likely to be responsible. In the office also are to be found bulletin boards, pictures, key racks or cases, and sometimes display cases. Although you are not expected to do the custodial chores, you need to keep all these areas and furnishings orderly, attractive, and in functioning order.

The school office should be both business-like and pleasantly informal. Drapes, pictures, and flowers soften the formal appearance of the callers' area; neatness and orderliness in room arrangement and working space provide the proper business aspect.

The waiting room. At times, the waiting room seems to exercise magnetic drawing power on such things as books, lunch boxes, playground balls, and undistributed packages and deliveries. To preserve a business-like appearance in the area, such things should not be permitted to remain there, even for a short time. A place where they can be stored should be established in a closet or elsewhere in the building.

You should have an adequate number of chairs in the waiting room and keep suitable reading material at hand. Keep the chairs and literature arranged in an orderly manner and check the area for neatness several times during the day. A magazine rack will help keep the periodicals in place.

The office counter. The visitors' waiting area of a school office is seldom large and is usually separated from the secretary's working space by a counter. A well-styled counter in the elementary school has a higher level designed to accommodate not more than one or two adults at a time and a lower level for small children who otherwise cannot be seen. High school counters are all of the same height and have small signs or placards to designate the type of services transacted.

The counter should be kept clear and uncluttered. Items not immediately in use should be placed in the spaces underneath. Any person in the working space who does not receive callers should be seated facing away from the counter or not so near to it that a visitor who does not get his attention feels he is being ignored.

The office bulletin board. The bulletin board in the office area is commonly used to inform school personnel regarding such items as organization activities and announcements, university classes, cultural events, and schedules of duties, special teachers, and special rooms. Your chief responsibility is to arrange the bulletin board so that it will be both attractive and functional.

Suggestions for bulletin board arrangement. Arrangement of the items according to subject matter such as given above seems to be the most practical method. Here are a few suggestions:

1. Space each item so that it is instantly visible.
2. Use interesting space arrangements such as diagonal, horizontal, or vertical divisions.
3. Use colored paper to attract the eye and emphasize important bulletins.
4. Place notices that require considerable reading close to eye level.
5. Avoid a cluttered, over-crowded effect.
6. Exercise constant vigilance regarding dated material. Remove promptly those that are past due. Remove everything at the end of the term.
7. Write teacher's room numbers or names across the bottom of bulletins that require reading by certain or all teachers. When all the room numbers have been checked or the names initialed, the bulletin may be removed. If there are one or two negligent teachers, the bulletin may be removed and placed in their boxes for checking.
8. Use topic headings or subject labels for bulletin items. Make labels easy to read, and uniform. Commercially made letters are easy to handle and always make a neat appearance. Block letters cut from colored paper are often effective.
9. Create interest by fashioning yarn, string, or colored thread into words. Observe spacing between letters and words.

10. Use separate bulletin boards or easels outside of the office area for special notices and posters pertaining to Red Cross, P.T.A., and Community Chest and similar organizations.

Office pictures. Framed pictures of good quality and children's paintings are suitable wall decorations in the office working space and waiting room. When commercial pictures are used, they should be carefully selected for appropriate size, color, and general subject appeal. At intervals, change pictures throughout the building to renew interest.

Suggestions for selecting and hanging pictures.

1. Use children's paintings and other artwork.
2. Use permanent wooden frames. They are not expensive and prove neater and easier to handle than do tag board mountings.
3. Place a small label in one corner of the painting to indicate the pupil-artist's grade level.
4. Hang pictures in relation to the wall space where they are placed, horizontal pictures on horizontal wall areas, vertical pictures on vertical areas, or use off-balance placements.
5. When more than one picture is used, align the edges of frames at either the top or bottom.
6. Group pictures close together.

Artwork and flower arrangements bring life and color into the office area. They must be skillfully arranged to give a pleasing and harmonious effect.

Flowers for the office. Often a large planter or indoor plant is more appropriate in the office area than is a "salt and pepper" effect of too many small flower arrangements. Although they require less frequent attention than do fresh flowers, plants cannot be neglected if they are to remain attractive. Remove all the dead leaves and stringy runners and see that the plants are regularly watered.

A good flower arrangement has distinction and qualities not found in a commonplace bouquet of flowers. Good color, suitable design, appropriate container, and a knowledge of when to stop are points that provide distinctive flower arrangements.

Suggestions for attractive flower arrangements.

1. Limit the choice of flowers to one of these color schemes: shades of from dark to light of *one* color only; similar colors such as orange-red, orange and yellows; opposite colors such as purple and yellow or blue and orange.
2. Use triangular, horizontal, or vertical arrangements.
   To create a *triangular arrangement,* choose the longest stem, preferably one with a bud or small flower, as the apex and place it in the holder. Put in the remaining stems one at a time, alternating on the left and right side of the first one. Maintain one main stem or line and let the others show less importance by their shorter and different lengths. Use the largest and darkest flowers at the base of the arrangement. Use the light colors and forms at the top for balance.

To create a *horizontal arrangement,* use a low bowl or container (best for desks and office counters). Avoid delicate vases that tip easily. De-stem heavy-petaled flowers such as gardenias, camellias, and dahlias, and float them in a flat dish. Use an odd number of blossoms. The rule of one, three, or five is a good one to remember when arranging flowers.

To create a *vertical arrangement* (effective against a wall space or heavy background), use gladioli, larkspur, and iris.

3. Use appropriate containers that match the texture of the flowers they hold: fragile containers, such as glass or fine pottery, for delicate flowers; heavier containers of pottery, metal, or wood for coarser flowers, weeds, and branches.

4. Select flowers approximately one and one-half times the height of the vase or one and one-half times the diameter of the container, if a low bowl. White, green, pale blue, and natural tones are the most ideal colors for containers.

5. Know when to stop. It is better to have too few flowers than too many. A courageous snipping of unwanted leaves and flowers often produces a better effect.

6. Use a good scissors or small pruning shears, several needle-point flower holders, an assortment of containers of different sizes, shapes, and tex-ture, and decorative accessories.

7. Add a festive note to the office area on the occasion of Easter, Halloween, Thanksgiving, and Christmas.

One or two centers of interest of considerable size are more effective in the office area than are many small ones. Expensive objects should never be placed on the counter, where they might tempt young fingers. Until they are needed, holiday decorations should be boxed, labeled, and stored where they won't be forgotten. This might be the top shelf of the supply room.

Desk management. Efficient office work starts with your own desk. Good desk management requires organization of materials. In organizing the flow of materials to and from the desk provide for (1) incoming materials, (2) work in progress, and (3) outgoing work.

The top of your desk is a work area. Only materials needed for work in progress should be permitted to remain on the surface. This is often easier said than done, especially since, at some time, nearly every item of school business will cross your desk.

Use the following principles as guides to help you in the daily routine of desk management:

1. Keep telephone books and directories off the desk and counter. Have a special place for them.

2. Allocate each drawer of the desk to a specific purpose: stationery, forms, your "personals."

3. Place "unfinished" or work-in-progress materials out of sight when not actively working on them. Check these materials every day; sort for items approaching the due-dates.

4. Handle a sheet of paper only once, if possible.
5. Develop routines into habits—same place for storing things, same hour for doing things.
6. Allow ample unscheduled time.
7. Assign a definite time for getting "must" things done.
8. Schedule work requiring many materials for a time when interruptions are less likely to occur.
9. If a job will take a long time, break it into steps and complete each step one at a time.
10. Gather all materials before beginning a job.
11. Place outgoing or completed work, such as reports to the central administrative offices and letters, on the principal's desk for his checking and signature. Provide a file basket or tray on yours or the principal's desk.
12. Place materials going to teachers in their mail boxes or deliver it by messenger to their rooms.
13. Place outgoing mail in the mail bag or at the regular place of pick-up.
14. Leave your desk clean and in good order. At the close of the day, dust and cover your typewriter.

Other helpful suggestions for good desk management include the following points:

1. Weigh down papers to prevent their being blown to the floor.
2. Keep anything that might tip over on the desk at a safe distance—opened bottles of ink, vases of flowers.
3. Keep desk well stocked with supplies.
4. Check file trays daily.
5. Discard all obsolete items.
6. Protect or cover items of a confidential nature.
7. Keep money in a locked file. (Some schools forbid keeping money in a school office.)

MAINTAINING THE SUPPLY ROOM

The school secretary will find many kinds of items stored in the office supply room and other storage areas of the school building. Paper, pencils, carbon paper, paint, crayons, and other consumable supplies are stored in the office supply room along with many other materials that are used regularly.

The materials in school supply rooms are distributed according to some well-established system. Schools adopt either the "open" or "closed" system of supply room management. Each system has certain advantages and disadvantages, and the choice frequently depends upon the principal or what works best in an individual school.

Open supply room. If your school has an "open" supply room system, teachers can enter the supply room and take whatever supplies they need at any time during the school day. This is considered by some principals to be a more democratic method of handling supplies than the "closed" system.

If your school has the "open" supply room system, fasten a piece of paper to a clipboard and hang it by the door. You should encourage and educate teachers to list the kinds and amounts of supplies they take. Then you can easily re-order by checking the items listed on the clipboard. Teachers soon learn that there is no necessity to hoard materials, and this procedure allows the school secretary more time for her other duties. This system also saves paper work on the part of the teachers, since they do not have to place a written order. Many teachers like the system because they are not restricted when unforeseen circumstances require particular supplies. The disadvantage of having an "open" supply room is that some teachers may take more materials than they need. Also, teachers may neglect to list on the clipboard the supplies they have taken, or may leave untidy piles of stock on the shelves or counters.

Closed supply room. If your school has the "closed" supply room system, teachers cannot enter the supply room to select or remove supplies. Only you or your principal can select and remove supplies. Teachers send their supply orders to the office at stated intervals requesting the items which they wish to receive from the supply room. You fill their orders (sometimes the principal lends a hand). Student messengers can help deliver these items to the classrooms. Heavy items, such as reams of large paper and clay, may be delivered by the custodian. The advantages of this system are that it reduces the hoarding of materials, facilitates accurate supply accounting, and keeps the supply room in a neat and orderly arrangement. The disadvantages of the closed system are that your valuable secretarial time is used to fill orders and consultation with teachers who do not always know the specifications of items they wish to receive. Also, emergency requests for supplies cause interruptions in your work.

Many school principals like to have the teachers return all unused supplies to the supply room at the end of the school year. If carried to extreme, this can become a nuisance. Most principals allow teachers to retain the necessary supplies for use when school opens in September.

Points for managing the supply room. The following points are among those suggested by school secretaries to make management of the school supply room easier and more efficient:

1. Store in one place all items of a like nature.
2. Keep most-wanted materials in the most accessible places.
3. Open only one package or one box of each item at a time.
4. Place items on the shelves so that labels may be read easily.
5. Use shelf labels to organize supplies.
6. Arrange only identical items in depth on shelves.

7. Dispose of empty cartons and boxes.
8. Maintain supply room for supplies, not as a catch-all for unwanted, unclaimed articles.
9. Keep counters clear for working space.

Controlling supplies. For supply items, a stock card (3 × 5) giving information concerning all the specifications, price per unit, purchase
reference, delivery, and so forth, should be kept on file for each item. The
stock card should show a *high limit* and a *low limit*. The limits may be
established by keeping a strict account of each item for a period of weeks
to determine a reasonable average. Periodically, every week or month,
you should check the supply room shelves. If an item seems low, check
the appropriate card from the stock card file or binder against the "low
limit" to determine if you should re-order. As the specifications are already listed on the card, very little time is required to re-order the needed
items.

You can use the file of stock cards for inventory purposes. Post the
supplies on hand on each card by noting the amount received minus the
amount distributed. You should take a complete physical inventory at
least once each school year. The best time to do this is just before the
annual requisition order is compiled.

Mimeograph room. Most schools keep the mimeograph or duplicating
machine in a room apart from the open office area. Sometimes it is in the
supply room. The mimeograph room should be equipped with shelves
for paper and inks, a fireproof container for rags, and a file for used
stencils and mats. There should be clothes hooks for aprons or smocks.
Rubber gloves should be used when putting on and taking off stencils,
although with a little care, a good operator will rarely get ink on her
hands. It is advisable for you to train only one or two students to run
the machine, or do the work yourself. If possible, there should be another machine in another location for teachers to use. When several
people use the same machine, it is not long before the machine becomes
mechanically defective. Furthermore, casual users of the room seldom
leave it in as good order as they find it.

WORKING WITH CLOCKS, BELLS, AND KEYS

The secretary performs many small services to help keep the school plant
running. These services are not necessarily related or routine but they
may include responsibilities regarding the clocks, bells, keys, and lockers.
Many other services might be added, according to the individual needs
of the school.

Clocks and bells. In most schools today, bells ring automatically at the
times punched on the time tape inside the office master clock. These times
are set by the school electrician to meet the needs of the school program.
If there is a reason to depart from the regular schedule, you will need to

ring the bells manually. Such departures might be a shortened day, rain during recess or lunch, or a breakdown in tape or electrical equipment. You will find that a "Minute Minder" (clock with a bell) is a useful gadget to nudge your memory when bells are to be rung at unscheduled times.

The accuracy of school clocks is generally the responsibility of the school custodian. If, during his early morning check, he finds the master clock stopped or the room clocks giving different times, he should call the electrician. If the power fails while school is in session, you should call the electrician as a service to the custodian.

In the interests of a quieter school, there is a trend to discontinuance of the practice of ringing the school bell to summon the custodian, nurse, or principal. Instead, student messengers summon personnel to the office; or, where the school plant includes a number of buildings, telephone extensions are placed in strategic locations. Another plan is to have the custodian and others check in at the office at hour or half-hour intervals. Such an arrangement satisfactorily handles most requests.

Keys and locks. Your responsibility for handling keys and locks may be limited to keeping them under lock and key and to issuing locks and locker numbers on request. Practices vary, but in many schools, you would be requested to issue keys to teachers, classrooms, and to make available keys for special rooms and cabinets. You may also need to issue duplicate or master keys.

Issue classroom keys to teachers at the beginning of each school year. A key case is sometimes kept in the office area, in which teachers hang their keys on numbered hooks when they leave school in the afternoon and pick them up in the morning when they arrive. However, teachers in some schools keep their keys until the end of the year. Teachers are seldom given master keys; master keys are usually given to only the principal, secretary, and head custodian, and are used only for convenience and for emergencies.

Marking special keys. Keys for special rooms and cabinets are frequently needed and should be readily available in the office. You must account for them when they are withdrawn. Such keys are less easily misplaced if tagged with a good-sized piece of chipboard or plywood. Write the number or use of each key on the tag. You will find that colored nail polishes are effective for marking the tags. Provide space on the check-out card of each key for the signature of the withdrawee and the date of withdrawal. Special keys may be hung in a key case or on hooks attached to the desk or table in the office area.

Keeping a record. You should keep an up-to-date record of all keys on hand in the school. Show in this record the location of the door, cabinet, or room which each key will open, the serial number, and the number of keys of each kind. With this type of record, you will find it comparatively easy to order replacements for keys which have been lost, stolen, or broken. All keys should be numbered, the number stamped or tagged on each key.

Storing keys. There are two good methods of storing keys whenever a large number of keys are used. One is to maintain a key storage cabinet apart from the one used by teachers. Each type of key is hung on a hook. The hooks may be numbered to correspond to the key record sheet, or a small tag may be placed near the hook with the same description that is on the record sheet.

A second method is to use a small 3 × 5 inch envelope for each key, typing on it the serial number, the lock which the key will open, and the number of keys on hand. It is also possible to use an envelope for all the keys for a given room, labeling the envelope with the room number as well as other needed information. The envelopes may be stored in a box by room number for ease in locating them. Duplicates of all keys should be kept in the key envelope.

Combination locks. Keep a list of all combination locks by serial numbers, and the combinations. You will find it helpful to use a separate card for each lock and to tag unassigned locks with the combination.

FIRE DRILLS AND EMERGENCIES

Fire drills. In some schools, your responsibility in the matter of fire drills is primarily to see that a fire drill is performed once during each school month and that a report of the drill is filed with the proper department. In other schools, additional duties may be assigned by your principal.

Although a fire drill is proper at any hour of the school day, every school avoids holding drills at times that will cause inconvenience or unnecessary interruption. You should be alert to what will be going on in the building when you are scheduling a fire drill. It is not a good idea to schedule a drill when you know there is a class in the auditorium, when a testing program is in progress, or when demonstrations or special events are taking place in the building. Unscheduled drills occur when meddling fingers tamper with emergency alarm units. If this happens, allow the fire drill to proceed according to the usual routine.

Making the report. Many schools require that a written report be sent after each fire drill to the district administration offices, and, frequently, to the fire department as well. You should include such items as date and time of drill, number of minutes required to clear the building, and an evaluation of the drill.

Other duties. Additional fire drill assignments may require you to do such things as block an exit, check pupil lavatories, close office doors, clock the elapsed time of evacuation, ring the bell to indicate end of the drill, and signal permission to re-enter the building.

Maintenance of fire equipment. The head custodian is usually responsible for the maintenance of fire extinguishers and emergency firefighting equipment in the school. Both you and the custodian must observe all fire regulations regarding the use and storage of inflammable materials in and on the school premises. In most places, regular school inspections are made by members of the fire department, and their recommendations for elimination of fire hazards must be fulfilled.

Emergencies. An emergency is an unexpected occurrence which calls for immediate action. While many people think of emergencies only in terms of accidents or sudden illnesses, there are other situations occurring during the school day that meet the definition. An emergency situation may arise when there is an operating failure of school equipment, such as the furnace, a motion-picture projector, or the cafeteria's electric range. Unscheduled requests from the district office for reports on school matters, such as classification, attendance, and text books, require your prompt attention. Your principal may make an unexpected request for a special typing service to be accomplished without delay. And, of course, emergencies due to accidents and sudden illnesses occur in every school.

In almost all cases, other people depend upon you to assume control of the situation and do something about it at once. While you cannot hope to anticipate every type of emergency, be prepared for some of them.

Routine emergency requests. You should know whom to call upon for help for those situations which cannot be handled in the school office. For emergency repairs, you should know who is responsible for what. Keep an up-to-date list of names and telephone numbers of the proper school departments. Red-line these names in your desk directory and note in the margin any information that may be useful the next time.

Handling emergencies in the absence of your principal. Only rarely does an administrative problem arise which is critical enough to require immediate decision. Have an understanding with your principal that he should phone the school office at a specified time while he is away. This will help you take care of any situation beyond your control. Tell callers that "Mr. Principal will phone in (check clock) minutes. If you will tell me your problem, I will ask him about it when he calls."

In emergencies, or for unusual circumstances, or for someone to "back you up," you may send for the substitute principal. In an elementary school this person usually is a classroom teacher designated to serve in this capacity. In extreme cases, you might refer an issue to the office of the assistant superintendent, but use this only as a last resort.

Emergency requests for reports or special typing service are inevitable in every office. Accept them in good spirit as part of your job.

Situations involving pupils and school personnel. For accidents and sudden illnesses involving pupils, you should refer to the home and emergency phone numbers listed on the pupil registration cards. Some schools maintain a supplementary card containing the name, telephone number, and address of an adult known to the family, and the employment address of the parents. For the faculty and other members of the staff, you should have the telephone of a relative or physician to be notified. Other telephone numbers you will need at your fingertips are those of a nearby doctor, ambulance service, and the receiving hospital.

Many school districts now require school secretaries to have training in a standard first aid course. If your school does not have a full-time nurse, this training will be invaluable to you.

7

Using the Telephone
in the School Office

In this age, when schools are highly public-relations conscious, the school secretary has the opportunity to create good will and win friends for the school by consistently maintaining a high standard of telephone manners and techniques. Many people, including most parents, have no personal contact with members of the school staff other than by telephone. Always respond to each call in a manner that will create a favorable impression of the school. A cordial, pleasant voice can be one of your greatest assets.

HELPING YOUR VOICE SERVE YOU

The voice on your end of the line. Every time you answer the telephone you are responding to a person who had a reason for calling that was important to him. Since you are not meeting face-to-face, he cannot see your smile or sympathetic changes of expression. Only by the warm friendliness in your voice can you convey the impression that you are ready to give service. Give the caller your full attention. Your voice can reflect your attentiveness; a lack of interest is easily detected.

Tone is important. A normal conversational tone of voice—neither too loud nor too soft—carries best over the telephone. Be as sincere and natural as you are in person. Speak directly into the transmitter, unhurriedly and distinctly. Avoid a tone which may reveal you consider your time more valuable than the caller's time. Whenever you are tired, upset, or have had a trying experience, be especially careful of your tone qualities. Remember, your caller doesn't know and probably doesn't care how "you" feel.

You can improve your voice by practice. Ask yourself frequently, "How do I sound?" Ask a friend whether your telephone voice is your natural voice. It is important to remember that over the telephone your voice is the school talking.

RECEIVING TELEPHONE CALLS

Courteous, efficient telephone techniques will go a long way toward helping the caller feel that his call is important and will receive proper attention.

Incoming calls. Incoming calls must be answered immediately; the ringing phone cannot be ignored. When you cannot talk to the caller at once, say to him, "Menlo Avenue School, one moment, please." Then return to the line as soon as possible and say, "Thank you for waiting. This is Mr. Principal's secretary speaking. May I help you?" Beware of using a tone that implies, "Here I am, go ahead and tell me." In all cases, the courteous and businesslike response: "Good morning, Menlo Avenue School. This is the principal's office, Miss White, the secretary," is preferable to an unrevealing, "Hello."

Calls for the principal. If the call is for your principal, say, "Just a moment while I connect you with Mr. Principal's office." In the event that Mr. Principal is not at his desk, say, "I'm sorry but Mr. Principal is not available; may I take a message?" If his line is busy, say "Mr. Principal's line is busy. Will you wait?" If the caller wants to wait, report at least every twenty seconds that "Mr. Principal's line is still busy." However, don't encourage a caller to wait. It is better to take a message and arrange for the call to be returned.

Calls for teachers. When the call is for a teacher during class time, explain that, unless it is an emergency, you will have to take the number and have the teacher return the call when she is free. Teachers should not be called from the classroom to answer the telephone unless it is an exceptional circumstance. If the teacher is called during a known free time and several minutes will be needed for him to reach the phone, explain this to the caller. Ask if he wishes to wait or leave a message.

Calls for pupils. If the call is for a pupil, ask for further information and say you will be glad to give the pupil the message. If it is an emergency, arrange to have the pupil call back. In any event, you or the principal must monitor the pupil's call.

Taking telephone messages. In taking a message over the phone, record as much information as you can concerning the call. A simple printed form that provides for such important items as caller's name, caller's name, telephone number, nature of the message, and time of call, is a useful time-saving device. When printed forms are not supplied, secretaries often make up their own message-slips on the duplicating machine. These message slips should be kept near the telephone where they are readily accessible. In a manner of speaking, you actually perform an answering service for your principal, teachers, and, occasionally, pupils. It is important that you take these messages correctly and deliver them promptly. You will also find it helpful to keep a notebook on your desk in which you record every incoming call (date, phone number, nature of call, time). This will serve as an excellent reference when a month later you are trying to "track down" some information.

Getting information correctly. Messages for the administrators often include dates, hours, and addresses. Listen carefully to the numbers that are involved and repeat the information to the caller so that he can verify the correctness. However, avoid repeating facts of a confidential nature whenever other persons are present in the office. Take care to place a memorandum for the administrator in a conspicuous place on his desk and weight it down so that a sudden draft will not blow it aside.

Using student assistants. When student helpers are used to answer office phone calls, they should be trained to respond according to an established procedure, such as the following: "Menlo Avenue School, Charles Ryan, student, answering. May I take your message? . . . Now, may I repeat the information to be sure I have it exactly right. Thank you. Good-by."

Securing the name and number of a telephone caller. When you handle an incoming phone call, keep in mind that securing the name and number of the caller are essential points in every telephone conversation. Securing this information frequently requires persistence as well as courtesy. Use expressions that request rather than demand. This technique proves to be more effective and pleasing to the person on the other end of the line. "May I ask who is calling, please?" is preferable to the blunt, "Who is this, please?" And, "If I may have your number, I will be glad to return your call," creates a better impression than, "What's your number?" You can tell by the tone of the caller if he wishes not to reveal his identity. They want to talk to your principal—not you—and they do not wish to leave messages. Usually they will say, "If you will tell me when Mr. Principal will return, I'll call back."

Callers who wish to remain unknown. Few, if any, mysterious calls from unknowns actually occur, and if they do, few officials deny the caller a chance to speak. You will be able to recognize a familiar voice. The legitimate caller is always willing to give his name. When it is necessary to know who the caller is and he has not or will not identify himself, you might say, "Is this Mr. Brown?" or, "Have we discussed this matter before, Mr. Brown?" This usually forces the caller to indicate whether he is Mr. Brown or Mr. Somebody Else.

If the caller remains adamant, you may have to refer the call to your principal. He may wish to handle the call himself, or you may be required to say, "I'm sorry but I have been instructed not to disturb Mr. Principal unless he knows the nature of your call." It may be policy to ask the caller to make an appointment or write a letter. It is not advisable to give information or enter into any discussion until the caller is identified.

When your principal cannot be reached. Calls for an administrator frequently come in while he is engaged with a visitor in his office or when he is occupied with school business. A good plan is to have an understanding with your superiors regarding their wishes on the matter of interrupting conferences or calling them to the telephone. You will want to know under what conditions they are willing to take a call and whom they will talk to, regardless. Use your judgment as to whether a visitor in the office should have precedence over a caller on the telephone.

How to postpone calls. If the official is not to be interrupted or called to the phone, explain to the caller without revealing confidences that your principal is not available at the moment but that you will have him return the call at his first opportunity. For example, you may say, "Mr. Principal is conducting an interview at the moment; perhaps I could help you." Or a more general, "Mr. Principal is not available now. May I take a message and have him call you?" In no case should the caller be made to feel that his business is of less importance than that in which the official is engaged.

The same technique is considered acceptable practice when the administrator is occupied anywhere on the school grounds or away from the premises on errands of a school nature. Even if he fails to inform you of his whereabouts, be sure to word your answers carefully. A response in such a case could be, "Mr. Principal is out of the office just now. I'll get in touch with him and have him phone you." Or, if the person has no phone, "I'll get in touch with him and you may call back in fifteen minutes." Comments such as "He left the office without telling me," "I haven't seen him this morning," or "I don't know where he is" may convey to the caller a wrong impression of your office procedures or relationships.

Terminating calls. Bringing a call to a close is as important as opening it. A careful choice of words and suitable inflection of your voice will often let the party know that you consider the conversation ended. This requires considerable tact and courtesy on your part so that the caller will not feel you are cutting him off. Expressions such as the following may be used to good advantage: "Thank you for calling us, Mrs. Gray." "I will call you back in a few days." "I believe that's all we need to know right now, Mr. Black." A courteous expression of regret or appreciation plus a friendly, "Thank you for calling," will help leave a lasting favorable impression.

GIVING INFORMATION

You are likely to get many calls from different people asking for the identical information. Every day parents will call the school regarding such matters as the nurse's schedule, holidays, lost articles, cafeteria prices, hours of dismissal. Any special event, drive, or program is apt to produce a flood of calls. Requests for information regarding these and similar topics of a school nature can usually be promptly answered from your own fund of knowledge concerning them. It is important to remember to treat the last caller as courteously as the first.

Answering common requests. There will be many calls from those in the business division, the supervisor's office, the personnel department, and other members of the school "family." Train yourself to learn the answers to common requests and questions. Be able to take care of these without referral to your administrators. In the beginning this takes conscious, deliberate effort. Your information will come from scanning every bulletin that crosses the principal's desk, from pre-reading every bit of official correspondence coming to the school office, from placing telephone calls, and from alert listening to the conversation of teachers, custodians, and children. Notes may have to be taken and memoranda made. Before long, though, it becomes second-nature and then you'll find yourself taking pride and pleasure in your special knowledge.

If you are asked something you can't answer quickly, say, "I'm sorry, Mr. Black, but I don't have that information available; will you wait while I get it?" If getting the information will take more than just a moment, say, "May I call you back, Mr. Black, after I have obtained the information?"

Referring calls to another source. When the call requires information that is beyond your province, put the caller in touch with the best available source of information. Do not attempt to handle the request when there are other offices that possibly can supply the information. A good rule is never to turn a person away without at least putting him on a track that will lead him to what he wants to know. There is no occasion for such responses as, "I'm sure I don't know," or "We had something about that, but it was a long time ago."

If you must refer a caller to another source of information, it is your responsibility to be certain to the best of your knowledge that you have supplied him with the correct name, department, or telephone number. Check with your telephone directory to be sure the number is 6134, not 6341.

If a caller tells you that he has exhausted his resources in trying to locate the proper source of information, then it is appropriate for you to endeavor to find the information, even though the subject is of no direct concern to your own school or office. There comes a time when letting a person ride the telephone merry-go-round must come to an end.

Requests for confidential information. Occasionally there are requests for confidential information, not to be revealed to an inquiring caller. These include calls for names and addresses of parents, phone numbers and addresses of teachers, pupil records, and teacher status. A good rule is never to reveal anything directly pertaining to an individual that may be considered a personal matter.

Requests for referrals. It is not a good idea for you to recommend any services, such as private teachers, piano tuners, clinics, or psychiatrists. Nor should you endorse a particular school product, merchant, or a commercial establishment dealing in school or other supplies. To requests for information of this kind, a courteous "I'm sorry, but I cannot supply that information," will usually prove adequate.

Protecting the administration. Your tone should imply that you don't know, not that it's forbidden information. It is your responsibility to protect the administrator even if he hasn't kept you completely informed. No information should be given out that will in any way "backfire" on the administrator or other school personnel, or convey the wrong impression. Never let the caller know that your superior hasn't kept you completely informed or that he just doesn't take you or his staff into his confidence. In making your reply, remember that it's not only what you say but how you say it.

How to make calls for information. Before placing a call for information, plan the points you want to cover. You will make a better impression when you have clearly in mind the things you want to ask. If records and facts are needed, get them ready beforehand and have them before you while you talk. If you do not know exactly whom to ask for, give the person at the other end of the line enough information to make an accurate referral of your call. For example: "May I please have the department that handles the moving of a piano from one building to another?" When your call is answered, identify yourself immediately by saying, "This is Miss White, Menlo Avenue School, the principal's secretary speaking."

Keep your conversation to the point, but do not sacrifice essential data for the sake of brevity. Be sure your problem is understood and that you receive sufficient information to satisfy your request. Close the conversation with an appropriate expression of appreciation.

PLACING TELEPHONE CALLS

Your school and personnel directories should supply most of the telephone numbers you will need to use. The school administrator will often be able to give you those for business outside the immediate school system. For all other numbers, consult the phone directories; call the information operator only as a last resort. Give the person you are calling ample time to answer before you hang up. When the person called answers, identify yourself immediately: "This is Miss White, Menlo Avenue School, secretary to Mr. Principal."

Placing calls for the principal. When you place the call, it is your responsibility to get the person called on the line before connecting your administrator. However, it is considered poor etiquette to place a call and then make the called party wait while the person calling comes to the phone. This occasionally is a delicate problem, as some school officials are not aware of the approved procedure. It may be necessary to call your administrator to the phone as soon as you reach the other person's office. "Mr. Principal, I have the Jackson School on the line; Mr. Green is coming to the phone."

When the person is not in. When placing a call and the person is not in, inquire when he will be available. Leave the name of the person who called the school, and the school number. For example, "Please say that Mr. Principal of the Menlo School called. His number is MOnroe 9–8251." The general subject of the message can be indicated, if requested and known, but avoid detailed information.

In answer to, "May I take a message?" you may say, "Mr. Principal is calling about courses of study for the new teachers." Usually, though, this is the prerogative of the administrator, not the secretary. Unless your principal has directed you to state the purpose of the call, it is wiser not to state it, even if you know it.

Providing pertinent information. When placing or taking a call for your superiors regarding a subject on which there has been correspondence, place this material where he can easily see it while he takes the call. If the call concerns availability of a date, place his and/or the school's calendar before him. In short, provide the factual information your principal will need to handle the call.

LONG-DISTANCE CALLS

Many school districts discourage the practice of making long-distance telephone calls. In some cases, they are to be made only by the central switchboard upon request. You will need to learn the policy of your school district regarding long-distance calls.

Direct-dialing service. The new direct-dialing service found in many areas makes long-distance calling as simple as local calling. Where this service is available, the telephone company usually furnishes a list of, and code numbers for, those places that can be reached from your phone.*

Station-to-station calls. Where there is no direct dialing system, long-distance calls must be placed by the long-distance operator. As a matter of fact, only station-to-station calls can be dialed direct. A station-to-station call is made when the caller is willing to speak to anyone who answers. This type of call has the cheapest rate. All long-distance rates are based on so much for the first three minutes and so much for each minute thereafter.

Person-to-person calls. Although station-to-station rates are lower, it is frequently more economical to make a person-to-person call when your call must be received by a specific person, or when the person

* See page 73 for a more complete explanation of direct distance dialing (D.D.D.).

called is difficult to reach. To make such a call, give the long-distance operator the name of the place you are calling. This permits her to start the call without waiting for the number and name. Always supply the number, if you know it. When you do not know the number, the street address should be given. State the name of the person you are calling last. Stay on the line until the call is completed, unless notified to do otherwise by the operator. If the connection cannot be made at once, the operator, at your request, will try at intervals to reach the party you want. It is not necessary to repeat the call to another operator.

It goes almost without saying that long-distance calls should be planned in advance. Be prepared with the materials you may need, and be concise in your conversation in order to make the most use of your time. If you need to keep a record of the charges, request the operator to furnish this information upon completion of your call.

Last, but not least, telephones should be available to qualified personnel only. Other persons, especially pupils, wishing to make phone calls should be directed to the nearest public telephone booth.

TELEPHONE COURTESY

The secretary who masters the art of telephone use plays a vital role in establishing friendly relations with all those who call her office. The following are suggestions that have proven helpful for most occasions.

1. When the principal, and other persons, are using the office telephone, try to make the room as quiet as possible.
2. Close the window or door to minimize outside noises, stop typing for a few minutes, and ask those people conversing near the telephone to move farther away. If the person using the phone has to be given information, write it on a slip of paper and pass it to him; speaking to him interrupts his conversation.
3. If the administrator is making an important call and someone enters the outer office, quietly close the connecting door. To avoid overhearing his personal calls, you may find it necessary to invent an excuse to leave the office.
4. Some schools have intercom systems instead of classroom telephones. There is a courtesy due the teacher who has an intercom amplifier in her classroom. Think twice before chancing an interruption of the teacher's lesson. Is the message that urgent?
5. If you must call, give preference to the very first or the close of the class hour.

Other points you should keep in mind are:

1. Be courteous, cordial, and business-like.
2. Use a natural, distinct, tone of voice.
3. Always identify yourself promptly.
4. Give the caller your undivided attention.
5. Always have pencil and note paper ready to take down messages.
6. Handle as much as possible of the call without referral.

7. Always know where the administrator can be reached.
8. Keep at hand a list of all important telephone numbers.
9. Plan your out-going calls.
10. Close the telephone conversation with appreciative courtesy.

THE TELEPHONE SWITCHBOARD

Effective communication, both inside and outside the school plant, is very important to the smooth operation of the school. Much communication is handled over the telephone, and most junior and senior high schools have installed a central telephone switchboard, so that telephone calls can be focused and controlled from one area. Elementary schools do not usually have a central telephone switchboard. The telephone switchboard may be referred to as the PBX, meaning Private Branch Exchange.

The telephone switchboard operator. The person who is regularly assigned to the telephone switchboard has probably been trained by the telephone company. She knows her job well, and she knows that although she may have other duties assigned, her first responsibility is to effectively operate the switchboard. Other duties may consist of light typing, routine, clerical duties, or acting as receptionist.

The regular switchboard operator, however, cannot be tied to the switchboard all of the time. During a normal working day, she will need relief periods for breaks and lunch time. In the course of a year or so, she will need someone to take her job when she is off on vacation or out for illness. Most schools have found that at least two or three other clerical employees in the school should know how to operate the telephone switchboard. This section is written primarily for those clerical or secretarial employees in the school who may be called upon to relieve the regular operator on the switchboard.

It would be ideal if the telephone company were to provide the new or relief employee with more thorough and up-to-date orientation on techniques of operating the switchboard. Unfortunately, this does not happen in many schools. The regular attendant or operator is assigned to teach the relief employee the elements of running the telephone switchboard. The following points and techniques are given to the relief employee so that she may be a more effective operator. Remember that the primary duty of a switchboard operator is to give service—and courtesy is a part of that service. Accuracy in handling the traffic on the telephone switchboard should never be sacrificed for speed.

The telephone switchboard. Basically there are two types of telephone switchboards—the cord and the cordless. The cord switchboard is one in which connections are made by extending cords from their original position to a selected outlet, or jack. A board with heavy traffic may have many "crisscrossed" or overlapping cords. The cordless switchboard performs the same function, except that connections are made by keys either in an upward or downward position. The direction of the keys (up or down) is called a *path*. For example, the rows could be considered as follows:

Top Row:	Keys up	—Path "A"
	Keys down	—Path "B"
Middle Row:	Keys down	—Path "C"
	Keys up	—Path "D"
Bottom Row:	Keys up	—Path "E"

Whether or not your school has a cord or a cordless board, the principles of operation are very similar.

Turning the switchboard on and off. Usually a type of buzzer or ringing system will indicate to the operator any traffic that is on the board. The buzzer should always be turned "on" unless the operator is constantly watching the switchboard and can watch the lights as they indicate calls. The following instructions apply to most cord and cordless switchboards:

CORD SWITCHBOARD

To turn board "on"
1. Turn the generator to "P."
2. Turn battery and buzzer switches to the "on" position.

To turn board "off"
1. Turn generator to "H" position.
2. Turn battery and buzzer switches to "off" position.

CORDLESS SWITCHBOARD

To turn the board "on"
1. Turn ringing switch to "key" and buzzer to "on."
2. Release "N" key (located on face of board and used with night connections) to normal position.

To turn board "off"
1. Turn ringing switch to "Hand" and buzzer to "off."
2. Turn "N" key to downward position.

Handling inter-office calls. Inter-office or station-to-station calls are made within the school plant when one person wishes to call another. Keep in mind the following points when handling inter-office calls:

CORD SWITCHBOARD

Condition	*Action*
Signal appears	1. Plug in the rear cord above the light.
	2. Push the corresponding listening key forward either at the same time or before plugging in.
	3. Acknowledge the call—say "Office."
	4. Repeat the request and close the listening key.
	5. Connect parties by plugging front cord of same pair to line requested.
	6. Observe the cord lights.

CORD SWITCHBOARD (*Cont.*)

Condition	Action
Front cord lamp lighted	7. Ring with front key (pull toward you).
	8. Ring at intervals of 6–10 seconds and give ringing report at end of 30 seconds. Say, "I am ringing."
Front cord lamp becomes dark	9. Take no further action.
Disconnect signal appears	10. Disconnect—front cord first (rear cord lamp is lighted).

CORDLESS SWITCHBOARD

Condition	Action
Station signal appears (visual flag)	1. Remove receiver from hook and locate idle path (preferably E).
	2. Operate Attd. and Sta. key in same path. Answer, "Office."
Order given	3. Acknowledge order and locate called station.
	4. Check all paths for busy before connecting.
If called station is not busy	5. Operate called station key in same path in which call was answered.
	6. Ring called station by operating ringing key directly below station in downward position for one second.
Called station busy	7. Give busy report—Disconnect.
Called station answers	8. Close Attd. Key.
Disconnect signal appears	9. Disconnect from left to right.

Handling outgoing calls. If a party within the school wishes to make an outside call, he will pick up his telephone receiver and request "Outside" or "a line." The following points should be followed when such a request is made:

CORD SWITCHBOARD

Condition	Action
Station requests "outside"	1. Acknowledge request and close listening key.
	2. Operate through dial key (the back key). If only one trunk line is available, it is permissible to plug into trunk first to hear dial tone. The through dial key must be operated before the station dials or a wrong number will result.
	3. Connect front cord to highest numbered idle trunk and disregard dialing flashes.
Disconnect signal appears (back cord lamp becomes lighted)	4. Disconnect front cord first, and restore through dial key.
	5. Disconnect back cord.

CORDLESS SWITCHBOARD

Condition	Action
Station requests "Out-side"	1. Acknowledge the request and close the attendant key.
	2. Connect the highest numbered idle trunk in path with the station.
	3. Hang up receiver and disregard dialing flashes.
Disconnect signal appears	4. Disconnect from left to right.

Handling calls on incoming trunks. Incoming calls are handled the same way as are outgoing calls. The following points should be observed when such a call appears on the board:

CORD SWITCHBOARD

Condition	Action
Trunk signal appears	1. Open the listening key.
	2. Plug a front cord into the trunk and answer with the name of your school.
Request is given	3. Acknowledge the request and close the listening key.
	4. Connect back cord to called station and observe cord lamps.
	5. Ring with back key, following the same ringing procedure as you would for station-to-station calls.
Call is completed	6. Disconnect front cord first. Failure to disconnect promptly may result in a seized trunk. (A trunk may be "seized" on an incoming call before the operator disconnects the previous connection.) A trunk line clears when the station hangs up, not when the operator disconnects. If you make disconnections promptly, you will avoid "seized" trunks.

CORDLESS SWITCHBOARD

Condition	Action
Trunk signal appears	1. Remove receiver, operate attendant key in idle path and operate the trunk key in same path. Answer with name of your school.
Request is given	2. Acknowledge the request and check station in all paths for busy. If clear, connect in path of the call and ring the station.
	3. Follow same ringing procedure as station to station call.

Making a board line connection. School districts consisting of at least seven or eight junior and senior high schools will have direct lines to the offices of the Board of Education. It is referred to as a "Board line." Thus, if an employee in your school wishes to call directly to the Board offices, he will pick up his telephone receiver and request, "Board line, please." The operator then connects this order to the Board line, rather than to an outside line. This is actually a time-saving technique as it permits one to dial the extension immediately.

Supervising a call. Supervising a call means that you give a report to the caller when the line requested is busy or doesn't answer. It is important that you make a report on these calls. Otherwise, the caller becomes annoyed, and may even hang up. The called party should answer within 30 seconds. If you find that a certain station is repeatedly slow in answering, you should either call his attention to it or refer the problem to your principal. Busy or ringing reports should be given every 30 seconds. Don't give a "don't answer" report too soon. You should give the station about 90 seconds (no more) to answer. Following are some remarks you might keep in mind for appropriate occasions:

"Mr. Brown's line is busy. Will you wait, please?" or "Station ___ is busy, will you wait, please?"

"Mr. Brown's line is still busy," or "Station ___ is still busy." "You may have Mr. Brown's line now."

"I'm ringing Mr. Brown now. Thank you for waiting." (Be sure that the calling party is still on the line before ringing the station.) "Mr. Brown doesn't answer. Do you wish to leave a message?" (When you record the message, don't forget to write down the calling party's telephone number and name. Then don't forget to deliver the message.)

Answering calls. When you receive a signal for a call, answer an inter-office call by saying, "Office." When you answer an outside call, give the name of your school, using a front cord. Always remember to open the listening key before you "plug in" for the outside call. Also, do not "plug into" a trunk call until you are ready to answer as this will stop the ringing signal for the calling party and he may hang up, being charged for the call.

Reversed trunk connections will occur, for example, if the back cord is connected to the trunk and the front cord to a station. This arrangement will destroy supervision. When you discover such a reverse connection, you will need to "listen in" to determine the status of the call. If you hear conversation, frequent checking may be necessary to determine when the call is terminated. If you do not hear conversation nor a dial tone, say, "Are you waiting?"

If cords are reversed on an incoming trunk call, both supervisory signals will be dark. If you have not rung the station, change the cords quickly and ring the station, using the back key.

Ringing a station. When ringing a station, check first of all the cord lamps. If the back cord lamp is lighted, ring with the back key; if the front cord lamp is lighted, ring with the front key. If you find that both cord lamps are dark, check to see if the cords have been reversed. To ring the station, move the ringing key toward you. To prevent ringing in the party's ear, be sure that you ring with the key corresponding to the cord with which you have made the connection.

Ringing power failure. To ring an extension during a ringing power failure, turn the "Ringing" switch to the position marked "Hand." Then hold the associated ringing position while turning the crank of the hand generator.

Handling the cords. It is important that the cords be handled properly when making connections and disconnections. Improper handling of the cords will cause them to break or fray, making a noisy connection or some other trouble. Always hold the cord by the base or shell of the plug. Do not press on the cord at the base of the plug while plugging into the jack. Neither should you remove the plugs by pulling on the cords.

Tracing the cords. Cords should be handled properly when disconnections are made. The following points should be observed to help prevent cut-offs:

1. Check to see if it is a disconnect and not a call on which the called station has not yet answered. To make sure, you may need to use the listening key.
2. Trace the cords by hand rather than by the eye.
3. Protect the overlapping cords. The cord on top of overlapping cords is the one most likely to be disturbed.

Dialing a number. Before dialing a number, you should first listen for the dial tone—if dial tone is heard, dial the number. Never force the dial back, as the number is selected as the dial returns. Forcing a dial return will interfere with the operation and a wrong number will be reached. Also, leave the listening key open until the last digit is dialed, or again a wrong number will result.

If you have made a mistake in dialing, you will need to redial from the beginning. On a cord switchboard, you will need to reinsert the plug; on a cordless switchboard, close the key and then open it.

Making long-distance calls. Schools generally try to discourage the number of long-distance calls. Instructors' calls are always limited to local calls unless they charge the call to their home phones. Therefore, long-distance calls are calls in the line of school business and are made by staff members.

If a staff member asks you to call a person long distance, first find out if the station call can be dialed direct. Many cities now have what is called D.D.D. (direct distance dialing) for convenient, fast, and less costly service. Obtain the telephone number before placing the call. You may have to call Long Distance and ask for information in that city. After obtaining the correct telephone number, check in the telephone book or your code card to find the area for that city. For example, if you were dialing Dover, Delaware, the code number would be 302; New York City, 212. Dial the code number, then dial the telephone number. Once you have started dialing, continue without hesitation until completion of dialing.

For those stations in which dialing cannot be direct, obtain the call by dialing Long Distance. Service will be faster if you give the information in the following order: type of call (station-to-station, person-to-person, collect); request charges, if required; name of called city and state; called telephone number; and calling party's name. If you need to signal the long-distance operator for any reason, remove and reinsert the plug in the trunk jack.

If you receive a long-distance call, try to locate the person called as soon as possible. If that station is busy, try the buzzer system or try to locate the person on the intercom. Say, "Mr. Brown, long-distance call." If you cannot locate Mr. Brown, take the number of the operator and the city calling and leave a message for Mr. Brown to call that operator.

Transferring a call. If you observe an incoming trunk connection which is flashing, this probably means that the caller wishes to transfer the call to another station. On the cord switchboard, open the listening key and say, "Office." Repeat the request, leaving the listening key open to avoid a possible cut-off. Then transfer the cord to the requested station and ring. On the cordless board, operate the attendant key and say, "Office." Repeat the request given, leaving the attendant key operated while transferring the call. Disconnect the station and then connect the new station. Operate the "H" key before leaving the lines unless the station answers.

If a station in your school has dialed an extension through the Board line, the call cannot be transferred to another phone through the switchboard. The person must hang up and then dial the desired station.

Making night connections. When the regular attendant is off duty, some arrangement must be made on the switchboard so that some phones in the building or in various campus locations will have an outside line. This makes it possible for those still working in the building (custodial staff or staff members) to have access to an outside line. In other words, these phones are given direct outside connections. To make night connections, be sure you have turned off the battery, generator or ringing keys and buzzer. Then connect the trunks and station as your principal has instructed. It is wise to put up a sign reading "Night Connections, Do Not Disturb."

Reporting emergency calls. If there is an emergency in your school that requires the fire, police, sheriff, or ambulance, the report will first come to the switchboard operator to locate help. You should dial the emergency number (always have it available) and ask for help. If the person reporting the emergency wishes to report directly, you should remain on the line and give any needed assistance.

If the emergency necessitates your leaving the switchboard, inform your supervisor or principal at once and quickly make the night connections to some of the more important stations. Listed below are the markings of the alarm signals and their indications:

P.S. (Permanent Signal) Usually an extension user has left the receiver off the hook.

SW. F.A. (Switch Fuse Alarm) A fuse has blown on equipment in the switchroom.

C.B. (Call Block) All line finder switches are in use.

RLS. MAG. (Release Magnet) A switch in the switchroom is not working properly.

L.F. GRD. (Line Finder Ground) Indicated trouble in the dial equipment.

PWR. BD. (Power Board) Usually a fuse has blown on the power equipment or ringing current has failed.

NOTE: An operated alarm signal (except P.S. signal) should be reported to the Telephone Company Repair Service immediately.

N.A. (Night Alarm) Turns the night alarm buzzer on and off.

P.S. (Permanent Signal Key) Turns the Permanent Signal buzzer on and off.

COMM. (Common Alarm Key) Turns all other alarm signal buzzers on and off.

BAT. (Battery Cutoff Switch) Cuts all battery from the PBX switchboard. It is operated to the "OFF" position only at times when the switchboard has been connected for night service.

NOTE: All keys should be turned to the "Off" position when the switchboard is connected for night service.

Some guiding principles. You will not be able to learn to operate a switchboard in a day or two. Remember that experienced operators have long periods of training and much practice. You can improve quickly, however, if you remain alert and careful in the performance of your job. If you have any questions, ask the regular operator, or ask the principal. Following are some suggestions and guiding principles you should observe when operating the switchboard:

1. Make your voice reveal a friendly, businesslike and conversational tone. While you are on the switchboard, you are the invisible receptionist for the school. Enunciate your words distinctly, and speak directly into the mouthpiece.

2. Do not "listen in" on conversations. The universal law concerning secrecy of telephone communications prohibits a person to willfully "listen in" on telephone conversations for personal reasons, or at the request of another to permit anyone to "listen in." Violation of this law may lead to

fine, imprisonment, or both. However, you may "listen in" if you suspect trouble on a noisy line or to determine if a conversation is progressing normally.

3. Report equipment malfunction promptly. You may discover some equipment not functioning properly or a station may report it to you. In any situation, report directly to the Repair Service of the telephone company or leave a memorandum for the regular operator explaining the nature of the difficulty. Before reporting, make sure the generator key is turned "On." If it is on, test it by ringing a nearby station.

4. Answer signals in order of appearance. Good service includes answering flashes, new calls, and taking down disconnects within *ten* seconds. You should answer signals in the following order: flash; incoming trunk; incoming tie trunk; station signal; disconnect.

5. Never place liquids at the switchboard. It may be tempting to place a vase of flowers near the switchboard, but the danger of spilling liquids should be avoided—in fact, all liquids, including fingernail polish, should be kept away from the switchboard. If liquid is spilled around the board, there is danger of breaking the circuits and causing the switchboard operations to be discontinued.

6. Keep a list of personal and frequently called numbers near the switchboard. It is a good idea for matter of quick reference to keep a list of frequently called numbers, both local and long distance.

8

Handling School Mail
and Deliveries

Principals are teachers converted to administrative duties. Few have had formal training in office routines or office management. Some take to their new tasks like a jet to supersonic speeds. Others are frankly dismayed with the restraining and detailed nature of correspondence and the tasks of scanning mail, making reports, and even writing signatures. They would just as soon, if they could, place the whole business on the shoulders of a capable secretary.

You'll be a very fortunate secretary, indeed, if you find yourself with a principal who has routinized himself to looking over the mail in advance, has a set time for you to come in for dictation, has adopted a uniform style for writing letters, and has a set procedure for handling deliveries of parcels and packages. The purpose of this chapter, then, is to suggest some helpful procedures for handling the school mail that will come to you for attention and processing.

HOW TO PROCESS INCOMING MAIL

The school secretary must coordinate mail to and from two sources: the postoffice, and the school mail or messenger service.

Mail delivery and service. You may have to pick up mail at the postoffice, but more likely the postman will make deliveries to your school. School systems with two or more schools usually have their own "internal" school mail service. Some school systems still require the school secretary on her way home to pick up the "new" school mail at the superintendent's office and bring it with her to school the next morning. This practice is falling into disuse, and most school systems of any size now employ a messenger to carry the school mail between the superintendent's office and the various schools.

Distribution of the mail. Everyone is more than anxious to get his mail, and it is not uncommon for teachers to form the habit of looking into their mailboxes, not once, but several times a day. Every school is equipped with teachers' mailboxes. Unfortunately, most are too small—if they are large, teachers tend to use them for lockers. There is no perfect answer. At any rate, get right at the business of sorting the incoming mail. You will find that pupils enjoy sorting the mail and putting letters in the boxes. Use the pupils as office monitors, but check them every once in a while until you know the quality of work they do. It goes without saying that mail addressed to teachers is to be placed unopened in their boxes.

By all means, thoroughly empty the school mail sack or envelope. Turn it upside down, even inside out; shake it, run your hand through it. There is nothing worse than to have mail go back to the superintendent's office because you failed to find it at the bottom of the mail sack! Many schools, especially the larger ones, clock in the mail. Special clocks are made in which the letter can be swiftly thrust into a mechanism which instantly stamps the date and time on the back of the letter. Such methods, especially in small schools, are not necessary.

TYPES OF MAIL

You will receive these types of mail: (1) letters addressed to teachers, or which clearly should go to teachers, (2) letters addressed to the principal, (3) letters which can be answered by the school secretary, (4) letters addressed to the library and other school offices, (5) letters addressed to pupils, (6) letters requiring forwarding.

Letters addressed to teachers. Letters for teachers should be placed in their mailboxes ("pigeonholes"), which should be labeled in alphabetical order. When a teacher is added to the faculty or when one leaves, the labels on the box should be moved around so that there are no vacant boxes between labels. This should be done at the end or beginning of the term. If a teacher leaves in the middle of the semester, have her substitute teachers use the same box for the balance of the term. Have a box for yourself, at the lower right-hand corner. Teachers quickly get accustomed to putting their reports and memos to you in your mailbox.

You will receive letters, too, for teachers long since transferred, even deceased, so maintain a card file of forwarding addresses. Pupils can write the forwarding addresses.

Letters addressed to the principal. Letters addressed to the principal if not marked "personal" should be opened and sorted. Some will require the principal's personal attention; some can be referred to other offices; some you can handle.

Sorting the principal's mail. Letters for the principal should be sorted with the "personals" on top, unopened, the others by date of addressing, and all placed in the center of his desk or in a file, as the principal prefers.

Most principals appreciate having their mail sorted into (1) "personal" letters and mail requiring immediate attention, (2) mail that can be deferred, (3) school bulletins, and (4) advertisements, announcements, and professional journals.

Opening and scanning the principal's mail. When removing the contents of an envelope, make sure that you check for enclosures and clip these to the letter. If the return address is written on the envelope, the envelope should also be attached to the letter. All letters other than "personal" should be opened and scanned for important facts. Underline the words and phrases that "tell the story." Note in the margin any necessary comments or facts that will be helpful to your principal.

Mail requiring immediate attention. Mail that requires immediate attention is usually—but not always—addressed to the principal by his name. This mail may be from the superintendent of schools, other personnel in the school system, and from parents or school patrons. This mail generally concerns the welfare of the school or activities of the principal, teachers, or pupils, and usually requires action or reply before a specified date.

Mail requiring attention within the week. Mail of the type which calls for information, requests attendance at a meeting, or invites reservations to dinners such as those sponsored by Phi Delta Kappa, the men's educational fraternity, or Pi Lambda Theta or Delta Kappa Gamma, the women's educational sororities, can be deferred for several days or even a week. Letters containing dates of association and committee meetings should bear a notation, "Entered on calendar," meaning that you have put the pertinent facts about the event—time, place, and address—on the principal's daily calendar. Also note any mail which the principal has yet to answer. It is partly your responsibility to keep your principal doing his correspondence chores—tactfully, of course. If you are in doubt as to whether a letter should be referred to your principal or to someone else, show it to your principal first.

Communications regarding the school's activities. School bulletins must be read as soon as received. No immediate action may be required, but most principals feel, and rightly so, that they must keep themselves informed of new policies, regulations, and data sent from the superintendent and from central administrative offices of the school district.

Letters requiring information from various sources. Some letters may require information from several persons or offices. Make an entry in your "Daily Mail Record," which can be a loose leaf binder, and attach to the letter a routing slip to the persons concerned. Be sure to indicate the date by which the letter is to be returned to you. A week is maximum time if there is no indication to the contrary. Be sure to look in your

Daily Mail Record each day to check on outstanding correspondence which needs your personal attention, or which should be followed by "tracers." The record should contain columns for (1) the date you made the entry, (2) a brief sentence describing the correspondence, including the sender's name, (3) to whom it was referred, (4) the action to be taken, and (5) the date for follow-up, or deadline for return. Draw a line through the entry when the correspondence has been completed.

Miscellaneous mail items. Most advertisements, particularly of textbooks, travel opportunities, and offers to lend money, are placed in a separate pile for the principal's casual reading.

Letters to be answered by the school secretary. You will soon be able to process many letters. This correspondence will be of a routine nature. If you have kept a collection of sample or model letters, you will have no trouble adapting these to most current situations. Letters of this type can be prepared by you for the principal's signature. As your principal gains respect for your judgment, he will welcome this service and recognize your ability. He may even delegate to you the responsibility for signing correspondence as the school secretary. Few letters, however, destined for higher authority, such as the superintendent's office, should be signed by the secretary, regardless of who did the composing. That's the sole prerogative of your principal. No one should be allowed to gain the impression that someone else is running your principal's office or doing *his* work.

Letters addressed to the library and other school offices. The library always receives an abundance of mail, newspapers, magazines, advertising circulars, posters, and announcements. Other offices, too, especially in a high school, receive much mail of this type. The attendance office, the counselor's office, the physical education department, the student store, and finance office all receive large amounts of mail. You may find it advisable to have larger boxes or mail sacks for these offices. You may wish to use a monitor to take the mail directly to the rooms or offices concerned, where the librarian and teachers can do their own sorting and answering.

Letters addressed to pupils. School policy in handling letters addressed to pupils varies. One good procedure is to have the letter forwarded to the pupil's teacher, in the case of an elementary school, with instructions to the teacher to have the child open the letter and read it to the teacher in her presence. In the case of high schools this may not be a practical procedure. The principal will have to designate someone—the vice-principal or perhaps you—to send for the pupil to open and read the letter in the presence of the school representative; thus protecting the pupil. In case the pupil does not choose to open his letter, it would be wise to notify his parents that the letter had been received.

Letters requiring forwarding. It is not uncommon for a school to receive letters intended for other schools, or which should be passed along to another school. The reasons are many: the teacher may have been transferred, the subject or course may now be offered by some other school, the names or addresses of schools may have been confused, and so forth. It is your responsibility to see that such mail is properly forwarded. No letter should be returned to the sender except as a last recourse. If you know your school district, you can generally forward most letters correctly. This knowledge comes with time and experience. Don't fret if you don't know what to do. Your principal or one of the experienced teachers usually can be helpful. Give them a chance to help you.

Routing communications and journals to the staff. Professional journals as well as circulars from the superintendent's office are usually routed to several people. Staple a routing list to the letter, or pencil in the upper right corner the names or initials of persons who should receive them. Recipients soon understand that they are to sign or initial the letter upon receipt of it, read it, then pass it along without delay. If experience tells you that some person is characteristically dilatory, place his name at the end of the routing list. A list should not contain more than five or six names. Long lists require too much time for the item to reach the person at the end of the list. Use a second routing list, or make additional copies of the correspondence.

Bulky or heavy mail. Bulky mail cannot be put in a teacher's box. Put a memo in the teacher's box asking her to pick up the package at the office. Deliveries such as films, recordings, and library books all must be handled in this way. You may wish to use a mimeographed form for notifying a teacher. Because such packages are seldom tidy looking, you may want to reserve a shelf or corner in the supply room for temporary storage of such matter.

Teachers' responsibility in returning items. You cannot undertake to notify teachers when audio-visual materials, library books, and similar teaching aids are due for return. That must be each teacher's responsibility. Most lenders of such materials usually affix a conspicuous due-date label on each item.

Telegrams and special deliveries. Telegrams and special delivery letters deserve your immediate attention. A notice in a teacher's mailbox is a first procedure, but is usually not sufficient. Send a monitor to the teacher's room with the telegram or advise her to call at your office as soon as possible. Make an entry in your "Daily Mail Record" of the receipt of such communications.

Signing for "specials," telegrams, and special deliveries. One of the most exasperating experiences you will encounter occurs when someone signs for a telegram, special delivery letter, or package and then forgets to tell you anything about it. Days, even weeks later, you find yourself challenged about it, and you will have no more trace of it than a shadow on a rainy day. You're positive the school never received it. The sender has the post office trace the receiver's name and signature. You learn from the sender that it was the relief gardener, the night watchman, or even your best friend, the custodian, who did the signing, and there it is, sure enough, right where he put it and forgot it.

How can you guard against such mishaps? Make sure that your principal has instructed everyone that no delivery of letters, telegrams, or packages is to be signed for anywhere except in the school office, and by someone else only when you cannot be reached.

HOW TO PROCESS OUTGOING MAIL

Many school secretaries keep two desk baskets or trays for outgoing mail. One is marked "U.S. Mail"; the other, "School Mail." These trays are usually kept on or near the office counter so that teachers may also reach them.

Mailings for teachers. Teachers are quite likely to use the "U.S. Mail" tray for their personal postings. The mail tray becomes a service and a convenience to them. Postmen generally are willing to cooperate by picking up outgoing U.S. mail, if there is not too much of it, when they make their deliveries. As secretary, you can spare yourself numerous inquiries from teachers by posting a label on the tray listing the pickup hours.

Preparing mail for the postman. It is a good idea to train a pupil to go through the U.S. mail just before the postman is due to arrive to see that letters are sealed and proper postage affixed. Furthermore, as teachers will expect to buy stamps from you, you may as well keep on hand a supply of 3¢, 4¢, 5¢, and air mail stamps, a few special delivery stamps, and some postal cards. Unless your school district provides you with a petty cash fund, you or your principal may have to advance several dollars, which is refunded as you sell the stamps.

Packages requiring postal service. You cannot accept for mailing teachers' packages, parcels, books, and other postings requiring parcel post service at the post office. "I'm sorry, Miss Jones," you will have to say in a firm tone and with a smile, "that will have to be mailed at the post office." Hand it back, and don't break this rule or you may regret the day you ever relented. Your principal will back you up on this.

Mailings for pupils. You can anticipate that the high school newspaper editors will be asking you to post the school newspaper for them. If these amount to no more than a half dozen or so, there will be no harm; but if more, no—a positive no. In any case, the students should do the wrapping, stamping, and addressing of the school newspapers. They can also deposit the papers in the corner mailbox, especially if the papers would make a clutter on your counter. Some schools pay the postage for the school newspaper when the paper has no revenue of its own from the sale of subscriptions or advertisements. Issue only enough stamps to take care of one edition at a time.

Providing stamp service for pupils. Whether you should sell stamps to pupils for their personal mailings is for you to decide. An occasional sale is permissible when there appears to be an emergency. The better practice, especially in a high school, is to arrange for the student store to sell stamps, or to provide stamp machines.

Official school mail. Requirements vary in handling official mail. What constitutes "official" mail? Anything that your principal or other school officer does not voluntarily describe to you as "personal." If a teacher prepares a letter which she tells you is "school business," that, too, is "official." You can supply the postage. Save your challenges for more expensive and more important items. If you think a teacher is abusing the opportunity, refer the matter to your principal for handling—don't attempt to settle the matter with her yourself.

In the case of official mail which has been approved for posting by your principal, you will have to contend with everything from postal cards to packages. Some school systems require that all official correspondence destined for U.S. mail be first routed unsealed through the school mail center where it can be run through a postage metering and sealing machine. (No paper clips inside the envelopes, please; they jam the machine.) Some school systems allow you to requisition or purchase stamps which you can affix to the envelopes; other schools issue precanceled stamps, good only for official mail.

Certified and registered mail. There are times when your principal will wish to be sure that a letter he mailed has been received. For a fee, the post office will do one of two things for you—secure a receipt from the addressee and keep it on file or secure a receipt and return it to the school. This is "Certified" mail—the post office "certifies" the delivery of letters on which the school places no commercial value. It "registers" letters on which there is a commercial value and will reimburse the school up to a value of $1,000 if the mail is lost.

Insuring packages. Mail other than letters, post cards, and periodicals —principally packages—should be insured if the school wishes reimbursement in case of loss. The post office will insure up to $200. Higher indemnities can be obtained if the mail is registered by the post office or by a private insurance company (not by but through the post office).

Certifying mail. The school secretary can obtain forms (POD Form 3800) from the post office for certifying mail. The numbered end of the receipt for certified mail (cost, 30 cents—60 cents if registered—in addition to standard postage) is torn off and affixed to the letter. The remainder of the form is kept for the school office record. When the certified letter arrives at its destination, the postal carrier obtains a signed yellow slip from the recipient, which, if a return receipt has been requested, is returned to the mailer. The post office will accept the signature of any person who normally accepts mail for the addressee. A higher fee is charged when the mail is sent "Deliver to Addressee Only."

Packages and bulky mail. Packages must be wrapped securely. You can train a monitor to do an acceptable job, especially if you keep a "dummy" sample on hand so the youngster can see how the package should look when properly tied. Also, if you type a sticker with the addressee's name and address and use a rubber stamp for the return address, a pupil can do the addressing for you—even to weighing it on the scales, which should be part of your office equipment. Books, photographs, and pictures must be protected and reinforced with cardboard. Save the cardboard backing of paper tablets or your menfolks' shirts. Sometimes you can use manila file folders, but these are seldom strong enough.

Specifications for parcel post. Parcel post packages cannot exceed 70 pounds in weight, nor exceed 100 inches in length and girth combined (72 inches if mailed overseas). They must not be sealed, glued, or taped (unless mailed at the first-class rate). Foreign mailings must bear on the outside wrapping a description of the contents.

Your principal's mailings. When you give letters to your principal for signature, separate those he dictated from those that you or someone else has prepared for his signature. Most schools still include the envelope, carbon copy, enclosures, and even the principal's original notes, when submitting a letter for signature. A considerable economy will be effected if you follow the practice of submitting only the letter itself for signature. You could then address the envelope from the carbons while the letters are being read and signed by your principal.

Signing the carbon copy. A sensible practice, for future reference, is to slip the first carbon copy about one-half inch to the right of the letter itself. Then your principal can initial and date the carbon as he signs the letter. A record of signed letters sometimes is valuable in refreshing memories. Of course you never file the carbon copy until after the letter is signed and you have made any necessary changes on all copies.

Proofing the letter before obtaining a signature. Many principals sign letters without proofreading them; others scrupulously go over each and every letter. Never submit a letter to your principal without first having carefully proofread it, despite the principal's propensity to scrutinize every comma and period. Never let him get the idea that you expect him to do your job.

Checking the mail. When correspondence has been signed, bring it back to your desk and assemble it for mailing. Check each letter for these three things:

1. Has the letter been signed?
2. Are all enclosures included?
3. Are the inside address and the envelope address the same?

Pick-up time. Don't delay the postman or school messenger when he calls for the mail. It is easy to fall into the habit of asking him to wait while you type the final paragraph to a letter. He has many other calls to make and a schedule to maintain. It is better that you post the letter yourself than detain him.

HOW TO PREPARE LETTERS FOR MAILING

Folding and inserting letters in envelopes. Letters written on full-sized letterheads for insertion in long envelopes (No. 10) should be folded as follows: one fold from the bottom, about one-third of the way up; a second fold from the bottom to within one-sixteenth of an inch of the top. Insert in the envelope, top up.

Full-sized letterheads. Letters written on full-sized letterheads for insertion in short envelopes (No. 6¾) should be folded as follows: one fold from the bottom to within one-quarter of an inch of the top; a second fold from right to left, about one-third of the way across; a third fold from left to right within one-quarter of an inch of the right edge. Insert with the right edge up.

Half-sized letterheads. Letters written on half-sized letterheads should be folded as follows: one fold from right to left, about a third of the way across; a second fold from left to right, leaving about one-sixteenth inch between the edges at the right. Insert in a short envelope (No. 6¾) with the right edge up.

Inserting letter in envelope. No matter how they are folded, letters should be inserted into envelopes without turning them over; that is, in such a manner that when the letter is removed from the envelope and unfolded, the type side is up.

Preparing enclosures. Enclosures govern the size of envelope to be used. Never submit to your principal a short (No. 6¾) envelope when it is obvious that a large (No. 10) envelope will be necessary.

Fastening enclosures to be mailed. When it is necessary to fasten enclosures together, use staples—not paper clips. Don't fasten the enclosed material to the letter—fold the enclosure, then fold the letter, and slip the enclosure inside the last fold of the letter. Thus, when the letter is removed from the envelope, the enclosure comes out with it.

When enclosures are considerably smaller than the letter, staple them to the letter in the upper left-hand corner, on top of the letter. If two or more enclosures are sent, put the smaller one on top.

Postage for enclosures. Sometimes the enclosure is a course of study or a research report. Postage is paid at the regular third- or fourth-class rate plus the first-class rate (4 cents) for the letter. Minutes of meetings, if not in duplicated form, must be mailed at first-class rates.

Making a card file of addresses. Schools frequently send the same letter, invitation, or notice to many persons or schools. The school secretary must constantly build her file of mailing addresses. Experience soon makes clear who are the recurring receivers of the school's letters.

Make a 3 × 5 card file of each person to whom your principal regularly or occasionally addresses a letter. Perhaps a bother at the time, this eventually becomes a welcome convenience when you are suddenly asked to prepare a list of everyone who should be invited to a Founder's Day, Christmas party, or American Education Week program.

Preparing the directory. School districts generally issue a directory of school principals and supervisors. Counties, state departments of education, and P.T.A.'s also issue lists, as do chambers of commerce, service clubs, churches, veterans' organizations, and others. Start collecting these directories, but note that many are reissued each year because of many changes. Occasionally you will be told to send letters to everyone listed. Other times you will be asked for a particular directory in which your principal will check the names of persons who are to receive a school communication.

Preparing addresses for multiple mailings. When several persons are to receive the same communication, each letter and envelope must be typed separately. However, if the letter is impersonal, carbon copies, if clear, can be used. Dittoed and mimeographed lists of addresses can be duplicated on gummed paper, cut apart and pasted to envelopes, thereby saving you many hours of labor and materially reducing the chance of error. An IBM duplicating machine, where available, can make multiple gummed labels of addresses. But never use one of these "address conveniences" when single letters are to be mailed. Any form of addressing short of individual typing has an excellent chance of reaching the wastepaper basket unread. This hazard cannot be risked in the case of individual letters, and sometimes not even for multiple mailings. Your principal will advise you.

Handling mail when the principal is away. The manner in which you should handle the mail when your principal is away from the school for several days, or during an illness or summer vacation depends, of course, upon his personal preference. You can adapt the procedure of mail handling recommended here to his wishes.

1. If your principal makes a practice of telephoning your school each day, sort the correspondence according to school matters and personal matters. Also jot down the gist of each letter so that you can report to him readily.
2. Telegraph or write air mail special delivery about anything urgent that requires his immediate personal attention.

3. Acknowledge all correspondence, whether personal or business, if your principal is to be away more than a few days.

4. Copy all mail that requires your principal's personal attention and forward the copies to him. Many principals instruct their secretaries to hold all packets of mail until their return. If the principal wishes these packets forwarded to him, number the packets consecutively as you send them.

5. If your principal is on vacation and does not want mail forwarded to him, hold the letters that require his personal attention and indicate in your acknowledgment when a reply might be expected.

6. Keep the accumulated mail in folders marked "Correspondence to be signed," "Correspondence requiring your attention," "Correspondence to read" (letters that have been answered but in which he will probably be interested), "Reports," and "General reading material" (miscellaneous items of advertising, and publications that he might want to read).

9

Filing in the School Office

EVERY SCHOOL OFFICE is dependent upon records. Each day, correspondence and materials are received, compiled, and placed in files for safekeeping and easy finding. Mere retention of them, however, is not enough —records must be filed in such a manner that they can be found without delay when needed. The filing of correspondence, records, and valuable materials is an essential part of every secretary's job. You will find that most school offices have fewer types of files and follow simpler routines than do business offices.

Filing systems. Records must be analyzed in terms of how they will be asked for and how they will be used—the determining factors in any filing system. Because records may be asked for in various ways, you must have various systems for arranging them. The four standard systems of filing are: (1) alphabetical, filed according to the most important name appearing on a document; (2) subject, materials filed by subject or title rather than by a name; (3) numerical, materials are assigned a number and go in a master file; (4) geographical, geographic location more important than name. The first two systems are widely used in educational offices; filing by subject is the more common. The installation of a subject file requires great care. The list of subjects should be long enough to be comprehensive, but brief enough to avoid confusion.

The handbook, *File It Right,** contains excellent suggestions for a subject classification usable in an educational filing system. Chapter 27 contains excerpts from this handbook.

MAINTAINING THE SCHOOL FILES

Physical set-up of files. It is rarely advisable or even physically possible to centralize the location of all files within the school office. A single four-drawer letter-sized file of good quality is considered adequate. A similar file or other types of files may be placed elsewhere in the building.

The location for the file in the office area should be determined on the

* National Educational Association, Educational Secretaries Department.

basis of accessibility and visibility. Files should be conveniently located to each work station. When the file drawer is opened, direct light should fall on the folders, not in your eyes.

Preparation of material for filing. A preliminary sorting (rough sort for major division) of material can be done at the desk. A second sorting will arrange the items in order behind each major division (fine sort). A flat sorter with tabs bearing the divisions of the alphabetical or subject classification will save much time and confusion.

Indexing and coding. Indexing is the process whereby you determine where a certain correspondence should go—in other words, whether you will file it by the recipient's last name, the company name, and so forth. Coding is the process whereby you note on a paper where it is to be filed. Important words or sentences may be encircled in colored pencil, and the time limit for retention in the file may also be marked.

Placing materials in folders. Before materials are put into folders, all tears should be mended and rough edges trimmed. Small clippings or materials of unusual shape or small size should be pasted to a plain sheet of paper of standard size. All pins and paper clips should be removed.

After the material has been sorted, the papers are placed within the folder with the top and left edges even, and turned to face the front of the folder. The letterheads should be at the left-hand side of the drawer. Materials that are too large should be folded—they should never extend out of the folder. Half sheets can be laid side by side so that the folder will not bulge at one end. Materials should be filed in chronological order with the latest correspondence placed in the front of the folder. Your principal will instruct you regarding priorities and immediate filing of materials.

Making a cross-reference sheet. Correspondence and materials that could be filed under more than one name or subject should be cross-referenced; that is, the letter is filed under the name or subject considered to be the most important. This name is written at the bottom of the correspondence reference sheet and the name of secondary importance is written at the top. Experience is the best guide in the use of cross-reference sheets. You will only waste time if you prepare a number of cross-reference sheets that are never needed. Colored cross-reference sheets in pads are available at any stationery store. A label of a different color than those on the regular folders helps to locate the cross-reference folders.

Starting a new folder. It is easier to thumb through the papers in one folder than to remove and examine the contents of a number of folders. Make a "Miscellaneous" folder for each main subject heading and file it after the last subheading for that topic. When five or ten papers have accumulated in the miscellaneous folder, check to see if a new subject or subheading is needed. An accumulation of 40 or 50 papers in one folder usually justifies the making of a second folder for the same subject. The heading of each folder should be labeled with the name followed by the numbers "1" and "2"; for example:

Barber, Albert R. (1)
Barber, Albert R. (2)

Using the files. All related papers are filed together both within the folder and within the file. Folders should not bulge. They should be kept upright and held together when not in use.

All file folder tabs should be uniform in size and in location. The extreme left hand side of the drawer should show primary guides and the middle of the drawer should show the sub-heading guides. About ten folders are filed back of a guide, and there should be about twenty-five guides to a drawer. There should always be space left in the drawer for expansion.

Using loose-leaf folders. Loose-leaf folders are ideally suited for filing materials frequently requested by your principal, teachers, or members of the school staff. Such items as institute programs, supervisory personnel records, administrative regulations, P.T.A. announcements, and school directories are available for quick and easy reference when placed in such folders. Moreover, they do not then occupy valuable space in the filing cabinet.

FILING SCHOOL MATERIALS

Correspondence. Generally speaking, school correspondence has less permanent value than do school records pertaining to students, personnel, and reports. It is often possible to maintain a single chronological file for all correspondence. When letters are placed in a folder, they are arranged by date, the most recent letter received being put at the front of the folder. Many letters are of temporary value, and should be destroyed when their purpose has been served. Correspondence to, from, or about members of the staff or members of the student body should be filed in name folders under the main heading of *Employed Personnel and Students*. In such filing, alphabetical filing is followed.

Pupil attendance. Attendance records of students, particularly in a high school, are taken periodically throughout the day; in some schools, twice daily. These are collected and brought to the office. Attendance records are very important, for state and local financial support of schools is often based on attendance, as determined from these records. It is important that they be accurate. In most schools, the clerical staff records his absences on the individual pupil's record. These attendance forms are then filed chronologically by date and maintained only for a short period of time. Their only value, after being recorded on the student record, would be for verification or checking purposes. Attendance officers, registrars, and deans may use these attendance reports to check on discipline cases. If a student questions the record on his individual card, it might be necessary to locate the original absence form.

The periodic attendance reports required by the administrative office are filed under the main subject heading of "Students," subheading of "Attendance."

Pupil personnel records. The system most generally used for pupil personnel records is the alphabetical name filing system. In the case of a major alphabetizing problem, one can safely follow the arrangement used in the telephone directory of any large city, although it is not a standard index reference guide.

Individual student records. In setting up a name file as a student record file, be very generous with guides. This will facilitate locating a desired record. Individual folders are prepared for each student and filed alphabetically. Many schools are now using the Cumulative Guidance Record, described in Chapter 16. In the folder are placed all records pertaining to the individual student. Student enrollment cards should be carefully and completely filled out, giving all personal data. The school record is sometimes the only proof of age that an individual is able to locate. Frequently, student records are used in legal actions.

Microfilming student records. Pupil records are usually copied in some manner and the duplicate copy maintained in a fireproof vault. Many schools are microfilming student records in order to conserve valuable storage space and to speed location and reading of records. Great care is needed in preparing records for microfilming. Most companies offering microfilm service will furnish detailed instruction. See pages 176 to 178 for a description of microfilming pupil personnel records and the Cumulative Guidance Record.

Filing equipment for student records. Visible filing equipment is widely used for current pupil personnel records. A visible file is a card system in which there is one card for each student on which is recorded the academic, attendance, health, and testing information pertaining to the student. The cabinet type is used where the system is large; the visible rotary or book unit is often used in smaller systems. The visible rotary file is used in many school offices for filing student schedule cards. The visibility feature of this type of file makes the cards instantly available, not only for reference, but also for record-making purposes. Although most concerns producing filing equipment have a number of record forms for these files, most schools plan their own card, keeping in mind the purpose of the record and the type of equipment to be used.

Student withdrawals. When a student leaves the school system, either by graduation, voluntary withdrawal, or by request, a folder of the student's records is prepared for the permanent file and filed alphabetically by name. Here again it pays to be generous with guides. A guide for every 10 to 25 folders will increase the speed of filing and locating.

Teacher personnel records. Most school districts handle teachers' records in the central office. However, many schools keep a duplicate set of records pertaining to a teacher. Among these are records of merit ratings, recommendations, and leaves of absence. The alphabetical name filing system is the most satisfactory system that can be used for the records of teachers and other school employees.

Preparing teacher personnel folders. The teacher's personnel record becomes a written image of the faculty member, and will need to be retained in a permanent file. This folder will include all items pertaining to a teacher's training, experience, and special honors. It will contain the teacher's absence record, retirement fund membership and payments data, federal Old Age and Survivors Insurance number and payments, and many other records that are mandatory under state and federal laws. Many schools are required to keep time sheets and accurate records of vacations, personal leaves, and dates when substitutes were employed.

Many state retirement plans are integrated with the federal Old Age and Survivors Insurance program, so the OASI record of each teacher must be retained. The payments recorded on the individual payroll records are used in the preparation of quarterly reports to the federal government.

Card file for new teacher. When a teacher is employed for the first time in any school system, it is necessary to collect many items of personal data. A temporary card file will help in collecting the necessary information. This card can be a mimeographed listing of the items needed; and, as the information arrives in the office, items can be checked off the card.

Name _____	Position _____
1. License or credential, including expiration date	5. Application form
2. Contract signed	6. Military service
3. Transcript	7. Address and phone number
4. OASI and/or retirement number	

The cards are filed alphabetically by name in a small file box located in the desk of the responsible person. This temporary card can be discarded when it has served its purpose, or it can be included in the teacher's personnel folder or jacket. During the summer months, when there is a large turnover in the staff, this card file is a time-saver and a good check on completed personnel files.

Most individual schools do not keep teacher employment applications —these are usually sent to the central office.

Financial records and reports. The financial records and reports of any educational office must be maintained in accordance with the requirements of state and federal laws. Payroll records, showing each employee's gross pay and deductions, are filed in accordance with the desires of the state or district auditing department. Most auditors require that all payroll records be filed alphabetically by name, each fiscal year separate, until the audit is completed. Then his records are placed in each employee's folder in his permanent file for future reference. Included in each employee's permanent file are contracts, rate of pay for each year, cumulative sick-leave records, retirement deductions, federal and state tax deductions, and other records.

Reports to central offices. The subject filing system is generally applicable to all school reports that go to district, county, and state departments of education. Subject headings for such reports should include such items as enrollment and attendance, courses offered, teachers employed, accident reports, and vandalism. Each report should be filed with the other materials dealing with the same subject, perhaps in an individual folder as some of these reports are bulky. Usually, reports for two years past are maintained in the active file; older reports are stored in a permanent file, if they must be retained indefinitely.

Inventories. File all inventories alphabetically under the general heading of *Inventories*. The individual file tab designates the school, department, or room listing equipment. Two inventories are usually maintained: one of all *instructional* (teaching) equipment in special rooms such as the music, business education, and homemaking rooms; and one of *noninstructional* equipment, equipment purchased and owned by students or student organizations such as band uniforms, athletic supplies, artwork, records, and television sets. Many schools find it advisable to segregate inventories of non-instructional equipment owned by student organizations from those belonging to the board of education.

School forms. Schools use innumerable printed forms for recording information such as registrations, withdrawals, accident reports, work permits, attendance, and school lunches. All too often these forms have no consistency as to size and shape or regularity of use. (See page 108 to 110 for suggestions regarding the design and control of forms.)

Library. You may be asked to care for printed matter such as courses of study, teachers' guides, district or superintendent's newsletters, periodicals, professional journals, and newspaper clippings. Rightfully, many of these belong in a library, but since elementary schools do not always have librarians or libraries, the school office becomes the logical place for such material. Books and bound volumes may be placed on shelves, grouped according to subject matter whenever possible. Magazines, handbooks, and newsletters are best kept in binders filed by year. Professional magazines, such as *NEA Journal, The Instructor, Phi Delta Kappan, Nation's Schools, The English Journal, School Management, School Board Journal,* may be filed in metal pamphlet holders until the end of the school year, when all the issues for that year or volume are removed, tied with string, and stored elsewhere in the building. You will find it convenient to keep a loose-leaf notebook of newspaper clippings pertaining to the school. Items are clipped immediately, pasted to an 8½ × 11 sheet of paper, and marked with the source and the date of publication.

Blueprints. Most educational offices are constantly supervising the building and remodeling of school plants. Blueprints and drawings present one of the most difficult filing problems, because of their large size. Folding blueprints causes them to wear at the folds. The most satisfactory method of keeping such large papers is in a wide, flat, shallow drawer. Papers filed in such drawers should have the title and descriptive information recorded on the visible edge. Each file drawer is labeled as to its contents.

Sometimes blueprints and drawings are rolled and placed on racks. This method causes such materials to soil and wear more quickly than if they had been placed in drawers. Blueprints and drawings are in constant use during the construction of a building. When construction has been completed, they are normally shelved for a long period of time until some major repair is needed. Availability of original blueprints for a building saves much time and money in making construction changes. Blueprints should never be destroyed until the building is razed.

Tickler file. A tickler file is a small file containing tabbed guides for each month of the year, and 31 tabbed guides for the days in each month. Reminders on cards or slips of paper are filed behind the appropriate daily guide. You can place recurring items on one card and move the card from week to week, month to month, year to year. The tickler file is used together with the desk calendar. Correspondence or material pertaining to special events occurring within the current month may be taken from the regular file and placed behind the daily guide of the tickler file.

The circular "Rolodex" type file is another useful small file that can be used to keep an up-to-date record of addresses and telephone numbers. Such information is placed on individual cards which can be easily removed and reinserted (on the circular drum) when any changes must be made. It should be kept close to your principal's phone. You will be amazed at the number of times phone numbers are changed by the telephone company and you will find that this is the most accurate file of its kind in your school.

10

Preparing School Records
and Reports

REPORTS AND RECORDS are indispensable to the successful functioning of a school. They should be informative, intelligible, and accurate, since they furnish the information determining school policy and the figures upon which school financing is based.

This chapter explains how to prepare school records and reports. The first section describes the general procedures to follow, regardless of the kind of report or record. The second section explains the procedures to use in filling out special reports or records which are common to most schools. The third section discusses the management of records. The final section explains form design and control.

GENERAL PROCEDURES

Each school district has its own method of keeping records and rendering reports. If there is only one school in the district, the responsibility for their preparation falls upon the principal and his secretary. This can also happen in larger districts. As secretary, your work is strictly clerical and secretarial. You may work closely with the school nurse, teachers, assistant principals, custodians, and department heads who will supply you with needed information. The centralized school offices of the county, the district, or the state may sometimes be of service.

Larger school districts usually develop the forms which are used in the individual schools, thus relieving the principal of this responsibility. Because of the complexity of larger school districts, they require more forms, more reports, and more copies of each. They also issue detailed and specific instructions so that the information from the various schools can be centrally compiled in a consistent manner. There is also a trend to handling records by IBM cards, particularly in large school districts.

Common responsibilities. Regardless of the number or type of forms used or the size of the school district, there are certain responsibilities which all school secretaries must perform. For outgoing reports, you must:

1. Notify those who are to provide information.
2. Collect data.
3. Tabulate the data and prepare the report in the required manner.
4. Assemble the various papers into the correct number of copies.
5. Check the information for accuracy and completeness, including the required signatures.
6. Transmit the completed forms on time to the proper office.

For incoming items, you are responsible for:

1. Noting and dating the records, reports, or forms which are received.
2. Distributing them promptly to the people who should receive them.
3. Filing copies of reports for future reference.

Knowledge of instructions. Familiarize yourself with all instructions regarding the use of the various records and forms that you handle. These instructions can be found in the school district's general manual, in the school policies, and in special bulletins which are issued from time to time. Confer with your principal regarding those reports for which he is responsible. He may have special instructions which you will need to know.

Keeping instruction sheets available. Since some reports are made only once or twice a year, you may not remember the necessary details to complete them satisfactorily. Keep all instructions near at hand so that you can find them as the need arises.

From time to time, you will receive deletions, changes, or new instructions which must be attached to those already on file. Date these memoranda and include the name of the person or office which supplied them. Correct or destroy previous instructions so that there will be no confusion. Too often secretaries clutter up their files with obsolete information.

Determine to whom you should talk when you need further information. Find out who "gives the orders."

Due dates. At the beginning of the school year, look through all bulletins, handbooks, or instructions for the due dates of all required reports. Record these on your desk calendar. It is a good policy to write a reminder on your calendar pad a few days in advance of the due date, the number of days depending upon the estimated length of time required to prepare the report. As due dates of other reports become known, write them in a like manner on your desk calendar.

If your principal is responsible for the preparation of a report, give him the due date in time for him to prepare it. Information or data which your principal will need and which you can compile should be given to him at this time.

In addition to the desk calendar reminder, it is a good idea to use a checklist showing the subject of the report and the due date. Provide a column for checking the receipt of information from members of the staff who are to furnish it.

Forward all records and reports on time. If a report is likely to be late, call the receiving office before the due date and explain the reason. This will avoid confusion, and they won't think you have overlooked the report.

Collecting the data. You will often find it necessary to ask teachers for data such as the number of boys and girls enrolled in a class, the number of textbooks on hand, the number of children who plan to attend a school sponsored event, an inventory of school maps or other school equipment, or the in-service meetings teachers have attended.

Owing to their busy schedule as well as to the fact that their primary duty is teaching, teachers should have their clerical duties made as easy as possible. There are several things you can do to help:

1. Make the request for data in plenty of time for the teacher to gather the information. Put frequent reminders in the school bulletin.
2. Print the due date on the request form. Your own "due date" should be a day or so ahead of the actual time you need to file the report for your school. This gives you time to compile the information and to correct any errors which you find.
3. Remind the teachers at least one full day before the information is due in your office. Do this even when the due date is written on the request form.
4. Make requests for data as simple as possible. Provide columns or spaces which can be filled in with a check, a number, or a one- or two-word answer. These are more likely to be answered correctly. It will also make it easier for you to assemble the data.
5. Use a checklist to record the teachers' reports as they come to the office.
6. Check the teachers' arithmetic immediately if you have requested figures.

Preparation of the report. The administrative offices of your school district may either send you a form to fill out or prescribe the manner in which you are to make the report. Complete the report to the best of your ability on a working copy. Proofread every figure and piece of information. Then prepare the final copy. After the final copy is made, compare it with the original data or copy. If other clerical help is available, have another person proofread the report again. It is easy to make careless errors when you are too familiar with the information. Type all final reports and records neatly. Use care in correcting errors.

Number of copies. Usually you will make more than one copy of a report. Be sure that the carbon paper is inserted correctly and is of good quality. If several copies are to be made, look at the last carbon after typing a line or so to see whether the typing is coming through clearly enough to be legible. Be sure to make a duplicate copy for your office file whether called for or not.

Accuracy and completeness. Records and reports are cold, factual things. They will be looked at objectively to determine whether they are complete and accurate.

If the records or reports are in any way related to the budget or financial matters, the importance of accuracy cannot be overestimated. This is particularly true when you are dealing with the taxpayers' dollars. Such records include inventory lists, attendance figures, losses or accidents on which insurance must be paid, supply lists, or figures which are concerned in any way with the receipt of state or federal monies.

Not only must the figures be accurate but they must be placed in the right spaces or columns of the report. Totals and subtotals must be correct. Become familiar with all symbols which are commonly used, and make sure that you use them accurately. A misunderstood symbol could cost the school district many dollars. In California, for example, the use of "E" (enrollment) in place of "ADA" (average daily attendance) would be a costly error. Records and reports which involve money are usually audited. If an auditor finds that you have made errors, you will have to do the work over again.

Signatures. When the report is completed, give it to the principal together with the work sheets and the raw data for final checking. If the report is accurately filled out, he should sign or initial it. This is sometimes overlooked. In no case should a report be forwarded before the principal or the person responsible for it has verified its completeness and accuracy.

Forwarding the report. Send the report to arrive at the proper office on or before the due date. If duplicate copies are to be forwarded to different offices, do this in good time also. If the instructions call for the removal of the carbon papers, be sure to do this before distributing or forwarding the report. A copy for the school should be detached and filed. It is also advisable to keep all original data until the receiving office has acknowledged the correctness of the report.

SPECIAL REPORTS AND RECORDS

There are so many types of reports and records used in school districts that it is impossible to explain all of them. Each school district develops forms to meet its own specific needs. However, many school districts use similar forms for reporting accidents, federal reports or surveys, enrollment, inventories, and so on. If you become familiar with these and follow the instructions given in the preceding pages, you should be able to handle almost any type of report or record without too much difficulty.

Examples of common types of records and reports are explained in the sections which follow.

Accident reports. The purpose of accident reports is to provide information for insurance companies and to record the number and kind of accidents which occur at a school. Work closely with the school nurse or school doctor in preparing these reports. Make at least three copies: one for the school, one for the school district's business office, and one for the insurance company. Fill out and forward accident reports as soon as possible after the accident, within 24 hours if you can.

Reporting forms. The insurance company usually provides the forms on which you report accidents to children. You will need the following information:

1. Date and time of accident.
2. Location of accident.
3. Name and address of injured child, as well as phone number.
4. Witnesses. At least two should be named, if possible.
5. The name of the teacher who was in charge of the child's activity when the accident occurred.
6. The nature of the injury.
7. The extent of first aid which was given and name of person giving it.
8. Contact with parents, if any, and their attitude towards the accident. If they are antagonistic, make a brief statement regarding their complaint.
9. What was done with the child after first aid was administered.
10. The result of any follow-up examination of the injury by the school nurse or the principal.

Approval and disposition. After the report is filled out, have the principal, nurse, or responsible teacher read the information and sign it. In no case should anyone, particularly the secretary, make any public statements regarding the school's or the teacher's responsibility in the accident. These statements should be made only to the central school office or to the insurance company.

In the case of employee personnel, make similar reports. The state compensation agency may supply forms for this. Forward copies to the central business and personnel offices of the board of education for processing. Keep a copy for your file. Retain accident reports at least two years.

Federal reports or surveys. School districts throughout the United States are eligible for federal funds under Public Laws 874 or 815, the Smith-Hughes Act, or other similar legislation. In such cases, strict compliance with the law and the method of filling out the forms is a necessity if the school district is to qualify for federal funds. You and your principal must work closely with the school district's business office and must follow their specific instructions to the letter. Accuracy is most important, since thousands of dollars in benefits to the school district may hinge upon the outcome of the report.

Securing data. Many times you will need to urge teachers to do their part in securing necessary data. Teachers generally do not like to do extra clerical and bookkeeping jobs, so be diplomatic when you ask them to help.

Public Law 874 funds, for example, are based upon information which parents provide regarding the location and dates of their employment. This information is gathered on questionnaires which are sent home. Children must be reminded to return these report forms. Instruct them to insist that their parents take the time to fill out the desired information which is of such importance to the school district. You, too, may have to call parents and remind them to supply the required information.

You may also have to compile records of scholastic achievement and attendance for children of deceased veterans. To secure such information, you will consult teachers or the school's registrar.

Retention of data. Retain the *individual* forms used by your school for a period of one or two years. The *total* figures for your school should be kept for a period of probably five years.

Vandalism reports. When your school has suffered vandalism or a burglary, notify the police as soon as the discovery is made. In addition, send a report to the central school office within 24 hours, or as soon as possible.

This report should give:

1. The date and approximate time of the incident.
2. A short description of the damage.
3. A list of any stolen items and their approximate value.
4. Other information, such as who discovered the vandalism, suspects, or possible motives.

Retain these reports for a two-year period.

Annual report. The statistical part of the annual report is one of the major bases upon which a school or school system justifies its allotment of state school funds. It contains figures on attendance and/or enrollment. You will probably compile the information which is required and make out the report for the principal's approval. Forms are usually furnished by the State Superintendent of Public Instruction, or some other similar central agency.

The following data are typically required for most annual reports:

1. Name and address of school and district.
2. Number of days of instruction.
3. Attendance data for kindergarten, elementary schools, secondary schools, special training classes, part-time education, and adult education classes.
4. Number of classes maintained.
5. Summaries of data.
6. Average daily attendance.

7. Number of teachers.
8. Number of double sessions.
9. Certification by teachers of class data.
10. Certification by principal of school data.
11. Name, summer address, and telephone number of both principal and secretary.

Since accuracy is important, be sure that all facts and figures are backed up by the original data. It is a good idea to keep annual reports on file for an indefinite period, since they provide a statistical history of the school and are a source of future reference.

In addition to the statistical information described above, some school systems require the principal to include a description of the major activities and the educational program carried on in his school.

Accreditation reports. The high school secretary often has to compile or assemble a yearly or biennial accreditation report for the use of colleges or universities. Information for this report comes from counselors, registrars, and assistant principals, as well as from office records. Information, such as the following, is usually requested:

1. School district; name and address of the school.
2. Enrollment and number of students in the senior class.
3. Number of teachers and their qualifications.
4. A list of the courses offered at the secondary school.
5. The provisions for laboratory science, including the facilities available.
6. The number of senior students planning to enter college, as well as a list of the colleges they expect to attend.
7. The academic record of former students who have already entered college.
8. An explanation of the library facilities available to students.
9. The grading plan, including the grade ranking of senior students.

Keep accreditation reports in the school office for a period of at least five years; however, the principal may want to keep them for a longer time as a record of the progress made or as a historical reference for college use.

Health report. This is a report of the incidences of illnesses such as chicken pox, measles, and so forth. It may also record the number of children who have physical defects of the eyes, ears, heart, lungs, bones, or other similar conditions. These cases are very important because they require special services. It is sometimes possible to receive extra tax money for them.

The school nurse and the physical education department usually compile such information and keep the records. This type of data is strictly confidential and is made available only to those who are specifically authorized to have it. Your duty is to type the health reports and forward them to the proper offices. Keep individual student health reports for a two-year period, or until the pupil graduates.

Corporal punishment report. Corporal punishment is handled by the principal or assistant principal. You will probably make out the report, usually on a special form which lists:

1. The name of the pupil.
2. The reason for the punishment.
3. The date and time of the offense as well as the type of punishment administered.
4. The signature of the principal or the name and signature of the person administering the punishment.
5. Whether the parent was notified. In some cases, a copy may be forwarded to the parent for his signature.

File one copy in your school, forward one copy to the district administration office, and place a copy in the pupil's Cumulative Guidance Record. Keep each report until the pupil concerned has graduated from school.

Suspension report. Suspensions are taken care of by the principal. The report you make indicates:

1. The name of the pupil.
2. The reason for the suspension.
3. The date and time of the offense causing the suspension.
4. What has been done previously to attempt to solve the problem.
5. The duration of the suspension, listing beginning and ending dates.
6. The date of the actual return of the pupil to school.
7. Contact with the parents and their reaction.
8. The signature of the principal and/or the person handling the case.

One copy should be filed in the school office, one placed in the pupil's Cumulative Guidance Record, and at least one copy forwarded to the school district guidance office. Keep this report on file until the suspended pupil has graduated from school.

Inventory record. Your main responsibility at inventory time is to distribute the inventory forms to members of the staff, give them any advice or instructions which are needed, and to collect the completed forms and check them for accuracy. When all forms are collected, make a master tabulation for the school and give it to the principal for final approval. File one copy in your office and send the original to the district business office. Inventory forms are used to list:

1. Instructional equipment such as record players, movie projectors, and the like.
2. Custodial equipment such as vacuums, mops, polishers.
3. Cafeteria equipment such as stoves, mixers, dishwashers.

4. Science equipment such as microscopes, Bunsen burners.
5. Science supplies such as alcohol, chemicals, batteries.
6. Athletic equipment such as basketball goals, stopwatches, starting guns, hurdles.
7. Athletic supplies such as footballs, volleyballs, whistles, uniforms.
8. Playground equipment such as swings, slides, tetherball poles.
9. Instructional supplies such as paper, pencils, paints. These are usually unopened supplies as those that are opened are not counted.
10. Office equipment such as typewriters, adding machines, file cabinets.
11. Nurse's equipment such as audiometers.
12. Nurse's supplies such as bandages, alcohol, antiseptics.
13. Furniture such as tables, desks, chairs.

Keep inventories for a two-year period, or until a new inventory is taken.

Budgeting. As secretary, you may be asked to help compile the budget for your school for the coming school year. To do this, you must canvass the various members of the staff or department heads to determine their needs. Your current file of supply and equipment requests are a further source of information upon which to predict your needs.

Although budget records need not be kept beyond the end of the school year, it is sometimes desirable to keep them for a longer period as a reference to guide your principal in making out future budgets. District budget records probably should be kept for a ten-year period.

Statistical reports. Statistical reports are lists of figures which are used for statistical purposes. They are often presented in tabular form. Each table should have a title, typed in capital letters, centered above the table. Do not use any terminal punctuation. If the caption is long, use other lines which should be shorter than and centered under the top line. See Figures 3 and 4 for samples of titles.

Headings of columns. All columns should have short, clear headings. Center them over the column, and keep them separate from the headings of other columns. Do not use any terminal punctuation. Capitalize only the first letter of the first word unless there are proper nouns.

Box headings in which the typed words are set off by typed or drawn lines are effective, and there is less chance of the words being run together. See Figure 4.

Arranging tabular material. Unless the tabular material is very short, place each table on a separate page. To determine the vertical placement:

1. Count the number of lines required to type the material, including titles and blank lines.
2. Subtract that number from available number of lines (66 for 11" paper), and divide the result by 2. This gives the number of blank lines needed above and below the tabulation.

DISTRIBUTION OF SUPERINTENDENT'S QUESTIONNAIRES AND RESPONSES OBTAINED FROM 57 UNIFIED SCHOOL DISTRICTS IN CALIFORNIA

Size of districts	Questionnaires mailed	Questionnaires returned	Per cent of Questionnaires returned
Small-size districts (1,000–3,000 average daily attendance)	25	15	60.0
Medium-size districts (3,001–10,000 average daily attendance)	18	13	72.2
Large-size districts (Over 10,000 average daily attendance)	14	12	85.7
Total districts	57	40	70.2

Figure 3. Example of a table.

NUMBERS AND PERCENTAGES OF CHILDREN WHO TESTED OVER 110 IQ ON CALIFORNIA TEST OF MENTAL MATURITY

GRADE	LINCOLN SCHOOL			WASHINGTON SCHOOL		
	Number tested	Number over 110 IQ	Per cent over 110 IQ	Number tested	Number over 110 IQ	Per cent over 110 IQ
First	102	15	14.7	97	14	14.4
Second	120	17	14.2	103	12	11.7
Third	101	13	12.9	95	15	15.8
Fourth	98	11	11.2	88	13	14.8
Fifth	85	12	14.1	79	9	11.4
Sixth	106	19	17.9	83	11	13.3
Totals	612	87	14.2	545	74	13.4

Figure 4. Example of a table using boxes to set off the headings and data.

To determine the horizontal placement:

1. Count the number of type spaces required for the longest line of each column and add them.
2. Determine the width of the finished tabulation. It must be wider than the sum of the column width, but narrower than the width of the page. In a letter or manuscript, it must not be wider than the other lines on the page, and it will look better if it is indented at least five spaces from both sides of the letter or manuscript.
3. Subtract the total width of the columns from the total width of the tabulation. This gives the type spaces available for the blank spaces between the columns. There will be one fewer of these than the number of columns of tabulated material. Therefore, divide the available type spaces by the number of columns minus one, to the nearest whole number. Extra spaces can be left in the outside margins or between two particularly wide columns. Now you have the width of each inter-columnar space.

Typing the columns. First, set the machine as follows:

1. Set margin stops for width of tabulation.
2. Set first tab at left margin figure plus width of first column plus width of first inter-columnar space.
3. Set second tab at first tab figure plus width of second column plus width of second inter-columnar space, and so on.
4. Check tab stops, and be sure that final tab plus final column width brings you to the right margin stop.

Second, tabulate. Using a card to keep the place on the copy, center the title and subtitle, center column headings over the columns, and tabulate. This means working across the page.

The dollar sign is written only at the head of the column and below a summation line. In listing figures, the decimal points must make a vertical line, and usually all figures are carried the same number of places to the right of the decimal, even if this means filling in with zeros. In tabulating numbers with varying numbers of figures, set the tab at the most common beginning point (not the dollar sign) and space or backspace for longer and shorter items. If a column has one or two extra-long items, you can use two lines, indenting the second if single spacing, single spacing them on a double-spaced tabulation.

Groups of columns or different relationships between columns can be indicated by varying the width of the inter-columnar spaces between columns.

Lining the tables. Use double lines at the top and bottom of tables. Make a single line under the column headings and above the totals, if any. These can be drawn with pen and ink, or by using the underline on the typewriter, rolling the platen a fraction of a turn for second lines. Some typewriters have a card holder in which you can insert a pencil. Make the line by holding the pencil steady and moving the typewriter carriage by hand.

Vertical lines are not usually necessary if enough space is left between the columns. If columns are close together, however, use vertical lines. Make these with pen and ink or if the typewriter carriage is a wide one, insert the paper sideways without folding and use the underline or use a pencil on the side of the card holder to make the lines.

Ordinarily, there are no horizontal lines between each figure in the column unless omission of the lines would result in confusion.

Proofreading. Check every figure in the table against the original data for accuracy. Errors can easily be made when long lists of numbers are typed. Since tabular material is usually research data, it is absolutely essential that the typing be accurate.

RECORD MANAGEMENT

As school secretary, you will usually have the responsibility for record management. This is because the control of record keeping should be in the hands of one person and centralized in one office. It is an old story that everybody's business is nobody's business.

Record management (1) provides for the filing of records and reports, (2) provides for proper protection and storage of the records which are of reference or legal value, and (3) provides for reordering as necessary.

Filing. The method of filing records and reports is explained in Chapter 9. Remember, however, whenever you file anything, to put it in the right place. Whenever you take a record out of a file, put a charge-out card in place of the removed card, or use a sign-out sheet. In any case, do not remove any paper without somehow recording the fact.

You are the only one who should put the record back in the file. At the same time, remove the charge-out card or indicate the return of the record on the sign-out sheet. Neither the administrator nor others should be permitted to refile records.

Observe the retention schedule so that obsolete records are not kept on hand to clutter up the office or the file cabinets. When feasible, have records microfilmed and indexed so that valuable space can be kept available for current records.

Records should be readily available. A drawer that is two-thirds full is much easier to handle than one which is so jam-packed that it is almost impossible to remove or replace a paper.

File cabinets. File cabinets should be of good quality with ball-bearing drawer rollers so that drawers can be opened and closed easily. Keep all records of value, or those which would be difficult to replace, in file cabinets which can be locked. Records such as personnel reports and Cumulative Guidance Records for pupils should most certainly be kept locked so that unauthorized persons cannot use them.

Storage of records. Keep current records or reports in file cabinets or file boxes which are readily accessible to those who need to use them. Store obsolete records or those which must be kept for a period of time but which have limited use in inexpensive cardboard file drawers or boxes. Mark these clearly with the code number, the title of the forms, and the inclusive dates covered.

Retention of forms and records. The retention time for specific records has been explained in the early part of this chapter. In general, the length of time that forms or records should be retained depends on how they are utilized and the legal requirements prescribed by the state, county, or school district. Some records do not need to be retained beyond the end of the school year. Others should be kept until the pupils concerned have graduated from school.

If pupils move to another school, either send their Cumulative Guidance Record to the other school, keep it in your file, or send it to the district administrative office, as determined by school district policy. Some records need to be kept for reference use only and the length of time will depend upon the use the school principal wishes to make of them.

Reordering forms. In many school districts you will requisition printed forms from the central school office once or twice a year, in others, you can order them as you need them.

Until you have become familiar with your school, you may have difficulty in predetermining the forms you will need. To help you, place on the last package a memo slip which states, "Before taking this package, be sure to order more forms." If the forms are loose or in stacks, place a colored sheet at a predetermined distance from the bottom with a similar notation. With experience, you will be able to order in time to have the necessary number of forms on hand.

A similar technique can be used for forms which you will duplicate yourself. The colored insert sheet can read, "Make 200 more copies when this sheet is reached." There is nothing so disconcerting as to be out of forms when they are needed.

Punched card forms. Since more and more school districts are using punched card forms for reporting certain types of information, use special care when handling them. They must not be bent, wrinkled, or folded.

Filing and indexing blank forms. Keep a record or log book of the forms used within your school, with headings for (1) the code number of the form, (2) the date the form is printed, (3) the title of the form, (4) the number printed or duplicated, and (5) the number ordered or reordered. Enter each form on a separate line in chronological order according to the date of the first printing or order.

Keep a copy of every form on file. One way of doing this is to place the forms in a manila folder, scrapbook, or looseleaf type of notebook.

Paste small forms on standard size paper so that they will be easier to find. Put the code number and title on each form. File them in chronological or numerical order in the same sequence in which they are entered in the record book. Make a notation on the form or on a card stapled to the form showing:

1. Quantity printed.
2. Quantity reprinted.
3. Office to which orders and reorders are sent, if you do not handle the printing.
4. Name of person ordering or using the form.
5. When to order or reorder.
6. Notations of suggested revisions.
7. Date revisions are made. Place a copy of the revised form in the folder or notebook.

Information which is entered in the record or log book need not be entered on this card nor on the blank form which you place in the folder.

The forms folder has three purposes: it establishes standards to follow, it is an up-to-date reference manual, and it becomes a training manual for new personnel or secretaries.

FORM DESIGN AND CONTROL

It is important that a program be developed to control the physical makeup of forms and the use to which they are put. You can establish a Forms Committee to develop such a program. It can consider such things as the physical makeup of forms, their size, placement of information on forms, coding, type of paper to be used, design of the form itself, identification of forms, periodic review of the use to which forms are put, and form revision. In large school districts, forms are usually developed at the district level by a committee representing all schools. The explanations which follow will help you whether you are a member of such a district committee or take the leadership at the school level.

Physical makeup of forms. Forms which are used in school offices are not always practical. They may have been used over a period of time without changes, additions, or deletions. Even when changes are made, they may not occur in the best location on the form for ease in using. Different forms which carry the same or similar information do not always have items in the same sequence. An example is the enrollment sheet which is made out for an entering pupil. The form might list the pupil's name, address, birthday, grade, and parents' names, in that order. When this information is transcribed to the attendance card, the same information might be called for in a different order. This is confusing and can lead to errors in transcribing information. It also takes a great deal more time to record accurately.

Placement of information on the form. Place the school's name at the top of every form. It can be printed or filled in with a rubber stamp. Include the school address, if the form is to leave the school premises. Place information in the most usable location and in the same sequence it is on other forms to which it may be copied.

If forms are to be filed by a pupil's or teacher's name, have that name within a quarter-inch of the top of the page, with no printing whatsoever above the name. This facilitates locating the desired record.

Form design. Forms that are properly designed will convey usable information, accurately and clearly stated. The Forms Committee should decide on the size and style of printing to be used. Printed areas should contrast with the areas to be filled in. The blank spaces should be easy to fill out, and spacious enough to permit longhand entries. Blocks or boxes are preferable to blank lines.

Amount of writing. The amount of writing required should be reduced to a minimum. Wherever possible, provide space for a check rather than the writing of a sentence. People are more likely to provide the needed information when writing is kept to a minimum.

Column headings. If column headings are used, beware of letting the width of the heading determine the width of the column. Some columns may need to be wide and some narrow. Place the heading flush with the left hand edge of the column instead of in the center.

Spacing. Space the copy you send to the printer so that the information called for in horizontal columns can be written in on the typewriter. Measure the distance between lines to fit typewriter spacing. Where several lines are needed to supply the requested information, allow space for them. It is a good idea to type in typical answers on the dummy copy to see whether the spaces provided are adequate. Instruct the printer to follow the instructions for form design very carefully.

Form identification. Give every form a name or title. Place it at the very top or at the very bottom, depending on the method of filing which is used. Where names are filled in, write the surname first if the name is placed on the left hand side of the paper, or last if the name appears on the right hand side.

Code number all forms for identification. There is no need for most schools to become involved in complicated coding, since the whole idea is to help locate a form. The simple use of consecutive numbers is usually sufficient, such as: Form # 1, Form # 2, and so forth. Assign numbers according to their chronological order. After the code number, you can show the number of copies ordered or reordered. Put the date on the line below the number.

Larger schools, particularly secondary schools, might want to precede the number by a letter symbol to identify the office or department which uses the form. For example, pupil accounting forms might use A-1 for the original enrollment blank, A-2 for the class assignment sheet, A-3 for the office card, and so on. You should become familiar with the code number of regular reports for ease in locating and handling them. Coding should never become too complex or too difficult to decipher.

Use of one side. Except on rare occasions, use only one side of a form. Where information does not always need to be read or is very rarely used, it may be placed on the back of the form.

Size of forms. The size of a form depends upon the use to which it will be put. Eight-and-a-half by eleven-inch paper is a standard size for many forms and reports and lends itself to easy filing.

Many school forms require only a small amount of information. Loan slips for lunch money, overdue book notices from the library, tardy notices, and referral of a child to the school nurse are of this type. You can duplicate these on small slips or cards, preferably 3×5 or 4×6 inches. Do not make them too small or they will be lost or too difficult to fill out and file. Form sizes for recording attendance, health information and so on are better if they are at least 5×8 or 6×9 inches in size.

Not more than three sizes of forms should be used, or filing and storage become a problem.

Paper. The weight of paper depends upon the use given a form. Forms which are used only once and then thrown away, and forms which must be in duplicate or triplicate, can be printed on bond paper. Forms which are to be sorted, counted, or thumbed in a file should be on heavier paper (usually bristol board). Different types of forms can be printed on different colored paper for easier identification.

11

Timekeeping and Payrolls

KEEPING a record of working time and making up payrolls for the people who work in the school are usually among the duties of the school secretary. The procedure followed in performing these tasks varies in different school districts. In most large districts, there will be instructions already available.

Although the policies and procedures for compensating school employees vary, certain provisions are common to most payrolls. These provisions include timekeeping, working on the payroll, distributing the pay checks, and procedures for processing employment termination records.

TIMEKEEPING

Timekeeping involves establishing and maintaining a record for payroll purposes of the working time of all school personnel. Time worked is recorded on time sheets or time cards.

Time sheets. To establish a time sheet, you will need to prepare a "sign-in" list of personnel who are authorized to work in the school. On this list, the employees enter their times of arrival at work and departure by recording the clock times or by placing check marks after their names.

Time cards. Time cards are used in school districts which require that a time clock be used. The employee drops his time card into a slot in the time clock which automatically stamps the time on the card. Some schools permit the teacher to sign a weekly or monthly card certifying the days present and absent. Other schools require teachers to turn in their school keys each night. A quick check of the key rack shows which teachers are absent, late, or have forgotten to leave their keys.

Time sheets and time cards are usually renewed for each payroll period. They may be divided according to whether the person is a teacher or other employee, whether he is on a monthly salary or works by the hour, or by the length of the payroll period.

WORKING ON THE PAYROLL

The payroll is a consolidated report of employees' working time, together with legal and other entries that affect their compensation. These entries include deductions authorized by employees for income tax, hospitalization, medical payments, retirement, life insurance, professional society or union dues, savings bond purchases, social security, and sometimes credit union payments. The payroll covers a specified time period for which pay checks are written and from which other accounting records are prepared.

Preparing time reports for payroll. You will need to prepare at least two time reports—one for teaching and administrative personnel, and another for clerks, custodial, and cafeteria personnel. You may also need to prepare separate time reports for unusual assignments, for overtime work, and for special or substitute personnel. The latter personnel may carry their own or duplicate time sheets or time cards for which special actions must be taken or special notations made on the payroll. The central accounting office of the school district may require you to send payroll or time reports at different dates during the month. Some time reports, such as those for athletic coaching and extra-curricular assignments may be prepared and presented only once a semester. If you need to prepare many payrolls, you may find it desirable to maintain a separate calendar or a tickler file as a reminder. The use of a calendar and a tickler file are described on page 94.

Time reporting basis. Working time may be reported on the payroll on a positive or negative basis.

Positive basis. The positive basis of reporting working time is usually applied to employees who are paid on an hourly basis, such as evening-school teachers and nonteaching employees. Their hours of work may vary from one payroll period to the next. The total number of hours actually worked is entered by date on the payroll or time report. Entries may also be shown for absences by type and overtime. Holidays and vacations are not usually entered unless compensation is to be paid for them.

Negative basis. The negative basis of reporting working time is usually applied to employees paid a monthly salary, such as regular teachers and clerks whose payroll period is consistently the same length in days or hours. The total days or hours worked for the period are shown with entries for holidays and other types of leave which add up to the total number of days or hours for the pay period. For instance, a teacher on a monthly basis is paid on a school-month basis of 120 hours (5 days a week times 6 hours a day times 4 weeks). If she has been absent, her hours worked are entered together with appropriate entries for hours absent so the total for the month equals 120 hours.

Symbols used in reporting. Working time may also be reported on the time record by symbols indicating regular days, institute days, vacation days, holidays, and sick leave or other leaves for which pay is granted. Full compensation or fractional compensation for such days may vary according to school board regulations. These regulations require special entries on the time report, such as "H" for holidays, "S" for sick, "T" for institute, and "V" for vacation.

Consolidating the payroll or time report. To make up the payroll, you will find it helpful to follow these suggested steps.

1. *Assemble needed materials.* To consolidate the payroll, you will need the following materials: timekeeping records, payroll forms, transmittal forms, absence forms, overtime records, overtime authorizations, employee's withholding exemption certificates (U.S. Treasury Department, Internal Revenue Service Form W-4), employees' authorizations for other payroll deductions, tables of deductions, personnel record cards, budget cards, and other personnel forms or copies. You should also have at hand a copy of the instructions for preparing the payroll, as well as the telephone number of the person authorized by the board of education to answer questions about unusual payroll situations.

2. *Check each employee's time record and status.* First, put the time records for the employees in the sequence that they are to appear on the payroll. If you are working from a time sheet that corresponds to the payroll order, your task may be minimal. However, if you are working from time cards, you may need to sort them into alphabetical or numerical order by specified categories for entry on the payroll form. Punch-card systems for use with electronic sorting and tabulating systems usually provide pre-punched cards printed with the name of each school, and sometimes with the name of each employee, for each payroll period. As you arrange the records in correct order, check to see that you have a time record for every employee on the payroll. Punch-card systems usually provide extra cards and instructions for contingencies that may arise.

When the time records are arranged in proper sequence, check each employee's time record for accuracy and completeness. You might wish to make up a checklist or series of questions based on your instructions similar to the one illustrated.

As you check through the time records, you may wish to clip on substantiating documents as reminders for the "remarks" section of the time sheet. If pre-punched cards are used, do not pin anything to them, or bend or mutilate the cards in any way.

3. *Compile the payroll or time report.* If you are using payroll sheets, fill in by typewriter the necessary heading entries for the school name and payroll period—and, perhaps, the categories of personnel to be listed. Below each heading, list the names of the employees in payroll order.

Subsequent payroll entries can be made alongside each employee's name for his total days worked, total absences, and symbols or explanations for personnel changes in the "remarks" or other appropriate section of the payroll sheet or pre-punched payroll cards.

PAYROLL CHECKLIST

Is each employee's time record completely filled in with the required entries, such as times or symbols?

Is each employee's name spelled correctly for payroll purposes?

Is each employee's payroll number (if any) correct?

Is each employee's position classification name or code correct?

Is each employee occupying a position properly authorized in the budget and the one recorded on his budget card or personnel record?

Are the legal documents (credentials, licenses, etc.) licensing the employee to do the work he does current and on file where they should be?

If an employee has been absent, is the completed form in order which attests to reasons for which compensation is to be paid or not paid?

Do an employee's dates of absence coincide with the work record of the employee who substituted for him?

If an employee is absent on leave, or is in some non-pay status, are the payroll entries correct for his status?

Are the forms authorizing deductions from the employee's pay check for income taxes, retirement contributions, group insurance premiums, and the like, currently correct?

If an employee has worked overtime, is the record accurate?

If an employee has worked overtime, is the authorization for him to work such overtime correctly made up and signed by the authorized official?

If an employee has been overpaid or underpaid on a previous payroll, have the forms or notations been made that rectify the situation?

If an employee is new on the payroll or has left the payroll, have personnel forms been completed that show that action?

If the secretary is to figure the amount of the pay check, does the employee's budget card show his correct salary or wage rate?

If an employee has been granted a salary or wage increase, has the amount of increase and authority for it been entered on his time or budget card?

If an employee is working in a status limited in the number of hours permitted by the board of education, such as a reading assistant or retired teacher serving as a substitute, is the time entered on the payroll within the allotment?

Computations on payroll. Should it be your responsibility to compute the payroll amounts, the following steps are suggested:

1. Enter, from the budget card, each employee's approved gross salary or hourly rate.
2. Multiply the hourly rate by the number of hours employee has worked.
3. From the tables of deductions for income tax, retirement contributions, group insurance premiums, and the like, make entries in the appropriate

sections of the time report. These deductions may already have been figured and entered on the budget or personnel card. In this case, transfer the data to the time report from this card.

4. Total the deductions, and subtract the total from the gross pay to ascertain the net pay entry.
5. Prove the totals of deductions and the net pay total on the adding machine before entering these items.

Checking the payroll. No matter how careful you are, errors sometimes creep in. Take your typed copy to a quiet place and check it to find any discrepancies, errors, or omissions. Then have another employee read off to you from the time records, other tables and original sources, the entries that should be on the payroll. When such a comparison has been completed, make any necessary corrections and attach any required supporting data. Then present the payroll to the person authorized to verify it.

Verification of time worked. The principal usually verifies and signs the payroll for the employees in his school. Some payrolls, such as those for cafeteria employees and custodial employees, may be verified by the supervisor of these employees. The full signature of the verifying official should appear. He is usually required to initial all erasures and corrections appearing on the payroll. In the verifying official's absence, there are usually regulations to be followed as to how and by whom the payroll must be signed. Never forward for payment an unsigned payroll. If the payroll is not verified and transmitted to the paying office immediately, keep it in a locked cabinet or safe. Check the rules and regulations for forwarding the payroll to the board of education office for authorization.

Payroll accounting records. The totals of employee payroll earnings and deductions reported to the government and to the employee are almost always prepared by the central accounting office of the school district. The school district must annually furnish each employee a statement in duplicate of his gross earnings and all taxes withheld from his salary (on U.S. Treasury form W-2, supplied by the Department of Internal Revenue). The school district may also furnish its employees with yearly statements of money withheld for retirement and other purposes. It may be your duty to deliver and explain these statements to those employees for whom you prepare the payroll.

DISTRIBUTING THE PAY CHECKS

The pay checks for school personnel may be delivered by special messenger, registered mail, or by school mail. Pay days may be on different dates for various classes of personnel. For example, teachers may be paid every fourth Tuesday; clerks may be paid the second working day of every month; overtime pay day may be the working day nearest the fifteenth of every month. School districts differ widely in their pay days.

Verification of pay checks. You or some other responsible school employee will be required to sign a receipt for the pay checks. This should be done only after the contents of the package in which they are received have been verified. In all likelihood, it will be your duty to verify the pay checks, take required action for incorrect or missing pay checks, distribute them, and return evidence of their delivery to the school accounting office. The pay checks are usually transmitted with a payroll distribution sheet which lists each check included in the package by employee name and check or payroll number, if any. Following each employee's name, there is a space for him to acknowledge receipt of his check by signing for it. He must usually sign his name exactly as the check gives it.

Direct banking method. Some districts have instituted a new method of paying in which the pay is credited directly to a bank account stipulated by the employee—thus eliminating the need for warrants.

Distributing pay checks of absent employees. You will notify the personnel whose checks you are holding to call at the office to sign for them on the payroll distribution sheet as they receive the checks. Employees who are absent may be permitted to have their checks delivered to another employee or responsible person who presents to you an authorization or proxy, properly dated and signed by the absent employee. When all checks that you have received are accounted for, you will return the signed payroll distribution sheet to the central accounting office.

PROCESSING AND TERMINATING EMPLOYEES

In most school systems, employees who come to the school to work for the first time will have been interviewed and their employment officially certified by the director of personnel for the school district or someone of equivalent authority. This official certification is sometimes referred to as processing. Processing includes the filing of an application, birth certificate, and teaching credential or certificate, taking a health examination, fingerprinting, and swearing to the oath of allegiance. You will undoubtedly have complete instructions as to the basic procedures to follow in putting the new employee on the payroll.

Obtaining personnel data. Certain minimum personnel data should be secured from every employee who goes to work in the school—information that may be entered on a small personnel card. These data should include the employee's correct payroll name, the payroll title of his job, address, a telephone number where he may be reached, the names and number of his dependents, whom to notify in case of emergency, and the date and hour he started to work at the school. In addition, you must ascertain that he has completed an employee's withholding exemption certificate to show the number of exemptions to which he is entitled for income tax purposes.

According to the school payroll system, you will either make out for the new employee a time card or enter his correct name on the appropriate time sheet and show him how, when, and where he is to record his time worked. You may also need to tell him to whom he reports for work and, if at all possible, introduce him to that person. How to go about introducing a new employee to his job is discussed on pages 29, 30, and 32.

Terminating an employee's services. When an employee's services have been terminated, you will ordinarily prepare a special form to show the action. This form sets forth identifying facts concerning the employee, the last date and hour the employee worked, his payroll status, and the reason for termination. In addition, it is customary to make an entry of termination details in the "remarks" column of the ensuing payroll report. It also is usual practice to rule off in colored pencil or ink on the payroll report sheet the time spaces during which the individual did not work.

In case of the death of an employee's near relatives, most central accounting offices require that their office be notified immediately by telephone of the dates when the employee will be off duty but in a pay status. When an employee dies, the central office usually requires to be notified of the date and time of the death, and the name and address of the next of kin.

3

The School Secretary and Her Special Functions

12

Handling School Finances

THE SCHOOL SECRETARY will be concerned, in some measure, with financial activities involving funds allocated to the school by the board of education for the instructional program and school plant. She may be more closely concerned, however, with funds, principally student body funds, which pass through the school. This chapter describes activities you may find in accounting for board of education and student body funds.

TYPES OF SCHOOL FUNDS

Every school handles three general types of funds: moneys belonging to the board of education or school district, monies belonging to the students as a whole or to student organizations, and trust funds held temporarily until transfer to the designees or for a designated use. Reports of the condition of these funds are submitted to the board of education at specified intervals. Certain records and reports are required by law, in some states.

Board of education funds. You will seldom be involved in the accounting for school district funds used for the operation of the schools and the construction of school buildings. However, you may receive funds within the school that belong to the board of education and for which an accounting must be made. Such funds might include fees for rental of the school auditorium, payments for lost books and damage to school property, and money from cafeteria sales.

Student body funds. Student body funds represent money contributed by the students or earned through their activities, such as the raising of funds through salvage drives and subscriptions to the school newspaper, or the sale of tickets to athletic events. Typical student body expenditures cover the cost of parties for the graduating class, student awards, athletics, band and athletic uniforms, and insurance to cover student body property. The income and outgo of these funds must be reflected in student body accounts. The spending of student body funds is usually controlled by law or board of education regulations. These funds must be used for activities and materials to promote the general welfare and morale of the pupils of the school.

By being aware of the policies of your district concerning expenditures of student body funds, you will be in a position to aid your principal in determining whether proposed expenditures may be approved or disapproved.

Trust funds. Trust accounts, or clearing accounts, represent money that may not belong to either the board of education or the student body. Such money is held in trust until it can be transferred to the person or organization entitled to it, or until it can be spent for a designated purpose. For example, trust accounts include scholarship moneys, club and class treasuries, faculty funds, contributions to the Red Cross, and sales taxes. Money which the school collects on behalf of the board of education is also held as a trust account until it can be transferred to the board of education.

HELPING WITH BUDGET MANAGEMENT

You can help your principal on budget management in various ways. Have your principal explain to you the purpose of school and student body budgets and how budget requests are prepared. You can be of help by performing some of these tasks:

1. Locating records and official sources of information for those who are preparing the budget. This may include records of past expenditures, copies of the past year's budget, purchase sources, prices, and similar information.
2. Compiling a calendar of dates or deadlines for those preparing budget estimates.
3. Compiling board of education and student body budget requests in approved form.
4. Offering to help those who have difficulty preparing their requests or justifying them in writing.
5. Reviewing previous budget requests with those responsible for preparing budgets, warning them to avoid lump sum requests.
6. Encouraging those preparing budgets to show their needs on a per pupil or per activity basis.
7. Advising those preparing budgets to have explanations ready for any proposed increase in their budget.
8. Compiling board of education and student body budget requests in approved form.
9. Assisting your principal in keeping both board of education and student body budget accounts within their prescribed maximums.
10. Anticipating needs in your own office, such as office stationery and salaries of clerical assistants.

Student body budget. You may be asked to assemble the student body budget by securing estimates of needs and anticipated income from the faculty sponsors of student organizations, athletics, merchandise, publications, and the like. You will find that the procedure is much the same as for the board of education budget. The principal difference is that you must include in the student body budget, estimates of student merchandise sales, proceeds from ticket sales, and items which pay for the student body activities.

Budget accounting. When the board of education has approved the budget, your school will be notified of the allocations allowed in the budget. Ordinarily, your principal will need to re-allocate the sum to the various departments, offices, and services within the school.

To keep expenditures within the limits allowed, you will need to maintain a set of budget accounts. Budget accounts are often kept on fillers in a binder, or on cards. When accounting for the budget, enter on the control record the amount allowed each budget account.

When a purchase requisition is approved, record it as an encumbrance or a charge against its specific budget account. The estimated value of the merchandise or service will be available for you to record. You must charge every requisition against some account. Then, subtract this amount from the allowed budget or from whatever remains in the account. This shows the unencumbered or uncharged balance that can be used for future requisitions. Then, substitute for the amount set up as encumbrance the exact charge from the invoice when the requisitioned goods are received. See Figure 5.

Keeping "within" budgeted accounts. You should discourage any individual or department from ordering a whole year's supply at the beginning of the first semester because of possible storage and obsolescence problems. You should notify each individual or department when its budget account gets to within 10 or 15 per cent of the end of its funds. Always keep your principal informed whenever money allotted for an item is exhausted or requisitions presented exceed allotted amounts.

You will ease the problem of living within a budget if you keep all budget records up to date.

Approved student body budget allocations are to be accounted for in the same way as the board of education budget accounts. However, a more usual method is to enter budget information on a line at the bottom of the related ledger account sheets.

HANDLING SCHOOL MONEY

Your handling of school moneys will include the following activities: issuing receipts for money received, making bank deposits, withdrawing

BUDGET ACCOUNT: SUPPLIES FOR PUPILS BUDGET AMOUNT: $2,000				
Date	Description	Encum-brances	Expendi-tures	Unencum-bered Balance
9/6	Ordered $500 worth of supplies	$500		$1,500
9/15	Supplies ordered 9/6 received; actual price $560	−500	$560	1,440

Figure 5. Budget account ledger sheet.

money from the bank, writing bank checks, and reconciling the bank statement.

Receipts for money received. Form the habit of issuing receipts for any money deposited within the school office. Write the receipt in duplicate—the original for the person who makes the payment, and the duplicate for the school records. Receipts should be in book form, pre-numbered with printed or stamped consecutive numbers.

If you make an error on a receipt, do not erase it. Write "Void" across both copies, leave them in the book for reference, and make out a new receipt.

Do not omit any items on the receipt. Check to be sure you have recorded the amount of money received, the date, the name of the payer, the fund or account to be credited, and the full name of the person receiving the money.

Bank deposits. Many school systems require that all money collected in a day be deposited in the bank the same day. You should take the money to the bank in a canvas sack or leather bag that can be locked and sealed. Roll the coins in wrappers obtainable from the bank. Arrange the currency with the largest bills on top, face up, and fasten them with a money clip, paper clip, or rubber band. Put the checks and deposit slips in the pass book. Whoever takes the money to the bank should give the bag to the bank teller to unlock, and the teller should count the contents in her presence.

Deposit slips. Prepare the deposit slips provided by the bank in triplicate. The original deposit slip is for the bank; the second copy is to be signed by the teller and kept in the school files. On the back of the second copy, you should record the school receipt numbers with the amount they represent in the deposit. The third copy of the deposit slip is a memorandum which you may destroy when the signed second copy has been returned.

Enter currency and coin on the deposit slip by amounts under the items listed on the deposit slip. List endorsed checks individually by the place each is payable or by its American Bankers' Association transit number, together with its amount. The transit number is the small printed number that appears on the face of the check near the name of the bank; for example, $\dfrac{1-8}{210}$.

Before you list a check on the deposit slip, examine it for agreement of the amount in figures and in words, the signature, and agreement of the endorsement and payee. Do not deposit an incorrectly drawn check. If you receive one, seek a correction immediately from the issuer of the check.

Endorsement of checks. The Association of School Business Officials recommends the use of a rubber stamp to endorse checks. Such a stamp should be worded, "Pay to the order of (Name of bank)" and carry the words, "For deposit only." If you don't have such a stamp, these words should be written on each check deposited. Write the endorsement on the blank side of the check directly beneath the beginning of writing on the face of the check. Write the endorsement as near the top as possible so that no other words may be inserted above them.

Since anyone may secure the funds for a check written to "Cash" or "Bearer," you should endorse all such checks immediately. Whenever possible, you should insist that checks be written to the order of the student body.

If a check is returned by the bank for some reason having to do with the account of the maker, such as insufficient funds, (mark NSF) notify your principal at once so that an effort to collect the check is started.

Withdrawing money from the bank. Customarily, the withdrawal of student body funds from the bank—either commercial or savings accounts—requires the signature of two of three authorized persons. These two authorized persons sign checks and withdrawal slips jointly. One of these authorized persons is the principal, whose signature is almost always required. Keeping on hand a series of checks presigned by one of the authorized endorsers is considered a poor, if not illegal, procedure.

Writing bank checks. Most schools have their own printed checks. Such checks give the school's name, address, and telephone number. Schools' printed checks are usually bound in large books, three checks to a page, with all checks pre-numbered. A stub or attached voucher is provided for each check. The voucher describes the goods or services for which payment is being made and is sent with the check to the payee.

Stub-type check. When you write a stub-type check, first fill out the stub with the amount of the check, the date, the name of the payee, the purpose of the check, and the name or number of the account or fund against which it is to be charged. Then, write the check on the typewriter or in ink. Next, compare the stub and check to verify the following points: the check number, the amount, the name of the payee, and the date. Last, arrange for signature of the check.

Voucher-type check. When using the voucher type of check, printed in duplicate or triplicate, the carbon copies of the check and voucher serve the purpose of the stub. It is customary to verify and staple all supporting documents to the duplicate voucher and file them by check number.

Errors on checks. No errors, alterations, or erasures of any sort are permitted on a check. Write "Void" across the check and stub or voucher and make out a new check whenever you find an error. Place all copies of voided checks in a numerical check file.

Used checkbooks. After all checks in a checkbook have been drawn, paste a label on the outside cover giving the name of the bank, the dates on which the first and last checks were drawn, and the first and last numbers of the checks in the book. Number the books, and keep them for at least four years.

Reconciling the bank statement. The school's bank account must be reconciled at the close of each calendar month. Reconciliation is a matter of checking the balance in your bank book for accuracy by comparing it with the bank statement, which shows all withdrawals, bank deposits, and bank service charges. It takes some time to have all the checks you write clear the bank; therefore, the balance on the bank statement will not usually be the same as the balance you have shown by your check stubs. Thus it is necessary for you to reconcile the two balances by taking into consideration the outstanding checks (checks not yet cleared through the bank), deposits made after the closing date of the bank statement, service charges made by the bank, and any errors you may find. If you find any discrepancy, report it immediately to the bank for correction.

Most banks have a reconciliation form printed on the back of the statement you receive. It explains a simple procedure for reconciling a bank account. If you have difficulty in implementing these instructions, ask the bank teller to give you some help.

HANDLING MONEY FOR SPECIAL SCHOOL ACTIVITIES

School activities usually require that you handle the monies or help others to do so. You might find the following helpful when dealing with petty cash, cashiering, pupils' school savings, selling tickets, and merchandise.

Petty cash. Of course, you know that no employee—not even the principal—is allowed to have board of education or student body funds on his person. The needs of the principal's office for cash for a minor emergency and incidental expenses are met from a petty cash fund. The procedure for establishing a petty cash fund is as follows:

1. Draw a check for a round amount such as $10 or $25.
2. Charge the check to "petty cash" as an expense of the day.
3. Cash the check and place the currency in a cash box.
4. Make certain as you make payments from the fund that properly signed vouchers or evidence of payments are made.
5. Enter all cash payments not supported by vouchers or receipts in a simple cash book, preferably one that fits into the cash box.
6. Ascertain that the total of these records, plus the cash on hand, always equals the original amount of the fund.
7. Draw a check for the total amount of the expenditures from the fund to bring it back up to its original amount at the end of the month, or whenever the fund is low.
8. Add the vouchers and memoranda for charging to the accounts they represent.
9. Staple these records together, date them, and file them in a "Petty Cash Reimbursement" envelope.
10. Make no further posting to the petty cash account in the ledger except when it is increased, decreased, or closed if the records are charged to the appropriate accounts.

In handling the petty cash fund, always remember the following points: (1) never mix petty cash with your own funds; (2) never make change from it unless you can make the exact change; (3) never borrow from the petty cash fund; (4) keep the petty cash fund locked up.

Cashiering. You may have the responsibility of making change, collecting and counting cash, reading cash registers, supervising student cashiers, and protecting school funds. When you receive cash, always count the money in the presence of the payer before placing it in the cash drawer. Whenever you pay change:

1. Keep the coins and bills in full view of yourself and the payer until the transaction is complete.
2. Repeat aloud the sum of money being paid.
3. Count the additional coins to reach a full dollar.
4. Count out bills until the total sum received is reached.
5. Put the payer's bill in the cash drawer immediately after the transaction is complete.
6. Handle only one transaction at a time.

So far as is practicable, cash should be collected only in the office. Count money, especially when it comes in large amounts, in a location safe from interruption. You should enlist another person to witness the counting if you can.

Cash register. You may be asked to read the cash register in the student store to verify the cash with sales registered by student cashiers or others. In this case, you should arrange to have the recording mechanism of the register you read kept locked up when not in use, and for all cash register tapes to be saved.

The school money drawer or cash register should have a lock, and there should be only one person authorized to have the key. At the close of the day, money should be counted and transferred to a safe or vault which can be locked. If the school system requires that all collections be deposited in the bank each day, arrangements must be made to clear the registers and make the deposit before the bank closes. No large sum of cash should remain long at the school. Professional entertainers and others should be paid by check. Notify your principal immediately if you discover a shortage in funds at any time.

Supervision of student cashiers. If you supervise student cashiers, you should insist that they be carefully screened by your principal and their teachers, that they be instructed to ring up each sale on the register as a separate transaction and not allow cash to accumulate to be rung up as a lump sum. See pages 218 to 220 for suggestions regarding cashiering in the school cafeteria.

Pupils' school savings. Many elementary schools encourage pupils to develop the habit of saving regularly. These schools designate one day in the week or month as Bank Day. On that day, the teachers collect the pupils' deposit envelopes and send them to the school office where they are picked up by the bank's messenger.

Most banks do not expect the school teacher or secretary to count the money being deposited. However, it may be your task to organize and prepare the pupils' deposit envelopes for Bank Day. If so, arrange the envelopes by each teacher's room. Place all the pupils' envelopes for each teacher in a large envelope bearing the teacher's name and room number. Also insert into the large envelope the bank books and supplies. Any envelopes not already sealed by the pupil or teacher when they are returned to you should be sealed.

As soon as the individual deposit envelope for a pupil is sealed, the money it contains is to all intents deposited in the bank. Any error is assumed by the bank.

Selling tickets. On occasion, you may sell tickets for school activities or other school purposes. More likely, you will be asked to supervise students selling tickets or issue tickets to a teacher who is charged with the responsibility. You may also make up a ticket sales report.

Whenever tickets are sold in the school, a ticket sales report must be made up and recorded for audit. This report lists:

1. The event or activity for which the tickets were sold.
2. The date of the event.
3. The price or amount of the ticket.
4. The quantity of complementary and duplicate tickets issued.

5. The first (start) number and last (stop) number of the tickets issued.
6. The quantity and numbers of tickets returned.
7. The amount of money supplied the seller for making change.
8. The amount of money received from ticket sales.
9. The signature of the ticket seller.

When issuing tickets to sell, record the first and last number of the tickets issued and the amount of money provided for making change. Impress upon the seller that the loss of tickets is a personal liability just like loss of money. However, those who lose tickets are seldom held accountable if the tickets are not presented at the occasion for which they were issued and the school suffers no loss in consequence.

13

Requisitioning and Purchasing

No DOUBT you have heard the old cliché that a log with Mark Hopkins on one end and the student on the other was the only necessary equipment in a school. This may have some truth in it, but on the other hand, the poorest school cannot operate effectively without purchasing thousands of items for the use of teachers and pupils. These items are classified as supplies and equipment, ranging from pencils and chalk to television sets and teaching machines.

The role of the secretary in the process of purchasing is primarily that of a supplies and equipment watchdog. This does not mean that the purchasing, control, and use of supplies and equipment should be so tightly controlled that members of the staff must beg for their rations. The secretary must have adequate background and information about supplies and equipment plus an organized and logical system for the effective use and control of supplies and equipment.

This chapter has been organized to help you with the purchasing and requisitioning phase of your job. It will first discuss the nature of school purchasing, then give you a list of steps in requisitioning and purchasing, and end with some guiding principles.

NATURE OF SCHOOL PURCHASING

When a school prepares a budget, many, many items are considered. Obviously, it would be an insurmountable task to enumerate every item that is to be purchased. In order to simplify matters, all of these items are grouped under special categories such as supplies, materials, equipment, equipment repair, and equipment replacement. Usually, for matters of convenience, a certain percentage of the budget is encumbered for these categories. In some instances, the various categories are broken down into smaller units. For example, supplies, materials, or equipment may be divided into instructional and non-instructional. In this way, the principal is aware of the percentages spent respectively on instructional and non-instructional items.

Supplies and equipment. As you work with the ordering of supplies and equipment you should be able to differentiate between them. Supplies are usually defined as those materials which are consumed in current use, which have a relatively short life of service, which have a small unit of cost, and which are frequently replaced without addition to the value of the physical properties. Equipment is usually defined as physical property of a more-or-less permanent nature, other than land, buildings, or improvements to either of these. Lists of standard supplies and equipment are usually made available to all schools. It is considered good practice to furnish the teachers with this list for reference when making their requisitions.

Differentiating for budget reasons. One reason you must differentiate between supplies and equipment is that school funds are budgeted separately for supplies and equipment. It is just a matter of good common sense that if one does not encumber certain items as a certain per cent of the budget, someone else might spend the complete budget on his own pet project. For example, a department might spend all its money on the purchase of new typewriters and have absolutely no money left to repair or replace old typewriters. Some states do not require the school to make these distinctions in their budget, but you will find that the same idea is accomplished in one way or another.

Trade-in items. Generally speaking, most districts do not purchase second-hand items or make trades (swaps) with other schools or businesses. Otherwise, it gets to be a most complicated procedure and schools are spending a great deal of their time in bargaining for the "best deal." Some items are traded in periodically, such as homemaking department equipment, refrigerators, and gas or electric ranges. Many schools have devised a plan whereby they trade in their typewriters every three to five years—an equipment item which takes a great beating in a school year.

Services. There are many occasions in a school when services must be arranged for and paid for when the service is finished. Examples of such occasions are installation of bleacher seats for a football game or graduation exercise, repair of typewriters or calculating machines, and contracting for the electrical wiring for a bazaar or pageant. In most states, it is the obligation of the school to provide for the laundering of towels, dry cleaning of the band uniforms, developing of photographic films, and many other services too numerous to mention.

How a school purchases. Schools usually purchase items either through a central purchasing office or directly from an outside supplier. Outside suppliers are frequently contacted when schools are purchasing very special items, not ordinarily stocked in a school supply room or the district warehouse.

Purchasing through central purchasing office. In large schools, the ordering of supplies and equipment is usually done through a central purchasing office of the board of education. This office decides from whom the supplies will be purchased. They also call for bids when the order on any single item is large enough. The warehousing of district supplies is also under the control of the central office.

Direct purchasing. In small school districts, there generally aren't enough schools to warrant a central warehouse or purchasing office. In such case, authority to purchase directly may be given to each school. If you are responsible for such a purchasing plan, you should follow the general steps in requisitioning and purchasing given in the next part of the chapter.

How to familiarize yourself with purchasing. Items are stored in the supply room of the school, in a department supply room, or in a teacher's supply cabinet. Many school districts have a central supply room or warehouses from which they make periodic distribution of supplies and equipment.

Visiting the storage areas. It will help you to understand requisitioning and purchasing if you make a visit to the various areas of the school where school materials are housed. Among such places are the school's stock and supply room, the library, the textbook room, the audio-visual storage room, the central tool room, the gardener's and custodian's supply room, and the various storage areas in the various classrooms and departments. Contact the head custodian to take you on a general tour of these areas.

Studying the office records. After your visit to the various storage areas of the building, take a look at the school's purchasing records. They will give you a better idea of your duties and responsibilities in purchasing. These records should include purchase orders, schedules for requisitions, and budget allocations.

Studying the catalog. If your school district has a centralized purchasing department or business division, there probably will be a catalog of standard stock items with description, unit designation (ea, pkg, bx), unit prices, code numbers, department, whether the item is stocked in warehouse, and the budget account to which each is allocated.

STEPS IN REQUISITIONING AND PURCHASING

When organizing a project or planning an activity, it is a good idea to have an over-all picture of each specific step from beginning to end. The following steps should serve as guide posts to help you in the complete process of requisitioning and purchasing:

1. Determine what is needed.
2. Determine availability of funds.
3. Prepare requisition or request for purchase order.
4. Consolidate orders.
5. Forward requisitions or requests for purchase order.

6. Place or let purchase orders.
7. Make follow-up.
8. Receive and verify deliveries.
9. Distribute deliveries.
10. Make payments.

Determining what is needed. The first step in purchasing is to determine just exactly what items are needed. In order to know what is needed in a school:

1. Set up a system of control for requisitioning and purchasing within the school.
2. Set up a method of communication whereby each teacher, department head, and other personnel in the school can let you know the materials they need.

It is from these sources of information that the superintendent prepares the next year's budget. After the budget is approved, you then prepare the necessary forms for ordering such equipment.

Special supply requests. Special equipment and supply requests are usually sent in by each department at a specified time each year. For example, the principal might set a deadline sometime in April of each year for each department to turn in its requests for special purchase. These requests would include special items needed for the coming year. Ample time must be allowed for delivery before the opening of the next school year.

Routine requests. Routine equipment and supply requests are placed each school year at a specified time. These requests usually originate from department heads, individual teachers, or from any member of the staff. A part of the budget is allocated and requests are most generally placed and approved sometime early in the calendar year so that they can become a part of the regular budget.

Emergency requests. Requests for emergency items may come anytime during the year. Approval and processing are handled in the same way as for routine requests, except it occurs at irregular intervals. Part of the budget should be left unencumbered to cover such situations.

Determining availability of funds. As explained previously, a budget is adopted by the board of education for the operation of the entire school year—usually defined as July 1 to June 30 of the following year. A certain percentage of the budget is allocated to supplies and equipment. A certain portion of money set aside for a specific purpose is referred to as being "encumbered." The purchase price for each item is an encumbrance when the request for purchase is approved.

It should be your responsibility to know at all times what amount of money has not been spent or is unencumbered for any particular budget account. To help you in determining this information, the following budget points will be helpful:

1. Keep all requisition information in one place (a looseleaf notebook makes a good filing system.) Use a leaf or card for each account or school department allowed to make purchases.
2. Enter the budget amounts allocated to each account or department.
3. Each time a requisition is approved and a purchase order issued, enter the date, the purchase order number, and the amount of the encumbrance.
4. Subtract the amount of the purchase order from the previous amount remaining in the account or to the department's credit.

This procedure will always give you a true picture of the unencumbered amounts for each item budgeted. Thus, you should have no difficulty in knowing or determining if funds are available to pay for any item requested from any department or for any account.

Preparing requisition or request for purchase order. First, you must differentiate between a budget request and a purchase requisition. A budget request lists those items that a school or department thinks it will need for supplies or equipment during the forthcoming school year. The estimated cost of these items helps determine how much money will be needed to run the school next year. A purchase requisition is a written, formal request to buy a specific item or piece of equipment. The necessary information is usually written on a standard form.

Requisition blanks. Most districts large enough to maintain schools of more than six to eight teachers use requisition blanks for all purchase orders. Usually the principal already has the form arranged so that it can be made out in duplicate or triplicate. In using a triplicate, one copy would be filed in the principal's office with the other copies going to the superintendent's office. One of the superintendent's copies would be returned later with exact information as to the cost of the items ordered, thus helping the principal to keep accurate records.

Requisitions to central warehouse. In larger school districts, the central warehouse is generally a reservoir of supplies and equipment for frequently used (so-called "standard") items. Usually the principal (unless he delegates his authority to other persons) approves all requisitions for items from the warehouse. The warehouse, in most cases, operates on a strict approval basis and will never issue anything without a signed requisition. In some districts, the requisition must also have the approval of the assistant superintendent in charge of instruction or the curriculum director and/or the business manager. In addition, the requisitioner should be informed of the disposition of all requisitions. The school should keep on file (usually chronologically) one copy of all requisitions as a reminder of what was ordered. A requisition is a document representing money!

Types of requisitions. Requisitions are of two types: general requisitions, and requests for purchase order. *General requisitions* are used when an item is carried in stock by the school or the district's warehouse. *Purchase order requisitions* are used when the item is not carried in stock and must be purchased from a manufacturer or supplier, oftentimes called the vendor. When an item has to be purchased from a vendor, the purchase is sometimes referred to as a "buy out." All purchase requisitions must pass through the principal's office, or through the superintendent's office in small school districts, for approval. The approved requisition is then forwarded to the proper budget or purchasing officer in the school district.

Purchase order. Sometimes a purchase requisition is called a "Request for a Purchase Order." See Figure 6. After it has been approved and the budget funds encumbered, a purchase order (P.O.) is issued. The purchase order is your authority to tell an outside company (vendor) that you can buy a certain item, and that the school or board of education will pay for it.

If a purchase order is issued from a central purchasing office, it must be done on the basis of a purchase requisition from one of the schools in that district. However, if the individual school issues its own purchase order to an outside vendor, it still has to be done upon a purchase requisition from a teacher or other school employee with the approval of the principal or his designated representative.

Consolidating orders. As you check through the approved list of supplies and equipment orders, you will find that some departments have requested identical or similar items. Such items should be sorted out and consolidated into one request for a purchase order. The same principle holds true if you are in charge of ordering different items from the same vendor or supplier. You can consolidate items obtainable from one company.

Specifications relating to purchases. In preparing specifications for an item to be ordered or for a service (e.g., printing service) to be rendered, you should be absolutely sure that you have included all the information required to assure receiving the identical item that was in mind when the request was made.

How does one go about insuring that all the correct facts are on the specifications? Here are a few checkpoints which you might follow:

1. *Check in the catalog of equipment or supplies.* Every school should have an assortment of catalogs from many supply companies. If you are in a large school, your central purchasing office will let you use the catalogs from which they order. If you have no up-to-date catalog, phone several supply companies and ask for the information or a copy of their most recent catalogs.

2. *Telephone supply companies or suppliers for information.* After you have telephoned supply companies, check with the teacher or the employee

REQUEST FOR PURCHASE ORDER FOR SUPPLIES OR EQUIPMENT

Date _____

To the Superintendent of Schools:

There will be needed by the _____ Department of the _____
High School the items described below.

To be purchased from:

_____
(Name of Vendor)

_____
(Vendor's Address)

_____
(Vendor's Phone Number)

_____
(Teacher or Dept. Head)

_____
(Principal)

Quantity	Description of Item (Catalog Number)	Replacement or Addition	Delivery Date	Budget Account	Est. Cost	Tax	Actual Cost

Figure 6.

requesting that particular item to see if the specifications you received over the telephone will meet the needs of the person making the request. Or, you might ask the person making such a request to get the information himself from the supplier so that the information can be verified before specifications are prepared.

3. *Telephone other school districts for information.* Many times other school districts have ordered identical equipment, and they may have the information you need.

Forwarding requisitions or requests for purchase order. It is very important that you keep an accurate notation concerning the forwarding of your school's requisitions or requests for purchase orders. Note the date the requisition or purchase order was sent and to whom it was transmitted. In the forwarding of requisitions, make sure that they are properly signed, that the correct number of copies has been made and directed to the correct places. Be careful that requisitions are forwarded in ample time so that delivery can be made before the item is to be used.

Placing or letting purchase orders. Teachers or other authorized school employees who wish to buy items for the benefit of the school or student body must have a purchase order. A purchase order properly endorsed by the principal, secretary, or other authorized person is valid and practically any merchant will honor one. Every purchase order carries a serial number. It is important that this number be given the vendor. He must have it when he makes his claim upon the school district for payment.

Method of purchasing. Purchasing may be made by telephone, in person, or by mail. When making a purchase over the telephone, be sure that you have recorded and checked all the information regarding specifications, delivery date, and the like, before you dial the number. This will save additional telephoning or digging for information while the other party waits. It is also a good idea to call different vendors for the same item to locate the best price for comparable quality. The vendor will quote you the price and any changes in specifications. Be sure to tell him the serial number of the purchase order.

Verification of order. After you have chosen a vendor and called the order in, you should follow up this communication by sending a written purchase order or verification. Sometimes a teacher wishes to place an order in person so that he can obtain immediate delivery. In this case, the teacher should know that he cannot make substitutions without authorization, and that he must present a receipt or bill of sale to the school. Most schools, however, do not allow teachers to use their own money or to make a later claim for reimbursement.

Purchase order blanks. Some schools, particularly large high schools, print up books of "Requests for Purchase Orders." These books are issued to faculty advisers of student organizations and activities. The Requests are in duplicate. When a purchase is to be made, the treasurer for the student body fills in a request, has it countersigned by the faculty adviser, and presents it to you for issuance of a purchase order. The duplicate copy is retained in the faculty adviser's book.

Following up requisitions. Time allowed for delivery is usually considered in the placing of requisitions or purchase orders. You can generally get an estimate of how much time to allow from the purchasing offices or from the outside vendor. However, there may be delays in central purchasing or delays due to unavoidable circumstances. When such a situation occurs, the company or the purchasing office will generally notify you if there is to be a delay in delivery so you may tell the teacher or the person making the request. Sometimes a requisition or purchase order has to be cancelled. When this happens, inform the company concerned immediately.

Delayed orders. If you have not been notified of a delay in delivery and an unreasonable amount of time has elapsed, it would be wise for you to either phone the vendor or drop him a reminder of the purchase order. If delayed delivery is a frequent occurrence, you may wish to mimeograph or ditto some postcards which will save you time in such a follow-up. You need only fill out the basic specifications of the item ordered and give the serial number of the purchase order. The vendor will undoubtedly respond in a few days. If the item is no longer in stock, the teacher or person making the request should be so notified. This type of follow-up can and should also be made if delays are occurring in the purchasing office of the school district.

The central office usually delivers items immediately. If an item is not delivered, it may presently be out of stock but is on backorder for future delivery. It will be delivered when it again becomes available. Generally, the central office does not want the secretary to reorder undelivered supplies or equipment unless she has been notified of a cancellation.

Receiving and verifying deliveries. Your job is not finished when all the supplies and equipment have been ordered. Whenever merchandise is received, it must be checked with the purchase order as well as the invoice for quantity, price, and quality. A custodian will be needed if there are heavy boxes to be taken to the stock and supply room, or if equipment is to be distributed to various areas of the building. All equipment should be tagged and numbered according to the inventory policy of the school.

Verifying the receipt of merchandise. In most schools, either you or the school treasurer must verify that goods have been received or services performed before a bill can be paid. All too frequently persons have signed for goods delivered to schools without verifying the contents of packages or without checking to whom they were sent within the school. Although one should verify the contents of a package before signing a receipt, such verification is not always practicable. Delivery men are frequently in a rush and do not wait for the receiver to verify the contents of boxes and packages. You should not sign a delivery receipt which says, "Goods received and found to be satisfactory," unless you have examined the goods. You may, in some instances, write or rubber stamp above your signature, "Received but not examined."

When goods are delivered to a school, determine who placed the original purchase order. The purchaser should be asked to make out a "request for payment" and to certify that the goods have been received. No bill should be paid until an invoice has been received from the vendor and approved by an authorized school person.

Checking for errors. There may be errors in quantity or quality. There may be substitutions and partial shipments. There may be wrong deliveries and duplicate shipments. It usually is up to you to discover such errors and to check with the principal what action is to be taken.

Checking the invoice. Deliveries are usually accompanied by an invoice or other shipping document. An invoice is an itemized list of the merchandise sent to the purchaser. Checking invoices is most important because the sender's shipping and packing department may have been inaccurate in filling your order. If discrepancies are found, make a report to the sender immediately. Any breakage, damage, shortage or overage should be reported, if the item came from the Board of Education warehouse. Phone them immediately.

Recording purchases. After the above check has been made, you should complete your records by making an entry in your office records showing that the items were or were not delivered. The shipping document or invoice should be stapled or clipped to your purchase order or requisition and filed in a folder marked "Purchase Order Deliveries Received" or "Requisition Deliveries Received."

Distributing purchases. The distribution of purchases is an important and necessary part in the handling of supplies and equipment. You are usually responsible for sorting the items and materials and making deliveries of their purchases to teachers and other personnel. The items received should be labeled, tagged, stored, shelved, or placed in the stock and supply room.

Most schools have roller carts which are ideal for making such deliveries and distributing supplies. They will save you many steps. In some schools, the teacher may send a pupil to pick up the supplies. In other cases, you may ask the Office Monitor to assist in the delivery of supplies to teachers and other users.

Allocating portions of the purchase. One of the problems which you will encounter in delivering supplies is distributing the amount requested by the teacher. For example, if a teacher asks for twelve sheets of moss green paper, that quantity should be counted out and sent to her, even though it means the remaining portion of the ream has to be stored in the supply room. Furthermore, if the shipment is a consolidated order, items have to be sorted and correct portions sent to the persons making the request.

Making payments. The best school financial practice requires that all disbursements and payments be made by check against the proper budget account and mailed directly by the school secretary or treasurer to the person or organization named on the check.

Cash payment. On-the-spot cash payments should be avoided. There is always a chance that a cash payment may be forgotten. Both pupils and teachers are inclined to want immediate payment for their legitimate claims. Sometimes they cannot understand why they may not be paid out of cash on hand.

If a person insists on being paid in cash, the approved practice is to prepare a check according to established procedure which is cashed after proper endorsement by the payee. This procedure protects you and provides a verification of the cash disbursement. For example, professional entertainers at student body events should always be paid by check.

Other types of payments. Requests for payment other than by an invoice or statement usually arise when a faculty sponsor has made a purchase on behalf of the school and wishes reimbursement, or when some person or group has rendered services, such as a dance band or a caterer. No purchase should be made or services contracted for by a faculty sponsor or staff member without prior authorization. If a teacher has purchased items on his own without approval, he is usually responsible for payment of the invoice. Persons who have made unauthorized purchases should be referred to the principal for the required approval. When the teacher or staff member has followed approved procedures for expenditures (has obtained a purchase order), there will be on file with you or the school treasurer proper authorization for payment. Sometimes the only authorization is the item in the approved student body budget. Ordinarily, however, the mere inclusion of an item in a budget doesn't automatically confer authorization for its purchase. A purchase order must be requested and the funds encumbered. Regardless of the nature or source of approval, the person who has made the expenditure should be required to complete a "Request for Payment" form.

Request for payment form. The Request for Payment form gives a description of the item or service purchased, the amount of money to be paid, the name and budget account or the activity to which it is to be charged, and the name and address of the payee. The completed form should be signed by the authorized person and principal. It should also bear the date and number of the check by which payment is made. Requests for payment are often made in duplicate. One copy is kept by the person or organization that makes the request, the other is filed with the school secretary or school financial officer. Requests for payment, as well as the purchase orders that precede them, should be for items that are chargeable to only one account.

SOME GUIDING PRINCIPLES

The school organization, as in any other type of business, must be run in an orderly fashion. There are always many little quirks to requisitioning and purchasing supplies and equipment, and you can probably learn them only through experience. However, here are some guiding principles that may help you toward a smoother operation.

Anticipate needs. One of the important things regarding the ordering of special supplies is to anticipate needs. Don't wait until the week before Christmas to order supplies that are needed for Christmas artwork, and don't wait until the day before Halloween to order the black paper needed to make the black cats. Send a note around to remind the teachers to get their orders to you early. Most secretaries suggest that the due date for orders in the principal's office be set at several weeks ahead of the time that the order must go to the central purchasing office. This gives you extra time to prod the individual who is always late.

Order at regular intervals. Generally, stock supplies are ordered periodically throughout the year. Usually orders are placed once a month. However, some districts do not have stated ordering times. You should then arrange with the principal to have orders spaced regularly. In any event, the teachers should be responsible for filling out the orders for supplies they will need for the coming month. Different schools may have different ordering dates so that the district warehouse will not need to fill all orders at the same time.

Anticipate opening of school. Adequate supplies should be on hand for the opening of school. This may be insured by having teachers make out requests for the first month's supplies before they leave for summer vacation. The principal then completes the order with your assistance and makes suggestions for the general office and school supplies. From the final list, you can fill out the requisition and place it on order.

Anticipate "due dates." You should be most careful to submit orders no later than the due date so that the school will receive its supplies when it expects them. Delays in the orders of one school also delay the orders for the succeeding schools. You should notify teachers a week ahead of the order due date that they should place their orders for the following month. Teachers should place their orders with you in the same manner in which you place the school order with the district business office.

Watch for overordering. You should note whether teachers are overordering. If you suspect that a teacher is ordering too much of any one item, call this to the attention of the principal. The teacher will probably be ordering legitimately ahead, but she may be wasting or hoarding supplies. In no case should *you* try to clear up a matter such as this. Never challenge a teacher!

Avoid shortages and overages. When ordering is done annually or semi-annually, there is the necessity to anticipate the needs for an entire year or semester. This is an impossibility! It always turns out that you run short of many items but have no funds to buy more. Therefore, it is advisable to order as little as possible for the beginning of the school year. This permits you to keep some money in the budget for unexpected items in the final months of the school year. You will avoid serious shortages and overages by studying the records of previous years, asking teachers and your principal to do the same.

14

Enrolling Pupils and
Registration Procedures

ENROLLING and registering students is a function that all schools from elementary to university must perform, and the processes are similar at each educational level. The clerical staff of every school is intimately involved in the work of opening school and assigning students to classes. You will feel particularly close to the heart of the school when it is time to enroll pupils and register students.

Secondary schools, in addition, must make a master schedule of classes and register each student into his own program of classes. Provision must be made for accommodating students who wish to change classes and those who wish to transfer into or out of the school. Enrollment and registration, whether they take place at the beginning of the semester or throughout the school term, probably involves more paperwork and clock hours of clerical time than any other aspect in the operation of a school.

HOW TO ORGANIZE FOR THE OPENING DAY OF SCHOOL

If you are in the elementary school, you may have a large share of the responsibility for planning the physical details of opening day. Most administrators are experienced in registration procedures and do everything possible to reduce the work on opening day; however, the work is nonetheless always heavy. Many principals, though, attend to all the major details themselves and will enumerate to you the duties they wish you to perform. In the junior and senior high school the principal, an assistant principal, the registrar, or counselor may handle arrangements. If you are in a secondary school, you may be assigned the duty of organizing and assigning all of your clerical staff to certain enrollment tasks or registration "stations." Guidance and attendance clerks have especially heavy duties on opening day.

Elementary school. New pupils and parents will descend upon the elementary school on the opening day. There will be little pupils, the kindergarten children coming to school for the first time, and big ones from other districts, other states, and from private and parochial schools. You will want to be ready for them! It is wise to make preparations several days or even a week in advance.

Preparing for registration. Select a room other than the office for registering new pupils. This may be the auditorium, the library, or an unused classroom. Post a notice on an easel near the school entrance indicating the location. A student helper may be asked to direct parents and children, especially if the school has several buildings.

Arranging the room. In arranging the room, try to plan a traffic pattern for those who will enter, wait, enroll, and leave the room. If there are two doors, make one the entrance and the other an obvious exit. An adequate number of chairs is a necessity. Chairs with tablet arms will make it unnecessary to move in extra tables. Put in a few primary class chairs for the small children.

Besides your own desk, you may wish to have a supplementary table or two on which to place the printed enrollment forms of your district, pencils, and even the telephone directory. A wall map of the boundaries of the school district may be desirable. You will want to have close at hand a desk tray or box for completed forms, and your log of the day's enrollment. Keep an uncluttered working space on the top of your desk.

Helping with enrollment. When you reach school on the opening day, go directly to the registration area. The new arrivals are likely to appear early. Greet each of them with a friendly smile and a cordial attitude. Remember, you are their first contact in their new school. Give the parents or pupils the necessary enrollment forms and let them do the writing. Save your energy for the work that will come later. When the completed enrollment forms are presented to you, check them carefully. This is the best time to get complete information. Correct spelling of names is important. Numbers for address and telephone must be accurate. If "Occupation of Father" is given as clerk or salesman, try to find out where he works. Emergency references and telephone numbers can best be obtained at this time.

Specific procedures for enrollment. The following procedures are suggested for enrolling pupils:

1. Enter each new pupil on your daily registration log. Write his name, grade and room assignment, date, and indicate school last attended. Many schools use an entrance symbol to indicate type or location of school last attended.

2. Make out a registration slip for the teacher to whose room the pupil is assigned. This may be considered as the pupil's membership or admittance card. It will include information recorded on your registration log. It is given to the parent or pupil.

3. Distribute information bulletins. Frequently, members of the Parent-Teachers Association invite new parents to have coffee and doughnuts with them elsewhere in the school building, but not in the registration

area. A form letter from the principal or a bulletin giving information pertaining to school hours, lunch periods, cafeteria prices, nurse's schedule, rainy days, and other matters of concern to new pupils and their parents may be given out at this time.

Secondary schools. Preparations for opening day in a junior or senior high school are similar to those for an elementary school. More students, more teachers, and more course offerings make preparations for opening day and week more elaborate in a secondary school, however. An administrator, counselor, or other faculty member will be in charge.

Preparing for registration. You will no doubt be instructed by your principal as to what duties you will have in the registration process. This most certainly will require that you check to see that every staff clerk and all student helpers are at their assigned places at assigned periods of time. You will also have the responsibility for providing each person and registration station with necessary supplies. Among materials needed will be copies of the master schedule of classes, student handbook of information, registration forms, tentative class schedule, class cards, health cards, student body membership or activity cards, eligibility form for state- and federally-aided students, envelopes for pre-addressing if the school mails report cards.

Opening day of registration. When the master schedule of classes has been well-planned and an advance or pre-registration has been held, the work on opening day is considerably reduced. Practically all schools now complete the programming and registration of "old" students before opening day. Other than providing for "old" students to pick up (if not mailed or given to them in advance) their schedule of classes, the two big problems are to take care of students who want a different program and to prepare class programs for new students. Most schools require that students who want a different schedule of classes make formal application, and many schools require that the student attend his planned classes until a new schedule can be authorized.

Preparing for new enrollees. In a fast-growing or rapidly changing district, caring for new enrollees can be a real problem. Principals anticipate this situation and you or the switchboard operator will need to be prepared to answer numerous telephone and in-person inquiries concerning enrollment. Most high schools have some area, perhaps the library or cafeteria, reserved for new enrollees. Counselors, department chairmen, and selected teachers will be on hand to work out and approve programs of study for individual students. Intelligence tests or other tests may need to be given to new enrollees. You may be called upon for assistance in administering such tests. Sometimes the guidance clerk is requested to assist.

Verifying student records. Either you or the guidance clerk must expect to search and verify student records for at least five situations. Verification will be needed for students (1) eligible to receive state or federal aid because of physical handicaps, or because they are war orphans; (2) eligible to be exempted or excused from certain classes for health, religious, or other legal reason; (3) eligible for advanced standing by reason of having attended summer school, carried additional courses, or having satisfied prerequisites; (4) eligible to attend the school by reason of living within the school's boundaries; and (5) eligible for removal from probationary status. Students may be placed on probation because they have been low in scholarship or have insufficient credits for full class standing, or for disciplinary reasons.

Holding classes on enrollment day. A shortened day undoubtedly will be held on the first day of school; that is, the duration of each class or period will be shorter than normal. Some schools may not have class at all on the first day of school. All teachers will be expected to report their class enrollments before the close of the school day. Either you or the guidance clerk will probably have the responsibility of checking to see that each teacher is at his post. Enrollment checks may be made every day of the first school week, and sometimes the second week.

Some problems and precautions. Unfortunately, the process of enrollment and registration is bound to strike some snags. Here are a few examples.

Age verification. Parents are required to furnish acceptable documentary evidence to verify the pupil's birth date, especially when he is first enrolled in kindergarten or first grade. Many states establish by law the minimum age for entrance. You will encounter those who "didn't know what to bring" or who "lost everything like that in a fire." If regulations permit, you may say that you can make a temporary enrollment, but instruct the parent to bring in verification as soon as possible. See pages 170 to 171 for acceptable legal proofs of age. It should be made clear to the parent that a permanent enrollment will be made only when this information is received. Some districts set a time limit upon temporary enrollments.

District-jumping. District-jumping, common in large cities, is an enrollment problem you must anticipate. Pupils who belong in an adjoining district may come to enroll in your school. This situation may arise because of lack of information or it may be deliberate for personal reasons. Be prepared with a large map that clearly indicates the boundaries of your school district and the location of schools nearby. If it is necessary for the pupil to enroll elsewhere, point out the proper school and give the parent a slip of paper containing the name and address, and directions if necessary. Permits which release pupils from one district to attend school in another are frequently given for justifiable reasons. If a permit has already been granted by the school district in which the pupil resides, the pupil can be enrolled without further question.

Change of grade level. There is also the problem of those parents, usually from out-of-state, who try to change the pupil's grade (always up) with the change in address. They present no report card, no transfer slip, but insist Bill was in the "high third" last year. He may look like a second grader to you, but it is wisest to take the information, and make a grade and room assignment. If the principal is not available to decide, take the pupil to the teacher and explain the situation to her. Then, ask her to stop in at the office at a later time to discuss the matter with the principal.

First day "rush" hour. Often a "rush hour" of the first day can become a real problem. It is desirable to enlist the services of various teachers to help in counseling and enrolling for this first period. In the elementary school, this is also a splendid opportunity for the teacher to meet the parents.

HOW TO HELP IN PROGRAMMING AND MASTER-SCHEDULE MAKING

If you work in a secondary school, you will undoubtedly be involved in programming students, making the master schedule, or both. Every high school student must be programmed into a full-schedule of courses every semester. This requires that a schedule of courses be developed for the entire school and that each student be programmed and registered into his proper courses. This is time-consuming, detailed work and calls for much paper handling and clerical effort.

The actual making of the school's master schedule and the approving of student's programs is the duty of a principal or counselor. The guidance secretary or clerk's role is to help the administrator with the details.

Tally, bin, punch-sort, and machine methods. No two high schools ever program in exactly the same way, yet there are only about four basic methods. These are referred to as tally, bin, punch-sort, and machine. There are advantages and disadvantages to each. Every administrator seems to develop his own preferred method and then becomes its protagonist. The guidance clerk learns the method her superior prefers and then develops her own little schemes and short cuts for doing the work assigned her.

The tally method. This method calls for tallying the number of students requesting each course. The method is slow and laborious, but it is accurate. Administrators have dreamed up many devices and schemes for speeding up the process.

The bin method. This method is in reality an adaptation of the tally method. There is a card for every pupil, for each period, and for each class. These cards are stored in bins or racks and then pulled or removed as the students are programmed into classes. This method is reasonably fast and accurate. Care must be used in handling class cancellations, additions, and counting to be sure that every student has a full program. Considerable work is involved in getting the cards ready, in building the bins, and storing them when they are not in use.

The punch-sort method. This method is a further refinement of the tally method which attempts to take advantage of the speed gained in the bin method without the disadvantage of a multiplicity of cards. There is only one card for each student. The method has been referred to as the "poor man's machine-sort." It requires a numerical code number for each student, teacher, and course. These cards must be hand-punched. The holes must be patched if there is an error or change. If there are numerous changes, it is better to make out a new card. The method requires much working space, and several clerks are necessary. The specially printed cards and other material can be expensive.

The machine-sort method. This method, usually IBM or Rand, requires all the coding and preliminaries of the punch-sort. The method is fast and eliminates the hand-typed lists needed in the other three methods. In fact, printing of all lists is one of its main values. Special machines and specially trained personnel are needed. It is expensive, and if one of the technicians is ill or the work backlogs in the key-punching, usually the main point of delay, the system bogs down. Program changes at actual time of registration are best handled initially by hand.

Methods for programming and schedule-making. From the above information the following points can be concluded:

1. All methods sound complicated, but all methods attempt to mechanize the process.
2. All methods must result in (a) a program of courses for every student, (b) a numerical list of all rooms with teachers and subjects, (c) an alphabetical list of all subjects by teachers and room, (d) an alphabetical list of all teachers by subject and room, (e) and an alphabetical list of all students, their courses, rooms, periods, and teachers' names.
3. All methods usually require the clerical assistance of almost everyone who can be made available to help.
4. All programming and schedule-making for the next term regardless of the method, must start five to eight weeks before the close of the term. Many schools allow three months or more.

Necessary registration information. All registration systems require that:

1. Students be given information regarding graduation requirements, college admission requirements, course offerings, and prerequisites, electives, and alternate choices allowable.
2. There be a list for each student of the courses he wants or must take.
3. The number of students to be enrolled in the entire school be estimated very closely.
4. The number of sections of each course to be offered be determined with exactitude.
5. The number of classrooms in the school, their special use, and the maximum number of students that can be seated in each be known.

6. The exact number of teachers that will be needed and the subjects that each will teach be known.
7. All lists of students, teachers, or classes be arranged alphabetically or by some numerical code.
8. Provisions be made for adding and cancelling classes or moving classes to another location.
9. Provisions be made for changing classes of students who have attended summer school or failed to remove deficiencies; or for programming at the opening of school new pupils who have not previously been in attendance.

Schedule-making calendar. The calendar of schedule making is usually divided into five phases: preplanning, schedule-building, advance or pre-registration, registration or enrollment, and finalization.

Preplanning. Proposals for classes and new course offerings are received, estimates of enrollments and class sections needed are made, and tentative assignments of teachers are proposed. Student's requests for courses are obtained, and counselor and parent approval of the program of each student are frequently secured.

Schedule-building. The number of sections of each class for each period of the day are determined. Each teacher's schedule of classes by room numbers is worked out in detail. Requests for additional teachers, if needed, are made. During this time, care is taken to keep a balance of classes every period of the day. Attention is also given to the demand for popular classes and single-period or section classes that might conflict or compete.

Advance or preregistration phase. Each student is assigned to his full schedule of courses with attention to his course or teacher preferences, his special abilities or handicaps. Notification is given to both students and teachers. Students nearing graduation, playing on athletic teams, those having physical handicaps or rendering special school services frequently are programmed first.

Finalization. In the final phase, classes are balanced so that teachers have equable teaching loads, program changes for students are approved, class rolls are declared permanent, and copies of each student's program are made out for various school administrators and school offices.

Helpful suggestions for registration and enrollment. A guidance secretary or clerk who wishes to be of fullest help to her principal or counselor should note the following suggestions:

1. Allow plenty of time for your part. Have an understanding at the beginning of each semester when you are to help in the programming and block out dates and time so there will be no interferences.
2. Assemble all materials and supplies you will need before starting your part of the schedule-making or programming.
3. Do one step at a time. Don't shuttle back and forth. If two steps must progress simultaneously, use two persons. If you are in charge of the

clerical staff, assign no more than one step at a time to a person. Avoid assigning two persons to the same step. There is always more chance for error when two persons are doing the same task, and neither accepts responsibility for the other.

Guidelines to accurate registration. When performing schedule-making, programming, and registration duties, you must be alert to the following considerations:

1. Assign students of the same scholastic ability to the same group or class. This is important if your school places fast-learning pupils into one class, slow-learners into another, and so forth.
2. Check to see that no omissions or duplications in tallies of whatever type occur.
3. Keep a balance in number of students enrolled in any class or group of classes. One class must not be allowed to become over-large while another in the same course, very small.
4. Immediately notify the person in charge of programming of any conflicts or errors which you discover. Report errors in writing. Use paper slips of same size and color.
5. Consult your administrator concerning any special notations or questions you may have. Do not second-guess!
6. Make all changes and tallies immediately, during active registration. Do not let them pile up. Every day must be complete with no holdovers!
7. Notify the teacher immediately if her class is to be discontinued, split, or shifted to another location. Indicate the exact time (date and period) when the change is to become effective. Some schools hold faculty or department chairmen's meetings at the end of each school day during registration to inform teachers of imperative changes.

HOW TO HELP IN MAKING PROGRAM CHANGES

Many high schools allow the guidance clerk or secretary considerable latitude in making routine changes in student's programs. There are changes which are obviously in error and must be corrected. There are others which just as obviously cannot be allowed or must have the special approval of the principal or counselor. How much independent authority you may have depends not only upon your own experience and training but upon the experience, purposes, and personality of your superiors. Never attempt to make a change, even if requested by a parent or teacher, without authorization of the counselor or principal. You may have the authority, but if there remains even a slight question in your mind, refer the request to your administrative superior.

Approving student's program on master schedule. Some schools are speeding up the approval process by making "miniature" copies of the school's master schedule of classes. The counselor writes the student's name across the top and OK's on the master itself the approved classes or periods.

Making program changes. When a student's program has been officially approved for changing, the following routines become the responsibility of the secretary or clerk. (1) Clear the student with his old and new teachers. It is recommended that the student himself be required to "run" the change of program; that is, that he should get the signatures of both old and new teachers. It is also recommended that the signature of the new teacher be obtained before the student checks out with his former teacher. Fewer students "get lost" when this order is followed. (2) Make the necessary changes in all the office student personnel records, particularly the Cumulative Guidance Record. (3) Notify all personnel concerned. The office most concerned will be the attendance office. Others will include the vice-principal, the counselor, the nurse, the librarian, and the home room teacher.

Waiting period for program changes. Some high schools require that there be a waiting period before a student's request for a change in classes will be considered. Many schools regard all programs as temporary until the permanent programs are made and signed by the class teachers.

Maintaining official set of student's programs. There is a trend toward further reducing paper work by having only one official copy of each student's class program. This official set of programs is generally placed in the attendance office, where it is most needed. Persons who want to know a student's program ask the attendance office. Schools advocating this procedure argue that few departments within the school ever keep their set of student programs up-to-date, and that the main office is always providing an answering service anyway.

One bit of advice: Do not let recording of student program changes accumulate. Do them daily, certainly, at the beginning of the term, and less frequently, about once a week, thereafter.

HOW TO TRANSFER PUPILS

A pupil may be transferred within the school from one grade or class to another; he may be promoted as a member of the sixth grade class in an elementary school to the seventh grade in a junior high school, or from the eighth or ninth grade to the freshman class of a senior high school; or, he may be transferred to a special class maintained by the school district.

Pupils also will transfer to other schools and cities. Some will withdraw with no intention of continuing their education, and a few will be expelled, for cause, from school.

Within-school transfers. For one reason or another, a principal may find it necessary to move a pupil from one teacher to another within the school. The transfer may be a promotion, it may be a retention in grade, a downward transfer, or just the balancing of the number of pupils in each of two teacher's classes. In any event, the transfer request originates with or has the prior approval of the principal.

You should notify the teachers concerned and advise them of the terminating and entering date and time. This is important to the avoidance of duplications in attendance accounting. The teachers usually exchange their own records. You are responsible for changing the school's office record and advising others concerned, such as the school nurse.

Class or grade transfers. In the case of sixth-grade classes transferring to junior high school and of eighth- or ninth-grade classes transferring to a senior high school, within the school district, it is a common practice to make the transfer or promotion for the entire class, not by individual pupils. Have each pupil make out an enrollment card in his classroom. Then assemble the cards alphabetically according to the various local high schools the pupils may be entering. Alphabetical lists are prepared in triplicate for each local high school. Two copies of each list and the enrollment cards are sent immediately to the high schools concerned. One copy is returned by the high school after the opening of the new term. The names of pupils who failed to enter are crossed off. You will then send, to the high school, the Cumulative Guidance Record, health card, and other personnel records of those pupils who actually entered the high school. The records of the other pupils are retained until officially requested by some high school or until the time arrives for permanent filing in the school archives. Most schools also check on non-enrollees who cannot be accounted for by telephoning the home or by referring their cases to the attendance supervisor, who will visit the last known home address to be sure they are not just skipping school.

"Special class" transfers. Transferring a pupil within the district from a regular school or class to a special class, such as a sight-saving, deaf, physically or mentally handicapped class, is often treated as a special transfer. Practices differ, but frequently the home school maintains certain records for pupils attending these classes. A special transfer is usually made upon the recommendation of the principal, counselor, or nurse.

Whenever a transferring pupil has attended a special class, such as speech or remedial reading, immediately give his teacher an official notice that the pupil has left the school. The pupil's vacancy makes an opening for the next one on the list.

Transfers-in. When a pupil has been legally enrolled in some other public school within or out of the state, he may be admitted and placed in the grade or class in which he was enrolled in his former school. It is customary to require pupils transferring-in to present evidence of their former grade placement and school. Most school systems provide printed forms with space for such items as name of pupil, name of school issuing the transfer, last date or attendance and grade, pupil's birth date, name of parent or guardian, old and new home addresses, and signature of the pupil's former principal.

Obtaining information from the pupil. Always ask the new pupil if he has attended a school in your district before; there may be records available at a former school. Pupils in large elementary districts frequently forget the name of the school. In such a case, you might ask, "Where were you living before you moved?" and name some of the schools in that area. If this fails to produce results, you might telephone a few schools to make inquiry. Careful checking at the time of enrollment may save trouble later. There are other times during the course of the school year when the name of the former school may be supplied on a form filled out in the classroom or heard in conversation.

Assigning new students. In assigning new students to a room or classes, make an effort to keep all classes at or near the same size. In general, a new pupil is assigned to the teacher who has the fewest students in her class. There will be exceptions, for various reasons. Among these reasons are ability of the student and the teacher's class, extra duties of the teacher, and special classes, such as music, which may require a special time schedule.

If there is no test data on the student, you may have the duty of giving the student an aptitude or intelligence test before he is assigned to a class. This can be done in the office or in the nurse's office, if necessary. Suggestions regarding tests are given in Chapter 17.

Transfers-out. When a pupil moves from one school to another, you will need to make out a transfer card if the pupil is in an elementary grade or a transcript of credit if he is in high school.

Elementary transfers. The elementary transfer card must show the pupil's full name, his most recent address, his exact date of birth, and the grade he was in at the time the transfer card was issued. School systems differ as to how much additional information they put on the transfer card. The transfer card is signed by the principal and is not given to a pupil unless the child is accompanied by a parent or presents a note of request from his parents. It is customary to tell the elementary pupil to see his teacher first so that he can clear his desk or table, return his books, and get his papers and classwork. You should have the pupil wait while clearing the office records. This includes "logging out" the pupil. You should keep a log book in which to enter the date the pupil was issued his transfer and the school or city to which he is being transferred. This log also serves as a reminder to assemble the pupil's health record, Cumulative Guidance Record, and other forms which may later be sent to his next school. These latter forms are never given to the pupil or parent and are only forwarded upon the request of the school receiving the pupil.

Junior high school transfers. The procedure for checking out junior high school pupils is essentially the same as for the elementary pupil. The difference lies in requiring the pupil to carry a check-out card or slip which must be signed by each teacher and the persons in charge of locks or lockers, gym clothes, guidance office, library, and textbook room. The teachers may also be required to issue a final grade or mark for each subject in which the pupil is enrolled.

Senior high school transfers. The transfer procedure for individual students in the senior high school is essentially the same as in junior high school except that more student personnel records are involved. Some schools allow the student to request his own transfer; other schools require a letter from the parent. The checking out process may include collecting for laboratory breakage, overdue library book fines, and fees for lost books. In addition, a transcript of credit may have to be prepared. No student should be checked out until all clearances are complete. Sometimes the student comes in at the close of the school day. He should be told to return the next day; as an alternative, he can be informed that his transfer card will be mailed to his home address and that his transcript of credit will be mailed to his new school when that school sends a request.

Graduating seniors. High school seniors planning to continue their education usually apply for admission to a number of colleges and universities. Requests for transcripts can get out of hand if they are numerous or allowed to come in at any time. To control this, some high schools place a limit (say, three) upon the number of transcripts they will prepare without charge, or they set a deadline for filing applications for transcripts. A school may charge a fee for additional transcripts or require the pupil to list at one time all the universities to which he is applying for admission. In any event, every school attempts to discourage irresponsible requests for transcripts that will not be used. Few if any high schools will, in the final analysis, refuse to prepare a transcript if it will be the difference in a graduate's being accepted by or refused admission to a university.

Withdrawals. The terms "withdrawn" or "withdrawal" are generally reserved to designate the termination of a student's school enrollment. Although the student may have moved to another city or enrolled in a private or parochial school, "withdrawn" usually means that the student has not transferred to another school and that he is no longer in attendance in your school, and probably not in any other school. "Left—Address unknown" and "deceased" are also in the category of withdrawals. Generally speaking, students who withdraw are students over the compulsory attendance age who have quit to go to work, who have joined the armed services, who have left to get married, or who have been expelled. Also some school districts permit pupils of compulsory school age to withdraw for reasons of severe illness or immaturity.

Procedure for withdrawing pupils. This procedure is similar to that for transferring pupils. Assemble in your office the student's permanent records, note date and reason for withdrawal, and place the material in the inactive student personnel file. These records are retained indefinitely or are microfilmed along with the records of graduating students. All staff persons affected by the withdrawal should be notified, and pertinent guidance information should be recorded on the Cumulative Guidance Record.

Suspension of pupils. Suspension is not considered a withdrawal because it is a temporary absence imposed by the principal for disciplinary reasons. It may be for an indefinite length of time. Its purpose is often to permit an opportunity for parents, teacher, principal or others to meet together and discuss the student's problem. You will need to know for attendance purposes the date on which a suspension begins and ends. During the period of suspension, it is the duty of the parents to keep the pupil off the streets and away from school. Frequently, you will receive reports of violations. You may call upon the principal or supervisor of attendance to investigate the matter.

Expulsion. Expulsion is a permanent dismissal from school for serious misbehavior in school or on school property. It is to be recorded as a "withdrawal." A pupil usually is expelled only by the authority of the board of education upon the recommendation of the central office to whom the principal has reported the case. Whenever a pupil is expelled, the date of the pupil's return is of no concern to you. No attendance record is involved; the school has no responsibility for the pupil. If infractions are reported, it is a matter for the police department.

HOW TO PREPARE AND SEND TRANSCRIPTS OF CREDIT

The transcript of credit is mailed directly to the school designated by the student. This should be done without delay, as the next school may not accept the student's word as to the courses he has completed. The transcript must show the exact courses the student has taken, the mark he received in each subject, and the credit allowed for each course. The transcript must be signed by the principal, or the secretary if she is authorized, and is usually impressed with the school's seal. Some schools now photostat the Cumulative Guidance Record or other permanent record of courses completed as a means of saving time.

Recording transfers of students to other schools. When a student transfers to another school before the end of the term, an entry at the time of departure should be made in pencil in the Cumulative Guidance Record of the date the pupil left your school and the marks he had received up to the date of his departure. When the end of the term is reached, these marks should be crossed out with ink. Should a student re-enter your school during the same semester, the marks can be erased and replaced by the new marks he is given at the end of the term (or at the time of his second departure). When a pupil transfers frequently during the term, so that he earns no marks or credit, a notation should be made on his records explaining the reason for his having received no marks or credit.

Receiving transcripts from other schools. Whenever a transcript of credit is received from another school, the original transcript should be kept on file for future reference. The Cumulative Guidance Record is a good place to retain this transcript. If a student enters from a non-accredited high school, make a notation on the Cumulative Guidance Record. For a listing of accredited high schools, you may refer to the *Directory of Secondary Schools in the United States,* a publication of the Office of Education, United States Department of Health, Education and Welfare, Washington 25, D.C.

Recording pupil information from official transcripts. When an official transcript of record indicating a pupil's marks in that school district is received from another school system, these should be entered in ink on the Cumulative Guidance Record. When the pupil is from a school system that uses a marking system different from that in your own school, it is important to record the marks he has received in his former school district with a notation explaining the equivalent values or system of record-keeping on the Cumulative Guidance Record. Some schools follow the practice of recording the mark from the other school district, using an equal sign to indicate the equivalent value in their own school district.

Handling records for pupils who had "no transcripts available." When the pupil has been enrolled in the school but has brought no report card or other record of his previous schooling, then an entry should be made to indicate the grade placement and the notation: "No transcript available; assigned to sixth grade by principal, 9–62." High school students allowed advanced standing may be recorded in two ways: "No transcript available; counselor allowed 60 semester periods credit for tenth grade," or "No transcript available; assigned to eleventh grade by counselor; credits not to be computed for tenth grade." You will be instructed as to the practice to be followed in your school.

Obtaining official records. You should make persistent effort to obtain an official record of the pupil's work in his former school. Most schools have a form which they send to the pupil's previous school. If there is no response in two or three weeks, it is necessary to write a letter. Return-address a blank of the transcript form used in your own school, requesting that it be marked and returned. Another technique is to notify the pupil's parents and urge them to request the former school to return the form directly to your school. It may be necessary to use the pupil's copy of his report card in place of an official transcript. In such case a notation should be made on the Cumulative Guidance Record that the marks were copied from the report card.

HOW TO HANDLE WORK PERMITS

Minors between the ages of 14 and 18 years of age may apply for individual work permits for out-of-school hours. You may be asked to prepare these forms for the principal's signature.

Obtaining vital statistics for minors. In some states, minors over 12 years of age may be issued work permits for vacations, Saturdays, or Sundays. The minor must prove his age by a birth certificate, or it can be verified from the school records. The school office must keep a record of each permit, showing the name, address, birth date, and grade of the minor. These are usually kept on hand at secondary schools or may be ordered from the pupil personnel office, the attendance-guidance office, or the child welfare office, depending on the procedure used in the school district. The board of education usually requires a report on the number of work permits issued.

Granting work permits for special industries. Minors may also be granted permits to work in special industries such as theatrical, movie, live television, or modeling productions. The minor usually takes the request for a permit to his school for recording of his school record. He then takes it to the place where the schooling is provided or to the tutor who will instruct him. Upon termination of his employment, the minor returns to his regular school, bringing the record of his school progress with him. In some cases, the teacher or tutor at the minor's place of work will contact the school and attempt to correlate his schoolwork with that in his regular class.

15

Keeping Attendance Records

KEEPING attendance records is a duty that belongs only to those secretaries and attendance clerks who are responsible for official records of pupil attendance. Pupil accounting, as this work frequently is called, is an area of specialized knowledge that is learned only through experience on the job. Most school secretaries have learned pupil accounting from careful reading of instructional bulletins issued by the superintendent's office, from studying and using attendance records, and from asking questions of the principal and experienced secretaries.

ATTENDANCE INFORMATION

Most states hold the principal and teachers legally responsible for the accuracy and up-to-date maintenance of all attendance records. The clerical aspect of pupil accounting, however, is performed by you or the attendance clerk.

Procedure for recording attendance. Every school has some method for keeping a record of each student's attendance. If you are new to the job, you will undoubtedly find your school has well-established ways which you will learn and follow. New procedures are usually prescribed by the central office of the school district to meet new requirements of the board of education and state law.

Need for accuracy. Attendance records are the substance of the attendance reports which determine the amount of money allocated to each school or school district from state funds. For this reason, it has been said that none of the tasks pertaining to attendance is really worth the doing unless performed with strict attention to accuracy and completeness in every detail.

Attendance reports. In some school districts you are required to prepare monthly attendance reports, others by semester or year. These reports, often called "statisticals," furnish a summary of the school's total attendance record. The information required for the statistical report is often compiled from the registers maintained by classroom teachers. The school register is a legal document most often to be found in elementary schools and occasional summer sessions of secondary schools.

The register. The register contains pages for recording each pupil's attendance on a daily and monthly basis. Any change in a pupil's enrollment status is also marked in the register. The register is submitted to you for checking and for use once each school month, or as often as required. In schools where the classroom teacher does not maintain a register, all attendance accounting is performed in the office by you or the attendance clerk. Large high schools and junior colleges will have a registrar or attendance officer in charge.

Responsibilities for attendance record keeping. Most likely, your part in attendance record keeping will involve assistance with clerical tasks, such as making out forms, recording attendance data, or helping at the "attendance counter" first thing in the morning when the rush of returning absentees is heaviest. You may have to give an hour or two each day to these functions, offer additional assistance when school attendance reports are due, or type necessary forms or correspondence concerning absence inquiries and referrals to the attendance supervisor. You may also be called upon to supply information regarding attendance regulations.

HOW TO POST ATTENDANCE

Registers, or no registers, it is common practice for the classroom or home room teacher to make a daily attendance check of those pupils in her class and report to the office the names of absentees. Some teachers do this on a simple sheet of paper that has been scored to indicate a place for the pupil's name and date of absence; other teachers and schools use attendance cards.

Elementary schools. Many schools have found that the individual absence card is especially useful because it provides in one place additional information that is helpful in checking the reason for absence. The top portion of the card furnishes the name of the pupil, grade, room number, name of parents, home address, telephone number, and other children in the family. The bottom two-thirds is lined by days and weeks forming squares in which to make entries of absence, usually by some established symbol. The cards of those absent are collected by an office monitor or sent to the office by a class messenger. The absence card has the added advantage of serving as a pupil's record of attendance for the entire school year. Many teachers use them to maintain their registers. These absence cards can also serve as a re-admission card following a pupil's absence.

Secondary schools. The procedure in keeping attendance may vary from school to school, but the following suggestions will be helpful to you if this responsibility falls to you. You will find that most junior and senior high schools use individual absence cards, usually collected by an office monitor. As soon as the absence cards have been collected in your office, they should be alphabetized. Then you can type a list of the day's absentees. This list should be duplicated and distributed to all teachers within the shortest time possible (one hour, say). Teachers of subsequent periods are thus notified of absentees from their respective classes. If other students are absent whose names are not on the list, the teacher must notify the attendance office. If a student whose name is on the absentee list appears in class, he must present a clearance or re-admittance card from the attendance office, or be sent immediately for a clearance card. The "absence card" can be used to serve the dual purpose of a clearance or re-admittance card.

Posting the attendance. As soon as the absence lists have been distributed, the attendance should be posted. This means that you or the attendance clerk will post or record the absences of those pupils on the absence list. A file is maintained in the school or attendance office with a separate card for each student. The law requires that fractions of a day of absence be recorded. Each period or hour the pupil is not in school must also be posted.

The student's attendance card must be arranged for the checking of days, weeks, and school months. A glance at any student's card will show the dates and times he was not in school in any given month. These attendance cards, if teachers' registers are not used, are the source of data for compilation of the school's attendance reports. You will find it advantageous to always complete posting of absences every day before leaving the office.

Checking reasons for absence. As early as possible in the school day, you will need to examine the absentee lists or cards and, when necessary, make inquiry regarding each absence. Some states, such as California, permit verified illness absence to be credited toward total attendance. Wherever this is legal policy, use a symbol, such as a circle, to identify illness absences. Time spent for medical, optometrical, or dental treatment, religious instruction, and work experience under certain conditions is often legally authorized as part of the pupil's school attendance.

"Days absent" are days or time of actual absence of any pupil for any reason excepting those specifically allowed by school law. For example, days of absence may be due to suspension from school, truancy, and religious holidays. In some areas, lack of suitable clothing or baby sitting duty may be real enough reasons for absence, but it is not a legal reason. Only legal reasons can be counted as attendance.

Junior colleges. Keeping attendance records in the junior college is simple compared with elementary or high school procedure. All that is required in the junior college is that the instructors turn in either weekly or monthly records of the days that each student in his class was absent.

If the student was absent for illness, a symbol worked out by the college is so indicated.

Reporting the attendance. Some states permit "negative" reporting. The assumption is made that the student is present unless he is reported as absent. The attendance clerk then merely subtracts the number of absentees from the total number of students registered in the class. Other states require "positive" reporting, in which each student must specifically be identified as having been present for each session of each class.

Posting the attendance. Each absence turned in by an instructor is posted on the student's attendance card (the one he filled out when he first registered). Unlike elementary or high school attendance keeping, there is no tracing done as to the reason why the student was absent. The student is assumed to be a mature individual voluntarily attending college. If he fails to meet his classes, he is the one who is penalized—his grade may suffer, or he may be dropped from the class roll.

The posting of attendance is similar to that in a high school, though junior colleges have devised many schemes for doing this. Attendance—or absence—must ultimately be recorded on each student's attendance record. The problem is different from elementary and high schools in that the number of classes or hours of attendance in junior college can vary with each student.

Computing the attendance. In elementary and high schools, all students, with a few exceptions that are especially indicated, attend the same number of class hours each week. This simplifies the computation of the total hours of student attendance. Junior colleges, on the other hand, must compute the number of hours of attendance for each student and divide this total by the number of legally required hours constituting a day or week's attendance. For example, if a student attends classes for 10 hours but 20 hours constitutes a regular week, then he can be credited with only half a week's attendance. On the other hand, if he attends classes for 25 hours and the regular week is 20 hours, does the school get credit for one-and-a-quarter week's attendance? Some states do allow a student to "earn" for the college more than a week's attendance credit per week; other states will not allow any college to credit itself with more than a day or week's attendance for each student, regardless of how many hours above the maximum he may attend class.

HOW TO TRACE ABSENTEES AND VERIFY ILLNESSES

Illegal absence and truancy are two problems that most elementary and high schools encounter. Keeping pupils at home for such reasons as caring for younger brothers and sisters, assisting with housework, or taking private lessons violates the compulsory education laws which require that all children of school age shall be in school. Truancy can soon become linked with delinquency if allowed to go unchecked by the school and parent.

Tracing and verifying absentees. Attendance has financial implications for the school or school district. Most schools depend upon you or the attendance clerk to perform the function of tracing absentees and verifying illnesses as part of the day's work. It is often time-consuming, but need not be a frustrating task.

Each morning after you have received the cards or lists of absentees from the classrooms, you should scan the names. If you find the name of a pupil who has a truancy record, trace this pupil immediately. In most cases, unless there is reason to question its validity, a first-day absence need not be checked.

Contacting the home. When a pupil's absence continues for more than two days, you should try to contact the home to learn the reason. A telephone call is the quickest method. Some parents may resent being questioned; others may prolong the conversation with small details. A good beginning is to say, in a friendly tone of voice, "This is the secretary of the Menlo Avenue School. We missed Bill at school today. Was he sick?" Or, another approach: "This is the secretary at the Menlo Avenue School. Mrs. Black, Bill's teacher, asked me to call about Bill who is not in school today. Is Bill sick?"

If the parent tells you that Bill is home because of illness, it is appropriate to make a sympathetic remark or two, then courteously close the conversation without pursuing the subject. Immediately following the call, you should indicate this reason for absence by the "illness symbol." The specific reason may also be recorded; e.g., cold, earache, or whatever. If the absence continues beyond a reasonable number of days, you should make a second call of verification. When you receive no answer to a home phone call in three trials during the day, it is reasonable to assume that the absence is due to reasons other than illness.

If the parent reports the child to be absent for a reason not legally acceptable, you should not challenge the parent's reason. If the practice becomes habitual, however, you should bring it to the attention of your principal. He may suggest that the case be reported to the child welfare or attendance supervisor.

Contacting other people. When you have been unable to make a contact with the parent by telephone and the absent pupil has a brother or sister in school, you may want to call upon him for information. However, you probably realize that youngsters in the lower grades are not always reliable sources of information. Often they really don't know, but they like to tell a good story.

Other procedures which may reveal to you the reason for the pupil's absence include calling a relative or neighbor, or inquiring from a neighboring school in which other children in the family are enrolled. Home calls are usually made by members of the staff. Often the urgency of your investigation will depend upon the reputation and address of the child's family. For children living in motels, trailer courts, and, in many cases, apartments, "days of absence" may actually become "days not enrolled" because the family is likely to be considered transient.

Re-admitting the pupil. Even though you have made contact with the home, many schools require the pupil to bring a note of explanation from his parent when he returns. In schools where a specific type of attendance card is used, the absentee usually brings his note to the person who handles the card. The attendance card becomes the pupil's permit for re-admittance to the classroom. When the pupil has been absent for a consecutive series of days, such as a full week, he may be required to report to the school nurse for clearance before he can return to class. Absence notes from home are usually saved until the end of the school year and then destroyed. One place to keep them is in the Cumulative Guidance Record.

HOW TO CHECK AND KEEP SCHOOL ATTENDANCE REGISTERS

Many school secretaries depend upon school registers to furnish the information needed to compile the school's total attendance report. Registers are legal permanent records of enrollment and attendance of pupils. They look like the ledgers kept by bookkeepers. The responsibility for filling in the register and keeping it up-to-date every day is usually that of the classroom teacher.

Checking for accuracy. On the last day of every school month, each teacher closes her register and delivers it to the school office. You should check the accuracy and completeness of these monthly registers before taking from them the data needed for the school's summary of attendance. It may take you a week or more to check registers, especially if your school has a thousand or more pupils. Your principal may choose to check the teachers' registers himself, or he may prefer to cover the office while you work behind a closed door so you will not be disturbed while checking the registers. However, this latter procedure does not always guarantee privacy. You may find yourself frequently interrupted to give answers to questions that only you may know. In any event, it is a good plan to work on the registers during a quiet time of the day when interruptions are least likely to occur.

Using a proof sheet. You can supply teachers with a proof sheet to be used for making their own check of their register. Such a proof sheet provides a tally of pupil names brought forward from the previous month, the number of new pupils enrolled, and the number who have transferred or withdrawn during the school month. It may require the month's total for days of absence, or attendance, and days not enrolled. The sum of these three items should be equal to the number of pupils on the monthly record multiplied by the number of days taught. This proof sheet may become your working copy of figures when you consolidate the reports from each teacher into the summary report of the total attendance in the school. Usually you will want to double-check each teacher's register for the following items:

1. Agreement of school enrollment or attendance card with register record for each child in the room.
2. Names of pupils brought forward from previous month.
3. Names of new pupils properly entered and dated.
4. Transfers and withdrawals properly dated and indicated.
5. Days not enrolled.
6. Accuracy of arithmetic.

Making reports. When you feel that, to the best of your knowledge, each teacher's register is in order, you will be ready to compile the attendance report for the school. The teachers' registers should not be in your hands for more than a week; certainly no longer than necessary to prepare and verify the school's attendance report. When you have done with them, you should return them to the respective teachers.

From time to time, you may be called upon to make other reports related to attendance. These may have to do with grade enrollment by months, a tally of the number of boys and girls, or the number of foreign-born pupils. If not readily available, the data for the report may be requested from the classroom teacher.

HOW TO ISSUE NEW REGISTERS

In addition to your obligation of checking registers, you will often find that school registers create additional responsibilities. These include preparing and distributing a new register each year to each teacher, instructing new teachers in the proper procedures, and giving answers to most of the questions asked by both experienced and inexperienced staff members.

Providing a cover. It is advisable to provide a protective cover for each register. Bright paper chosen from a wallpaper sample book brightens up an otherwise rather drab document. Some secretaries take pride in producing or selecting artistic cover material. The material should be cut large enough to provide a generous overlap on the inside of the register. A skimpy cover tends to come off easily. The teacher's name and room number should be placed on the outside front cover for ready reference.

Explaining procedures for keeping the register. Although instructions for keeping registers are frequently given on the first few pages of each register, some new teachers find that formal directions can be overwhelming. You will find it worthwhile to take a few extra minutes to make sure that each teacher understands the register-keeping procedure and the need for accuracy. A good plan is to arrange with your principal for a demonstration at a faculty meeting. A sample register page may be drawn on the chalkboard to show all the items that must be included each month, such as name and sex of each pupil, calendar dates of the school month, signatures, and enrollment practices. At this time, the teacher's attention may be directed to any violations of established procedure or recent changes in regulations. Teachers should be admonished to keep the register in a safe but convenient place. Some schools require this place to be uniform in all rooms throughout the school. This practice is a help to substitutes and others who may need the register during a teacher's absence.

Teachers with problems relating to attendance accounting frequently will ask you questions. In many cases, the answers to their questions may be found in the register or printed instructional material, but you should be willing to give each teacher the benefit of your knowledge without referral. Often a question may concern the case of an individual pupil about whom the office has received recent and pertinent information.

HOW TO COMPILE ATTENDANCE REPORTS

All schools are expected to make monthly, semester, or annual compilations of their attendance. Some school districts require daily reports, especially during the first days of a new school term. From time to time additional, special reports of attendance may be required, such as those for Public Law 874 regarding unusual attendance caused by the installation of federal defense plants or activities.

Attendance records and procedures may vary, but all attendance reports, or "statisticals" as they are likely to be called, generally will include these items: names of teachers, the total number of pupils enrolled, the total number of days the school was in session, the total days of pupil absence, the total days of pupil attendance, the average daily attendance, and changes in enrollment, including transfers and withdrawals.

Using the tally sheet. Preparation of attendance reports usually proceeds faster and more accurately when the secretary or attendance clerk has prepared in advance a tally sheet showing the principal time periods and the teachers' names or subject breakdowns for the final report.

Two people working together—one recording and one calling off the data—can usually complete the tally sheet quicker than one person working alone. If there are no built-in checks of figures to show whether or not the report is in balance while still in the tally-sheet form, the recording should be checked. When two people are working together, they may exchange tasks occasionally. A second tally sheet or a different color pencil may be used for recording the check of the figures. If the report is related to any figures or estimates for an earlier time period or report, the earlier report must be compared with the current one, and any necessary explanations or reconciliations made.

Completing the report. When all details have been accounted for, the final report may be typed with the required number of carbons. When accurate and complete records of attendance are maintained daily, you should encounter little or no difficulty in compiling the school's attendance report. When proofs can be used, you should prove the totals. When you have completed and checked the report, give it to the principal for his inspection and signature. Then send it to the district office for compilation with reports from other schools. In one-school districts, the statistical report is sent to the county or some central office. A duplicate copy should be retained in the school as a reference and a permanent record of attendance growth or loss.

16

Helping the School Counselor

THE MODERN SCHOOL is not satisfied with just teaching the pupil. It also is concerned that each pupil shall do the utmost with his capacities and, in addition, develop his abilities to his maximum potential. The school attempts to help him solve his school problems and surmount his learning difficulties.

As the school secretary, you will be called upon to assist. Your responsibilities will include assisting the school counselor or guidance counselor, keeping pupil personnel records, microfilming, and maintaining guidance information files. Scoring tests and computing simple statistics also are essential parts of the school guidance program, and are treated in the chapter that follows.

THE GUIDANCE CENTER

The function of guidance is becoming so important in the modern school that terminology is used which helps to convey the concept of its broad scope. Although the term counseling office is common, more and more schools are referring to it as the Guidance Center.

Providing receptionist service. Probably nowhere in the school is a more concerted effort made to treat the pupil as a person than in the guidance center. Even the most mischievous pupil is given the same friendly greeting and attention as is the most popular leader in the school. The pupil may be a truant or a little demon to a teacher or a vice-principal, but to the school counselor he is a youngster who needs help, even affection. Your part is to see that there is a welcome mat at the door of the Guidance Center. It should be a place that is as attractive and comfortable as possible.

Few elementary schools have a guidance center or even a counseling office as such; however, most high schools have some kind of guidance facility. In an elementary school, you may find that the school office doubles as the counseling office, and that you will share with the principal the role of a guidance aide.

The guidance program starts on the day the pupil enrolls in the school and does not end until he leaves—and, sometimes, not even then. Many schools now conduct follow-up studies on their pupils.

The student seeking a counselor. Students come to the counselor's or principal's office for a variety of reasons. Some want a change in their classes, some want to quit school, some are sent by a teacher who feels they belong in another course, some merely want to talk to a friendly adult. The reasons are almost without end. No doubt, you will be the first to greet this student, to make an appointment if one is necessary, and to see that the student is properly occupied while awaiting his turn with the counselor.

"May I help you?" "Do you wish to enroll?" "Would you like to speak to the counselor?" These are good greeting remarks, provided the tone of voice is friendly and helpful. Frequently the student does not need to talk to the counselor. He may only wish to ask some informational questions or to look at a college catalog. (Pages 43 to 45 also give some helpful hints in receiving office callers.)

Providing the counselor with students' records. You can aid the counselor by listing the names of students waiting, together with their grade and the problem they wish to discuss. However, you should never press a student to tell you his problem. Simply pull the Cumulative Guidance Record and other relevant records and present them to the counselor before or at the time the student enters for his interview. These records should be promptly refiled, not later than the close of the same day. Entries concerning new data about the student should be made at once. Information scribbled on various pieces of paper should never be allowed to accumulate.

Authorizing hall passes. The high school student generally will need a hall pass or permit to return to his class. You can authorize this pass and note the time on the pass. With the advice of the counselor, you can devise a suitable hall pass if one does not already exist. This form can be mimeographed on a distinctively colored paper.

Maintaining appointment lists. Some schools maintain appointment lists for the counselors. These lists generally are mimeographed with the date and counselor's name at the top and, along the side, hours or periods when the counselor will see students. As students make appointments or are assigned a follow-up interview, write in the student's name. A new interview list is made for each day. Before starting a new list, you should check with the counselor concerning the hours he will not be available, and block off these hours. Then you can make appointments for that day.

Include appointments with parents. Parents are usually worked into the interview schedule without prior appointments. This is accomplished by saving at least 15 minutes of each hour or period for screening interviews and unanticipated callers. You should make notations by the names of those students who fail to keep their appointments.

Using "request to leave class" memos. Some schools follow the policy of using a "request to leave class" memo to secure advance permission of the teacher so that the student may be absent from his class to keep a counseling appointment. When these request memos are placed in the teacher's mailbox on the afternoon before the scheduled interview, the teacher is reasonably sure to see it upon his arrival the next morning. If the teacher decides that the student isn't to be released from class, the teacher places the request memo in the counselor's mailbox immediately, usually with some explanation. A rescheduling of the appointment then becomes necessary, and the teacher has the responsibility of telling the student that his interview has been cancelled. If the teacher approves the appointment, the student uses the request memo as a hall pass when going to the counseling office. If the counselor fails to endorse the request memo, you may do so at the conclusion of the interview.

PUPIL RECORD SERVICE

Pupil record service includes preparing a Cumulative Guidance Record or pupil personnel form for each entering or new student, sending requests to the pupil's former school for his records, and sending the original or duplicate copies of records of pupils transferring to another school.

At the high school level, the pupil record service may include the following responsibilities:

1. Receiving, filing, and evaluating the credit transcripts of pupils transferring from other schools.
2. Preparing transcripts of credits for graduates and pupils transferring to other schools.
3. Recording final marks or grades on the Cumulative Guidance Record or other pupil personnel records.
4. Preparing class lists of pupils.
5. Helping in the preparation of the master schedule of classes.
6. Recording class and program changes.
7. Assembling and distributing report cards or blanks to teachers.
8. Receiving report cards from teachers for posting, filing, and mailing.

You might also be asked to perform a similar service in regard to teacher's roll books. They must be distributed promptly at the beginning of each term and in most schools are collected at the close of the semester or year.

Pupil program cards. Several sets of pupil program cards are maintained in every junior and senior high school. These cards list the student's name, address, grade, the periods in which he takes each course, and the teachers' names. These cards are alphabetized by boys and girls, by grade, or by some other method. The sets of cards serve as quick reference for the location of every pupil in school.

THE CUMULATIVE GUIDANCE RECORD

The Cumulative Guidance Record is a large card or folder on which is recorded important personal information about the pupil and his school progress. The "cum" (rhymes with *broom*) card is made out when the pupil first enters school, and presumably follows him all the way through elementary and high school. Of course, this does not happen if the pupil's family moves from city to city, or if the school fails to send the cum to the pupil's next school, or if the school does not use cum cards.

Cum cards, however, are coming into broader usage. A large part of your responsibility is filling out the card when the pupil enrolls in school, and keeping it up to date.

Handling and securing students' records. The Cumulative Guidance Record eventually contains much information about the pupil and his history in school. It therefore becomes a highly confidential document that must be protected from the prying eyes of other pupils and those who have no business knowing about the pupil. In fact, the cum card in some states is a legal document that is subject to court challenge, and may not be erased or altered without proper authority. Some states are now permitting, even requiring, that the cum card be made available, upon request, to a parent. This, however, is not your duty. The counselor or the principal himself usually is the only one to explain the contents of a cum card to a parent.

Many elementary schools allow teachers to keep the cum cards in their classrooms provided they are kept under lock and key. High schools usually retain the cums in a file cabinet in the counseling office. It therefore behooves you to make a note of the names of the pupil, his teacher, and the date when you release and receive cum cards. This procedure is to protect you and enable you to trace misplaced cum records.

Schools differ in their procedures for filling out the Cumulative Guidance Record. In the absence of instructions to the contrary, the procedures outlined below have proven satisfactory. It is advisable to use a typewriter or black ink, both of which photograph well. A medium- or broad-point pen is recommended. Do not use green or blue ink or lead pencil. Red ink usually, but not always, is satisfactory.

Recording biographical information. When the pupil first enrolls in your school, he will submit certain biographical information. The following suggestions should prove helpful in recording this information:

1. *Pupil's name.* The pupil's full name should be entered, last name first. If a pupil's name is changed, the old name should be crossed out only lightly so that it is still readable, and his new name and the date of change entered alongside or beneath the former name. The legal name should be followed by the word "legal" in parentheses. Actually, it is wise always to record the pupil's name as it appears on the document ac-

cepted as proof of his age. Subsequent changes can be entered as recommended above. If the child is known by a nickname, as "Billy," use quotation marks around it. If he has a second or preferred name, underscore the name by which he wishes to be known. If there are two pupils with the same name in the school, type in red—"Watch."

2. *Pupil's date of birth.* The pupil's birth date should be recorded only as shown on the document accepted as proof of his age. State laws vary as to what documents are acceptable proof. A certificate of birth, baptismal certificate, passport, and health office or vital statistics record of birth are commonly accepted proofs of age. The nature of the document and serial number, if any, should be noted on the Cumulative Guidance Record. Do not use symbols to indicate the information. Symbols are too easily misinterpreted at later dates. When no acceptable documentary proof of birth can be obtained, the parent may sometimes be allowed to file an affidavit certifying the pupil's date and place of birth. In such case, a notation should also be made on the cum, as "birth certificate not obtainable." When recording the place of birth, enter both the city and state or, if the student is foreign-born, the city and country.

3. *Names of parents or guardian.* The father's first and middle names should be recorded, in that order. Record the mother's maiden name (surname) and the first name in that order. If either parent is deceased, divorced, or separated, write "dec." or "div." or "sep.," respectively, in parentheses, after the father's middle name, or after the mother's maiden name. If there is a step-parent, write "step" and the step-parent's name directly beneath the father's name or the mother's maiden name, as appropriate. If the child does not live with his parents, record the last, first, and middle names, in that order, of the adult responsible for the child.

4. *Occupation of parents or guardian.* The occupation of the parent or guardian should be entered as specifically as possible. For example, "linotype operator" is preferable to "printer," "automobile salesman" to "salesman," "typist" to "office worker," "lathe grinder" to "mechanic."

5. *Names of brothers and sisters.* The first and middle names of brothers and sisters, together with their birth dates, should be entered. If a brother or sister has a surname different from the pupil's, this name also should be entered. Teachers should be solicited each term to bring this section up to date.

6. *Pupil's age.* The pupil's age should be recorded in years and months. Some schools require that this be done each term for convenience in computing test results and other reports. To avoid errors in date of birth, use numbers for month, day, and year, with dashes between them; e.g., 4–29–51. Some schools use Roman numerals for the month only (IV–29–51).

Recording subsequent information and changes. As the pupil progresses through grades, additional information will have to be added to the cum card to keep it up to date. Of course, there will always be changes which must be noted on the cum card. The following suggestions should prove helpful to you in recording this information:

1. *Change of home address.* Changes of home address should be recorded immediately, as should the telephone number of the parent or guardian. Record "none" if there is no telephone.

2. *Change of room or school.* Each time the pupil changes rooms or transfers schools, the date entered and left should be recorded. It is advisable, if school regulations permit, to have the pupil's record dated as leaving one day and entering the next day. This will help avoid counting the pupil twice if tallies of pupil enrollment and attendance are made. It also is recommended that the date be recorded if the pupil changes teachers even though he may remain in the same school.

3. *Attendance record.* The number of days present in school and absent from school may also have to be entered on the Cumulative Guidance Record. This total, if for the full term, must agree with the totals shown on the pupil's report card and in the teacher's class register. Usually elementary teachers are responsible for computing and recording each pupil's attendance, but you may be required to cross-check the totals on the cum and on the teacher's class register.

4. *Intelligence test scores.* Intelligence test scores, as indicated elsewhere, may be variously disguised by designating them as "scholastic capacity test score," "index," "serial number," or other such cryptic terms. If you are in a high school, you will be responsible for entering test data on the Cumulative Guidance Record. In the elementary school, the teacher may do the entering of test scores on the records of her own pupils.

For intelligence tests, the date (month and year) the test was given as shown on the test booklet should be entered, as should the pupil's grade, the name of the test, the level, if any, of the test (such as "elementary," "primary," or "non-language"), and the form (as L or M or A, B, C, or K, 1st). All of these data are shown on the cover of the test booklet or on the cum itself from earlier testings.

The intelligence quotient (IQ) as shown on the test booklet should be recorded together with the pupil's chronological age (CA), which was his actual age in years and months at the time he took the test, and the pupil's mental age (MA) which also is shown on the test booklet cover. Some schools also provide that the expectancy age (XA), which indicates the grade the pupil should achieve for his age and intelligence, be entered.

5. *Achievement test data.* Educational achievement tests tell how well the pupil does in such subjects as arithmetic, reading, language, and spelling. The month and year should be recorded to indicate the date the

pupil took the test. A date stamp may prove a time-saver. The name of the test, the level, and the form of each test must be recorded. In recording elementary school test scores, it is customary to record the grade placement rather than the raw score; for example, "4.3" would mean the fourth grade and the third month of that grade. High schools generally use percentiles (as 25th, 50th, 75th) to indicate student achievement.

6. *Curriculum and major.* Record the curriculum and major that the student is following each semester. A curriculum usually carries some broad designation, such as academic or college preparatory, industrial arts, homemaking, and business education. The major is usually a subdivision of a curriculum. Foreign languages, mathematics, science, and social studies are typical majors within an academic or college preparatory college curriculum; stenography, bookkeeping, and salesmanship are typical majors within a business education curriculum.

7. *Faculty adviser.* In high schools in which the student has a different teacher each class or period, it is customary to designate the person who serves as the student's adviser or counselor. Most Cumulative Guidance Records provide a place for this information. If not, an entry should be made somewhere on the card to indicate the name of the person who was primarily responsible for advising the pupil and for approving the curriculum and major he is taking. Some high schools require parents to sign a form indicating approval or acknowledgment of the courses being taken by pupils. This form is filed in the Cumulative Guidance Record and held until the student graduates or the cum is placed in the school archives.

8. *Teacher's observations and comments.* In this section the teacher records information she thinks important for understanding the pupil and helping him to get along in school. This information covers matters of health, emotional problems, seating arrangements, study habits, relations with other children, and a host of other things. These entries may be made only once or twice a year. Your most important obligation is to see that each entry is dated and initialed or signed by the teacher. Cumulative Guidance Records with no notations should, upon the advice of the principal, be returned to the teacher for her comments. You might need to remind the principal to call in the cums several weeks before the close of the term, so that you can do the necessary checking of entries. Some schools require that each teacher sign a slip vouching all items on the cum card have been completed.

9. *School marks.* Although the trend is toward maintaining a single record of the marks a student receives in his courses, you must see that these are properly entered in whatever record the school keeps and that they are in exact agreement with the marks shown on the report card. Below are some practices which have proven helpful to other secretaries.

If your school has not adopted its own procedures and practices, the following may prove helpful:

a. Record the titles of the subjects as listed in the catalog of authorized courses or other official documents of the board of education. It is important to be consistent in the use of the titles of courses so that there can be no confusion from one semester or year to the next.
b. Record every subject the pupil has taken. The best procedure is to record the periods or subjects in the order in which the pupil takes them daily, or the order in which they appear on the report card. Some Cumulative Guidance Records, however, have their own special arrangement or sequence, as English, social studies, mathematics, science, and physical education.
c. Check again to be sure that no course is omitted from the pupil's record. One way to be sure that all courses have been recorded is to count the number of courses shown on the report card. Then compare this total with the total number of courses appearing on the pupil's permanent scholastic record, the Cumulative Guidance Record, or whatever record your school uses.

Some high schools require that the number of units or periods taken daily by the student be recorded. At the high school level, it is especially important to indicate the grade (ninth, tenth, and so on) and whether the semester is the first or second term.

10. *Incompletes.* When a pupil receives a mark of *incomplete,* this is normally recorded "inc." Allow sufficient space above the abbreviation to record, at a later date, the mark given if and when the course is completed. If the work is not made up by the time the cumulative record is removed from the class files, the notation "N.M." should be recorded above the "inc." to indicate that no mark has been given and the time for removal of the incomplete has expired.

It is common practice to assign a zero (0) for all courses marked "incomplete," "no mark," and for subjects to be repeated. If the student's total number of credits or hours taken does not add up to the customary total, a notation should be made explaining why the total is different from that normally expected.

11. *Retention.* Retention indicates that the student was required to repeat a grade or subject because he did not measure up to standards of achievement. This is normally recorded under semester or year in which the repetition took place. For example, when a seventh grade course in history is repeated by an eighth grade pupil, it should be recorded under the eighth grade with a notation "History (seventh)." When an elementary pupil repeats a grade, the word "Repeat" should be written in *heavy print* and *underlined* with the beginning and ending months and year of the term or semester repeated; for example, "**Repeat: 9–61 to 1–62.**"

12. *Acceleration.* When a pupil has been accelerated so that he skips a grade or course, an explanation should be entered on his personnel

record. For example: "Double promoted, fourth to sixth grade, 6–62," "Credit granted Spanish II, 6–62." Unless there is reason to the contrary, it is advisable to use as a date the last school month of the term before the pupil is accelerated.

13. *Shortened program.* When a pupil takes less than the normal daily program, an entry also should be made to indicate that the program is a shortened one. For example, "Carried 4 subjects, 9–61 to 1–62," or "Carried 20 semester periods, 2–62 to 6–62," or "Carried 2 units, 9–61 to 1–62."

14. *Summer school credit.* When a pupil takes work in summer school or secures credits by some other procedure, it is necessary to record the marks received together with a notation of the summer school attended and the date.

15. *Graduation requirements.* Some Cumulative Guidance Records have a place for indicating whether the pupil has completed certain specified requirements for graduation. Among such required courses are likely to be courses in United States history, American government, physical education, and, possibly, first aid and driver education. If such a place is provided in the pupil personnel record used in your school, you should make sure that he has completed such required courses. A check mark (or an "OK") is not sufficient. You should indicate the completion of a requirement by some positive word or abbreviation such as "Completed," or "Comp."

Emptying or disposing of "cum" contents. Most Cumulative Guidance Records are folders. Throughout the year, the teachers and counselors provide many notes, anecdotal records, report cards, and similar memoranda to be filed in the pupil's permanent record. Sometimes the cum becomes so bulky that it is actually cluttered, difficult to file, and the contents in danger of falling out. Under these circumstances, you should affix some of the more important items to the cum, perhaps using paste, or glue; exercise discretion in this practice, however, because the space on the Cumulative Guidance Record is usually so crowded that to affix anything to it means that some important material may be obscured. Also, there is the possibility of damaging the card when removing something that has been affixed to it. Do not use staples. Photographs may be a possible exception to material that is authorized to be affixed to the cumulative record. Photographs should be attached with rubber cement or glue.

Condensing and storing cum items. You or the counselor should condense or purge the cum every so often, perhaps once a year, and certainly once every third year. The usual practice is to discard any material which is not written directly onto the cum card. If the material is important enough to keep, it should be transcribed onto the cum so that there is no need to keep any note or memorandum.

At the end of each school year, some schools staple together all the loose items and affix a small label or sticker bearing the school year, as "1961–62." This bundle is dropped into the cum folder. For each year the student is in school, then, there is a bundle of memos. There is less likelihood that bundles will be lost, and much time is saved, particularly at the high school level, in locating any given item or notation.

Handling confidential items. Occasionally some item is so confidential or perhaps inimical to a student's welfare that the school will not allow it to be placed in the Cumulative Guidance Record. Typical of such are psychiatric reports, court probation orders, and notations of arrest. A way to alert an authorized user of the cum that such documents exist elsewhere in the school is to make some such entry on the cum card as: "See principal, 4–61." The title indicates the administrator who holds information in a special file, and the date indicates when the notation was made.

Filing records after graduation. Items usually retained in the Cumulative Guidance Record after the student has been graduated or has left the school permanently include his health (nurse's) card and his attendance file card (if that is not kept elsewhere). Each school usually provides you with a list of documents to be retained and those that may be destroyed. The principle to be followed is to retain only those items that might be needed to identify the student or to substantiate or explain an action taken by the school that seriously affected the student's normal progress in school. The cum and its contents should then be ready for microfilming or permanent filing in the school's archives.

MICROFILMING SERVICE

Schools are adopting microfilm to insure absolute accuracy, eliminate typing, and save time in making transcripts. Microfilming, too, saves much-needed storage space. You will find that microfilmed materials are more accessible than original documents. Machines for making microfilm copies of student and other school records can be purchased or rented. Readers for scanning and reference are available, too.

A 24-to-1 reduction is recommended as efficient and satisfactory. A school must decide which forms or documents are to be retained and microfilmed. The most important student documents probably will be the Cumulative Guidance Record (and other promotion slips or pupil personnel records) attendance record cards, health cards, "contracts" for the completion of graduation requirements, and military service information, if any.

Preparing for microfilming. The following procedures are recommended for the preparation of materials for microfilming:

1. Alphabetize cums and other records. If a numerical system is used, an alphabetical cross-reference list or numerical index also must be supplied.

2. Establish an order or sequence of forms for each student.

3. Discard forms not to be duplicated. If in doubt about a form, it should be retained and microfilmed.

4. Turn all forms in the same direction so that the student's name shows at or near the top or always from the same side.

5. Remove all staples, clips, and tapes.

6. Check ink and trace over or retype doubtful lettering. (Pencil and red and blue ink are questionable in their reproducing or photographic quality.)

7. Over-large cums may have to be cut in two with a paper cutter in order to fit them into the copying machine. Be sure student's name appears on both halves.

Microfilming. The records are now ready for microfilming.

1. Start photographing each film roll with a card on which is lettered or typed:

> Serial number of the roll or spool.
> Name of school or school district.
> Year or years being microfilmed.
> Name of first student.

2. Skip two, preferably three, frames between every student and each alphabetical divider or identification card. This makes for easier location of each student's record and permits splicing in corrected film or retakes. A black card the size of the largest document is recommended in making the "skips."

3. Conclude roll—the last frame photographed—with:

> Serial number of the roll or spool.
> Name of school or school district.
> Year or years covered on roll.
> Name of last student on roll.

Some schools also photograph on each roll an authorization, such as "This certifies that this microfilm is an exact copy of the documents shown hereon and was photographed by authority of the superintendent of schools and the board of education." The date and signature of the administrator in charge are appended.

Send each roll to the photographer for processing as soon as microfilmed. Request both a positive and negative copy.

Verifying microfilm. As soon as the developed roll is returned, check it on the reader for imperfections (out of focus, doubled-over corners, poor readability, and the like). Rephotograph documents imperfectly reproduced.

It is recommended that retakes be spliced into their proper sequence, but note that some states may not permit "breaking" the film. If this is so, then the names of students whose documents have been refilmed must be listed on both the spool wrapper and the box which contains the spool. Microfilm should be filed with the spool left in the box. The box must be identified exactly as per the first and last frames on the roll.

Setting time intervals for microfilming. It is recommended that microfilming be done each year. A longer interval results in alphabetization problems. The documents of withdrawn and transferred-out students for the past school year should be alphabetized with those of graduates of that same year. When a search for a student's records has to be made, it is easiest to have only one alphabetical list.

A school must expect that transcripts have to be made while the microfilming is in progress. It is better to pull the necessary records, using "out" cards, than to delay either the microfilming or the transcript making. The documents can be quickly returned to the file after the transcript is made, with little time lost.

Original documents should not be destroyed until the microfilm has been checked and its quality has been certified to the superintendent of schools or other qualified authority.

GUIDANCE INFORMATION SERVICE

One of the most desirable guidance services, that of filing guidance information materials, often is the most neglected. This is quite understandable, because the pressures of other services are regarded as more important in many schools. On the other hand, it probably is true that the availability and use of guidance information materials is the best clue to the nature and effectiveness of a school's guidance program. Guidance materials can be broken into two broad classifications: those to be read by students, and those to be used only by counselors and teachers.

Accessibility of materials. The placement and accessibility of materials must be arranged with the user in mind. Many schools, particularly high schools, maintain the basic student occupational file in the school library and an abridged file in the counseling office. Sometimes a good file of occupational and educational information materials is set up in the waiting room area of the guidance office so that students feel free to use it at will. Individual counselors are provided files of essential reference materials.

While you have no particular obligation for the guidance file in the school library, you should provide the library with duplicate copies of materials you receive. Cooperation in both directions is very important.

With few exceptions, the informational file in the guidance office is almost certain to be a responsibility of the guidance counselor. That responsibility should be extended to the maintenance of attractive bulletin boards and displays of career-book jackets. These boards and displays might well be changed every second week to attract student interest and stimulate use of the guidance office services.

Categories of guidance information. Guidance information materials can be grouped into seven categories: (1) college catalogs and directories; (2) occupational materials—pamphlets, briefs, and monographs; (3) educational material—brochures and pamphlets; (4) scholarship announcements; (5) employment announcements; (6) professional literature; and (7) tests.

College catalogs and directories. The guidance secretary should solicit all state and nearby universities, colleges, junior colleges, and technical or business institutions in the spring of each year for their latest catalogs and directories. A copy for each counselor, one for the student's shelf, and one for the library should be requested. As soon as the new edition is received, last year's copy should be discarded. About every second week the guidance secretary or one of her student monitors should re-alphabetize these catalogs and directories. The student file in the reception area should be checked more often, and the more often it needs re-alphabetizing the more satisfaction the secretary should take, for that is real testimony that the catalogs are being used.

Occupational materials. Occupation materials generally are filed in three-, and four-drawer cabinets. There are two broad categories; individual occupations, and industries. "Surgeon" and "surgery" are examples of occupations; "medicine" and "health services" are examples of industries.

Ask yourself this question, "Is Mr. Jones a _____ or does Mr. Jones do _____?" If your answer makes good sense, file the material in your "occupations" file. If your answer won't make a sensible reply, file it in your "industry" file. Be sure to write the occupation or industry under which you are filing the pamphlet, together with the month and year, in the upper right-hand corner of the cover. There are many methods for filing occupational materials, some of them available commercially in the form of ready-printed dividers and file folders. The alphabetical file is about as good as any. At least, the students and counselors can find the material. Insist upon re-filing the material yourself. Many pamphlets, aside from salary data, do not become obsolete so quickly as publishers would have you think. Consult your head counselor before discarding occupational briefs and monographs. Don't throw something away unless you have a replacement.

Educational materials. Educational materials are grouped into two broad categories: by individual subjects (as trigonometry or Spanish), and by areas or departments (as mathematics or foreign languages). Again, file alphabetically and do the re-filing yourself. Students should be allowed to browse through the informational files in the reception area. Subject materials are difficult to collect. Some of your materials may be five years old yet still be substantially up-to-date.

Scholarship announcements. Scholarship announcements usually are made by an institution, sponsoring agency, or subject area. Many of these, for a time at least, should be displayed on the bulletin board. Single sheet announcements and thin folders might be placed in a loose-leaf binder, to be discarded at the close of the school year. Books and monographs about scholarships should be placed on a shelf. They should not be discarded without specific authorization.

Employment announcements. Job announcements and employment circulars should be treated like scholarship materials. Display them, hold them until the expiration date or close of school, and then discard.

Professional literature. Professional guidance journals, publications, and research reports should be filed where they will be seen and used by the counseling staff. You probably will receive only a single copy at a time. Immediately send each copy on to the professional staff. Use a routing slip, with your name last. When it is returned to you, file it on a shelf, in a container or drawer. At the close of school each year, tie a string around a year's volume of issues and stow them away in some corner. Check with your counselor about retention of loose odds and ends. They may or may not be wanted for future reference or as a source of speech material.

Tests. File your tests alphabetically under one of the categories described earlier in this chapter. File a copy of each form, the test or examiner's manual, scoring key, scoring stencils, and norms with each test. Stamp "Office copy—do not remove" on at least one copy of each item. Always keep these tests. There is no telling when they will be needed. Keep all the catalogs of test publishers in one place. Discard the old catalogs when new ones are received.

17

Testing and Simple Statistics

As PART of the counseling and evaluation program, elementary and high schools routinely give tests to their students. This testing service involves you in certain responsibilities, such as knowing the types of tests used in your school, administering tests, scoring tests, and working simple statistics.

TESTS AND TESTING

Kinds of tests. You will soon become familiar with the different types of tests used in your school. Many of these tests are called "standardized" tests because there uniform conditions for administering the test have been established, and uniform methods of interpreting the test results are used. A large number of individuals all over the United States have been tested in the same way to provide norms against which any particular test score is compared. An equally good name would be "commercial" tests; that is, tests prepared and sold by commercial publishers as distinguished from those prepared by a teacher for her own use. Your concern will be almost exclusively with the standardized tests. You are not likely to be asked for assistance with tests a teacher writes, except perhaps to cut stencils and do the mimeographing.

In the case of the standardized tests you are likely to be asked to order the tests; to stock, inventory, and issue them; perhaps score the tests, and tally the results. You may even be asked to do some simple arithmetical calculations of class averages.

Types of tests. There are five general types of test which you may have to handle. They are intelligence tests, achievement tests, aptitude tests, interest inventories, and personality inventories. Aptitude tests and interest and personality inventories are usually used for vocational guidance; that is, to help a student find a suitable field for vocational training or employment. The last three test types are used almost exclusively in high schools and higher educational institutions.

Intelligence tests. Intelligence tests measure the pupil's native capacity to do school work, usually of the mental or intellectual type. Intelligence tests predict how well the pupil will learn.

Achievement tests. Achievement tests measure what the pupil actually knows or has learned in school subjects. Achievement tests look backward to find out what the pupil has learned.

Aptitude tests. Aptitude tests are similar in function to intelligence tests in that they predict what the person is capable of doing. Aptitude are generally of two types: the vocational aptitude, and the scholastic aptitude. These tests measure such capacities as dexterity of the fingers, ability to differentiate colors, skill in recognizing musical notations, ability to visualize how a house will appear by looking only at the blueprints. As yet, aptitude tests are not in as common use as are the other types of tests.

Interest inventories. Interest inventories are used to estimate how well a person likes to do certain activities or occupations. They do not tell how capable a person is likely to be in doing a job; they merely indicate whether he is likely to be satisfied or happy doing certain types of jobs or taking certain types of courses.

Personality inventories. Personality inventories indicate in general how a person is likely to react or behave toward others under certain conditions. They estimate such traits as cooperativeness, concern for other people, perseverance, and aggressiveness. Interest and personality measures are called inventories because the answers are not marked "right" or "wrong" as in the case of tests. A list of *Publishers of Standardized Tests* is given at the end of this chapter, p. 194.

How to administer a test to a student. Occasionally a guidance secretary is asked to administer a "paper and pencil" test, especially to a new student having no test data. These tests are always the group-type test though given to an individual student. These tests can be administered in the principal's or counselor's office, the nurse's room, an empty classroom, or the library. The test booklet should be examined and all marks erased. In your spare time, study the manual of directions and become familiar with the plan of the test, the sequence, and the responses. You might even wish to take the test yourself. The following points should be observed when administering a test:

1. Follow the directions carefully, but don't be too rigid or too formal in doing so. The results are valuable only if the test is administered under standardized conditions.
2. Maintain a pleasant, easy manner.
3. Be sure that lighting, ventilation, and temperature are adequate.
4. Have a supply of pencils and scratch paper ready.
5. Have a stop watch, timer, or wall clock.
6. Place a "Testing—Do Not Disturb" sign on the outside of the door.

7. Give no assistance on test items. Answer direct questions with a "Do the best you can" or "Do just as it says."

8. Make notes of unusual behavior during the test.

9. Be sure that all personal data (name, age, and so on) are filled in by each pupil.

How to score tests. The scoring of tests often becomes, in part, your responsibility. While every teacher is responsible for marking her own tests, it is not uncommon to find that intelligence tests and certain printed achievement tests are scored by the "office"—meaning *you.*

The tests which you may be called upon to score will be those which the teacher or school counselor may give as part of the guidance or general evaluation program. Practically never will you work with the tests which the teacher gives as part of her daily instruction. Hence, your help may be available for marking tests in which the counselor, principal, or superintendent may have a special interest.

Follow manual of directions. In scoring tests, the first thing to do is to read the manual of directions. Every test manual has special instructions for scoring the test. These directions must be followed meticulously. As you may have surmised, you are not expected to know the answers to the tests. The publishers of the tests always provide an answer key with the test. The key will be found with the manual of instructions. One key is packed with each package of tests. There are generally 25 or 35 tests in a package.

There are two common types of score keys: the answer key, and the answer stencil, sometimes called a "template." The answer key is usually used for tests in which the pupil writes his answers directly upon the test booklet. The answer stencil is usually used for tests in which the pupil makes all his answers on a single answer sheet.

1. THE ANSWER KEY. The answer key is placed alongside the pupil's answers in the test booklet. The key is so printed that the correct answers fall into exactly the same position as the pupil's answers on the test booklet—if the pupil answered correctly. A glance shows which of the pupil's answers are correct and which are not. The answer key is frequently printed with vertical lines separating columns of answers. The key can be folded on these lines so that the answers in each column can be placed exactly alongside the pupil's answers. It is customary to count all the right answers and neglect incorrect or omitted answers. A few tests require that the number of incorrect answers be subtracted from the correct answers. If this is the case, the test booklet will plainly show a place to mark the total correct answers, the total incorrect answers, and the place for subtracting the two. When a pupil gives two answers for the same question, the usual practice is to give him no credit even though one of the answers may be right.

2. THE ANSWER STENCIL. The answer stencil is usually a thin cardboard

with a scattering of holes punched to indicate answers. The stencil is used when answers are marked on a single answer sheet. These are generally designed for scoring on an electronic scoring machine and have to be marked with special pencils containing a large amount of graphite. However, when there are only a hundred, or even two hundred tests, it may be more practical to score the tests by hand. In this case, you place the answer stencil or template over the pupil's answer sheet in the position marked and count the spots or rectangles appearing in the holes, which denote correct answers. Incorrect answers are covered up by the stencil. The number of correct answers is the pupil's raw score. You then proceed to look up the pupil's norms.

It is recommended that you do not completely score one pupil's test booklet before going to the test booklet of the second pupil. Instead, open all the pupil's test booklets to the same page; for example, page two. Score page two for every pupil. Then turn every pupil's test booklet to page three, and score all the pages three at once. This is much faster and more accurate. You will almost know the answers after the first few booklets.

Record total scores. Having marked the answers for each test booklet, you should next transfer the total scores to the space provided on the front or back of the test booklet. (Some test booklets are printed with every other page upside down to prevent the pupil's reading ahead or going back.) Sometimes the scores on several pages or sections of the test must be added together and these partial totals or "sub-totals" added to make a grand total. Be sure to check your arithmetic for accuracy. Adding and subtracting are the greatest sources of serious errors. (Also be very careful to recheck or proofread for accuracy scores you transcribe from the inside to the cover or front page.) These sub-totals and grand totals generally have to be looked up in the manual of directions to find the norms. "Percentiles" usually have to be computed.

1. NORMS. Norms signify the age, grade placement, or percentile to be assigned to each pupil's score. Norms are used as a basis of comparison. You can compare an individual pupil's score with the scores of comparable pupils. Total scores, or raw scores, mean nothing in themselves. Occasionally there are separate norms for boys and girls. In some instances, different percentiles are assigned to the same score for pupils of different ages or grades. For example, a pupil 9 years old who scores, say, 27 may get a higher percentile than a pupil 10 years old who also scores 27 on the same test.

2. PERCENTILES. Percentile really means per cent. Suppose there were exactly 100 pupils tested. A pupil in the 37th percentile would be one who did better than 36 of the pupils, but 63 pupils did better than he. The better his performance on the test, the higher the percentile.

After you have finished scoring and recording the total scores, you will need to enter the test data on the pupil's Cumulative Guidance Record or personnel card and submit a list of the test scores to the appropriate counselor, administrator, or teacher. The used test booklets must ultimately be stored or disposed of in accordance with school policy. On the basis of the test results, intelligence quotients, percentiles, grade placements, class averages, and other simple statistics are computed.

How to order tests. When ordering tests, whether directly from publisher or from the central office of your school district, the following information must be given: (1) test title, (2) test form, (3) battery, school or pupil level, code or catalog number, if any, (4) number of test booklets needed, (5) whether for hand or machine scoring, (6) number of answer sheets needed, (7) number of scoring stencils needed, (8) number of manuals needed, (9) number of special pencils needed, and (10) date all this is needed.

Allow two weeks, preferably three, for shipment. If the purchasing office of your school district is to place the order, inquire from them how long the delivery will take. Sometimes it helps to include the name of the publisher, street address, city, postal zone, and state, on the requisition to your school's purchasing agent.

Ordering directly from the publisher. If you order directly from the publisher, be sure to include (1) the name of your school, (2) the name of the person in your school to whom the tests are to be delivered, (3) the school's street address, (4) city, (5) postal zone, and (6) state. Your school telephone number should also be included. Be sure to indicate who is to be billed for the tests, or enclose a purchase order or remittance.

Most intelligence and achievement tests are packaged 25 or 35 to a package together with a manual and an answer key. Test orders, therefore, are usually specified in terms of packages, not single copies. Answer sheets usually are packaged in lots of 500. Lots of less than 500 can be purchased, but usually it is cheaper by the 500.

Checking number of tests on hand. Before placing your test order, check your shelves of tests to see how many tests and answer sheets are already on hand. Be very sure that you check the title, form, and level. It is always wise not to break open packages until the time when the teachers or counselors will be testing. Most miscounts can be traced to broken packages and mixtures of different forms of a test in the same pile. It will be helpful if you can teach those handling tests to open the packages at the unlabeled end so that unused portions of a package of tests can more easily be identified on the shelf. Answer sheets look very much alike, especially the IBM type. Be sure that the answer sheet is exactly the one needed for the test!

Estimating the number of tests needed. How can you estimate how many tests will be needed? Check the pupil enrollment in the grade or class to take the test. If there are 35 pupils, probably two packages of

35 each should be ordered. The extra tests take care of spoilage and unforeseen needs. If there are 350 pupils in the ninth grade class, order 12
packages of 35 each. This assumes that all 350 pupils will take the test
at the same time. If the testing is to be spread over several days or periods and the tests are not scored in the test booklet itself, the tests can
be reused. A smaller quantity therefore will be needed. Ordinarily it is
wise to order enough tests to take care of the maximum number of pupils
to be tested on any given day or period.

Preparing a yearly schedule for testing. Most schools eventually work
up a yearly schedule of tests. This is helpful to a guidance secretary who
wishes to place her test orders well in advance of the testing date. Two
months is not too long a time to allow. Most schools eventually keep
one full testing supply always on hand; then they are never caught short.
This method requires that there be a secure place to store the tests.
Test booklets can cost as much as a dollar apiece, so each should be
serially numbered and carefully checked out and checked back in at
each testing.

How to prepare for group testing. Most school counselors work out
a schedule of dates, hours, and rooms for giving group tests. Sometimes,
especially in a high school, the guidance secretary is expected to provide
a list of rooms (with number of pupil stations) that are vacant at any
given period.

Distributing test materials. The counselor will tell you how many tests,
answer sheets, pencils, and manuals will be needed. Count these out
and place them in piles by the names of the counselors or teachers who
will administer the tests. The tests and all accessories, including sheets
of special instructions, for each tester can be placed in large manila
envelopes. If they are too numerous for an envelope, the test materials
should be tied with a cord. A list of the testers' names should be made
and checked off as the tests are picked up or delivered. The same list
can be used for checking in the tests.

Collecting test materials. When the test materials are returned to.you,
the tests should then be alphabetized by the students' last names. Many
schools require that incomplete tests be removed. Also remove any used
scratch paper returned. Absentees and students with incomplete tests
may be retested on another date set by the school counselor. Teachers
usually are required to supply a list of absentees. To such lists are
added the names and answer sheets or marked test booklets of students
whose tests are incomplete.

As test materials are returned to you, you should also check in test
accessories—pencils, manuals, and the like. Resharpen the test pencils
so that they will be ready for the next group to be tested.

How to prepare tests for machine-scoring. Many tests, especially those
given to high school students, are scored by machine, but few high

schools are large enough to have their own test scoring machines. Some school districts have a test-scoring machine, but most schools rely upon a commercial test publisher or other agency to provide this service.

Checklist for machine-scoring. The following points will serve as a checklist to help you in preparing the tests for machine-scoring.

1. Scan all answer sheets for proper type of marks. Marks must be solid black within each pair of dotted lines. Faint marks may have to be blackened up. Crosses, dots, and checks do not score properly.
2. Erase stray pencil marks. If more than one mark is found in any given row, erase all marks in that row.
3. Verify completeness of all identification data, such as last name first, birthday (day, month, year), teacher's name, and grade or class. Incomplete tests and tests without full identification data may need to be removed. Also some schools follow the practice of not scoring achievement tests of pupils below 75 or 80 IQ. Ask your counselor or principal whether the tests of such pupils should be removed.

   If the pupil or his teacher inserts either or both birth date and chronological age, these should be checked. Many errors in computing the IQ can be attributed to an error in birth date or chronological age.
4. Insert any required identification data such as the IQ and chronological age. The IQ is obtainable from the cum card, unless it is an intelligence test that is being scored. The chronological age is found in tables that list birth dates by year and month.
5. Do not fold or bend any answer sheet.
6. Type a list of services wanted:
   a. scoring only (whether total or part scores), by raw score, actual grade placement, or percentiles
   b. alphabetical or high-to-low listings of test (total or part scores) results by teacher, class or subject, grade, or school (also called "Class Record Sheets")
   c. insertion of expected (anticipated) age or grade placement
   d. averages and frequency distributions of total or part scores by teacher, class or subject, grade, or school for raw scores, percentiles, actual grade placements, or expected (anticipated) age or grade placements (usually 50 or more tests are necessary)
   e. right-response record showing by class or individual pupil performance on specific items or questions within the test
   f. item-analysis record showing the number or per cent of answers given selected items or questions in the test
   g. pressure-sensitive gummed labels for attaching to each pupil's cumulative guidance record, his raw score, grade placement, expected or anticipated grade placement, percentile or standard score
   h. local school, grade or class norms
   i. duplicate set of interpreted, punched IBM cards for each pupil
7. Keep a record of date tests were sent for machine scoring. List name of test, form, number of tests, class and teacher, date test was given. If time permits, make a list of those pupils who were tested.

8. Keep a record of the date in which the tests were received from machine scoring. As soon as received, verify that all the services you requested have been supplied. Notify persons concerned at once if any tests are missing or if not all the services have been performed. Commercial test publishers usually promise completion of test scoring services in two to three weeks. Central offices of school districts usually require four to five weeks.

SIMPLE STATISTICAL SERVICES

After you or the guidance clerk have gained experience in other guidance office duties, you may be called upon to do some simple statistical computations, such as computing class averages and percentiles, calculating grade-point averages, calculating class rank, and estimating teacher grade or mark distributions. All these are done by simple arithmetic processes which you probably learned in elementary school.

When all the tests have been marked, it is customary to make a record of the scores obtained by the class. This record is prepared in one of two ways. First, the tests can be arranged alphabetically by the pupils' last names. This is a good method for the teacher who wants to transfer the test scores into her roll book. Most teachers arrange their roll books alphabetically. The second method is to arrange the tests with the highest score first and the lowest score last. This method is good when the teacher wants to know the average median of the class or the ranking of her pupils, highest to lowest.

Sometimes the teacher wishes to know whether the boys did better or more poorly than the girls. Or perhaps the principal wishes to compare the averages of two four-grade classes in his school. You, as the school secretary, may be called upon to figure these averages.

Should you have forgotten your arithmetic, the sections below explain step-by-step how to do these "statistics." Don't let the statistical terms frighten you; they are part of the guidance jargon and are quite elemental. You will find yourself using them with ease and skill in no time.

How to figure averages. Add up all the scores. Divide the total by the number of pupils tested. There is an exception: you must omit the scores of those pupils who were not present in school to take the entire test or who left out whole sections of the test. Obviously, the test scores of such pupils are incomplete and should not be included.

Other uses for figuring averages. Besides computing the average score on tests, the principal may ask you to estimate the average age of children in the first grade, or the height of pupils in the sixth grade, or the average money contribution of each child to the Junior Red Cross. In any event, the procedure is always the same. Add up each age, each height, or contribution and divide by the number of pupils or items.

Most school offices have adding machines, so the only work you have to do with pencil and paper is the division. If you happen to have a calculator, you can do the division by machine. Ask the teacher in the business department or the company representative to demonstrate this simple process.

A *shortcut*. On some tests you may find that several pupils have the same scores. This may happen when the test is very short or there are many pupils. In such cases it is advantageous to sort the tests from highest to lowest scores. Then you can write each score and tally the number of pupils getting that score. The tallying is done just as votes are tallied in an election. Your tally may look something like this:

Score	Tally	No. Pupils (f)	Score No. Pupils (f)
10	1 1	2	20
9	1 1	2	18
8	1 1 1 1	4	32
7	1 1 1	3	21
6	1̶1̶1̶1̶ 1 1	7	42
5	1̶1̶1̶1̶ 1 1 1	8	40
4	1 1 1 1	4	16
3	1 1	2	6
2	1	1	2
		Total no. pupils = 33	197

$$\text{Average is } \frac{197}{33} = 5.97$$

The number of pupils receiving each score is designated f for *frequency*, as shown in the tally. Each score and the number of pupils (f) receiving that score are multiplied. That is, $10 \times 2 = 20$; $9 \times 2 = 18$; $8 \times 4 = 32$; and so on. These are then added; in the example, 197. This sum (197), which is the total of each score times the number of pupils (f), is divided by the total number of pupils (33). The quotient (5.97— actually 5.969) is the average.

$$\text{Average} = \frac{\text{Sum of all scores}}{\text{Total number of pupils}}$$
$$= \frac{197}{33}$$
$$= 5.969 = 5.97$$

Average and mean. School people are apt to refer to the average as the *mean*. These words, in practical usage, are the same. Your principal may tell you to compute the *mean*. He is telling you to compute the average. Also, it may be well to know that the total number of pupils or scores is sometimes designated N, for *number*. These symbols are a form of statistical shorthand.

How to figure percentiles. Sometimes your principal will wish to know which pupils were in the upper half on the test, or even in the top quarter or 25th per cent. In our example, could we assume that any pupil who scored better than 5.97 was in the "upper half" on the test? No, because by counting we find that 18 pupils received a score of 6 or better. It would appear that more than half the class ($33\!\!/\!_2 = 16.5$) did better than the average. The low scorers apparently pulled the class average down. Therefore the middle or 50 per cent must be higher than the class average of 5.97. This is so, as we shall see.

The 50th percentile, which exactly divides the class in half is the number of pupils or scores (33) divided by 2 (that is, $33\!\!/\!_2$), or 16.5. If we count the (f) column from the bottom upward, we find that 15 pupils ($1 + 2 + 4 + 8$) received scores of 5 or less; therefore the 16.5th score must be among the seven pupils with a score of 6. In other words, the score of 2.5 pupils must be added to those of the 15 pupils we have already counted to make the required 16.5. As this requires 2.5 of the 7 pupils who received a score of 6, we divide 2.5 by 7. This gives us the proper proportion of those who received the score 6: $2.5\!\!/\!_7 = .357$, or .36. We add the score 6 and the .36 to get 6.36, which is the score of the 50th percentile that exactly divides the class in two. Sometimes the score of this 50th percentile is called the *median*. The symbols for median are *Md* or *Mdn*.

Summary of steps in figuring percentiles. If you have difficulty in figuring percentiles, check your work through the following steps:

1. The percentile score is found by multiplying the per cent by the number of tests or pupils, for example,
$$.50 \times 33 = 16.5$$

2. Starting from the lowest score, this number (16.5) of pupils or test scores is counted upward until the score is reached in which the percentile (50%) must fall. In the example, the 50th percentile falls in the score 6.

3. The difference between (a) the number of pupils (15) counted to the score 5 which is next below that in which the 50th percentile falls and (b) the additional number of pupils (2.5) to reach the 50th percentile (16.5) is divided by the number of pupils (7) receiving the score in which the 50th percentile falls; for example,
$$\frac{2.5}{7} = .36$$

4. Add this to the score in which the 50th percentile falls, for example
$$.36 + 6 = 6.36$$
to give the correct percentile score. Thus, 6.36 is the score of the 50th percentile.

All percentiles are computed in the same manner. Take, for example, the 25th percentile which separates the lowest one-fourth from the remainder of the class ($.25 \times 33 = 8.25$). By the method shown, the 25th percentile occurs at score 5.28. And another example: the 75th percentile separates the top one-fourth from the remainder of the class (.75 × 33 = 24.75). Thus, the 75th percentile occurs at score 8.19.

How to figure class rank and grade-point average. Many high schools are asked to report the class rank or standing of students in the graduating class. This information often is requested by the universities to which graduates are seeking admittance. Class standing frequently determines whether a student will or will not be awarded a scholarship or other honor.

Class rank. Most high schools eventually develop their own tables of class standing based on the average grades or marks awarded students over a period of years. These tables are consulted for most students, but in the case of the highest ten students, or perhaps the top 5 per cent of the class, standings are computed.

A student's class standing or rank usually is based on the grades or marks he has received during his entire high school career, though some schools count only the senior year. Other schools exclude physical education, study, hall, incompletes, and sometimes courses in art, music, and other special-subject areas. In any event, a numerical value must be assigned to each mark.

Grade-point average. If your school uses an A-B-C-D-Fail system of grading, a value of 4 may be assigned to an A; 3 to a B; 2 to a C; one to a D; and zero to an F. Other schools may assign: 3 to an A; 2 to a B; 1 to a C; zero to a D; and zero to an F. However, there are fewer clerical errors when the former system is used, every grade having a different numerical value. Whatever the values assigned, the procedures for computing grade-point average are the same as figuring class standing:

1. Count the number of A's a student has and multiply by A's numerical or grade-point value. Repeat for the B's, the C's, D's, and F's.
2. Add all the grade points together to obtain the total grade points which the student has accumulated. ("Grade points" are also called mark-points, honor-points, and similar names.)
3. Divide the student's total grade points by the number of courses he has taken. This will be his grade-point average.

Let us assume that the following grades or marks were received by a student in a three-year senior high school which divides each year into two semesters.

Course	Grade or Mark	
	First Semester	Second Semester
English I	A	A
English II	B	B
English III	A	C
Spanish I	C	B
Spanish II	B	C
Spanish III	C	B

	Grade or Mark (Continued)	
Course	First Semester	Second Semester
Algebra I	A	B
Geometry	B	B
Algebra II	B	A
Biology	D	C
Chemistry	C	B
Physics	B	A
Physical Education I	F	C
Physical Education II	D	D
Physical Education III	C	B

This student's scholastic records summarizes as follows:

Grade or mark	Number of each grade or mark received		Grade-point value		Grade-point
A	6	×	4	=	24
B	12	×	3	=	36
C	8	×	2	=	16
D	3	×	1	=	3
Fail	1	×	0	=	0
Inc.	0		—		—
	30 (Number of courses)				79 (Total grade-points

$$\frac{\text{Total grade-points}}{\text{Number of courses}} = \frac{79}{30} = 2.63 \text{ (grade-point average)}$$

This student probably would be reported as a B-minus student, where "A" carries a value of 4.

A school giving a value of 4 to an "A" probably would follow some such interpretation as the following:

Student Classification	Grade-Point Average
Straight A	3.76–4.00
A minus	3.51–3.75
B plus	3.26–3.50
B	2.76–3.25
B minus	2.51–2.75
C plus	2.26–2.50
C	1.76–2.25
C minus	1.51–1.75
D plus	1.26–1.50
D	0.76–1.25
D minus	0.51–0.75

If a student's class average is computed, it is wise to carry out the average to at least two decimal places. When a student repeats a course to raise a grade or eliminate a failure, he is not charged with an additional course.

Some schools add up a student's grade-points each semester or year. This does speed up the process in the final year but has the disadvantage of requiring the computation of points of many students who will never graduate.

If your school assigns differing units or credits, also called "semester periods" credit, to various courses, these units must first be multiplied with the point value of the grade the student receives. For such schools, it is advisable to compute the grade-point value of each course separately and total rather than to group all the A's, B's, C's as explained above. Also, to obtain the grade-point average, the number of units or credits is substituted for the number of courses. The formula then becomes:

$$\frac{\text{Total grade-points}}{\text{Number of units}} = \text{Grade-point average}$$

To obtain the class rank or standing of a student, his total grade points are listed or ranked from highest to lowest and then numbered 1-2-3-, etc. (The same can be done with grade-point averages, but unless grade-point averages are needed, they can be omitted.) If the student stands first or has the greatest number of grade points in, for example, a class of 250, he is reported as 1/250; if he stands twelfth, he is reported as 12/250; if he stands last, he is reported as 250/250.

How to figure the distribution of grades or marks given by teachers. Both elementary and secondary schools are interested in knowing the proportion of high and low grades given by teachers. The teachers of some grades or subjects are more generous in giving grades than others. While few principals ever interfere with grades given by teachers, they know, as do experienced teachers, that if the grades of one teacher get out of balance with those of other instructors teaching the same grade or course, there can be repercussions of various sorts. One way to let teachers know that they or their departments are out of line in giving grades is to compute the percentage or proportion of each type of grade given. This is also called computing the "distribution" of grades.

The percentage distribution of grades is computed by subjects. Separate subjects—say, English and arithmetic—though taught by the same teacher, are computed separately. Two classes in the same course, if taught by the same teacher, are generally added together.

A tally is made of the number of A's, B's, C's, and so on in each course. The total number of grades given is divided into 100 to obtain the percentage value of each grade. The number of A's given is multiplied by this percentage value. This is repeated for the B's, the C's, etc. As a check, the resulting percentages are added to see that they total 100. The percentages may be rounded to one decimal place.

For example, the grades given by Miss Jones in algebra are as follows:

Grade or mark	Number given		Percentage value of each grade		Percentage Distribution (Rounded)
A	5	×	3.125	=	15.625 = 15.6%
B	10	×	3.125	=	31.250 = 31.3
C	10	×	3.125	=	31.250 = 31.3
D	5	×	3.125	=	15.625 = 15.6
F	2	×	3.125	=	6.250 = 6.3
Inc.	(4)	do not count			

32 (total number of grades given)   100.000 = 100.1%

$$\frac{100\%}{\text{Total number of grades given}} = \frac{100\%}{32} = 3.125\% \text{ (percentage value of each grade)}$$

PUBLISHERS OF STANDARDIZED TESTS

Bureau of Educational Research and Service, Extension Division, State University of Iowa, Iowa City, Iowa.

Bureau of Publications, Teachers College, Columbia University, New York 27, New York.

California Test Bureau, Del Monte Research Park, Monterey, California.

College Entrance Examination Board, 475 Riverside Drive, New York 27, New York; Box 27896, Los Angeles 27, California.

Educational Testing Service, Educational Publishers, Inc., Los Angeles Office, 4640 Hollywood Blvd., Los Angeles 27.

Houghton Mifflin Co., Park St., Boston 7, Massachusetts; 777 California Avenue, Palo Alto, California.

Psychological Corporation, 304 E. 45th Street, New York 17, New York.

Public School Publishing Company, 345 Calhoun Street, Cincinnati 19, Ohio,

Sheridan Supply Co., P.O. Box 837, Beverly Hills, California.

Science Research Associates, Inc., 259 E. Erie Street, Chicago 11, Illinois.

Stanford University Press, Stanford University, California.

C. H. Stoelting Co., 424 North Homan Avenue, Chicago 24, Illinois.

Vocational Guidance Centre, 371 Bloor Street, W., Toronto, Canada.

Harcourt, Brace & World, Inc., Tarrytown-on-Hudson, New York.

18

Helping in the Library and Textbook Room

THE SCHOOL SECRETARY may be asked to assist other personnel in various phases of the school program. Although most large schools have personnel regularly assigned to special areas, you should know about the operation of the school library and the textbook room, and the use of audio-visual materials.

THE SCHOOL LIBRARY

In high schools, the library is usually managed by a librarian. Elementary schools sometimes assign a teacher as library chairman. Clerical duties in the library may include helping to arrange books on the shelves, making book cards, ordering books and magazines, scheduling class visits, circulating books, and mending magazines and books.

The elementary school library is about half fiction, including picture books and easy books. High schools have a larger proportion of nonfiction books.

Practically all schools use the help of pupils who volunteer their services. Some high schools allow pupils credit for library service. Elementary schools use pupils from the fourth grade up to assist in the handling of books. Pupils are trained to circulate books, shelve books, "read shelves," review books, and do many small chores that keep the library orderly and attractive.

Processing library books. Before a new book can be placed on the shelf, it must be processed. Processing, sometimes called accessioning, covers unwrapping the book, cataloging, numbering, and stamping it, and placing it on the appropriate shelf. In processing library books, use the following suggestions as a guide until you learn the complete process.

1. Check each new title against the invoice or shipping list to see that the author, title, edition, and number of copies received are correct. Return imperfect books, and report shortages immediately.

195

2. Open each book so that the back will not break and it will lie flat when open. This is done by placing the spine of the book (that part of the cover or binding which conceals the sewn or bound edge of the book) on the table, pressing the front cover down until it touches the table. Then, gently press down a few of the front leaves of the book. Do the same for a few pages in the back. Repeat this process with a few pages near the front, then a few pages near the back, and so on until all pages have been opened.

3. Identify each book with an appropriate classification number, reading symbol (elementary schools only), copy number, and the name of the school. Then prepare shelflist and catalog cards.

4. Assign each nonfiction title a classification number which represents the subject of that book. Most school libraries use the Dewey Decimal System. Under this system, an outline of classifications is used. Figure 7 outlines the main classes of the Dewey Decimal Classification, 8th abridged edition.

Elementary school libraries also indicate the reading difficulty of a book by a series of symbols. Three symbols are recommended:

A star (*) indicates a picture book suitable to read to children in primary grades.

A circle (○) indicates a book with a vocabulary suitable for beginning readers (first and second grade).

A triangle (△) indicates a book with a third-grade or easy fourth-grade vocabulary.

Figure 7

Dewey Decimal Classification

*Second Summary: Divisions**

000	*GENERAL WORKS*		200	*RELIGION*
010	Bibliography		210	Natural theology
020	Library science		220	Bible
030	General encyclopedias		230	Doctrinal theology
040	General collected essays		240	Devotional & practical
050	General periodicals		250	Pastoral theology
060	General societies		260	Christian church
070	Newspaper journalism		270	Christian church history
080	Collected works		280	Christian churches & sects
090	Manuscript & rare books		290	Other religions
100	*PHILOSOPHY*		300	*SOCIAL SCIENCES*
110	Metaphysics		310	Statistics
120	Metaphysical theories		320	Political science
130	Branches of psychology		330	Economics
140	Philosophical topics		340	Law
150	General psychology		350	Public administration
160	Logic		360	Social welfare
170	Ethics		370	Education
180	Ancient & medieval		380	Public services & utilities
190	Modern philosophy		390	Customs & folklore

400	*LANGUAGE*
410	Comparative linguistics
420	English & Anglo-Saxon
430	Germanic languages
440	French, Provençal, Catalan
450	Italian & Rumanian
460	Spanish & Portuguese
470	Latin & other Italic
480	Classical & modern Greek
490	Other languages

500	*PURE SCIENCE*
510	Mathematics
520	Astronomy
530	Physics
540	Chemistry & allied sciences
550	Earth sciences
560	Paleontology
570	Anthropology & biology
580	Botanical sciences
590	Zoological sciences

600	*TECHNOLOGY*
610	Medical sciences
620	Engineering
630	Agriculture
640	Home economics
650	Business
660	Chemical technology
670	Manufactures
680	Other manufactures
690	Building construction

700	*THE ARTS*
710	Landscape & civic art
720	Architecture
730	Sculpture
740	Drawing & decorative arts
750	Painting
760	Prints & print making
770	Photography
780	Music
790	Recreation

800	*LITERATURE*
810	American literature in English
820	English & Old English
830	Germanic literatures
840	French, Provençal, Catalan
850	Italian & Rumanian
860	Spanish & Portuguese
870	Latin & other Italic literatures
880	Classical & modern Greek
890	Other literatures

900	*HISTORY*
910	Geography, travels, description
920	Biography
930	Ancient history
940	Europe
950	Asia
960	Africa
970	North America
980	South America
990	Other parts of world

* Reprinted with permission of Forest Press of Lake Placid Club (N.Y.) Education Foundation, owners of copyright.

Give every book a consecutive copy number so that the book can be identified for business purposes. Copy numbers are helpful in preparing inventory records and are used also to identify lost or mutilated books.

Preparing the identifying book cards. If such cards are not supplied, prepare an author card, a title card, and subject card on 3 × 5 cards.

An *author card* is the most important catalog card made for a book. In preparing this card, follow the form given below. Capitalize only proper names and the first letter of the first word.

1. Type at the top on one line the classification number, the reading symbol (if any), and the author's name, last name first.
2. On the next line, indent three spaces below the author's last name and type the title of the book, the name of the publisher, and the date of publication. (Obtain the title from the title page.)

3. Skip one line and type the number of pages and the number of illustrations, if there are any.

4. One inch from the bottom of the card, type consecutively an Arabic numeral and subject (for each subject card that is prepared) and a Roman number (I, II, etc.) followed by the word "title" for each subject card. This is called a "tracing" and insures that all catalog cards are withdrawn from the catalog when a book is lost or permanently removed from the library.

737.4   **Reinfeld, Fred, 1910-**
    Catalogue of the world's most popular coins.   **Sterling** 1956
     268p illus

  "Lists virtually all foreign coins the average collector wants to know about, with the current value of each and pictures of many of them. With a . . . Coin Finder section for the beginner." Retail bookseller
  Quarto volume

1 Coins ɪ Title ɪɪ Title: World's most popular coins   **737.4**

1-4-57   (W)   The H. W. Wilson Company

(Author card)

Ready-prepared catalog cards can be purchased from the H. W. Wilson Company. These cards make classification of books much easier in cases where clerical help only is available. Check the list of book titles for cards wanted.

A *title card* shows the title of the book on the top line. The second line gives the classification number, the reading symbol (if any), and the author's last name; on the final line the number of pages, as 58p., and the abbreviation "illus." if there are illustrations.

A *subject card* is usually used by both junior and senior high schools, and is prepared as follows:

1. Type the subject, in red, on the top line of the card.
2. Type the classification number and the author's name, last name first, in black, on the second line.
3. Type the title of the book on the third line.
4. Type the number of pages on the fourth or subsequent line, as 58p. and the abbreviation "illus.," if there are illustrations. Be sure that all subjects are traced on their respective author cards so that they can be found if the book becomes lost or is permanently removed from the library.

Catalogue of the world's most popular coins

737.4   Reinfeld, Fred, 1910-
Catalogue of the world's most popular coins. Sterling
1956
268p illus

"Lists virtually all foreign coins the average collector wants to know
about, with the current value of each and pictures of many of them.
With a . . . Coin Finder section for the beginner." Retail bookseller
Quarto volume

1 Coins ɪ Title ɪɪ Title: World's most popular coins   737.4

1-4-57   (W)   The H. W. Wilson Company

(Title card)

Handling other identifying library cards. Some school libraries keep
a record of the books added to the library by entering consecutively each
new title into a journal of accessions, but others are using shelflist cards
for each new book. This card is kept in the librarian's own desk file and
is not placed in the general card catalog. The purpose of these cards is
to record the books owned by the school library. It is invaluable when
you are taking a library inventory. The card is similar to the author
card explained above, but, in addition, it supplies information about

COINS

737.4   Reinfeld, Fred, 1910-
Catalogue of the world's most popular coins. Sterling
1956
268p illus

"Lists virtually all foreign coins the average collector wants to know
about, with the current value of each and pictures of many of them.
With a . . . Coin Finder section for the beginner." Retail bookseller
Quarto volume

1 Coins ɪ Title ɪɪ Title: World's most popular coins   737.4

1-4-57   (W)   The H. W. Wilson Company

(Subject card)

copy numbers and the date when each book was added to the library. There is only one shelflist card for each title. Duplicate copies of the same title are listed on the same card. When preparing these cards, it is helpful to use the following suggestions:

1. Type on a single line at the top of the shelflist card the classification number, the reading symbol (if any), and the author's name, last name first.
2. On the next line, indent three spaces below the author's last name and type the title of the book.
3. Skip two lines, then type the copy number and the month and year (in numerals) the book was added to the library. (Immediately below, record the copy numbers and dates of duplicate books.)

737.4   Reinfeld, Fred, 1910-
         Catalogue of the world's most popular coins. Sterling 1956
         268p illus

       No. 6, 1/6/62
       Nos. 7-12, 2/1/62

                                      737.4

   1-4-57   (W) The H. W. Wilson Company

(Shelflist card)

Other catalog cards may also be prepared. The catalog cards of biographies substitute the symbol B for the classification number. The catalog cards of fiction carry no classification number, but they may have a brief description of the story. If this is not supplied, the librarian probably will omit the description. Fiction may also have an *illustrator's card*. This card is the same as the subject card, but shows the name, last name first, of the illustrator typed at the very top, immediately above the name of the author.

Identifying the library books. Records of all books must be kept. Each book should be identified with the school's name and given a number.

1. Stamp the name of the school and the copy number of the book at the top of the inside front cover, at the lower right corner on the title page, and at the top of page 25. (Actually, any page will do, but it must always be the same one. This facilitates rebinding.) You will need a num-

bering machine and rubber stamp showing the name of the school. "THIS BOOK IS THE PROPERTY OF _____ SCHOOL."

2. Place the classification number (nonfiction) or copy number (fiction) on the title page above the copy number and on the spine of the book. The number on the spine is usually placed two and one-half inches from the nearest printed lettering already there, if possible. It usually bears the title and frequently the author's name. Use white ink on dark bindings and black ink on light bindings when using a Stud-point pen. Many libraries are now using an electric pencil writing on transfer paper.

3. Place the "reading" symbol on the spine and on the title page immediately above the classification number.

4. Type a book card and pocket, and paste the pocket on the inside front cover. The head of the book card and pocket shows the school name, the reading symbol, the copy number, and the classification number; also, the last name of the author, the title of the book, and the price of it. Fiction, of course, has no classification number. The book card has printed lines for entering the name of the borrowing pupil and the date when the book was borrowed.

5. Book plates, if used, should be pasted on the inside back cover.

Sorting library books. Use as many library tables as necessary for the initial sorting of books before placing them on the shelves. Start by sorting the nonfiction from the fiction. Group nonfiction books according to the classification numbers. A separate table or area can be set aside for each hundred classification numbers (000–099, 100–199, and so on). The 900–999 numbers may require additional space because of the large number of titles in this grouping. If there are many books to be sorted, a sign with large numbers should be placed at each area. Biography, fiction, and picture books can be set aside for later sorting.

Check the classification number on the spine of the book, then place the book on the proper table. When all the books have been sorted by 100's, with the spines visible, arrange them in numerical order from lowest to highest numbers. Classification numbers are read figure by figure, as 973.8 (nine-seven-three point eight.)

When there are several books in the same classification, arrange them alphabetically by the last name of the author within the classification. Example:

Classification	Author	Title
580	Dickinson	First book of plants
580	Miner	True book of plants we know
580	Webber	Bits that grew big
580	Zim	What's inside of plants

When there are several books by the same author in the same classification, they are arranged alphabetically by title. Example:

591.5	George	Masked prowler
591.5	George	Vision, the mink
591.5	George	Vulpes, the red fox

Now sort the biography books. Arrange them by the last name of the biographee—the person who is the subject of the book, not its author. When there is more than one biography of the same person, arrange the books alphabetically by the last names of the authors.

When sorting fiction and picture books, label tables for each letter of the alphabet. Provide areas for picture books (*), first and second-grade books (○), and third and easy fourth-grade books (△). When all the fiction books have been placed on their proper tables, arrange them alphabetically by the last name of the author. When there is more than one book by the same author, arrange them alphabetically by title.

When arranging books by authors whose last names begin with "Mc" or "Mac," the books are arranged as if all the names were spelled "Mac." They are shelved after "Mab." Example: McCloskey, MacDonald, McGraw, MacGregor.

Arrange picture books (*) alphabetically by the last name of the author. Do the same for the first and second-grade books (○), and then for third and easy fourth-grade books (△).

Shelving library books. When transferring the books to shelves, begin with the 200 group and transfer it to the shelf in the same order as it is arranged on the table. Continue with the rest of the classification groups, the fiction, the picture books, and easy books.

Books are placed on the shelves from left to right moving from the top to the bottom of each section of shelves. Books should stand upright and be placed even with the front edge of the shelf. Do not use more than two-thirds the length of the shelf. Begin each new general classification on a separate shelf; for example, if the 400's end in the middle of a shelf, begin the 500's on the next shelf. Leave the bottom shelves free for oversize books.

Each section of shelves containing fiction should likewise be labeled with the inclusive letters of the alphabet shelved within that section. Example: A–B. The section containing reference books should be labeled "References." Picture books (*) should be labeled "Picture Books." Easy books (○ and △) should be labeled "Easy Books" or some similar designation that will not discourage slow-reading upper-grade pupils from using them.

Shelf labels may also be used. The names of the Dewey Decimal Classification numbers can be used, but omit the numbers. Consult the Children's Catalog. Do not use a shelf unless there are several shelves that can be covered by the same shelf label. When a library's collection of books is small, use only general headings on shelf labels.

Discarding library books. Books that are no longer being used or which are worn out and not worth rebinding should be discarded. A check should be made to see if some other school in your district can use the books. If not, the superintendent's office should advise you about how to discard the books. In some schools, policy on discarding books is the responsibility of the librarian. Some school districts will not allow school books to be sold or given away. Each discontinued book, if it is still an active title, should be stricken from its book inventory card by cancelling its copy number.

A list of the discarded book titles and quantity of each should be given or submitted to your principal. Make a copy for your own records.

Inventory cards of obsolete books should be marked "obsolete" and placed in a dead file. Books to be discarded should be packaged and tagged for delivery to the office or person responsible for disposing of them.

THE TEXTBOOK ROOM

In schools furnishing free textbooks to pupils, either you or the textbook clerk is assigned the responsibility of controlling the textbooks and the textbook room. The textbook room is a centrally located room, usually near the library, where textbooks are checked in and out to pupils and teachers. The control of a textbook room requires at least three types of record:

1. A record and annual inventory of all textbooks belonging to the school.
2. A record of all books lent to each pupil.
3. An account of all funds received for lost or damaged books, and the disposition of such funds.

Schools that have inventories of 25,000 or more textbooks generally employ a textbook clerk on a 12-month basis. The textbook clerk is responsible for the collection of textbooks and should keep the room locked when it is necessary for him to be away. However, the textbook room should be available to each teacher throughout the year so that he can browse around to see if there are any shelved books that he would like to use. A looseleaf notebook, with a page for each teacher, kept in the textbook room is a convenient record for charging supplementary textbooks out and in. Teachers usually make arrangements among themselves for using supplementary textbooks. If this is the case, it is well to prepare and post a rotation schedule of supplementary textbooks in the textbook room.

Many schools operating a textbook room find it necessary to employ a textbook room clerk, so we will assume that the textbook room is in charge of a textbook clerk. However, you might be asked to perform these duties in some schools.

Determining books needed. The determination of books needed will be handled through department chairmen, a faculty textbook committee, the principal, or the dean. This is usually done once a semester or once a year.

In large school systems, the city or the state may issue a list of authorized textbooks. In this case, textbooks would be selected from this list and then requisitioned from the school district's central purchasing office. Whatever the procedure, an administrator (the principal or a supervisor) is usually responsible for determining the quantity of books needed for each grade level or subject. It is up to each teacher to let the principal know how many titles he has of every book, together with the condition of those books. If a book is worn out, it should either be rebound or replaced. On the basis of such information, the principal can then decide whether to rebind or replace.

In an elementary school, you may be asked to prepare a mimeographed form to help the teachers in reporting this information to the principal. This form should include spaces for the teacher's name, room number, and the date; the list of titles (exact) of all textbooks used, together with the number of each which are in good condition or unusable, and the number of additional copies needed.

After the above information has been gathered, it should be consolidated into one list so that the total number of books needed for each subject and grade level is easily ascertained. The list is then ready for the principal's approval.

Requisitioning new titles and adoptions. When making out the requisition for textbooks (new titles or adoptions), be sure that you copy the information exactly, such as the title, author, publisher, edition, date of publication, number of copies needed, the list price, and tax, if any. Workbooks usually require separate requisitions. The same rule applies when ordering for the opening of new rooms or replacements for books.

After the requisitions have been prepared, they should be sorted by grade and by subject. Check to be sure you have not listed a title more than once. Then consolidate your order as to quantity. You will also need the principal's approval for this step.

When requisitions are made for new titles, new adoptions, or revised editions, this should immediately indicate to you another problem. What will become of the old books? Teachers usually do not have enough space in their rooms to store discarded books. You will hear all kinds of rumblings from staff members about the lack of space and "When are they going to pick up these discarded books?" You should arrange for the books to be taken away from the school. In some districts, this becomes a standard procedure and pickup trucks are sent around regularly for discarded equipment, books, and whatnot. You may find that you need to be firm with your principal: "We have these discarded books stacked in the corridor. When are we going to get rid of them? The fire department will not let us keep them there, as they constitute a fire hazard!"

In some cases, however, the teachers may indicate to you that they wish to keep a discontinued reader in the elementary grades. These books might provide excellent supplementary reading material for homework because, in many schools, pupils in the primary grades are not permitted to take the regular readers home.

Placing or letting orders. In school systems that operate through a central purchasing office, the ordering of books is done by requisition from the adopted list. In other schools, you will be responsible for placing the textbook orders directly with the publishing company or the student store. The number ordered should be based upon the needs indicated by the textbook requisitions and upon the approval of the principal. If book orders are placed twice a year, you should make sure that the requisition is filed early enough so that books will be available for the new semester. Book orders for September should be placed before March, and book orders for the second semester should be placed not later than October. However, requisitions for State textbooks for the next year generally can be placed anytime after January 1, if enrollment and textbook needs can be estimated reliably. The requisition form should show the name of the school district, the exact shipping address, and the signature, title, and address of the superintendent, principal, or otherwise authorized district official. Requisitions should also show enrollments.

Following up requisitions or orders. You will know from previous orders about the length of time required for book orders to be filled. If you feel that an unreasonable amount of time has elapsed since your order or requisition was placed, it would be wise to investigate the matter. If the company is located in the city, call them on the phone. Sometimes the delay is due to their negligence in misplacing an order or it may have become buried on someone's desk. Keep needling them. "The semester is going to open; the teachers need the books on the opening of school. What shall I tell them?"

Obviously, you would not make it a practice to call companies out of the city. You would want to send a follow-up inquiry to trace the cause of delay in shipment. If this type of delay becomes a frequent occurrence, you might want to mimeograph or ditto some follow-up forms on postal cards. Save yourself time in any routine task.

Receiving and processing the textbooks. Textbook forms are used to enable a librarian or textbook clerk to handle books more efficiently. A *distribution record card* which is used for recording the routing of the book should be made out for each textbook title. It can be alphabetized by author-and-title or by title-and-author. Each teacher's order for books for her pupils is recorded on this card at the time the order is filled. When the books are returned, a credit is indicated on the card. Losses are also shown on this card, which simplifies the preparation of the annual "Lost Textbook Report."

A **textbook inventory card** is prepared for each title. Notations are made, by date, of the number of books received, transferred to another school, lost, and disposed of.

Processing the textbooks. You will find it helpful if you follow a routine in receiving and processing incoming textbooks. The following suggestions have been devised as a checklist:

1. Count the books and check that the quantity agrees with the invoice or packing slip accompanying shipment of books.
2. Check this number with your original requisitions.
3. Date the requisition, opposite the title, to show date received.
4. Attach the invoice or packing slip to the requisition.
5. Report any shortages immediately to the purchasing office of your district or to the publishing company.
6. Use the invoice to revise (if need be) your list of prices.
7. Return imperfect books to the shipper with a note indicating the imperfection. Give the school name to insure replacement.
8. Stamp and number each book in three places: on the inside of the front cover, on the title page, and on two or three pages scattered throughout the book (or pick out a specific page, perhaps page 25, and use the same page number for stamping all the books).
9. Give each textbook a copy number. Refer to the textbook inventory card for the last copy number used, if the title is a replacement.
10. Fill out a textbook inventory card and a distribution record card if the textbook is a new title.

Shelving the textbooks. Textbooks should not be unpacked or untied unless they are ready to be processed and shelved. This prevents losing copies and confusing them with other books.

1. Shelve the titles as they appear in your textbook list (list of all the authorized textbooks used in the school).
2. Shelve the books horizontally, five with spines to the front and five reversed. This method simplifies counting when taking inventory.
3. Shelve obsolete or discontinued titles in the back of the textbook room.
4. Keep a reference shelf of all your authorized textbooks. This should always be kept up to date. Each book title should be stamped "Reference." Stamp "Reference" on the three places where the copy number would appear: inside front cover, on the title page, and on another selected page; say, page 25. Use the same page for each book.

Issuing textbooks. Many procedures are in use for the issuance of textbooks to students. You should find that procedure which suits your school best, and then work out the necessary forms for textbook accounting. The following procedure could be modified for use in any school system.

1. Two basic forms are recommended for the control of textbooks. A *teacher textbook order card,* to be used by the teacher when ordering books, and a *student textbook receipt card,* to be made out by the student when he receives a textbook. These cards are needed when making an accounting of textbooks.

2. Each teacher should order her books for the opening of school by filling out a teacher textbook order card in duplicate (teacher's copy and a textbook room copy). The same card is also used to order additional copies of the same title. The card shows the teacher's name, room number, title and author of book needed, the date of the order, the number of copies desired, the course title, and a place for recording the return date. Every teacher should use a separate teacher textbook order card for each title. The teacher should fill in the card in duplicate and send it to the textbook room clerk. The textbook room clerk should fill the order, keep one copy of the card, and return the other to the teacher along with the books. The textbook room clerk should also send along enough student textbook receipt cards to equal twice the number of books charged to the teacher.

3. The teacher should have each student fill out, in duplicate, the Student Textbook Receipt Card. Information should include the teacher's name, condition of the book, and book number.

The teacher can have a class monitor collect the cards and alphabetize them by the students' names. The cards should be carefully checked for book number, condition of book, and teacher's name before the cards are returned to textbook room. This is a teacher responsibility. She should also check to see that each pupil has signed his name, written in the teacher's name, the classroom number and date on the label that is pasted in front of the book. The teacher should retain one set of the cards and send the other set to the textbook room clerk. This should be done on the same day the books are delivered to the teacher.

When a student changes his program or checks out of school, his teacher should collect the book and in return give to the student the teacher's copy of the student textbook receipt card. This is the student's receipt to prove that he returned the book. The teacher must then return the book to the textbook clerk and receive in exchange the clerk's copy of the student textbook receipt card. No teacher should reissue the book to another pupil without having a new card made out in duplicate.

This procedure places responsibility upon the teacher to do the actual issuing and receiving of textbooks to students. This is necessary when there is only a small office staff in the school. Furthermore, the teacher is more likely to be in contact with the student than is the school secretary or textbook clerk.

The pupil who is leaving school shows his student textbook receipt card to you when presenting his withdrawal or school check-out card.

Before the last week of the school term, either you or the textbook clerk should have each teacher verify the quantity of books charged to her accounts. On the date set for return of textbooks, the teacher should collect all books from her students and give each his student textbook receipt card on file with her. The teacher should check the copy number against that shown on the student textbook receipt card. The teacher should send the textbooks to the textbook room along with her copy of the teacher's textbook order card.

Transferring of textbooks. Sometimes estimates for textbooks are miscalculated, and a shortage will occur after the semester has opened. In this case, the textbook clerk or school secretary probably can locate the needed books in other schools. This results in a "transfer of books," either on a temporary or permanent basis. You will no doubt use the telephone in locating a school willing to lend or transfer books. Give the information accurately over the phone, including the name of the receiving and lending school, the number of copies, author, and title.

Procedures should be worked out for the transfer of books, both on a lending and borrowing basis. Whether you lend or borrow on a temporary or permanent transfer, the procedures are very much the same. Suggested procedures for the transfer of textbooks include:

1. Check to see that a transfer form for both temporary and permanent transfer is received and completed for the school records.
2. Do not sign transfer forms until the books have been received. Upon receipt of the books, transfer forms should be signed and forwarded to the lending school.
3. Check to see that a sufficient number of carbon copies for the transfer form were typed by the lending school. Indicate on this form when the books are to be returned if it is a temporary loan.
4. Do not stamp or number books (borrowing school) if the loan is made on a temporary basis. The borrowing school should use the copy numbers in the book for charging purposes. Some indication should be made to the student (on the student textbook receipt cards) specifying the name of the lending school.
5. Return books on time. The return date should be recorded on the file copy of both the lending and borrowing school. Books lost or damaged should be replaced or paid for by the borrowing school.
6. Prepare the textbooks for transfer between schools. Tie the books firmly, using a slip knot, in small bundles not more than 12 inches high. Use new shipping tags for addressing to the receiving school. Tie the tag securely around the knot, in the center of the top bundle of books. The tag should clearly show the name of the receiving school and be marked "Attention: Textbook Clerk," and the name of the sending school.

Delivering textbooks to teachers and pupils. An exact record should be kept of the textbook and its itinerary. (See section on How to Issue Textbooks, pages 206 to 208.) A textbook may be in the hands of the teacher, the pupil, or on the textbook room shelf. If the textbook is lost or damaged, you will have some way of determining who is responsible.

Normally, textbooks are issued to the students through their teachers. The teacher requests a suitable number of textbooks for her classes. The textbook clerk or secretary filling this order should keep a record of this transaction. Usually the teacher or a monitor will come to pick up the books. However, in some schools the books that are to be used the next semester are left in the teacher's room. Returning all such books to the textbook room each semester would be a waste of time and energy.

Inventorying books. Books are easily lost. A strict account of all books should be maintained, and an inventory should be taken of all textbooks at least once a year. Teachers should check carefully the numbers of all books released to them. When books are returned to the textbook room, the numbers should correspond with the original list. Teachers should see that numbers are recorded when textbooks are issued to the pupils. The return of a textbook with another number should not fulfill the pupil's obligation.

An inventory of all textbooks should be taken each year during the summer months. The following procedure is suggested:

1. At least a week before the close of school, teachers should ask pupils to check their lockers for lost books. The school custodian should recheck the lockers the week following the close of school.

2. A list of lost books (by title and copy number) should be prepared before the opening of school in the fall.

3. All books in the textbook room and in the cupboards of the teacher's classroom should be counted and the quantity of each title recorded on the annual textbook inventory list.

4. The list can be arranged with the title on the left side and verti-columns across the rest of the sheet. The inventory date can be placed at the head of a column and the number of copies on hand can be written in the column opposite the proper title. The same list can be re-used year after year by the addition of new titles. Pamphlets are not usually listed on the annual textbook inventory report.

Processing lost and damaged books. In most states, the pupil who willfully damages, defaces, or loses property belonging to a school is legally liable for the cost of replacement. Therefore, most school districts hold the pupil responsible if he has lost or damaged a textbook. Moreover, some schools delay issuing a transfer or diploma until the student's textbook record is clear.

Schools differ in their policy of charging teachers for lost and damaged books. Some school systems consider textbooks issued to teachers to be consumable and in the same category as office supplies. In such cases teachers are not charged.

When the textbook clerk finds that some pupils have neglected to clear their textbook record for lost or damaged textbooks, a letter should be sent to the parents of those pupils.

Collecting fees and fines. Students who lose books are charged according to the condition of the book at issue; damage is assessed at return. A record of the condition of a book is usually kept by means of a coding system. One large school uses the following procedure:

1. Books in "A" condition (new or newly rebound) are valued at list price.
2. Books in "B" condition (used but clean) are valued at 75 per cent of list price.
3. Books in "C" condition (well worn) are valued at 50 per cent of list price.
4. A maximum charge of $1.00 is made for lost or discontinued authorized textbooks; $0.40 for supplementary books.
5. Two receipts are issued after the student has paid his fee: one to the student as record of payment for the lost book, and a duplicate as a notification to the teacher that the student has paid for the book.
6. Books lost during the semester are to be paid for before a new book is issued.

If the student states that he has lost his book, or that it has been chewed up by the dog or his baby brother, he is charged according to the school policy, is given a receipt, and the book then becomes the property of the student. The copy number of the book must be stricken from the textbook inventory card and the distribution record card.

If the student finds his book after he has paid for it, he should present his book and his receipt to the textbook clerk, who should issue him a "Request for Refund." The student would then present this form to the student body manager or student book store for refund. Sometimes a fine of 5 or 10 cents is charged for processing the recovery of a lost textbook. However, in some states, a charge of this type is illegal.

Miscellaneous points concerning textbooks:

1. Book inspections should be conducted once a semester to disclose defective books. Those books which are mutilated, imperfectly bound, or in need of rebinding should be identified for replacement.
2. Books that have been discontinued for classroom use should be declared inactive and should not be rebound.
3. Books should be rebound only once. Tie books to be rebound in bundles, turning five each way, and tag for the bindery.
4. Books are usually sent to the bindery once a year, at the close of the school year.
5. For emergency mending, use regular book mending tape, not transparent tape.
6. Books from homes under quarantine for communicable diseases should be fumigated or destroyed.
7. Pupils who do not attend school regularly or who may wish to borrow a book over the summer vacation should be required to deposit in escrow the full list price of the book.
8. Keep a reference shelf of authorized texts for ready use. It should be kept up to date. All discontinued titles should be removed once a year.
9. Keep a record of all classroom sets of books by title, copy number, and date issued to and returned by teachers. The number of copies of classroom sets, of books in a high school is usually equal to the maximum number of seats in the teacher's room. Elementary class sets, if the title is printed in several levels of reading difficulty, may be about 15 copies

of each level of reading difficulty. (*My Weekly Reader* is typical of magazines published in several editions to fit the reading abilities of the pupils.)

AUDIO-VISUAL MATERIALS

Audio-visual materials are not new; only increased emphasis on their use and increased variety of materials for teaching are new. Schools using audio-visual materials are adding another dimension to their instructional services. These materials cover a wide range of supplementary teaching aids, including books and magazines, maps and globes, wall charts, public address systems, motion pictures, transcriptions, kinescopes, film strips, 35 mm slides, screens, opaque projectors, overhead projectors, radios, television sets, teaching machines, tachistoscopes, mineral exhibits, dioramas, framed reproduction of art works, flags, mounted specimens, models, study prints, and transparencies. Although all of the above mentioned materials are in classroom use, you are likely to find that the majority of teacher requests are for films and filmstrips.

Ordering of audio-visual materials is usually done through catalogs. In large school systems, requisitions of audio-visual materials are made to the central audio-visual center of the school district. This central office furnishes each school with a complete catalog of all their available services and audio-visual materials. The catalog is kept up-to-date by supplements published each month or semester. In schools where a central office service is not available, much of the same material is available through companies who produce educational audio-visual materials.

It would be impossible to list all of the film titles and sources in a volume such as this. For a comprehensive list, check the *Educational Film Guide* and its supplements.

Determining film and equipment needed. Film and equipment for school use are usually determined by the faculty and administration. Most schools employ an audio-visual chairman or representative whose primary duty is to counsel and advise his colleagues in the selection and utilization of teaching materials. This representative is also expected to carry out the following specific duties:

1. Organize, train, and supervise the school projection crew. This crew is composed of boys and girls who are competent to assist the teacher in using audio-visual materials.
2. Order motion pictures from the audio-visual central library or from outside companies.
3. Schedule the showing of films in the classrooms.
4. Schedule motion picture projector reservations to correspond with film showings. Schedule other equipment as requested by teachers.
5. Advise and instruct teachers in selecting, ordering, and utilizing materials.
6. Assist teachers who wish to learn to operate equipment.

7. Maintain equipment and make minor repairs and adjustments as necessary.

8. Keep teachers informed of new materials which are available for their use, as well as new developments in the audio-visual field.

9. Solicit the continuing cooperation and support of the faculty audio-visual advisory committee. This is usually a group (two or three members) appointed by the principal who have shown an interest in the use of audio-visual materials and equipment, competence in using such materials, and willingness to serve.

If your school does not have an audio-visual chairman, it might be that you will be the logical person to handle some of these tasks.

You will get your information concerning film and equipment needs through the faculty, administration, and students. Students sometimes request movies and equipment for a special student assembly or club activity.

Those persons who wish a film or other kind of audio-visual material should be asked to request it periodically (once or twice a semester). The catalogs, film titles, and film sources should be kept either by the secretary or the school librarian.

A film requisition form should be distributed to the teachers so that when they have selected their film titles, they can fill in the pertinent information, such as catalog number, film title, black-and-white or color, running time, producer, and first, second, or third preferred dates for showing. By this procedure, film and audio-visual materials and equipment needs can be scheduled to avoid conflicting dates. Remember that the requisition should be approved by the principal and should be in accordance with the budget set aside for audio-visual materials and instructional services.

Processing long-range and urgent requests. Ask your principal what the policy is on long-range and urgent requests for audio-visual materials. Then see that the policy is put into and kept in practice. Most teachers plan ahead for film requests (possibly six weeks to a semester or a year in advance of proposed showing). However, there are teachers who seem to operate on an emergency basis and ask that their requests be specially expedited. You should have such urgent requests approved by the principal; however, he may delegate that responsibility to you, and it is up to you to use your own judgment. Sometimes you will be fortunate in obtaining a film on short notice; other times, it will be quite impossible. Your faculty members should be aware of the imposition on you.

Long-range requests are processed either on requisition through the central audio-visual office of the school district, or by contacting outside companies who produce and rent educational audio-visual materials. In general, use the same basic procedure as described below in renting, purchasing, or borrowing.

Renting, purchasing, or borrowing. A basic rule to remember is that no audio-visual material should be rented, purchased, or borrowed unless it is requested by a teacher, student, or school personnel for instructional purposes and has the prior approval of the principal. Requisition forms should be used. In large school systems the volume of requests is so great that the central office may employ IBM booking cards. In this case, each school will be provided with a box of film cards containing a separate card for each film title. The audio-visual chairman in each school, or you, will be in charge of this box. Then periodically, usually each month, you can pull those cards which represent the film titles requested. These cards can be placed in separate envelopes for each week of the month and then forwarded to the audio-visual center.

Unfortunately, most schools are not equipped with IBM booking cards. Most schools must deal directly with outside film agencies. You should place the order with a particular company to either rent, purchase, or borrow. It is assumed that a faculty committee or the individual teacher ordering the film has previewed and evaluated company films before showing them to their classes. If faculty members do request free films, they should understand that the good films are popular and extremely difficult to schedule, especially if ample time for the request has not been allowed. Whether you use a central audio-visual center in your school district or deal directly with outside film agencies, the procedure for renting, purchasing, or borrowing is similar.

Following up your order. After your order or requisition is received by the film agency or by the central office, a confirmation notice will be sent to you which will state one of the following:

1. The film is available and will be sent on the date you requested.
2. The film is not available on the date you requested. (They may either confirm it for you on your second or third preference dates or ask you to choose another date.)
3. The film is obsolete and has been withdrawn from circulation.

In any of the above three instances, a follow-up is needed. You should notify the teacher that the film has or has not been confirmed for a given date. Also, you should keep a record of all scheduled films by date of showing. A small tickler file can be used. The teacher's notification probably can be on a mimeographed form. You will find that teachers appreciate a second reminder when the film arrives, as they may forget the date of showing. From the tickler file of confirmed showing dates, chart a master schedule with room locations.

Announcing and recording film showings. Announce through the school bulletin the titles of the films which are confirmed for the coming week. Even though you have confirmation on a certain film, it still may not be sent because the company or the audio-visual center may be unable to keep the booking date. This is usually because some other school failed to return the film at the due date. Again, keep your teachers posted!

Teachers usually show films in their own rooms if the room can be suitably darkened. In some schools, however, classes have to be moved to the auditorium or to a special blackout room. You may need to keep a day-by-day record of rooms suitable for film showing, together with a schedule of dates, periods, and names of teachers showing films.

Delivering and receiving. When the films are delivered to the school, they should be stored at once in a central audio-visual room, the library, or the school office. The films should be returned, according to your master schedule, on time so that if other teachers in the school wish to use them they can be re-routed. Teachers should not be allowed to pass film directly to other teachers. If a teacher insists or is in the habit of taking films home, this practice should be reported to your principal so that he can deal with the situation as he chooses. It is illegal in most states for any audio-visual material or equipment to be used outside of the school unless there is school sponsorship. Insist that the teachers return the films on time! Since many films are from booking agencies and must be returned on a definite date, it penalizes the teachers and pupils at some other school when materials are overdue. Audio-visual materials should be assembled and ready to turn over to the delivery man or in the school mail on the date due.

In some high schools, teachers check out films and equipment from the department chairman. In most instances, however film are handled through you or the audio-visual representative. The teacher is responsible for return of the film.

The trend is to encourage teachers to learn to operate the projection machine and to obtain an operator's license. Some teachers, however, need a trained projectionist, usually a student. In such cases, a trained student projection crew, each with a projectionist's license, may do a very adequate job. They are usually under the supervision of a teacher.

Lending, storing, and returning audio-visual material and equipment. If you are in charge of audio-visual materials and equipment, you should catalog all materials. Teachers should be required to be prompt in returning materials and equipment to the proper place. Films are usually scheduled for a week and other audio-visual materials for two weeks or longer. Special audio-visual equipment can often be borrowed from the central office of the school district. Such loans are on a monthly, semester, or yearly basis.

When film or equipment is to be returned, you must see that it is properly packaged and mailed or shipped to the lender. Most film should not be rewound before it is returned. In most schools, teachers who fail to return their film on the due date are charged with the responsibility of returning it themselves.

Inventorying equipment. The method of equipment control in this section also applies to any other equipment in the school. Each piece of equipment should have a number. In some cases, the serial number will be sufficient. In others, it may be necessary to have each item code-numbered. In any case, the method of keeping track of equipment should not be so time consuming that it is too costly to keep accounts in minute detail. It is possible in record keeping to spend too much time in high-priced man hours in keeping track of a possible loss of a few items. On the other hand, nothing should be done which will encourage laxity on the part of the staff in taking care of equipment.

The best method of keeping track of equipment is to make two 3 × 5 file cards for each item. These cards should list the name of the item, the model, serial and/or code number, date purchased, cost, and where located. One card should be filed alphabetically and the other by room number or departments. Nothing should be moved from one room to another without office notification and approval. At this time, the room location of the item should be changed on the inventory card. These cards make an always up-to-date inventory. They are invaluable when there is a loss due to damage, fire, or theft.

Processing damaged equipment. It is a good idea to pull the card from the file when it is sent in for repair. The date and extent of the damage should be noted on the card. This also provides an easy means of determining which type of equipment is unsatisfactory, such as a record player which constantly breaks down. It also provides a ready means of determining when a piece of equipment needs to be repaired. When the equipment is returned to the school, the date should be noted and the card refiled.

Returning unused orders. Even after second notices, some teachers still forget to pick up the audio-visual materials they have ordered. If this is a common occurrence, you should keep a carbon copy of the confirmation sent to the teachers. Then you are covered. You may then return the film unused.

19

Helping in the School Cafeteria

THE SERVICES that the school secretary will be called upon to perform for the school cafeteria are never arduous. Schools today usually employ a cafeteria manager and other help to do the food preparation, handling, serving, and cleanup chores. Your services, except for the smallest of schools, will be related, at most, to ordering food supplies, checking upon deliveries, scheduling use of the cafeteria by school clubs and similar groups, typing of menus and requisitions, and cashiering during the lunch hours. Secretaries of schools which regularly employ cafeteria personnel will seldom be called upon except for emergency assistance.

ORDERS AND REQUESTS

Cafeteria purchases or orders fall into three categories: stock items which are more or less the same week in, week out; perishable items which are seasonal in nature or which cannot be preserved any length of time; and laundry, linen, and equipment.

Ordering food. Most cafeteria managers assume the responsibility for ordering food, but may bring you a food list for phoning to the vendor or market. School systems comprising several schools may have contracts with vendors who make regular deliveries of specified food items. You should maintain in your address file a list of the authorized vendors, their addresses, telephone numbers, names of the managers, the types of food supplied, and delivery dates and times. Such contracts usually are awarded annually before the opening of the fall term.

Handling telephone requests. If you are to telephone requests for deliveries, you must arrange for a fixed hour on specified days of the week when the cafeteria manager is to supply you with a list of items to be ordered. You also must have a similar understanding with the vendor or market concerning the time for placing and delivery of these orders. Between 2:00 and 3:30 P.M. are considered suitable hours.

Requests to the laundry to pick up soiled laundry and linen can be made by telephone also. It is not uncommon that aprons, uniforms, napkins, table cloths, and towels may be sent to different laundries. Be sure you know what goes where.

Requesting equipment. Equipment requests or requisitions are likely to be presented at any time. It is suggested that a schedule for requisitioning cafeteria equipment be worked out similar to that for instructional equipment and supplies. This will help to reduce the number of demands made upon your time. Requests for emergency cafeteria repair service also should be handled as are repairs to other parts of the school plant. See Chapter 13 for suggestions concerning requisitioning and purchasing.

DELIVERIES

Deliveries are generally made directly to the cafeteria. Your most important responsibility is to receive the deliveries during hours when no one is available in the cafeteria.

Arranging for deliveries. The usual plan is to have an arrangement with the vendor whereby deliveries are to be left, if, for example, at night. A school copy of the invoice or delivery slip is left with the merchandise, and a second copy, signed by the driver, is returned to the vendor. Some vendors require that the school copy of the invoice be signed the following day, either by you or the cafeteria manager.

Accepting the delivery. If you are still on duty and are accepting the delivery, you should sign the invoice or delivery slip with your full name. Initials are not adequate. Judgment must be exercised in checking upon the merchandise received. Delivery men should not be detained while a check is made of a large delivery. If shortages, overages, incorrect substitutes, or damaged goods are later discovered, a telephone call to the vendor usually is adequate. If the vendor takes exception to your report, then at future deliveries, you have no choice but to detain the delivery man.

Storing the delivered items. Perishables should be placed under refrigeration at once. Meat should be unwrapped so that air can reach all sides. Perishable food must be refrigerated at or below 50°F. Milk and dairy products also must be placed in the refrigerator.

Fresh fruits and vegetables in sacks or boxes must not be left standing on the floor, but be placed on racks or shelves. Flour, cereals, sugar, and other foodstuffs that can be damaged or contaminated by water must be stored on racks above the floor. Insecticides, detergents, chemicals, and the like are to be stored separate from food. Do not place anything on top of a refrigerator, cabinet, or kitchen range.

Incidentally, never lift heavy weights without help. If the delivery cannot be broken into parcels light enough to handle easily, let them stand. Vendors have a responsibility for making up orders so that they can be handled properly.

FOOD SERVICE IN THE CAFETERIA

The scheduling of groups for use of the cafeteria is generally a joint responsibility of the school office and the cafeteria manager. The responsibility of the school office is to determine, first, whether the group is one privileged to use the cafeteria; second, to check whether the cafeteria is willing to undertake serving the group.

Securing approval to use the cafeteria. The school principal must always give his approval for the use of the cafeteria. Schools usually differ in their procedures as to how the matter is handled. One method, less desirable, is to have the group make the initial contact with the cafeteria. The better procedure is for the initial contact to be made with you. The purpose behind the procedure is to give the office a chance, if necessary, to refuse the group. In this way, the office "protects" the cafeteria. One of the things for which the principal is paid is to keep employees and departments within the school from being overworked or exploited.

The contacting of the cafeteria, if necessary, should never be done in the presence of the applicant. Some schools establish in advance days when the cafeteria is or is not available. Most schools insist upon the use of regular days. Pupil groups usually deal directly with you. Out-of-school groups should be referred to the principal. If the cafeteria is willing to undertake the service, then the group or its representative can be told to see the cafeteria manager so that dates, menus, and price can be arranged.

Scheduling extra services. Many groups, as it frequently turns out, also wish more than just food service. They may wish special seating arrangements, decorations, entertainment, microphones, student waiters, tickets, printed programs, publicity, and a host of other services. In anticipation of such requests, many schools, particularly high schools and colleges, have a check list or questionnaire that can be completed by the applicant. It is quite probable in schools large enough to receive such requests that a teacher or administrator will be assigned to work upon the details. Then you need only to refer the applicant to the proper school representative, and the minimum number of persons guaranteed. Two days' notice usually is considered necessary when telling the cafeteria how many people are to be served.

CASH REGISTER SERVICE

If you are in an elementary school, you are more likely to be called upon to handle the money at the cash register or "cashier" in the cafeteria than if you were in a secondary school. Performing this service calls for promptness. Regard this as an opportunity to see the pupils in another light, an occasion to get to know them better.

Some schools sell lunch tickets, others collect cash. Printed, pre-numbered tickets should be used and an accurate record must be kept of the tickets sold. See pages 38, 39, 121, 122, 123, and 128 for suggestions on handling student monies.

Prices in school cafeterias. Prices in school cafeterias generally are lower than in restaurants. Many boards of education run cafeterias at cost and often take a loss so that no pupil will be deprived of noon nourishment. Surplus food also is supplied by the federal government which helps materially in holding costs to a minimum. One large school system estimates its prices on the basis of 45 per cent for food, 45 per cent for labor, and 10 per cent for other costs.

Making change. Begin your cashiering duties by counting the change on hand, by checking the amount of tape in the cash register, and by checking to see that the cash register is working properly.

Elementary pupils generally present no problem in the cafeteria line and usually have the correct change with them. Often there is a teacher assigned to cafeteria duty to help maintain order. Elementary schools, with a limited menu, frequently have but one or two standard lunches at a fixed price, and parents learn to give their children the exact sum. A method that facilitates collecting is to teach the pupil to place his money on the lunch tray so that you, the cashier, can reach it.

Standard practice when making change is to place the pupil's money on the ledge of the cash register until his change is counted out to him. This eliminates argument as to the amount given the cashier. The money is placed in the proper coin compartments before the next pupil is served. In the interest of speed, many cashiers do not count out the change to the pupil, but it is educationally sound to teach pupils to expect to have their change counted to them. Start counting the change by stating the cost of the lunch, then add pennies to round the amount to the nearest multiple of five or ten, then add nickels, dimes and quarters.

When counting the cost of individual items on a tray, train yourself to work from one side of the tray to the other. However, with experience, you will be able to tell at a glance the total cost. Most states exempt the lunches of pupils and teachers from sales tax. Sales tax, if required, is added in last.

Policy on charging meals. Most schools discourage charging meals and never permit pupils to do so. Pupils who have lost their money can usually borrow from the office. Checks should not be cashed during the serving of lunch. Names of pupils who receive their lunches through the courtesy of the P.T.A. or other agencies should be known to the cashier or she should keep a list of the names at the cash register.

Pupils' diets. One of the responsibilities of the cashier will be to see that the pupils select a balanced lunch. A lunch of all sweets or several desserts is not permissible. Tell the pupil, "You can have only one dessert.

Take the other back." A complete lunch generally includes a main dish (hot or cold), bread or muffin, butter or fortified margarine, and milk.

Many schools now have a "nutrition" service in mid-morning. Frequently this is for milk or fruit. Other schools may offer a limited breakfast service.

CAFETERIA HELPERS

Some pupils will receive lunches in payment for services performed in the cafeteria. These pupils are allowed a stipulated amount of food. Food in excess of the allowance must be paid for. Pupils who work in the cafeteria should be taught to observe the following rules:

1. As soon as you reach the cafeteria, put your books, purses, and wraps in the locker or assigned place, wash your hands, and put on your apron and hair net or cap.
2. Keep your hands and nails clean. Hair must be combed before reporting for duty. Girls should not apply make-up while on duty.
3. Avoid unnecessary conversation and loud talking while on duty.
4. Do not eat or drink while on duty.
5. Do not help yourself to food while on duty.
6. When your work is finished, put your apron and cap in the place assigned, take your belongings, and leave the cafeteria. Do not loiter with the people who are on duty.
7. If you are absent from school, telephone the cafeteria or school office before 10 o'clock. This is absolutely essential if you expect to keep your cafeteria assignment.
8. When you have a cold, do not report to work. If in school, report to the cafeteria manager so that a substitute may be appointed to fill your place temporarily.

Cafeteria records. Your cashiering duties may require preparation of a daily sales report. If the cafeteria has a cash register, the tape should be removed each day to compile the report. At the end of the lunch period, the amount in the cash drawer should equal the total shown on the tape plus the cash which was initially in the cash register. Funds must be banked daily.

Cafeteria reports usually show the income from pupil lunches, adult lunches, and income from other sources, such as the sale of candy and ice cream. The number of lunches served usually must be shown grouped according to the total lunches for pupils, for adults, and for pupils served free or at reduced rates.

Typing and posting the menu. A final, or perhaps an initial, duty may be to type up the daily menu. The cafeteria manager probably will supply this to you on a mimeographed form. Several copies of the menu should be typed and posted at the entrances to the serving line and on the cash register. Some school districts issue weekly, semi-monthly, or monthly menus. These may also be posted in each classroom.

4

The School Secretary
and Typing Services

20

Typing School Correspondence

No SECRETARY really feels she is a secretary unless she types letters. This is as true of the secretary in a school as it is of a secretary anywhere else. The only difference, if any, is that other duty demands of a school may be so numerous and pressing that you, as a secretary, may let correspondence have but a second- or third-place priority. This should not be. Correspondence should be handled promptly, daily. You may even need to badger your principal, or else he, too, may be inclined to put off his letter-writing chores.

This chapter discusses the basic instructions needed to typewrite school letters, letter forms or styles, the parts of the letter, and the preparation of inter-school memoranda.

SCHOOL LETTERS

You will generally see correspondence first—even before your principal. Unless a letter is marked "personal," you are expected to open it and familiarize yourself with the contents. If an incoming letter concerns matters on which there has been previous correspondence, you should present the correspondence file with the latest communication.

Secure basic instructions. Whether the school principal dictates or writes his letters longhand, he probably will want a "rough" draft of it for editing purposes. Schools are and should be exceedingly careful about not only the composition and tone but about the spelling, punctuation, and other matters of sentence structure. You will need to know whether you are to submit a rough draft of the letter and whether you or your principal will do the editing. Also, there are some letters that you can compose yourself (the chapter that follows describes how to write school letters).

Secure address and determine salutation and complimentary close. You will need to know to whom the letter is being addressed and the salutation to be used. In a letter of reply, the addressee's name and address are usually indicated. The signature on the sender's own letter, as well as his salutation and complimentary close, are clues to the form to be used in the school's letter of reply. In the case of other letters, the principal may not know the correct spelling of the addressee's name, his initials, title, or his exact address. You are expected to look these up. You can consult the telephone book, school directories, previous correspondence, and college catalogs. You may even make a telephone call to the addressee's own secretary to get the necessary information.

Every experienced school secretary builds her own file of addresses. Every time a letter is typed to some new person, that address should immediately be recorded in your address file.

Determine number of copies. Now that copying machines have come into common use, any failure to type the correct number of copies is not as serious a time loss as previously. A copy can be quickly duplicated. You should, however, check with your principal at the time the letter is dictated or written to determine the number of copies to be made, where they are to be filed, and the persons to receive duplicate copies. Occasionally your principal may not wish any notation to appear on the addressee's copy of the distribution being made of the letter. (See page 238 for instructions covering blind copy notations.)

Secure enclosures. It is not uncommon for reports, questionnaires, announcements, and informatory bulletins to be enclosed with school letters. You should obtain these at once and include them with both the rough and final drafts of the letter.

Set time for typewriting. All letters should be handled promptly. Most letters can and should be answered within 24 hours. At most no letter should go unanswered for more than a week, and then only upon specific instruction from your principal. Your principal should indicate at the time of first reading when he wants the letter answered. An occasional letter must be given "rush" attention. Always tell your principal in advance of any work in progress that may have to be set aside to do the "rush" typing.

If your principal is away and cannot reply to a letter, it is in order for you to write a letter stating this fact. Part of the problem in typing correspondence lies in timing. It is possible that you have not set a time each day for typing. Ask your principal to work out a calendar of daily duties with a set hour for typewriting. Usually this should be right after he has examined his correspondence and has finished dictation.

Decide upon stationery and envelopes. Most schools and school systems have determined one standard size letterhead, generally 8½ × 11 inches. Two sizes of envelopes are often used. A No. 6¾ envelope (3⅝ × 6½ inches) is used when there is only one sheet to the letter and not more than one small enclosure. A No. 10 envelope (5⅛ × 9½ inches) is used when the letter contains two or more pages or there are several enclosures which would make a bulky letter in the smaller envelope.

Various size stationery and envelopes. Some schools also have "half sheets," measuring 5½ × 8½ inches. These are "personal" letterheads for use of the principal, if he chooses, in writing letters of thanks, sympathy, appreciation, commendation, regrets, and quasi-social correspondence. This letter size, folded into thirds with creases parallel to the lines of typing, goes into a No. 6¾ envelope. It should be noted that the printing on the "executive type" letterhead may be confined to the name of the school and a second line reading "Office of the Principal" or similar identification. The address on this letterhead is placed beneath the complimentary close and the signature, and is aligned flush with the left-hand margin. The title of your principal may be omitted below his name if the word "office" is printed on the letterhead.

Reusable envelopes. Most school districts having their own mail room supply large reusable envelopes for inter-school correspondence. When using these, write on the next available line the addressee's name and school, bend the clasp prongs down or coil the string around the fiber button to hold the flap in place, and put the envelope in the school mail.

LETTER FORMS OR STYLES

There is no standard form or style for school letters. Schools use the full-block, semi-block, and personal styles in accordance with your preference or your principal's. Most principals tend to accept any style so long as it is neat.

A few school districts have adopted an "official" form; most have not. Some schools suffer from allowing several typists to use different letter styles. You should take the initiative on this point! Recommend to your principal one style and then see to it that all letters from your school conform to this style.

The National Office Management Association (NOMA) has recommended a "simplified" form, which is the full-block style, omitting the salutation, and substituting a subject or attention-catching line. Few, if any, school systems, have adopted this format. Schools tend to be conservative and traditional. They would rather err on the side of being overly conservative than being thought too modern. (For examples of the full-block, semi-block, official, and simplified styles of letters, see pages 226–229.)

PARTS OF THE LETTER

Every letter has the following structural parts: letterhead, date line, inside address, salutation, body, complimentary close, signature, and responsibility marks. In addition there may be an enclosure mark, a carbon copy or blind copy notation, a line for continuation sheets, an attention line, and a reference line.

Letterhead. Practically all school systems provide printed letterheads

Prentice-Hall, Inc.

Englewood Cliffs, N. J.

WINDSOR 7-1000
AREA CODE 201

EXECUTIVE OFFICES

July 16, 1961

Miss Sheila Jones
The Modern School for Secretaries
12 Harrington Place
Greenpoint, New York

Dear Miss Jones:

You have asked me to send you examples of letter styles being used in offices throughout the country.

This letter is an example of the full block style of letter, which has been adopted as a standard at Prentice-Hall. We have reproduced it in our Employee Manual so that everyone will be familiar with the form and the instructions for its use.

Since Prentice-Hall is a leading exponent of modern business methods, we naturally use the most efficient letter form. This style saves time and energy.

As you see, there are no indentations. Everything, including the date and the complimentary close, begins at the extreme left. This uniformity eliminates several mechanical operations in typing letters.

Our dictaphone typists always use this form unless the dictator instructs otherwise. The dictator is at liberty to alter the form if a change is desirable for business reasons.

As the dictator's name is typed in the signature, it is not considered necessary to include his initials in the identification line.

Sincerely,

Martha Scott
Correspondence Chief

cf

Figure 8. Full-Block Style of Letter. The distinguishing feature of the full-block style is that the inside address and the paragraphs are blocked without indentation, flush with the left-hand margin. The salutation and attention line, if any, are aligned with the inside address. The date and reference line are flush with the left-hand margin. The typed signature is aligned with the complimentary close, both flush to the left. Open punctuation is used.

Prentice-Hall, Inc. *Englewood Cliffs, N. J.*

WINDSOR 7-1000
AREA CODE 201

EXECUTIVE OFFICES

July 16, 1961

Miss Sheila Jones
The Modern School for Secretaries
12 Harrington Place
Greenpoint, New York

Dear Miss Jones:

    Most companies have a definite preference as to letter style. Many leading business corporations insist that all letters be typed in semi-block style. This style combines an attractive appearance with utility. Private secretaries, who are not usually concerned with mass production of correspondence, favor it. Here is a sample to add to your correspondence manual.

    This style differs from the block form in only one respect— the first line of each paragraph is indented five or ten spaces. In this example the paragraphs are indented ten spaces. As in all letters, there is a double space between paragraphs.

    The date line is flush with the right margin, two or four spaces below the letterhead. The complimentary close begins slightly to the right of the center of the page. All lines of the signature are aligned with the complimentary close. Open punctuation is used in the address.

    No identification line is used in this example. As the dictator's name is typed in the signature, his initials are not necessary. The typist's initials are shown on the carbon copy.

        Very sincerely yours,

        Martha Scott
        Correspondence Chief

Figure 9. Semi-Block Style of Letter. The distinguishing feature of the semi-block style is that all parts of the letter begin flush with the left-hand margin, but the first line of each paragraph is indented five or ten spaces. The typed signature is aligned with the complimentary close, both to the right-side of the letter. The date is typed in the conventional position. Open punctuation is used.

Prentice-Hall, Inc.

EXECUTIVE OFFICES

Englewood Cliffs, N. J.

WINDSOR 7-1000
AREA CODE 201

July 16, 1961

Dear Miss Jones:

Every correspondence manual should include a sample of the official style. It is used in many personal letters written by executives and professional men, and looks unusually well on the executive-size letterhead.

The structural parts of the letter differ from the standard arrangement only in the position of the inside address. The salutation is placed two to five spaces below the date line, depending upon the length of the letter. It establishes the left margin of the letter. The inside address is written block form, flush with the left margin, from two to five spaces <u>below</u> the final line of the signature. Open punctuation is used in the address.

The identification line, if used, should be placed two spaces below the last line of the address, and the enclosure mark two spaces below that. As the dictator's name is typed in the signature, it is not necessary for the letter to carry an indentification line. The typist's initials are on the carbon of the letter, but not on the original.

Sincerely yours,

Martha Scott
Correspondence Chief

Miss Sheila Jones
The Modern School for Secretaries
12 Harrington Place
Greenpoint, New York

Figure 10. Official Style of Letter. The distinguishing feature of the official style is that the inside address is placed below the signature, flush with the left-hand margin, instead of before the salutation. The identification line and enclosure notations, if any, are typed two spaces below the last line of the inside address. Open punctuation is used. This style is especially appropriate for personal letters related to quasi-social and courtesy matters. If available, "half sheets" (5½ by 8½ inches) should be used.

NATIONAL OFFICE MANAGEMENT ASSOCIATION
12 East Chelten Avenue
Philadelphia 44, Pa.

June 16, 1961

Mr. N. D. Edwards
Robertson-Davies Company
35 Fifth Avenue
New York 11, N. Y.

MUCH ADO ABOUT SOMETHING

Your interest in better business letters, Mr. Edwards, makes writing to you a real pleasure. Especially when you give me an opportunity to discuss NOMA's Simplified Letter.

The SL is really just a sensible way of putting a soft collar on business correspondence — a way of combining dignity with informality at a low cost in keystrokes and typewriter manipulation. Yet it incorporates the same sound principles that good letter writers, like you, have demonstrated for years.

Physically, I suppose, the dropping of the meaningless salutation and close, and the use of the left block format will first catch your attention. This letter actually looks as the typewriter was made to make it look.

But, more important, the philosophy behind the SL seeks to reduce slow starting — a long windup and a wobbly pitch. It seeks to combine sincerity and simplification without sacrificing friendliness.

Every letter becomes a challenge. Every letter echoes the sound of the writer's own thinking. As I write to you I'm acutely aware of that sound. I hope you won't think me presumptuous in trying to demonstrate the endless possibilities of this way of letter thinking.

I'd be glad to send you more detailed suggestions on the SL, and to receive your report of experience in trying them out.

Your letter was a happy reminder that letters, too, invite inquiring minds — invite much ado about something simplified.

VAUGHN FRY - PUBLIC RELATIONS

Miss Besse May Miller, Mr. W. H. Evans

Figure 11. Simplified Letter. The distinguishing feature of a Simplified Letter is that the salutation and complimentary close are omitted. "Copy to" is also omitted before the names of persons to whom carbon copies of the letter are to be sent. All structural parts of the letter are flush with the left-hand margin. The subject line is placed between the address and the body of the letter. Open punctuation is used.

for each school. Some of the large school districts do not do so for their elementary schools. In such instances the name of the school system or district is printed on the letterhead and a blank line is supplied for insertion of the school's name.

Date line. Dates should always be accurate! Date the letter the day it is dictated, not the day it is typed unless there has been a lapse of several days between the dictation and the transcription. Use figures for the day of the month and the year (July 1, 1961). Do not use the ordinal form (21st, 22nd) for the day of the month. Do not abbreviate or use figures to designate the month.

Inside address. The inside address and the address on the envelope should be the same. The address contains the name of the addressee, his position title, his school or organization, his street address, city postal zone number if available, and state. You can obtain a guide to zone numbers from the post office. Principals, of necessity, are prone to give partial addresses. You must find the complete address by looking in the telephone directory, in various school directories, or in professional periodicals. Guessing at initials and titles is inexcusable. Maintain your own file of recurring addresses by using an address book or typing 3 × 5 inch cards each time you type a letter which is likely to be followed by others to the same addressee. When it is not known whether the addressee is a man or woman, you should use the form of address appropriate to a man. If you are not sure if the woman is Miss or Mrs., the modern trend is to use the abbreviation *Ms.* It stands for both.

Name and title. The following instructions for writing the name and title of the addressee are standard:

1. If it is short, the addressee's position title may be placed on the same line with his name.
2. If the addressee holds two or more offices, use his highest title or the one that appropriately fits the subject of the letter.
3. If the letter concerns the addressee's special capacity, as "Program Chairman, School Administrators' Association," he may be so addressed.
4. The personal title of *doctor* is given to holders of earned and honorary doctor's degrees (as Ph.D., Ed.D., LL.D., D.Sc.) awarded by accredited or recognized universities and colleges.
5. A personal title (*Mr., Dr.,* or *Professor*) may precede the name; or, if not used, the abbreviation for the doctor's degree may follow the name, but not both.

Right	*Wrong*
John R. Blank, Ph.D.	Dr. John R. Blank, Ph.D.
Mr. John R. Blank	Mr. John R. Blank, Ph.D.
Dr. John R. Blank	Dr. John R. Blank, Ph.D.
Professor John R. Blank	Professor John R. Blank, Ph.D.

6. Some universities use only the personal title *Mr.* even though the person holds a doctor's degree, reserving the professional title *Dr.* for physicians and dentists.

7. Degrees below the doctorate (B.A., B.S., M.A., M.S.) are not used in combination with the personal name except in a listing of the members of a faculty or department of instruction, or regents of a university.

Right	*Wrong*
Mr. John Blank	John R. Blank, B.A., M.A.

8. A woman member of a board of education or school trustees is addressed by her own name.

Right	*Wrong*
Mrs. Mary Blank	Mrs. John R. Blank

9. A woman holder of an earned doctorate in Education (Ed.D) should be addressed: Dr. Mary Blank or Mary Blank, Ed.D. Having first accorded her personal title in the address or salutation, it is then permissible for purposes of variation in the letter to refer to her as Miss Blank, or Mrs. Blank. When the letter is informal, reference to the degree may be omitted: Mrs. Mary Blank. In any case, follow her preference, if known.

10. When addressing a husband and wife who both hold doctor's degrees, it is permissible to use the following:

   Dr. Mary A. Blank, and
   Dr. John R. Blank or The Doctors Blank

   My dear Doctors Blank:

11. When addressing a married couple in which the wife holds a doctor's degree and the husband does not, reference to the wife's degree should be omitted.

   Mr. and Mrs. John R. Blank

12. If a husband and wife are being addressed in their individual professional capacities, use separate letters and separate envelopes.

13. When addressing joint invitations to a wife and husband in which the latter is an official no distinction ordinarily is made. When the wife is the official, the distinction may be made:

Members of the Board of Education	(If a man) Mr. and Mrs. John R. Blank (If a woman) Mrs. Mary Blank and Mr. John R. Blank
Superintendent of Schools	(Formal if a man) Superintendent and Mrs. John R. Blank (Informal if a man) Mr. and Mrs. John R. Blank (Formal and informal, if a woman) Mrs. Mary Blank and Mr. John R. Blank
School Principal	(If a man) Mr. and Mrs. John R. Blank (If a woman) Mrs. Mary Blank and Mr. John C. Blank
University President	(If a man) President and Mrs. John R. Blank (If a woman) Mrs. Mary Blank and Mr. John R. Blank
University Professor	(If a man) Professor and Mrs. John R. Blank (If a woman) Professor or Mary Blank and Mr. John R. Blank (Optional) Mr. and Mrs. John R. Blank

14. The position title (as *superintendent* or *principal*) follows the name. It does not take the place of a personal title (Dr., Mr., Miss, or Mrs.), which should be used and should precede the name.

Right	Wrong
Mr. John R. Blank, Superintendent	Superintendent John R. Blank
	John R. Blank, Superintendent

15. Do not abbreviate position titles, such as *Principal* and *Superintendent*. Mr. (or *Dr.*, *Miss*, or *Mrs.*) is a personal title and precedes the individual's name, even when the position title is used. If a person's position title is short, place it on the first line; if it is long, place it on the second line.

Right	Wrong
Mr. John R. Blank, Principal	Mr. John R. Blank, Prin.
George Washington High School	Geo. Washington High School
Cleveland, Ohio	Cleveland, Ohio

The modern trend is to omit the position title, particularly if it makes the address run over four lines.

16. Hyphenate a position title that represents two or more offices.

Right	Wrong
Secretary-Treasurer	Secretary Treasurer

17. If a letter is addressed to a particular department in a company, place the name of the company on the first line and the name of the department on the second line.

18. When addressing an individual in a firm, corporation, or group, place the individual's name on the first line and the company's name on the second line.

19. Women in official or honorary positions are addressed just as men in similar positions, except that *Madam, Mrs.,* or *Miss* replaces *Sir* or *Mr.* See Figure 12 on page 235.

20. When writing to a man and a woman in their joint capacity, address them by their respective titles, placing one name under the other.

> Mrs. Jay S. Russell
> Mr. Adam L. Matthews

The same form applies when addressing two women or two men in their joint capacity.

21. When writing to a woman and a corporation in their joint capacity, place the woman's name first, follow by *and,* and place the corporation's name on the next line.

> Miss Jan Jones and
> The Bank & Trust Company
> Co-Trustees of the Jones Scholarship Fund

The same form applies when addressing a man and a corporation.

Address and city. The following instructions for writing the address of the street and city are standard, although various authorities give different rules.

1. Do not precede the street number with a word or a sign

Right	Wrong
70 Fifth Avenue	No. 70 Fifth Avenue
	#70 Fifth Avenue

2. Spell out the numerical names of streets and avenues if they are numbers of 20 or under. When figures are used, do not follow with *d*, *st*, or *th*. Use figures for all house numbers except the single numerical *one*. Separate the house number from a numerical name of a thoroughfare with a space, a hyphen, and a space.

Right	*Wrong*
123 East Twelfth Street	123 East 12th Street
123 East 21 Street	123 East twenty-first Street
	or East 21st Street
One Fifth Avenue	1 Fifth Avenue
123 - 22 Street	123 22 Street
	or 123 22nd Street

3. If a room, suite, or apartment number is part of the address, it should follow the street address. This position facilitates mail delivery. If the address is an office building instead of a street, the suite number precedes the name of the building.

Right	*Wrong*
700 Baylor Drive, Room 289	Room 289, 700 Baylor Drive
1010 First National Bank Building	First National Bank Building, Suite 1010

4. Never abbreviate the name of a city. States, territories, and possessions may be abbreviated, but the better practice is to write them out in full.
5. The postal zone number follows the city and is separated from the state by a comma.
6. If there is no street address, put the city and state on separate lines.
7. Use a post-office box number, if there is one, in preference to an address. *Never* use both.

Salutation. Letters to and from school officials use the same salutation as letters to personnel in business or government. The same rules apply. There is this exception: letters to elected government officeholders, when addressed formally, may employ the title Honorable, as "The Honorable John R. Blake, Governor." The trend in Education is away from this formality and to address the person by his personal title, as Mr. or Dr., even though he is an elected officeholder.

School trends in salutations. There also is a trend in school correspondence toward selecting a form of salutation and complimentary close on the basis of whether the letter is formal or informal, whether the addressee is a stranger or an acquaintance, or whether the addressee is a casual acquaintance or a close friend. The trend in school correspondence is to give preference to the informal salutation. There must be a correspondence between the salutation and the complimentary close. See Figure 12 on page 235. When in doubt as to whether the addressee is a man or woman, use the salutation appropriate for a man.

First names. Many principals, well known to each other, tend to use first names. You can be guided by the salutation used in the sender's letter to the principal and by the sender's form of signature. In letters originating with the principal, he should indicate to you the form he prefers. The signature must be in agreement with the salutation. A first name in the salutation calls for a first name in the signature.

Selecting and typing the salutation. The form of salutation varies with the tone of the letter and the degree of acquaintanceship between the writer and the addressee. See Figures 13–19 on pages 242 to 248 for the correct salutation to use in letters to people in official or honorary position.

1. Type the salutation two spaces below the inside address, flush with the left-hand margin. If an attention line is used, type the salutation two spaces below the attention line. Capitalize the first word, the title, and the name. Do not capitalize *dear* unless it is used as the first word of the salutation.

2. Use a colon following the salutation. A comma is used only in social letters, particularly in those written in longhand.

3. *Mr., Mrs., Ms.,* and *Dr.* are the only personal titles that are abbreviated.

4. A personal title in a salutation must be accompanied by the surname.

Right	*Wrong*
Dear Professor Blank	Dear Professor:

5. Do not use a position title in a salutation, except when the formal salutation "My dear Mr." is used.

Right	*Wrong*
Dear Mr. Blank:	Dear Superintendent Blank:
My dear Mr. Superintendent	My dear Superintendent:
Dear Mr. Blank:	Dear Mr. Secretary:

6. When the letter is addressed to an individual, make the salutation singular, for example, *Dear Sir:* If the letter is addressed to a company, make it plural; for example, *Gentlemen:* or *Dear Sirs:* The former is preferable.

7. When the letter is addressed to a school or board of education to the attention of an individual, the salutation is to the school or board of education, not to the individual.

Right	*Wrong*
Los Angeles City Schools	Los Angeles City Schools
Attention: Director of Housing	Attention: Director of Housing
450 North Grand Avenue	450 North Grand Avenue
Los Angeles 12, California	Los Angeles 12, California
Gentlemen:	Dear Sir:

8. If you are not sure whether or not the woman you are addressing is single or married, use the abbreviation Ms. It stands for both Miss and Mrs.

Right	*Wrong*
Dear Ms. Blank	Dear Miss or Mrs. Blank:

9. If the letter is addressed to a group of women, the salutation is Ladies: or Mesdames: Do not use "Dear" or "My dear" with either of these salutations.

10. The salutation to two women with the same name is *Dear Mesdames Blank:* (if married); *Dear Misses Blank:* (if unmarried); *Dear Mrs. Blank and Miss Blank:* (if one is married and the other unmarried).

11. The salutation to two women with different names is *Dear Mrs. Blank and Miss Smith.*

SALUTATIONS AND APPROPRIATE COMPLIMENTARY CLOSES

	Salutations	Complimentary Closes
Very Formal (Impersonal.)	My dear Sir: Sir: My dear Madam: Madam:	Respectfully Yours respectfully, Respectfully yours, Very respectfully yours,
Formal	Dear Sir: Dear Madam: Gentlemen: Mesdames:	Very truly yours, Yours very truly, Yours truly,
Less Formal (The trend today is to use less formal forms in school correspondence rather than the formal forms.)	Dear Mr. Blank: My dear Mr. Blank: Dear Mrs. Blank: My dear Mrs. Blank: Dear Miss Blank: My dear Miss Blank:	Sincerely, Sincerely yours, Yours sincerely, Very sincerely,
Personal (Implies personal acquaintance or previous friendly correspondence.)	Dear Mr. Blank: Dear Mrs. Blank: Dear Miss Blank:	Yours cordially, Cordially, Cordially yours, Most sincerely,

Figure 12.

Body of the letter.

1. Single space unless the letter is very short. Double space between paragraphs.

2. Always indent paragraphs when a letter is double-spaced. The address may be single-spaced, but if it is double-spaced, the indented style should be used.

3. When the block style is used, begin each line flush with the left-hand margin of the letter. When the indented, semi-block, or personal style is used, indent the first line of each paragraph five to ten spaces.

4. If a letter is more than one page, do not start a new paragraph at the bottom of a page unless there is space for at least two lines. Avoid ending a paragraph at the end of a page. Also, do not carry fewer than two lines of the paragraph over to the next page.

5. When the day precedes the month, it is permissible to write the day out. For example, *fifth* of March. If the day follows the month, use the figure without the ordinal abbreviation; i.e., *March 27.* It is advisable to use the day (as *Wednesday*) with the date.

6. Indent enumerated material five spaces from each margin of the letter—more, if necessary to center the material. Precede each item with a number, followed by a period. Or the number may be enclosed in parentheses. Begin each line of the indented material two spaces to the right of the number. Carry over lines are flush with the first line of the item. Single space the material within each item, but double space between items.

Letter Punctuation. An examination of school letters reveals a decided preference for the "open" form of punctuation. This means that (1) a period is omitted at the end of the date line, (2) commas are omitted at the end of each line of the address, (3) a colon is used after the salutation, (4) a comma is used after the complimentary close, (5) the comma is omitted after the sender's name, and (6) a period is omitted after the sender's title. The "open" form does not necessarily have any reference to punctuation of sentences within the body of the letter. The usual rules of punctuation apply, even to the comma before the "and" in a series.

Complimentary close. The form of the complimentary close varies with the tone of the letter and the degree of familiarity between the writer and the addressee. The degree of formality of the complimentary close should correspond with the salutation. "Yours truly" is relatively formal. "Sincerely," or any variation, as "Sincerely yours," while less formal, is becoming increasingly popular. The use of "Cordially" and its variations, also "Most sincerely," are considered informal or personal, implying personal acquaintance or previous correspondence.

A safe procedure when replying to a letter is to use the same salutation and complimentary close as the sender used in his letter. However, if you have chosen a standard style, it should be used most of the time. Blind imitation of other's letter formats and styles shows very little imagination. Punctuate the complimentary close as follows:

1. Capitalize only the first word of the complimentary close.
2. Follow the complimentary close with a comma.

Signature. School correspondence is usually signed by the writer, followed by his position title, usually on a separate line. Some boards of education or school superintendents require that the name and title of the superintendent first be typed in, followed by the name, title, and signature of the actual writer. Ordinarily the typed name and title of the writer can be omitted if they appear on the letterhead.

The inclusion in the signature of the writer's title or position indicates that he is writing the letter in his official capacity. However, if your principal writes a letter on school stationery about a purely personal matter, his position is not included in the signature.

Instructions for typing the signature. The following instructions should be observed:

1. When the school name is included in the signature, type it two spaces below the complimentary close, your principal's name four spaces below the school name, and his position either in the same line or on the next line. When the school name is not included, type your principal's name and position four spaces below the complimentary close.

2. When the inside address is typed in block form, align the signature with the first letter of the complimentary close. When the indented form is used in the inside address, align the signature with the third or fourth letters of the complimentary close. No line of the signature should extend beyond the *right-hand* margin of the letter.

3. Type the signature exactly as your principal signs his name. Initials with the surname are now considered inappropriate. The first name is spelled out. In accordance with your principal's preference, his middle initial or name should be used.

4. The title *Miss* or *Mrs.* enclosed in parentheses may precede the typed name of a woman to indicate her marital status, in which case no personal title need precede the written signature.

5. It is not customary for a Doctor of Education or Philosophy to follow his signature with the initials Ed.D. or Ph.D. This practice is permissible in the case of educators and psychologists engaged in private business or clinical practice in which the degree has a professional connotation. When you sign your principal's name to a letter, you should place your initials immediately below your principal's surname.

6. When your principal's name *is* printed on the letterhead and you sign a letter in your own name as secretary to the principal, do not include the principal's initials unless there is another person in the school who has the same name. Always precede your principal's name by a personal title as (Dr., Mr., Mrs., or Miss).

Right	*Wrong*
Elizabeth Smith	Elizabeth Smith
Secretary to Mrs. Blank	Secretary to Mrs. J. R. Blank
(or)	
Secretary to the Principal	

7. When your principal's name *is not* printed on the letterhead and you sign a letter in your own name as secretary to the principal, your principal's name and position should be indicated.

Right	*Wrong*
Elizabeth Smith	Elizabeth Smith
Secretary to Mrs. Blank, Principal	Secretary to Mrs. Blank

8. When you are authorized to sign your own name as school secretary, there is no need to indicate your principal's name or position.

Right	*Wrong*
Elizabeth Smith	Elizabeth Smith
School Secretary	School Secretary
	Mrs. J. R. Blank,
	Principal

Responsibility marks or identifying initials. The responsibility marks, also known as the "identification line," show who dictated the letter and who typed it. These marks are only for reference use by the school. Because the dictator is usually the person who signs it, there is no need to repeat his initials in the identification line. Unless school rules require otherwise, the recent trend is that only your initials should be typed, preferably in lower case. These should be flush with the left-hand margin. When the person who signs the letter has not dictated it, the dictator's initials should be included and typed first, and followed by a colon and your initials.

Enclosure mark. When a letter contains enclosures, type the word *Enclosure* or the abbreviation *Enc.* flush with the left-hand margin one or two spaces beneath the identification line. If there is more than one enclosure, indicate the number (Enc. 3). If the enclosures are of special importance, identify them (Enc. special prints with technical illustrations). If any enclosure is to be returned, make a notation to that effect (Enc. transcript—please return).

Carbon copy notation. When a carbon copy is to be sent to another person, type the distribution notation flush with the left-hand margin, below all other notations. If space permits, separate it from the other notations by two spaces.

> sre:ng
> Enclosure
> Copy to Mr. S. A. Williams

The abbreviation *c.c.* may be used instead of "Copy to." No colon is necessary.

Blind copy notation. Type the blind copy notation in the upper left-hand portion of the letter on the carbons only. This indicates that the addressee of the letter does not know that a copy was sent to anyone else.

Continuation sheets. When a letter is more than one page in length, all pages except the first should be written on paper without a letterhead. Some schools, however, print the name and address in small type at the top center of the continuation sheet, or near the top left-hand margin.

Continuation sheets should be of the same size and quality as the letterhead. Order them when ordering the letterhead. Comparatively few letters run more than one page; the percentage varies with the school and office.

If no printed heading is used, the heading of the second page should contain the name of the addressee, the number of the page, and the date. Leave space between the heading and the body of the letter.

> Mr. R. H. Smith   -2-   September 12, 1962

If possible, let the last line on the sheet be a fragment of a sentence, thereby forcing the reader's attention to the next sheet.

Attention line. Strictly speaking, school letters should be addressed to a school or business, not to a person. A second, or attention, line directs the letter to the attention of a school official or department. This practice marks the letter as a business matter rather than a personal letter and insures that it will be opened in the absence of the individual to whom it is addressed. An attention line should be used when it is more important that the letter be acted upon than that it be received by a specific person.

Type the attention line two spaces below the address. The word *of* (attention *of*) is not necessary. The attention line has no punctuation and is not underscored (Attention John Blank). When a letter addressed to a school or firm has an attention line, the salutation is *Gentlemen*. It is permissible to direct the letter to the attention of an individual without including his given name or initials, if they are unknown.

Reference line. If a file reference is given on an incoming letter, repeat this reference line in your reply, whether requested or not. Place your own reference, if any, beneath the incoming reference.

When letterheads include a printed reference notation, such as *In reply please refer to,* type the reference line after it. If the letter also has a subject line, type the reference line to the right side of the letter, about four lines beneath the date.

NEW DEVELOPMENTS IN BUSINESS CORRESPONDENCE

A study conducted recently by John L. Rowe, University of North Dakota, Grand Forks, was concerned with determining current typewriting styling practices in business correspondence. After an analysis of some 10,000 business letters from all over the United States from both large and small companies, the following developments were apparent.

1. *Abbreviations:* Abbreviation is becoming obsolete. Apparently the only satisfactory abbreviations are: a.m., p.m., Mrs., Mr., and C.O.D.

2. *Address:* The name of the state is also spelled out rather than abbreviated (California for Calif.). Generally, you would not see a name in the address typed as Mr. K. P. Blank. The first name is usually spelled out and the middle name indicated by an initial. The trend toward the elimination of abbreviations seems to indicate an era of formalism in letter writing.

3. *Paragraph indentions:* The trend toward uniform indention of five spaces is going out. Rather, today the development is toward indenting each paragraph to the colon in the salutation. Also, another form of paragraph indention is to begin the paragraph at the same place as the date, especially when the date is centered.

4. *Salutation:* The Dear Sir or Dear Madam form of salutation is being replaced by more direct salutation, such as Dear Mr. Blank or Dear Mrs. Blank. Apparently the reason behind the direct salutation is to establish immediate contact.

5. *Complimentary close:* The trend in the complimentary close, as in the abbreviations, seems to be more formalized. "Sincerely yours" is gen-

erally the most common form of complimentary close that is used rather than "Sincerely," "Yours truly," and other less formal styles.

6. *Body of the letter:* The trend today in business letters is to say what you have to say in as few words as possible. Over 50 per cent of the letters contained 75 words or less. Now letters open with a direct message and eliminate wornout statements such as: "we have your request," "we received your letter of." Also, letters today contain a greater percentage of numbers. This is generally accounted for by increased mechanization and centralization of business activities.

7. *Dictator's initials:* Generally, the typed name of the dictator eliminates the need for the dictator's initials. Another trend is toward the elimination of the dictator's initials from the identification line. Rather, the transcriber indicates her initials only.

8. *Stationery:* The trend is toward using one uniform length of paper for short, medium and long letters because odd sizes tend to become lost in the files. Colored stationery is becoming obsolete in business letters today, although it is used occasionally for duplicated material enclosed with the letter.

9. *Type:* Colored type is gradually disappearing. Today, black type is preferred in most business letters.

10. *Letter styles:* Over 55 per cent of the letters studied showed the popularity of the semi-block style. Along with this, the trend toward blocking the address and indenting the complimentary close was also seen.

INTER-SCHOOL MEMORANDA

There is a trend toward the use of inter-school memoranda for correspondence between schools and offices within a school district. It should not be used in correspondence addressed to people outside the school or school district. Essentially, it is a speed form of letter.

The headings of a memorandum list the school or department's name, centered, and typed in capitals, flush left, on separate lines.

DATE:

TO:

FROM:

SUBJECT:

"To" line. This line lists the name of the person being addressed. The title (as Chairman, English Department) can be used. When several persons are to receive the same memorandum the names of each person can be listed on a separate line. Each addressee's name can be checked off on his memorandum. It is a courtesy to include Dr., Mr., Mrs., or Miss with the full name. Surnames without the first name are not considered acceptable form.

Sometimes the names are listed and numbered in order of circulation. The notation can be inserted: "Please initial, date, and pass to next person." If the sender wants the memo returned, he can list his own name as the last recipient.

"Via" line. This line indicates that the memorandum should be seen by an intermediary person before it reaches the addressee. Few schools use a *via* line. Its use might well be considered as a means of keeping correspondence in proper channels and all interested parties informed. The person named on the *via* line should initial the memo beside his name before forwarding it to the addressee.

"From" line. This line lists both the last and first name of the sender. It usually does *not* include Dr., Mr., Mrs., or Miss as a personal title, although the position title of the sender may follow his name. The sender should always initial his name in lieu of a signature. A typed "From" line name is not adequate evidence that the sender has approved transmittal of the memorandum.

"Subject" line. The subject is stated briefly, usually in topic form. Key words, such as would be used in filing, are placed first, followed by common or explanatory words. (*For example: Physical education, girls'.*) A memorandum of reply usually repeats the subject as given on the incoming memo.

Paragraph numbers. The paragraphs can be numbered 1-2-3 for easy reference. The content should be written as tersely as possible.

Figure 13

Letters Addressed to State and Local Government Officials

Personage	Envelope and inside Address	Formal Salutation	Informal Salutation	Formal Close	Informal Close	1. Spoken Address 2. Informal Introduction or Reference
Governor of State	*Formal* The Honorable the Governor of California Sacramento 14, California *Informal* The Honorable John R. Blank Governor of California Sacramento 14, California	Sir:	My dear Governor:	Respectfully yours,	Sincerely yours,	1. Governor Blank (or) Governor 2. Governor Blank (or) The Governor (*Outside his own state:* The Governor of California)
Lieutenant Governor	The Honorable John R. Blank Lieutenant Governor of California Sacramento 14, California	Sir:	My dear Governor Blank:	Respectfully yours, (*or*) Very truly yours,	Sincerely yours,	1. Governor Blank 2. The Lieutenant Governor of California Governor Blank (The Lieutenant Governor or Governor Blank)
Secretary of State	The Honorable John R. Blank Secretary of State of California Sacramento 14, California	Sir:	My dear Mr. Secretary:	Very truly yours,	Sincerely yours,	1, 2. Mr. Blank
Attorney General	The Honorable John R. Blank Attorney General of New York Albany, New York	Sir:	My dear Mr. Attorney General:	Very truly yours,	Sincerely yours,	1, 2. Mr. Blank
State Representative or Assemblyman	The Honorable John R. Blank House of Representatives Nashville, Tennessee	Sir:	My dear Mr. Blank:	Very truly yours,	Sincerely yours,	1. Mr. Blank 2. Mr. Blank (or) Representative Blank
Mayor of a City	The Honorable John R. Blank Mayor of Memphis	Sir:	My dear Mayor Blank	Very truly yours,	Sincerely yours,	1. Mayor Blank (or) Mr. Mayor 2. Mayor Blank

Figure 14

LETTERS ADDRESSED TO UNIVERSITY OFFICIALS AND PROFESSORS

Personage	Envelope and inside Address	Formal Salutation	Informal Salutation	Formal Close	Informal Close	1. Spoken Address 2. Informal Introduction or Reference
President of a University	John R. Blank, LL.D., Ph.D. (*Use only highest degree unless degrees are in different fields*) (*or*) **Dr. John R. Blank** President, Lake Forest College Lake Forest, Illinois (*or*) President John R. Blank Lake Forest College (*if no doctor's degree*)	Sir:	Dear Sir: (*or*) Dear President Blank:	Very truly yours,	Sincerely yours,	1. President Blank 2. Dr. Blank
Catholic President of a University	The Very Reverend John R. Blank, S.J., D.D., Ph.D. President, Fordham University New York 10, New York	Sir:	My dear Father Blank:	Very truly yours,	Sincerely yours,	1, 2. Father Blank
University Chancellor	Dr. John R. Blank Chancellor, University of Alabama University of Alabama	Sir:	Dear Sir: (*or*) Dear Chancellor Blank: My dear Dr. Blank:	Very truly yours,	Sincerely yours,	1. Dr. Blank 2. (*formal*) The Chancellor, Dr. John R. Blank
College Professor	John R. Blank, Ph.D. (*or*) Professor John R. Blank (*if no doctor's degree*) Department of Sociology University of Tennessee Knoxville, Tennessee	Dear Sir: (*or*) My dear Sir:	Dear Dr. Blank: (*or*) Dear Professor Blank:	Very truly yours,	Sincerely yours,	1, 2. Dr. Blank (*or*) Professor Blank 1, 2. Mr. Blank (*or*) Professor Blank

Figure 15

Letters Addressed to University Officials and Professors (Continued)

Personage	Envelope and inside Address	Formal Salutation	Informal Salutation	Formal Close	Informal Close	1. Spoken Address / 2. Informal Introduction or Reference
Dean, College or University	Dr. John R. Blank / Dean (Assistant Dean), / School of Commerce, / University of Mississippi / Oxford, Mississippi / (or) / Dean John R. Blank / (if no doctor's degree) / School of Commerce / (or) / Miss Mary Blank / (if no doctor's degree) / Dean of Women	My dear Sir: / (or) / My dear / Dean Blank: My dear / Miss Blank:	Dear Sir: / (or) / Dear Dean Blank: / (or) / Dear Dr. Blank: Dear Dean Blank: / (or) / Dear Miss Blank:	Very truly yours, Very truly yours,	Sincerely yours, Sincerely yours,	1. Dean Blank / 2. Dear Blank / (or) / Dr. Blank, the Dean / (Assistant Dean) of the / School of Commerce 1. Dean Blank / 2. Miss Blank
College Lecturer or Instructor	John R. Blank Ph.D. / (or) / Mr. John R. Blank / (if no doctor's degree) / Lecturer / Department of Education / University of Washington / Seattle, Washington	My dear Sir: My dear Sir:	Dear Sir: / (or) / Dear Dr. Blank: Dear Sir: / (or) / Dear Mr. Blank:	Very truly yours, Very truly yours,	Sincerely yours, Sincerely yours,	1. Dr. Blank / 2. Mr. Blank 1, 2. Mr. Blank

Figure 16

Letters Addressed to Elementary and Secondary School Officials and Administrators

Personage	Envelope and Inside Address	Formal Salutation	Informal Salutation	Formal Close	Informal Close	1. Spoken Address 2. Informal Introduction or Reference
State Superintendent of Public Instruction	John R. Blank, LL.D. (or) Dr. John R. Blank Superintendent of Public Instruction State of California Sacramento 14, California	Sir: (or) Dear Sir:	Dear Dr. Blank: (or) My Dear Dr. Blank: (or) My dear Mr. Superintendent:	Respectfully yours,	Sincerely yours,	1. Mr. Superintendent 2. Dr. Blank
County Superintendent of Schools	Dr. John R. Blank (or) Mr. John R. Blank (if no doctor's degree) Superintendent of Schools County of Los Angeles Los Angeles 12, California	Sir: (or) Dear Sir:	Dear Dr. Blank: (or) Dear Mr. Blank:	Very truly yours,	Sincerely yours,	1. Mr. Superintendent 2. Dr. Blank (or) Mr. Blank
City Superintendent of Schools (public schools)	Dr. John R. Blank (or) Mr. John R. Blank (if no doctor's degree) Superintendent of Schools City of Los Angeles Los Angeles 12, California	Sir: (or) Dear Sir:	Dear Dr. Blank: (or) Dear Mr. Blank:	Very truly yours,	Sincerely yours,	1. Mr. Superintendent 2. Dr. Blank (or) Mr. Blank
City Superintendent of Schools (Catholic schools)	The Reverend John R. Blank, S.J., Ph.D. (or) The Reverend John R. Blank (if no doctor's degree) Superintendent of Schools Archdiocese of San Francisco San Francisco, California	Sir: Sir:	Dear Father Blank: (or) My dear Father Blank: Dear Father Blank: My dear Father Blank:	Very truly yours, Very truly yours,	Sincerely yours, Sincerely yours,	1, 2. Father Blank

Figure 17

LETTERS ADDRESSED TO ELEMENTARY AND SECONDARY SCHOOL AND JUNIOR COLLEGE OFFICIALS AND ADMINISTRATORS

Personage	Envelope and Inside Address	Formal Salutation	Informal Salutation	Formal Close	Informal Close	1. Spoken Address / 2. Informal Introduction or Reference
President (Director) of a Junior College	John R. Blank, Ed.D. (or) Dr. John R. Blank (or) Mr. John R. Blank (if no doctor's degree) President (Director) Junior College of Connecticut Bridgeport, Connecticut	My Sir: (or) My dear Sir:	Dear Dr. Blank: (or) Dear President Blank: (or) Dear Director Blank:	Very truly yours,	Sincerely yours,	1. Dr. Blank or President (Director) Blank 2. Dr. Blank (or) Mr. Blank, the President (Director) of the Junior College
Dean (Assistant Dean) of a Junior College	Dr. John R. Blank (or) Mr. John R. Blank (if no doctor's degree) Dean (Assistant Dean) Junior College, Texas	My dear Sir: (or) My dear Dean Blank,	Dear Dr. Blank: (or) Dear Dean Blank:	Very truly yours, / Very truly yours,	Sincerely yours, / Sincerely yours,	1. Dean Blank 2. Dean Blank (or) Dr. (Mr.) Blank, the Dean (Assistant Dean) of the Junior College
Instructor, Junior College	John R. Blank, Ph.D. (or) Mr. John R. Blank, Instructor, Chemistry Dept. Sands Junior College Tucks, Florida	My dear Sir: (or) My dear Dr. (Mr.) Blank:	Dear Dr. Blank (or) Dear Mr. Blank:	Very truly yours,	Sincerely yours,	1, 2. Dr. Blank / 1, 2. Mr. Blank
School Supervisor	John R. Blank, Ed.D. (or) Mr. John R. Blank (if no doctor's degree) Supervisor of Social Studies Los Angeles City Schools Los Angeles 12, California	My dear Sir: (or) My dear Dr. Blank: (or) My dear Mr. Blank:	Dear Dr. Blank (or) Dear Mr. Blank:	Very truly yours, / Very truly yours,	Sincerely yours, / Sincerely yours,	1, 2. Dr. Blank / 1, 2. Mr. Blank

Figure 18

Letters Addressed to Elementary and Secondary School Teachers and Administrators

Personage	Envelope and inside Address	Formal Salutation	Informal Salutation	Formal Close	Informal Close	1. Spoken Address 2. Informal Introduction or Reference.
School Principal (High School or Elementary School)	Mary Blank, Ph.D. (or). Dr. Mary Blank (or) Miss Mary Blank (if no doctor's degree) Principal, Washington High School Shreveport, Louisiana	Madam: (or) My dear Madam:	Dear Dr. (Miss) Blank: Dear Miss Blank:	Very truly yours, Very truly yours,	Sincerely yours, Sincerely yours,	1, 2. Dr. (Miss) Blank 1, 2. Miss Blank
School Vice-Principal, Assistant Principal (or) Dean	Mr. John R. Blank (if no doctor's degree) Vice-Principal High School Cleveland, Ohio	My dear Sir:	Dear Sir: (or) Dear Mr. Blank:	Very truly yours,	Sincerely yours,	1, 2. Mr. Blank
Teacher, High School or Elementary School	Miss Mary Blank, Teacher Elementary School Lincoln, Nebraska	My dear Madam:	Dear Madam: (or) Dear Miss Blank:	Very truly yours,	Sincerely yours,	1, 2. Miss Blank
Single woman holding a doctor's degree	*(Formal)* Mary Blank, Ph.D. *(Informal)* Miss Mary Blank	My dear Madam:	Dear Dr. Blank: (or) Dear Miss Blank:	Very truly yours, Very truly yours,	Sincerely yours, Sincerely yours,	1. Dr. Blank 2. Miss Blank
Married woman holding a doctor's degree	*(Formal)* Mary Blank, Ph.D. *(Informal)* Mrs. Mary Blank	My dear Madam:	Dear Dr. Blank: (or) Dear Mrs. Blank:	Very truly yours, Very truly yours,	Sincerely yours, Sincerely yours,	1. Dr. Blank 2. Mrs. Blank
Husband and wife both holding doctor's degrees	*(Formal)* The Drs. John R. Blank *(Informal)* Mr. and Mrs. John R. Blank	Dear Sir and Madam:	Dear Drs. Blank: (or) Dear Mr. and Mrs. Blank:	Very truly yours,	Sincerely yours,	1. The Drs. Blank 2. Mr. and Mrs. Blank

Figure 19

Letters Addressed to Elementary and Secondary School Officials and Administrators (Continued)

Personage	Envelope and Inside Address	Formal Salutation	Informal Salutation	Formal Close	Informal Close	1. Spoken Address 2. Informal Introduction or Reference
Husband without doctor's degree and wife with doctor's degree	Mr. and Mrs. John R. Blank	Dear Sir and Madam:	Dear Mr. and Mrs. Blank:	Very truly yours,	Sincerely yours,	1, 2. Mr. and Mrs. Blank
President, Board of Education	Mr. John R. Blank, President, Board of Education, City of New York, 110 Livingstone Street, Brooklyn 1, New York	Sir: (or) Dear Sir:	Dear Mr. Blank: (or) My dear Mr. Blank:	Respectfully yours,	Sincerely yours,	1. Mr. President (or) President Blank 2. Mr. Blank president of the Board of Education
President, Board of School Trustees	Mr. John R. Blank, President, Board of School Trustees, Montezuma School District, Tuolumne County, Sonora, California	Sir: (or) Dear Sir:	Dear Mr. Blank: (or) My dear Mr. Blank:	Respectfully yours,	Sincerely yours,	1. Mr. President (or) President Blank 2. Mr. Blank, president of the Board of School Trustees
Member, Board of Education	Mrs. Mary Blank, Member, Board of Education, City of New York, 110 Livingstone Street, Brooklyn, New York	Madam: (or) Dear Madam:	Dear Mrs. Blank: (or) My dear Mrs. Blank:	Very truly yours,	Sincerely yours,	1. Mrs. Blank 2. Mrs. Blank, member of the Board of Education
Member, Board of School Trustees	Mrs. Mary Blank, Member, Board of School Trustees, Montezuma School District, Tuolumne County, Sonora, California	Madam: (or) Dear Madam:	Dear Mrs. Blank: (or) My dear Mrs. Blank:	Very truly yours,	Sincerely yours,	1. Mrs. Blank 2. Mrs. Blank, member of the Board of School Trustees

21

Writing the School Letter

A LETTER from a school or school principal, to all but the initiated, can appear an awesome thing. It usually is not; but people often feel that way. Psychologists would say that the recipient opening a letter from a school or principal may, for the moment before he reads the contents, feel like a fearful child called to the teacher's desk not knowing the reason why. The reader often reacts to school letters as he does to unopened telegrams.

Recipients of school letters. School letters are written to parents, teachers, non-teaching employees, to professors, other schools, professional organizations, law enforcement officers, to social agencies, merchants, and to building contractors.

Purpose of school letters. School letters are written to accomplish some definite purpose. They may concern a variety of school matters, from a protest over the eligibility of an athlete to the appointment of faculty advisers for school activities, a request for a scholarship for a worthy student, the retirement of a teacher, the appointment of a school nurse, the purchase of school supplies, or a question of research. When the writer knows what action he wants the reader to take or the information he wants him to understand, half the task of letter writing is completed. School letters usually give or request information, or request or specify action. They also praise and commend.

You may think that you shouldn't be concerned with composing school letters. That's supposed to be the principal's job. Yes, but! First of all, there are the routine letters which he will expect you to handle. All secretaries do. Then there are those letters you can answer as well as your principal. In fact it's highly doubtful if he's had as much training in handling letters as you. (Of course you will never tell him so.) These are the letters you can start learning to compose. They'll cover such topics as the opening and closing of school, policies regarding contests and the use of school premises, confirmation of meeting dates and speaking engagements, letters of thanks and appreciation. Many of these letters become form or guide letters. A school will be able to use them over and over with minor changes here and there. There's a danger, though, in the repeated use of a letter. It may undo the intended goodwill if it is received or read more than once by the same person.

In time your principal may learn to lean heavily upon you and your judgment and stock of school knowledge. It is inevitable that you should share in the appraisal and composition of school letters.

THE PARTS OF A SCHOOL LETTER

The opening paragraph, the body of the letter, and the closing paragraph are the custom-made parts of a letter. These, plus a plan for checking the quality of the letter, demand the attention of the secretary and principal. Usually the salutation and complimentary close of a letter give the writer little concern. (Figure 12, page 235, and Figures 13–19, pages 242 to 248.)

The beginning paragraph. The opening paragraph of a school letter is like removing one's hat and coat. It indicates the identity of the writer. It is the reader's opportunity to have an indirect look at the school or the principal. From it the reader forms his initial and perhaps lasting impression of the writer and the school. The effect you should create in a letter is that the school and faculty are considerate, friendly, and attentive, but also firm, direct, and impartial. The tone of a letter is set in the beginning paragraph.

In the first paragraph the writer tells the reader why he is writing, what his purpose is, what he wants to know, or what he wants the reader to do. When the writer has clearly in mind the subject and purpose of his letter, the question of how to begin almost answers itself. Go straight to your point. Don't waste words. Don't try to "soften up" the addressee.

If a natural, easy beginning is still not forthcoming, the writer might try one of these beginnings: Ask a question, make a request, or state a fact.

QUESTION: "Does your school system have annual or semi-annual promotions?"

REQUEST: "Would you help us to obtain some information about annual and semi-annual promotions."

STATEMENT: "The schools of this city are considering the advantages and disadvantages of annual and semi-annual promotions."

It is always wise to avoid if possible the "I" approach. The use of "I" may cause the reader to feel that the writer is thinking of himself only or from only his point of view. Usually "this school," "our faculty," "the students," and similar third-person expressions can be used in place of the first person, "I."

The body of the letter. Imagine yourself talking directly to the reader. In a letter, that's exactly what you do: speak directly to the reader. In addition, you must come to the point swiftly. In the opening paragraph you have already made clear to the reader what his role or relationship is with reference to the purpose of your letter. In the body of your letter you support your purpose with information or explanation. These supporting facts must be arranged in some purposeful order.

Arrange supporting facts. If you are giving information about a meeting or speaking engagement, you could do no better than to check whether the body of your letter has answered the questions who?, what?, where?, why?, and how? Perhaps you recognize these as the newspaperman's ready-reference check list.

If your purpose is to request a service or to give an explanation, you'd be wise first to jot down your reasons, arguments, or points. Then number these in some logical fashion, according to their importance or strength. Remember, importance depends not upon how you feel about it, but how the reader feels; upon what he values most highly, not upon what concerns you most.

Start with strong points. When writing, start with your strong points, saving a good clincher for the end. Four or five points should be maximum. If you can't command action with them, it's doubtful if five hundred more could do better.

Check for repetition. Re-read the body of your letter. Is each point really a separate point, or are they the same point re-stated in another form? Repetitiousness is a major weakness in the letters of educators. Teachers are so skilled in the art of repeating themselves for the benefit of their pupils that they tend to do the same thing in their letters.

Set stage appropriately for type of news. When you have good news to convey, you can use a terse, newspaper headline style. If your information is not too pleasant, you probably should be more discursive. You can set the stage, give the events or incidents leading up to the present situation, or you can state the school's concern or position; then you can come to the action or stand you are taking. It's also wise to let such a letter cool for awhile; then try it for fit. Let some colleague read it for his reaction. Watch how he reads. Does he recoil? Does he nod his head in agreement? Rewrite the letter until it has the right tone. Tone is especially important when negative information must be given. Be alert to avoid unnecessary bluntness or officiousness.

Check for logical presentation. The main thing in composing a letter is to get your points down on paper first. While we have argued for a logical, orderly form of presentation, most people do not think or write this way. For them it is best to let their ideas, feelings, and purposes tumble out onto scratch paper any way they will.

These facts, impressions, and reactions become your raw writing material. Having said what you want to say *without* regard to arrangement, order, sentence form, spelling, capitalization, or paragraph organization, you can go over your heap of paper and ideas and sort them out for purpose, fact, and point. Read them over to see if you really have made your point.

Re-think purpose of letter. Now stop and see if you can write for yourself in one sentence what the purpose of your letter really is. If you can, you're ready to start writing your letter. You'll have no trouble in getting to the point of your letter and stating your facts in a sensible, convincing order. Only after you have said what you need to say and have captured the right tone are you ready to edit your spelling, punctuation, and capitalization. Those "mechanics of English" are the last to be smoothed out.

The closing paragraph. The best ending is simply to stop when you have written what you want to say. A complimentary close, the principal's signature, typed name and title complete the letter. Florid or superfluous closings are no longer in vogue. One no longer says, "I beg to remain" or similar statement.

A letter can also be ended by summing up in a sentence the main idea of the letter or by making a suggestion or courteous request for action. *Summation:* "I can recommend Mr. Blank to you without qualification." *Request:* "Will you please have your secretary telephone my office not later than February 15 to say if we may have the pleasure of your presence." "I would welcome an opportunity to discuss this matter in person with you."

Checking the rough and final drafts. Every letter, except those so routine that the first draft can be the final draft, needs to be checked for tone, pedagese, and preciseness.

Re-read letter for tone produced. Read your letter for tone. Is it earnest? Is it pleasant, even buoyant? Is it dull and tedious? Is it dignified and forceful? Is the letter a pedagogue talking down to his class? Is the letter an introvert afraid to open his mouth and speak up? Read your letter out loud. Hearing the words is different from seeing them. How would you react if you were to receive your letter in the mail? Is the tone argumentative or contentious? If so, wring out the emotional content. Does the letter lay down the law? If so, smooth it with the soft glove instead of the harsh club.

Re-read letter for possible effect to be produced. The ultimate test of any letter is the action it causes or the effect it produces. Every letter should reach the reader's "soft" spot. People respond to those who respond to them, who are interested in the things that interest them: the children they love, the ideas they cherish, their picture of themselves, their success. They're sensitive, too, about what they know or don't know, what they've done or haven't done, what they've achieved or haven't achieved. There's no need to puncture the skin.

Check letter for "pedagese." "Pedagese" is slang for words and expressions over-used by school people and which frequently have meaning only to them. Among over-used pedagese expressions you will find these: frame of reference, child-centered school, environmentalism, stereotype, prestige symbol, value judgment, guilt-feelings, experience curriculum, group acceptance, group dynamics, test validity, and a host of others. If you must use these or other jargon of the professional educator, be sure your reader can infer their meaning from a reading of your letter.

Check letter for preciseness. Preciseness in a letter covers your choice of words, sentence length, accuracy, completeness. Simple and short words are the rule.

Check letter for pedantic vocabulary. Non-school persons may expect school correspondence to contain pedantic vocabulary. Professional educators, in contrast, are easily annoyed by a letter that seems to parade the writer's knowledge of words.

Check length of sentences. Sentences should be brief. Sentences containing twenty or more words can be difficult to understand. Sentences of more than thirty words can be very difficult.

Check for accuracy and completeness of facts. Facts must be accurate and complete. If an educator states a fact, few people will question its accuracy. To them it is true because an educator said it. Because people react this way, you and the school principal must lean over backwards to be exact and correct. Trusting your memory isn't enough. Guesses will never do, and being close isn't good enough either. Even if extra work is necessary, check your records and reports for the *exact* figures.

Check letter for conciseness. Conciseness is another quality to be observed. Have you already established your point? Then stop—don't overwrite. On the other hand, don't be so concise as to be painfully brief. Terseness is desirable, but brevity can be close to rudeness.

Check to see that a carbon is filed. Always make a file copy of every letter. Letters concerning teachers or pupils should be placed in the appropriate personnel file.

22

Rendering Typing Services

PRINCIPALS vary greatly in their school activities. Some give more speeches and do more writing than others. Your role will vary accordingly. A school secretary might be asked to type the rough drafts and the final copy of the articles which the principal writes for publication. Also, your principal and teachers may assist in preparing curriculum materials, instructional outlines, or manuals intended for district publication. Typing these materials is a responsibility which you have as an employee of the school district and as an accommodation to your principal or the teachers.

Other special typing activities you may be asked to perform might include preparing school bulletins, typing speeches, and typing schedules.

TYPING ROUGH DRAFTS

All manuscripts go through several typings. This is such general practice that you should not feel discouraged when you have to type a paper several times. In typing these rough drafts, use a format as nearly like the finished copy as possible. Don't worry too much about strike-overs or corrections at this stage. A rough draft is just that—a rapid, rough typing of the material to get it down on paper. If you use colored "second sheets," rough drafts won't be mistaken for the finished copy. It is also a good idea to write the word "Draft" at the top.

This is about the usual procedure:

1. First rough draft. This is usually edited by the writer to polish it up.
2. Second rough draft. This is also edited by the writer.
3. First tentative copy. This is submitted to others for their suggestions and comments. It sometimes carries in one corner the notation, "For committee use only" or "Not for official release." This copy can be mimeographed if several opinions are desired.
4. Approval copy. This is submitted to the superintendent or other superior for approval before the manuscript is released.
5. Final copy.

Sometimes there are fewer typings, sometimes more! Many inexperienced typists get exasperated at the many retypings. Remember, however, that school people, of all writers, cannot afford to publish anything short of the most carefully worded and grammatically correct paper.

TYPOGRAPHICAL SPECIFICATIONS

Paper. Type all copy on plain white paper, using only one side. Paper that is 8½ by 11 inches is most commonly used. Use bond paper of good quality rather than thin, highly glazed paper, since it will take corrections better and will stand up to wear. Type carbon copies on thinner paper or onionskin. Needless to say, keep the typewriter keys clean so that all letters, regardless of the kind of paper used, will be sharp and clear.

Carbon copies. Some editors like to receive two copies of a manuscript since they may send it to more than one person to edit. The extra copy speeds up their editing. You should also make a carbon copy for the writer to keep.

Use carbon paper that is hard, black, and non-greasy. This type of carbon, while not as black as others, makes a sharper letter and is less likely to smudge than those with a soft or medium finish. It is difficult to say how often you should change a carbon paper since your typing touch and the condition of the typewriter are determining factors. Every six to ten pages, look at the carbon copy to see how it is faring. In any case, change the carbon paper often enough to keep the letters sharp and of the same degree of darkness.

Determining length of the manuscript. To estimate the length of a manuscript, count the number of words in each of several lines and average them. Multiply this figure by the number of lines on a page to determine the number of words on a page. When this figure is multiplied by the number of pages, you will know the approximate number of words in the entire manuscript.

Determining format of the text. The placing of the typed text on the page, which also affects the margins, depends somewhat on its length. For pica type, use a 40-space line for manuscripts of 100 words or less. Use a 50-space line for manuscripts of 100 to 200 words. For any manuscript of more than 200 words, use a 60-space line. If your typewriter has elite type, the lines should consist of 50-, 60-, or 70-spaces. The purpose of the line width is to present the manuscript in its most attractive manner, centered on the page.

Manuscripts less than one page in length should be centered on the paper. Rather than becoming involved in complicated word counting to determine the placement of a short manuscript on the page, type a rapid, rough draft (which is sometimes good practice anyway). With experience, you will become proficient at judging the placement of a manuscript on the page.

Margins. Leave a margin of 1¼ inches on each side of the paper. On the first page of the manuscript, leave a top margin of 2½ inches and a bottom margin of 1½ inches. All succeeding pages should have top and bottom margins of 1½ inches. This marginal space allows room for notations to be made by the editor or printer.

If a manuscript is to be bound at the top, leave an inch more margin at the top than on the other three sides. If it is to be bound at the side, leave an inch more at the left than on the other three sides.

Spacing. There are three types of spacing which you must consider.

1. Sentence spacing. Space twice after Roman numerals or a capital letter indicating a main heading, and once after an Arabic numeral or a small letter indicating a subhead. Space twice after periods and colons.
2. Line spacing. This is called "leading" by printers, vertical spacing by others. Double space all lines. Use triple spacing if the editor requests extra space for editing purposes.
3. Paragraph spacing. Double space between all paragraphs and above and below all headings. Triple space below titles. It is effective at times to triple space between paragraphs or between the end of a paragraph and the following heading.

Indenting. It is good practice to indent all paragraphs six to eight spaces. This is true whether or not the paragraph begins with a heading. Some secretaries prefer to indent ten spaces.

The first line of quoted material is indented the same number of spaces as are the first lines of the paragraphs. All subsequent lines of single spaced quotations are indented four spaces from the left-hand margin.

Numbering pages. The first page of a manuscript of more than one page and the beginning page of each chapter should have the page number at the bottom of the page, three spaces below the last line. Number all pages after the first alike—at the center or right-hand top margin, on the seventh line-space, unless the manuscript is to be bound at the top. In this case, number at the bottom three spaces below the last line. Page numbers are called "folios" by printers.

Headings. Use headings to set off and identify the various ideas presented in a manuscript. Arrange them so that major points have the most prominent headings. This use of headings to indicate paragraphs which are of descending importance accomplishes the same purpose as an outline. Ideas which are of equal importance should have the same type of heading. The following style of typing headings is recommended by the authors. However, you should be aware of the fact that different offices may use individual variations.

Center heads. These primary headings are always centered on the page and are typed in one of the following ways, using no punctuation:

<u>CENTER HEAD—CAPITALS UNDERSCORED</u>

CENTER HEAD—CAPITALS

<u>Center Head—Capitals and Lower Case Underscored</u>

Center Head—Capitals and Lower Case

Side heads. Side heads are called subheads. Two types are commonly used.

1. Flush left side heads. Place these secondary headings on a separate line flush with the left-hand margin to identify major ideas of lesser importance than center heads. Do not indent nor use terminal punctuation. Type them in one of the following ways:

SIDE HEAD ON SEPARATE LINE–CAPITALS UNDERSCORED

SIDE HEAD ON SEPARATE LINE–CAPITALS

Side Head on Separate Line–Capital and Lower Case Underscored

Side Head on Separate Line–Capitals and Lower Case

2. Run-in side heads. Use these third-value or paragraph headings to point out ideas of lesser importance than flush left side heads. Indent them the same number of spaces as paragraph indentations. Run these headings into the text of the paragraph and place a period at the end. Type them in one of the following ways:

PARAGRAPH HEAD–CAPITALS UNDERSCORED. This type of subhead is run into the paragraph. It is called a "run-in" side head.

PARAGRAPH HEAD–CAPITALS. This type of subhead is run into the paragraph. It is called a "run-in" side head.

Paragraph head–first letter of first word capitalized; others lower case, underscored. This type of subhead is run into the paragraph. It is called a "run-in" side head.

Paragraph head–first letter of first word capitalized; others lower case. This type of subhead is run into the paragraph. It is sometimes called a "run-in" side head.

Be sure to type all headings and subheadings in the manuscript in a uniform style. If there is any doubt about which grade of heading is which, once the manuscript is typed, mark each heading with a letter— "A" for center heads, "B" for flush left side heads, and so on. Provide the editor with a key.

TYPING OUTLINES

Outlines are usually used in schools for instructional purposes. Your principal or the teachers will probably develop the material for instructional outlines. They should be kept simple and not have too many subdivisions or the thought may be lost. Your job is to type the rough copy in correct outline form.

"Outline" defined. An outline is a short way of putting ideas or thoughts on paper. It is characterized by its arrangement and form. There are two types of outlines. One is a topic outline in which the ideas are expressed by a very few words or topics. This type is commonly used for a first draft. After all ideas are organized, the outline should be rewritten in sentence form, which is the second type of outline. It is well to remember that an outline is not a succession of headings in its final form. It should show relationships and sequence.

Capitalization. *Capitalize all letters in the title.* Capitalize the first word and all other important words of a main topic, but capitalize only the first word of subheads.

Punctuation. Use a period after all topic numbers and letters except those in parentheses. Do not punctuate items which are not complete sentences. Use periods after sentences in a sentence outline.

Spacing. Leave two spaces after Roman numerals or capital letters which indicate main headings, but only one space after Arabic numerals or small letters indicating subheads.

Triple space below the title. Double space above and below main headings and secondary headings. Single space between items subsidiary to secondary headings. In a sentence outline or an outline with such long items that two lines are required for many of them, double space between the items.

Alignment of numerals. Type all numerals, whether Roman or Arabic, so that the right-hand figures in columns form a straight vertical line. Use the tabulator key. For example:

1	I
6	III
15	IV
306	VIII
2627	X

Margins. Set margins wide enough so that each item will fit on a single line, if possible. In figuring this, remember that some of the subheads may begin several spaces in from the left-hand margin.

Tabulating. Set the tabular stop so that each subletter or figure stands below the first letter of the first word of the topic next above it in rank. Whenever an item takes up more than one line, start the second and succeeding lines with the first letter under the first letter of the first line.

Example of a topic outline. The form shown below is a simple one in common usage. However, there are a number of variations which can be used. Consult your principal regarding the exact form he desires. For example, some people prefer to indent subtopics five to seven spaces.

```
    I. First Main Topic
       A. First subhead of first main topic
          1. First subdivision
          2. Second subdivision
             a. First item of subdivision
             b. Second item of subdivision
                (1) First item
                (2) Second item
       B. Second subhead of first main topic
```

II. Second Main Topic
  A. First subhead of second topic
  B. Second subhead of second topic
    1. First subdivision
    2. Second subdivision
  C. Third subhead
III. Third Main Topic

If the outline is correctly constructed, the word *and* could be used to connect I, II, and III. A and B could also be connected with *and*. Likewise, 1 and 2 and *a* and *b* could be connected with the word *and*. This test will show whether proper relationships are correctly placed in the outline.

Sometimes, such as in making notes for a speech, the complete outline form which has been explained may be too formal, and a simple jotting down of main ideas in brief outline will be more effective. In any case, the form you use should be consistent throughout the outline.

TYPING QUOTATIONS

You may be given an article to type which contains quotations. Become familiar with the recognized method of typing these into the manuscript, taking into consideration the spacing and the length of the material to be copied.

"Quotation" defined. A quotation is a word-for-word copy of material from a previously published work. It may also be taken from a speech.

Typing procedure. When the quotation is short, three lines or less, type it into the text and enclose it in quotation marks. If the quotation is longer, set it off from the text. In this case, indent the first lines six to eight spaces and all other lines four spaces from the left-hand margin. Do not use quotation marks when the quotation is indented in this manner. When the quotation is to be used in an article for publication, use double spacing, regardless of the length. Copy and paragraph all quotations exactly as they appear in the original source. Punctuation must also be the same.

Use the ellipsis to indicate the omission of any words. The usual sign of ellipsis is three dots alternating with spaces to indicate omissions up to one paragraph in length.

All quotations whether they are included in the text or set apart by indentation should be followed by an index number or an asterisk, raised above the line. This calls attention to the footnote or the bibliographical reference from which the quotation was taken. Precede each footnote by the same index number or asterisk, also raised above the line. This credit is necessary to meet the legal requirements of the copyright law. In addition, if the article is intended for publication, be sure that the writer has secured the permission of the author or publisher to use the quotation. The procedure for doing this is to copy the quotation, explain how it is to be used and who is to publish it. Send this information to the publisher of the original article and request permission to use it.

TYPING BIBLIOGRAPHIES

You will probably not compile the original material for the bibliography but may be given the notations or books from which to type it. To do this, record the information on cards, organize the cards, and then type the bibliography.

"Bibliography" defined. A bibliography is a list of books or references which has been used in the writing of a manuscript. It contains the author's name, the title of the work, publication data, and the number of pages. It is placed at the end of an article, chapter, or book.

An annotated bibliography is one which has a brief comment about the major theme of each work, or states the importance of each reference.

Gathering the data. Cards are a must when compiling a bibliography. If notations are brief, use 3 × 5 inch cards. If this size is too small for the necessary comments, use larger cards. Some people prefer slips of paper cut to size. Paper is thinner, goes into the typewriter more easily, and costs less than cards. However, paper is not as easy to handle when it comes to filing. Whatever is used, be consistent and use the same size and weight throughout.

Put only one reference on any one card, regardless of the temptation to do otherwise. Record the publication data in complete form on the cards which should be kept in alphabetical order. The bibliography or footnotes can then be compiled by simply copying the information from the cards.

When you prepare bibliography cards, be sure that every item is accurate as to spelling, punctuation, and page references. Avoid abbreviations. Prepare each card in the same manner.

Books. Record the author's surname first, followed by a comma, his other names or initials, and a period. Next, record the title *exactly* as it appears on the title page with the first letter of all important words capitalized. Underscore each word and put a period at the end of the title. The publication facts appear next: place of publication followed by a colon; name of publisher followed by a comma; date of publication followed by a period. The number of pages appears last with a period at the end. Here is a bibliographical reference to a book:

Mee, John F. Personnel Handbook. New York: The Ronald Press Company, 1952. 1167 pp.

When two or three authors are listed, record everything in like manner except that with the exception of the first author, all surnames are given last. The following is an example of how this is done:

Elsbree, Willard S., and E. Edmund Reutter, Jr., Staff Personnel in the Public Schools. Englewood Cliffs: Prentice-Hall, Inc., 1954. 438 pp.

If more than three authors are listed, the words "et al." or "and others" should follow the first author's name, the names of the other authors not being listed.

In the case of reference books, the author's name is recorded as previously mentioned. Each important word of the title is capitalized, but is enclosed in quotation marks and is not underscored. The name of the reference work is underscored and is followed by the editor, year of publication, volume number, and inclusive page numbers.

Magazine articles. For magazine articles, the author's name is given with the surname first, followed by a comma and his other names or initials. The title of the article is given in full with the important words capitalized and enclosed in quotation marks but not underlined. It is followed by a comma and the name of the periodical, underlined. This, in turn, is followed by the volume number, a colon, the page number(s), a comma and the month and year of publication separated by a comma. Here is an example of a magazine article reference:

Essex, M. W. "Practical Personnel Policies," National Education Association Journal, 41:369–370, September, 1952.

If the author is not known, the title of the article appears first. The reference is then listed alphabetically by the first word in the title. For example:

Educator's Dispatch, Arthur C. Croft Publications, New York City, April 7, 1955.

Special reference materials. For information regarding special types of bibliographical references, such as essays, encyclopedia articles, government publications, and so on, you should refer to such sources as A Form Book for Thesis Writing by William Giles Campbell, Writing Term Papers and Reports by George Shelton Hubbell, or A Manual for Writers of Dissertations by Kate L. Turabian.

Bibliography page. The bibliography is placed at the end of the manuscript. The heading should read BIBLIOGRAPHY, in capital letters centered on the page ten spaces from the top margin. Skip three spaces before making the first entry.

List all entries in alphabetical order. These can easily be typed from the cards previously described. The first word of each entry should be flush with the left hand margin. Indent other lines three or four spaces. Single space each line. Double space between each entry. If the bibliography is annotated (short comments about the value of the reference), double space between the entry and the annotation. In preparing manuscripts for a publisher, double space all lines.

In the event there are several entries by the same writer, the name is not repeated for succeeding references. Instead, place an unbroken line, seven spaces long, flush with the left hand margin. This line is followed by a comma and the title of the work.

If the article is not footnoted, number each entry on the bibliography page consecutively. Place this number, instead of the first letter of the author's name, flush with the left hand margin. When this method is used, all references to the bibliography are then made in the text by a number. This number is typed after the text reference and is enclosed in parentheses. If the reference is to a particular page, put a colon after the number and follow with the page number or numbers. Thus (6:45–46) refers to pages 45 and 46 of bibliography entry number six.

TYPING FOOTNOTES

"Footnote" defined. A footnote is a bibliographical reference which is put at the bottom of the page instead of at the end of the manuscript. Footnotes are referred to in the text by asterisks or index numbers (sometimes called superior numbers) which are raised above the line of type. Number them consecutively.

Typing the footnote. Type a line fifteen spaces long two spaces below the last line of the text. Start it at the left hand margin and extend it toward the center of the page. Begin the footnote a double space below this line. Type the name of the author with the surname last. Enclose the facts of publication in parentheses. Show the exact page or pages of the reference. Use no punctuation after the title. Otherwise, the footnote is written as in the bibliography. For example:

[8] George C. Kyte, The Principal at Work (New York: Ginn and Company, 1952), p. 36.

When more than one footnote appears on a page, double space between each entry. When sending a manuscript to a publisher, double space footnotes.

Precede each entry with an index number raised one-half space which refers back to the material in the text having the same raised number.

You can omit the facts of publication after the first citation in a chapter, using only the author's last name and publication title, with the specific reference, and need not use the publication facts at all if a complete bibliography is included.

Abbreviations. Repeated references to the same entry requires the use of abbreviations which are taken from Latin words. Use the abbreviation *ibid.*, underlined, when there are immediate references to the same work even when on different pages. Page or volume numbers must follow the abbreviation if different from the preceding one. For example:

  [9] Ibid., p. 16.

Use the abbreviation *op. cit.*, underlined, when references to the same work are near each other but are separated by other citations. Give the author's last name followed by a comma and the abbreviation, underlined. If page or volume numbers are different from preceding citations, they must follow the abbreviation. For example:

  [6] Jones, op. cit., p. 67.

Use the abbreviation *loc. cit.*, underlined, when a second reference is made to the same entry including the same page previously cited. Use the author's last name, followed by a comma and the abbreviation, when the reference is on a different page and other entries intervene. Do not use the author's name when the citation is on the same page as the previous entry. For example:

  [15] Loc. cit., p. 45. (This abbreviation refers to the same page in the reference as the previous one and appears on the same page in the text.)
  [22] Pittinger, loc. cit., p. 162. (This abbreviation refers to the same page in the reference but appears on another page in the text.) The abbreviation *loc. cit.* has a limited use. Use the abbreviations *ibid.* and *op. cit.* when possible.

These are the most common footnote abbreviations. For others, or for more complicated uses of these, refer to the books by Campbell or Turabian, previously mentioned.

Placement of footnotes. You may find it difficult to leave enough room at the bottom of the page for footnotes. It is a good idea to type several trial pages until you become familiar with the number of lines you must allow.

You can determine where to start the footnotes by using a guide sheet a half inch wider than the typing paper. Place marks on this guide sheet at the extreme right where it extends beyond the regular paper to indicate the top and bottom margins. Write the number "1" opposite the place where the first typed line will appear. Number each succeeding line to the bottom typed line.

Place this guide sheet back of the pages to be typed and align it so that the extra half inch with the numbers extends beyond the paper.

Whenever a footnote number is encountered in the manuscript, note the number of lines in the corresponding footnote. Refer to the footnote card which you made to find the number of lines you need. Deduct this number, plus two more lines for the separation from the text, from the total number of lines to be typed on the page. This locates the line at which to stop typing the text. If more than one footnote is to be typed, count the lines needed for each and add one more space for the separation between each footnote.

Sometimes a footnote appears on the last line of the page. This will cause difficulties unless you look ahead and anticipate this possibility. In such a case, shorten the page by one line and type the footnote reference on the next page.

Underscoring. Whenever the title of a book, periodical, or other publication is used, underscore it, even when it appears within the text of the manuscript. To the printer, this means that the title is to be printed in italics.

TYPING EXHIBITS

Exhibits are tables, charts, figures, or pictures which are used to explain the text. Fit small exhibits into the text in logical sequence. If larger, put them on a separate page and refer to them by the exhibit number. Always refer to exhibits by number rather than by page since pages may be changed at the printers and cause inaccuracies. If the exhibit is quite a ways apart from the reference, it is sometimes advisable to use the page number also.

"Tables" and "Figures" defined. Tables refer to statistical data which are placed in tabular form. Figures refer to materials presented in graphic or visual form. They may be graphs, maps, charts, photographs, drawings, or other such types of illustrations.

Numbering. Number tables consecutively throughout the manuscript with Roman numerals (there is a trend toward the use of Arabic numbers). Put the number a double space above the title and center it midway between the two side margins. Type the word TABLE in capital letters, without underlining. For example:

TABLE XI

Number figures consecutively from first to last with Arabic numerals. Place the number in the center of the page two spaces below the illustration and above the title. Use capital letters without underlining. For example:

FIGURE 52

You can give exhibits temporary numbers to place them properly in the text to help the editor identify them. Never paste, clip, or staple, exhibits in the manuscript. If you know where the exhibit is to be located when the final typescript is made, indicate it right in the manuscript. For example, if FIGURE 26 belongs on page 242, type "FIGURE 26 here" on page 242 on a separate line, centered from left to right with a few lines of space above and below it. If you have not decided where an exhibit is to be placed until after the typing is completed, insert a circled note in the margin to show where the exhibit should go.

PREPARING SCHOOL BULLETINS

School bulletins serve two purposes. They are a means of communication (1) between the school office and the pupils or staff and (2) between the school and the home. You will probably prepare most of them. To do this, you must collect the material to be included in the bulletin, type it, duplicate it, and distribute it.

Announcements or information which can be put into bulletins include chorus rehearsals; athletic, social, and special events; assemblies and programs; Red Cross and other drives, if authorized by the School Board; student body activities; supply order reminders; scores of games or athletic events; compliments to pupils and staff members for outstanding achievements; and meetings of clubs, the P.T.A., the School Board, committees, and the teachers' club. Reminders of things that have been overlooked or forgotten may also be included.

Bulletins which are sent home could explain school activities which are of interest to parents, safety rules, methods of grading, or general school information.

Individual items should be concise and to the point. They should answer the questions "what?" "who?" "when?" "how?" and, perhaps, "why?" Bulletins should give directions and explanations, particularly the date, time, and location of activities. Avoid publication of orders, since they are likely to arouse resentments. It is better to give orders orally.

Collecting the copy. Copy for the bulletin may come from the principal, memoranda from the central office, notices from teachers, librarians, heads of departments, sponsors of clubs, or others who have information of general or specific concern.

Look at all schedules pertaining to teachers so you can put reminders of such things as yard duties, bulletin board assignments, and meetings in the bulletin. Call the attention of committee chairmen, club sponsors, and special event leaders to the fact that they have activities coming up which should be mentioned in the bulletin. Remind your principal of activities, events, notices, or explanations which he should write for the bulletin.

Set a deadline for information which is to be placed in the bulletins. Enforce it without exception. In most cases, this deadline should be late in the afternoon of the day preceding publication. This will give you time to organize, type, and duplicate the bulletin.

Use a desk tickler in which to collect bulletin items as they come into your office. Put these notes into the section of the tickler corresponding to the date it is to be published. In this way, you are less likely to misplace needed information. Small notations left on your desk or placed in drawers often become lost.

Typing the bulletin. School bulletins are meant to be read. To achieve this purpose, they must be attractive and interesting.

In some cases it is a good idea to divide the school bulletin into two sections, one for teachers and one for pupils. If this is done, center the words "Teacher's Section" or "Pupils' Section" in underlined capitals at the top of each section.

Bulletins which are to be sent home should be addressed, "Dear Parents" or "Dear Fathers and Mothers." A sketch or an interesting drawing will help give the bulletin a "read me" appearance.

For identification, center the name of your school in capital letters at the top of the page. Some schools devise attractive nameplates for their bulletins.

Type a short, simple heading for each item in capital letters, flush with the left-hand margin and underlined. Sometimes it is better to list items by date rather than by topics. Type the date flush with the left-hand margin and underline it.

Leave a double space between the heading and the body of the item. Single space the item and indent the first line seven spaces. Another method is to place the headings at the left-hand margin and indent the text fifteen to twenty spaces in from the margin. This method uses more paper but sets the headings off for easy identification.

Do not crowd bulletins on a page or they will appear too wordy. Type the headings about one and a half inches down from the top of the page. If the first line of the heading is typed on the eighth line, the spacing comes out about right. Make the left-hand margin at least an inch and a quarter wide and the other margins at least an inch wide. An attractive looking bulletin is more likely to be read than one which is poorly spaced, poorly centered, and poorly typed.

Capitalize or underscore key words or phrases. Enclose special short announcements of particular importance in a box the better to attract attention.

For reference use, place the name of the responsible person and his title at the right-hand margin of each item below the last line. Type the date and bulletin number, along with your initials at the bottom of the page at the left-hand margin. This helps to identify it for future reference.

Keep daily bulletins to a maximum of one page, if possible. However, it is better to use two pages rather than to crowd the material. Head following pages with a brief title and the date, as: DAILY BULLETIN,

March 4, 1962. Place the page number in the upper right-hand corner flush with the right-hand margin. If the last item on a page cannot be finished, it is better to put the entire item on the next page, even though extra room is left at the bottom.

Duplicating the bulletin. After proofreading the stencil and making necessary corrections, duplicate the bulletin. Make enough copies for all who are to receive them. This should be done either the afternoon before distribution or the first thing in the morning.

Distribution of bulletins. Distribute one copy to each home room or classroom, one each to the principal and other persons who should receive it. It might be a good idea to give a copy to the bus driver, the custodian, the nurse, the cafeteria workers, and others who are connected with the school. Even though they are not personally concerned with the items, it is a good idea to keep them informed about all school affairs. Deliver school bulletins the first thing in the morning. Except for emergencies, this should be the only class interruption for passing out information to the teachers or pupils. Bulletins which are to be sent home should be given to the pupils the last period in the day so that they have a better chance of getting home.

All personnel who are to receive bulletins should have a folder labeled "SCHOOL BULLETINS" or a 3-hole notebook of good quality in which they can place them for ready reference. If a notebook is used, duplicate all staff bulletins on 3-hole punched paper.

You should maintain an office file of all bulletins, chronologically arranged. If bulletins are published by topics, it may be a good idea to maintain a cross reference file, filing them by subject matter as well.

TYPING SPEECHES

In most cases, you will probably not write a speech. But you may be given the rough notes to type into the form desired by the speaker, usually your principal.

Deciding the form to use. If the speech is to be read (heaven forbid), it should be written out in its entirety. Type it on letter size 8½ × 11 inch paper. If copies are to be sent to the press or if the speech is to be quoted directly, it must be written out in complete form or even mimeographed.

When the speaker is to speak from notes, it is usually best to use cards, 3 × 5, 5 × 8, or even 6 × 9 inches. If the notes are rather complete, it is better to use the larger size cards. This is especially true if the speaker wears glasses or is an older man.

Letter size paper or large cards may be used if a podium or a table is available on which to put them. If the speaker has to hold the speech in his hands, it is better to use smaller cards.

FRANKLIN ELEMENTARY SCHOOL

Daily Bulletin, March 5, 1961

TEACHER'S SECTION

IN-SERVICE MEETING

The in-service meeting for all fourth grade teachers will be held at the Lincoln School in room 7. Time: 3:30 p.m. Be prompt so that we can dismiss at 5:00 p.m.

John Smith, Principal

TEACHERS' CLUB DUES

This is a reminder that all dues should be paid to me by Friday, March 10. We'd like to have 100% participation this year as we have had in the past.

Louise Jones, Building Representative

PUPIL'S SECTION

BANK DAY

Tomorrow is Bank Day. Remember to bring your money and bank books.

Mrs. Robertson, Secretary

BASEBALL GAME

The Yankees from room 12 are playing the Indians from room 15. Time: 3:30 p.m. this afternoon.
Place: Baseball diamond no. 3.
Come out and root for your team.

Mr. Jeffries, Coach

PAPER CLEANUP

Many thanks to Mrs. King and the children in room 6 for taking time yesterday to pick up the papers around the building. We appreciate their work in keeping our school clean. But let's all do our share by putting all papers and lunch bags in the garbage cans at the ends of the halls. KEEP FRANKLIN CLEAN!

Mr. Smith, Principal

3/5/61
No. 4
cr

Figure 20. Example of a daily bulletin.

Typing the speech. Speeches are typed somewhat differently than usual typing. For one thing, it is a good idea to use larger type. The letters of elite type are too small for the speaker to refer to while he is talking. If he wears glasses or is an older man, it may even be necessary to use large kindergarten or primary type.

Leave a wide margin so that the speaker can insert notes if he thinks of changes or new ideas. Ordinarily you will double space the text although it is sometimes a good idea to triple space and leave even more room. The speech is easier to read when it is not crowded on the page.

Indentations should be ample, perhaps 15 or 20 spaces, for example. This makes it much easier to pick out the parts of an outline, the paragraphs, or the thoughts.

Pages or cards *must* be numbered, either in the middle or the upper right-hand corner. Set the numbers far enough apart from the text to be easily identified. Pages or cards which get out of order can cause a great deal of embarrassment and that is the last thing the speaker wants to encounter. Before giving the pages or cards to the speaker, see that they are in the proper order.

"**Tricks of the trade.**" There are a few things which you can do to help the speaker. Unless he is a polished speaker, every little trick will help put him at ease. Key words, phrases, or even sentences may be underlined, either with the typewriter, or better yet, with a red pencil. Be sure to use a ruler whenever a pencil or crayola is used to make lines.

Another trick is to put a red arrow in the margin pointing at a key phrase or sentence. Key points may also be indicated by consecutive red numbers in the left-hand margin.

TYPING SCHEDULES

A schedule is a list of activities or events that are to take place at regularly scheduled times. It is like a timetable and lists the date, time, and location of the activity. It is usually typed in tabular form and is similar to a table.

From the data which is given to you, organize the schedule so that it will have meaning to those who are to use it. It is important to make the headings of columns clear and the dates accurate. Leave enough space between columns so that the schedule is easy to read and does not cause confusion between columns. In case there is any doubt about what a number or a column means, type an explanation at the bottom of the page. Use lines to separate headings and the various parts of a table if there is the slightest possibility of misunderstanding.

It is a good idea to type a rough draft to organize the format before typing the final copy or the stencil (if the schedule is to be duplicated) unless you have had experience in doing this type of work. Examples of schedules are shown on pages 270 to 272.

DAILY SCHEDULE MULTIPURPOSE ROOM ROOSEVELT, 1960–61

TIME	MONDAY	TUESDAY	WEDNESDAY	THURSDAY	FRIDAY
9:00 9:30		Beers – Keefe	Sixth	Music	
9:30 10:00		Beers – Keefe	Sixth	Music	
10:00 10:30					
10:30 11:00					
1:00 1:30					
1:30 2:00	First	Second	Science		Science
2:00 2:30	First	Second	Third		
2:30 3:00 3:30	Square Dancing	Fourth	Girls P. E.		

as/10 27 60

Figure 21. Schedule for use of multipurpose room.
Blank spaces are left for others to fill in as the need arises.

270

FOURTH GRADE BOYS

NOON ACTIVITIES—KICKBALL SCHEDULE

Play Area	Jan. 7 Tues.	Jan. 8 Wed.	Jan. 9 Thurs.	Jan. 10 Fri.	Jan. 13 Mon.
1	1 vs 6	8 vs 9	—	1 vs 5	2 vs 3
2	7 vs 10	3 vs 4	2 vs 5	7 vs 9	10 vs 8
3	2 vs 5	1 vs 6	8 vs 9	6 vs 4	1 vs 5
4	—	7 vs 10	3 vs 4	—	7 vs 9
5	3 vs 4	2 vs 5	1 vs 6	2 vs 3	4 vs 6
6	8 vs 9	—	7 vs 10	10 vs 8	—

NOTE: The numbers in the columns under the dates correspond to the numbers assigned to the teams. All games are to start promptly at 12:20 p.m.

Figure 22. Example of a noon athletic schedule.

MINOR LEAGUE NOON SCHEDULE

BOYS

Games	Area	Dates				
		5/6/59	5/13/59	5/20/59	5/27/59	
Fistball	35	1 vs 2	5 vs 7	3 vs 9	4 vs 6	
Dodgeball	26	7 vs 8	3 vs 4	2 vs 10	1 vs 5	
Four Square	32	3 vs 4	8 vs 10	5 vs 6	2 vs 9	
Diamond H.B.	16	5 vs 9	1 vs 6	4 vs 8	7 vs 10	
Tetherball	29	6 vs 10	2 vs 9	1 vs 7	3 vs 8	

NOTE: The numbers under the dates refer to the team numbers. All games are to start promptly at 12:30 p.m.

Figure 23. Another arrangement for an athletic schedule. (Noon athletic schedule.) The dates could just as well have been listed down the left-hand margin and the play areas across the top. Each individual school will develop the form best suited to its needs. The important thing to keep in mind is that play areas, dates, and teams be properly and clearly identified.

272

LOWER GRADE YARD DUTY SCHEDULE 1960–1961	9/12 11/7 1/16 3/13 5/15	9/19 11/14 1/23 3/20 5/22	9/26 11/21 1/30 4/3 5/29	10/3 11/28 2/6 4/10 6/5	10/10 12/5 2/14 4/17 6/12	10/17 12/12 2/20 4/24	10/24 1/3/61 2/27 5/1	10/31 1/9 3/6 5/8	
BURNS	CL	C	R	O	EN	M	WM	O	
STRINGHAM	O	CL	C	R	O	EN	M	WN	
WOOD	WN	O	CL	C	R	O	EN	M	
WALKER	M	WN	O	CL	C	R	O	EN	
ALLEE	EN	M	WN	O	CL	C	R	O	
DUKE	O	EN	M	WN	O	CL	C	R	
VAUGHN	R	O	EN	M	WN	O	CL	C	
LANTRIP	C	R	O	EN	M	WN	O	CL	

M: Morning 8:40–9:00 am
O: Off duty
C: Cafeteria 11:20–11:50
CL: Cafeteria Line
WN: West Playground 11:50–12:20
EN: East Playground

R: Recess 10:00–10:15
11:15–11:20
1:20–1:30
2:30–2:35 (third)

Figure 24. Sample of a yard duty schedule for the entire year.

CORRECTING CONSTITUTIONS AND BY-LAWS

The Parent Teacher Association, student clubs, or professional organizations to which the teachers or your principal belong may periodically revise or correct their constitutions or by-laws. These changes are made by the executive body of the organization or club and are usually approved by the total membership.

You may be given these changes in rough form and asked to type them. The following pattern is used to set forth any changes:

1. Words that are to be deleted are marked out with a series of hyphens. (Now is . . .)
2. Words that did not appear in the section being considered, but are proposed for addition, are underlined. (This Constitution shall may be amended . . .)
3. Words that are to remain unchanged are printed without alteration. (This Constitution may be amended . . .)

Figures 25, 26, and 27 illustrate the method of typing deletions and additions to constitutions or by-laws.

SECTION 2. The officers and governors of the Association shall be elected at the Annual Meeting. The retiring immediate past President shall automatically become a member of the Board of Directors for the following year for the one-year period following the conclusion of his term of office as President.

Figure 25. Additions and deletions in constitutions and by-laws.

SECTION 5. ~~Nominations for Honorary Life Memberships in the~~ ~~California Association of School Administrators will be considered by~~ ~~the Board of Governors from members who have retired after having served~~ ~~with distinction in the field of educational administration for twenty or~~ ~~more years.~~ Any member of the Association who has retired after having served with distinction in the field of educational administration for twenty or more years may, at the discretion of the Board of Governors, be awarded an Honorary Life Membership in the California Association of School Administrators. Such awards shall be based upon criteria approved by the Administrative Policies Commission.

Figure 26. Replacement of an entire section of a constitution by a new section.

SECTION 5 3. Institutional membership shall be limited to State and County Departments of Education and legally organized California school districts upon proper action by the school board under the provisions of the Education Code, Sections ~~4361 and 4862~~ 1131 and 1132, and to institutions accredited for teacher education in the State of California. ~~or to educational institutions that qualify for membership~~ ~~by the action of their duly authorized agents.~~

Figure 27. Additions and deletions in a constitution.

23

Agendas, Meetings, and Minutes

SECRETARIES in schools probably have less need to take and type minutes than have secretaries in the central offices of a school district. However, you should know how to perform this service. It is the kind of service that makes a secretary invaluable to her principal and may well put her on the road to a promotion.

Minutes are the official record of a meeting and the actions taken. They indicate what happened or what was decided. Many questions arising at later meetings are settled by reference to the minutes of a previous meeting. If you are responsible for the minutes of meetings in your school, you will want to know more than merely how to write shorthand. The preparation for a meeting, the development of an agenda, and the final writing of the official minutes so that they are clear, accurate, and well-organized are all important aspects of a well-managed district and school.

THE AGENDA

Most school meetings are set up on the basis of an agenda, which is simply a list of items to be discussed. Not all school meetings, however, have agendas. Sometimes groups of instructors get together just to share ideas, to "brainstorm," or to "feel the tone" of a group. If you do have the task of preparing an agenda, you should first of all know why school meetings are held so that you can more effectively help your principal plan, prepare, and collect the agenda items.

Purpose of school meetings. Most matters that come before a school meeting are for the purpose of helping the principal reach a decision, getting information for a policy or procedure formulation, informing the teachers of a policy or procedure, helping the staff understand a situation or problem, motivating the staff to undertake some project, or gathering new ideas or suggestions.

Noting agenda items. The following list of suggestions should help you in organizing, collecting, and thus noting agenda items for future scheduled meetings:

1. Form the habit of scanning reports of the superintendent, supervisors, and others.
2. Note memoranda, bulletins, and report deadlines.
3. Re-read the minutes of the previous meetings.
4. Observe the pet projects of your principal and the problems that seem to puzzle him.
5. Canvass department or grade chairmen for items they wish brought before a meeting.
6. Develop the habit between meetings of listing items or topics that might be considered at the next meeting.

Each time an item comes to your attention, note it on a 3 × 5 card and place it in your meeting file for attention of the appropriate committee or the faculty chairman. Always do this immediately; don't wait until the day before the meeting to trust that your memory will recall the item. When the time is at hand to prepare the agenda, take your file cards to your principal and go over them with him. He will decide which ones to use.

Estimating time allowed for each item. Many school principals allow five, ten, or fifteen minutes for each item and indicate in the left-hand margin the hour when the item probably will be considered. You will often have the task of making the estimate of this time schedule. The weakness in these estimates is that they do not allow enough time. A rigid time schedule usually hinders free discussion and members of the group begin to feel regimented. It would also be safe to follow the procedure of not scheduling any agenda item for less than ten minutes. If uncertain about the length, add another five minutes. It is far better for the meeting to end early than to run overtime.

Some principals indicate the time a meeting is to adjourn. You must divide the available time among the items to be considered. You may have to propose to the principal that some items can and should be postponed to the next meeting. A typical agenda might be as follows:

3:25   Report of testing committee;
        Miss Amelia Wayside, chairman
3:35   Report of field trip committee;
        Mrs. Harriet Hammond, chairman
3:45   Routine business:
        a. curriculum and instruction
           1. classroom sets of supplementary textbooks
           2. plans for Open House
        b. guidance and pupil personnel
           1. no item
        c. auxiliary services
           1. no item
        d. personnel
           1. teachers—next pay warrants
           2. pupils—smoking

        e. buildings
           1. schedule of window washing
           2. keys and lockers
3:55   New business
4:00   Adjournment

Including factual information. Under a heading "Announcements" can be listed the dates, times, locations, and subjects of important events or meetings. You will save yourself much unnecessary follow-up work by taking a few last minutes before the meeting to go over the latest mail. It is not uncommon for a superintendent's bulletin or some important bit of information to appear in the mail with an announcement that could be read by your principal at the meeting. If your principal misses the opportunity to handle the matter at the meeting, you may find yourself mimeographing a special bulletin or sending notes hither and yon to get the word around.

Securing approval of the agenda draft. After you have made a draft of the agenda, take it to your principal for his approval or correction.

A typical agenda. Most books on parliamentary procedure contain a recommended order of business. The bylaws of some groups also list the authorized order of business. A typical agenda for a school meeting could include any or all of the following:

1. Opening of meeting
2. Flag salute
3. Approval of minutes of previous meeting
4. Additions to the agenda offered from the floor
5. Special presentations or reports
6. Reports of officers (as treasurer and secretary)
7. Reports of committees
8. Routine business
   a. curriculum and instruction
   b. guidance and pupil personnel
   c. auxiliary services
   d. employed personnel
      (1) certificated
      (2) non-certificated
   e. buildings and transportation
   f. supplies and equipment
   g. payment of bills
9. Signing of documents
10. Adjournment

Some boards of education and schools assign code numbers to these categories. For instance 8a:1024.62 would refer to a curriculum and instruction item considered at the October 24, 1962, meeting. These are indexed for future reference. Schools might wish to follow this practice.

New business. Currently provision is seldom made for "New Business" in a board of education meeting. This is because most boards of education now require advance notice of any new business to be presented.

The proposed business is then placed on the agenda under its proper subject heading as an educational presentation, report, or as a matter of consideration under one of the categories listed above.

Most meetings of teachers, by way of comparison, do include a place in the agenda for new business to be introduced from the floor. There are some indications, though, that councils and cabinet meetings of long-standing are moving toward the practice of a "closed" agenda and insisting upon advance notice of any new business to be brought before the meeting.

THE "TOOLS" OF A MEETING

You can help your administrator or school principal preside successfully by having on hand all the tools to successful chairing and minute-taking. The tools of a meeting are actually any reference which is or might be referred to during a meeting. It would then be your responsibility to collect all of these tools which would help your principal be more effective in his meeting. These "tools" should include most or all of the following items:

The minute book. The minute book is an up-to-date book containing the approved minutes of all previous meetings of the current year. Minutes of school faculty, department, and committee meetings ordinarily are kept in a minute book and are not duplicated for each member. There appears, though, to be a trend toward supplying committee members with personal file copies of minutes. When only single copies of minutes are maintained, minutes may be kept in a loose-leaf binder with dividers for agendas, resolutions, and reports. The pages of each section, separated by a divider, should be numbered consecutively with a contents page listing each meeting date and the page number of the respective minutes. The original copy of the minutes should be on durable white bond paper. You should be insistent that the president, chairman, or principal sign and date the minutes that have been approved at the meeting before he leaves the meeting room.

Reference books. Reference books might include adopted policies and procedures, official correspondence, copies of routine records and reports. You should be so prepared that you would not need to leave the meeting to get file copies of previous minutes, a copy of the school directory, the book of state school law, or similar references. Check with the meeting chairman, school principal, or department head concerning possible reference books that may have to be consulted during the course of the meeting. Particularly important are books on school law, policies, procedures, and parliamentary law.

There will be many informal and casual meetings that will require nothing more than a copy of the minutes of the previous meeting. On the other hand, regularly scheduled committee and faculty meetings need a number of reference books near at hand. If these books have to be carried any distance, use a library truck or cart for transporting materials to be used or distributed at the meeting.

Roster sheet. Almost all minutes, except those of large faculty groups, indicate the names of members present and absent. A roster sheet or an "attendance roll sheet" can be prepared in advance which lists the names of all members. At the top of the sheet, type the name and date of the meeting, and a notation such as: "Please sign (or initial) your name. Will the last person to sign kindly return this attendance roll sheet to the secretary. Thank you."

Times of arrivals and departures. Elected bodies, such as a board of education, are meticulous in all details, even to the time a member takes his seat after the meeting convenes and the time he leaves prior to adjournment. This procedure has proven necessary in questions whether a member was or was not present when some action was taken or decision reached. This is not done in any but formal meetings of elected bodies. If it is necessary or desired, the time of arrival and departure of a member may be noted in the proper chronological place in the minutes by some such notation as: "Miss Blank arrived at 8:25 p.m. and took her seat." "Mr. Blank withdrew from the meeting at 10:15 p.m."

Names of visitors. Some boards of education ask that the names of visitors be listed in the minutes. This list can be obtained by circulating a sheet headed "List of Visitors" with the name and date of meeting. The sheet should contain blank lines on which to sign. Someone in the audience usually will accommodate by circulating the list for you. Ordinarily, however, a record of visitors present is not made for meetings of teachers or school administrators.

The agenda. The agenda is simply a list of items to be transacted in a prescribed order. Bring to the meeting enough copies of the agenda for the anticipated number in attendance, even though you may have sent out the agenda items previously.

Reports and reference information. Reports and reference information refer to any item of informational nature which must be acted upon but usually requires prior study by the members participating in the meeting. Most persons attending a meeting are not ready to decide on short notice matters that are brought before the meeting. School districts and individual schools are trying to meet this condition by sending out advance copies of the meeting agenda together with reports, résumés, and data that will help members to make more careful decision on matters to be voted. This procedure assumes that members will study the agenda and read the supplemental references before they come to the meeting. The practice is gaining acceptance, especially when the chairman hews to the agenda and the references truly help the member to make up his mind.

Preparing the informatory data. Your part in preparing the reports and informatory data is (1) to arrange them in the same order as they will be needed on the agenda, (2) to number consecutively the pages of these reports, (3) to key the agenda items with the appropriate page numbers of the supplementary reports. For instance, suppose item 8a on the agenda is "Curriculum and Instruction" and the meeting is asked to approve a list of new science and mathematics textbooks. The titles, authors, and publishers of the textbooks to be approved are placed in the supplemental report. These books may be on pages 18 and 19 of the supplemental report. The agenda would then read:

8a. Curriculum and Instruction.

The textbook committee adoption of new science and mathematics textbooks. (See pages 18 and 19.)

Assembling the report. Some secretaries find it more practical to duplicate first all the supplemental reports. After placing the reports in the order shown on the agenda, you number the pages of the reports consecutively by means of a hand-numbering machine. After this numbering is done, the agenda, usually quite brief by comparison, is typed with the proper page numbers of the supplemental reports inserted at the same time.

Another suggestion is to use a manila file folder for the agenda and reports. This folder is opened and the agenda stapled on the right-hand side, the supplemental reports stapled on the left-hand side.

A list of bills to be paid. Unless the agenda is for a P.T.A., Student Council, or Faculty Association meeting, it is not likely that "Bills To Be Paid" will be an agenda item. Faculty and department meetings seldom have to consider such an item. Boards of education, on the other hand, regularly have to approve financial matters and requisitions for purchase. Almost all financial matters require supplemental reports. These should be handled as explained in the foregoing section on "Reports and Reference Information" and should be made an integral part thereof.

Resolutions. Resolutions may commend a person or establish a course of action. A copy of any resolution to be acted upon is usually included, in proper agenda order, with supplementary "Reports and Reference Information." Resolutions to be acted upon are sent out to the members in advance. For convenience in locating resolutions that have been acted upon, it is recommended that each resolution be numbered serially by years. For example "18–62" would be the eighteenth resolution acted upon during 1962. You should keep a file of resolutions and the date of the meeting at which each was endorsed. Actually, schools seldom pass resolutions except in the case of some retiring teacher, superintendent, or similar occasion.

Skeleton outline of minutes. Many committees and faculty groups are now using agendas which are in fact skeleton outlines of the minutes of the meetings. If you have to keep the minutes of a faculty or committee meeting, you should prepare in advance your own skeleton outline of the minutes. All you need do, then is to check names of members as absent or present and to fill in, on the spaces provided, the exact wording of any motion or action. The name of the maker of the motion, the name of the second, and the result of the vote taken can also be inserted on the blank lines provided.

Before and after the meeting. In addition to preparing the agenda and gathering the necessary informational data that is discussed above, you may have other responsibilities in preparing for a meeting. These may include:

1. Setting the time of and reserving a location for the meeting.
2. Making sure that room and equipment are in readiness.
   a. chairs
   b. tables
   c. chalkboards
   d. chalk
   e. stationery, gavel
   f. room unlocked, tidied-up, aired, or heated
   g. lecturn or podium
   h. ash trays
   i. microphone, extension cords, projector, screen
3. Sending meeting notices, including preparation of a mailing list and securing names and addresses of invitees.
4. Notifying or reminding speaker or guest
   a. location
   b. directions for reaching meeting place
   c. parking facilities
   d. confirming topic
   e. processing papers if speaker is to be paid
5. Arranging for sending out publicity, if any.
6. Securing advance copies of reports.
7. Securing and serving refreshments (also arranging for collecting money to pay for refreshments and for cleaning up).

Besides getting ready for the meeting, you will have work to do after the meeting is over:

1. Sending letters of thanks to speaker, guests of honor, and special workers.
2. Sending reminders to teachers assigned special duties.
3. Notifying persons affected of actions taken.
4. Notifying committee members of their appointments.
5. Placing important dates decided upon on the principal's and the secretary's own calendar.
6. Bulletinizing important dates and announcements.

THE MINUTES

The secretary to the superintendent frequently has the responsibility for maintaining the minutes of meetings of the Board of Education. Secretaries to principals and other school administrators receive practice in the all-important function of minute-taking by performing a similar service in the case of cabinet, council, and committee meetings. The school secretary may be asked to keep minutes of faculty meetings, department meetings, or school committee meetings.

Content of the minutes. Following is a check list of instructions for the preparation of minutes:

1. Begin with the date and place of the meeting.
2. State that the meeting was called to order, by whom, and at what time.
3. List the names of those present and those absent.
4. State that the minutes of the previous meeting were read and "unanimously approved," "approved as corrected," "approved as submitted," or that "The reading of the previous minutes was omitted."
5. Follow with a clear, accurate, and complete report of all business transacted, arranged in the order listed in the agenda (unless agenda order was changed).
   a. State all motions, the name of the maker, the seconder, and the action taken. Motions not seconded should be omitted.
   b. List all the major points in a discussion, if a school faculty, committee, or workshop meeting. Omit names of persons making each point.
6. List items of unfinished business on agenda.
7. State the time of adjournment.
8. List the important dates and facts to be remembered.
9. Use a complimentary close, "Respectfully submitted," and sign your name. Insert date the minutes were typed.
10. Type in a space for the chairman's signature of approval and date.

Recording of motions. Minutes of formal meetings, such as those of boards of education, usually contain only motions formally acted upon. All discussion, pro and con, is omitted.

A sample motion that was approved might read:

"Vice-President Marie Mendenhall moved that the Board instruct the architects to proceed with the working drawings on the proposed junior high school. Mr. Edwin Thormodsen seconded the motion, which was unanimously carried."

Board of Education and other formal meetings are meticulous in naming persons making and seconding motions. Although this is always a good procedure, many schools do not feel that the names of the maker and seconder are so important. What is always important is to record correctly the motion itself. Before the vote is taken, read back for immediate approval the wording of the motion as you have recorded it. Few motions are acted upon at a school faculty or committee meeting; many times, no motions are made.

Recording of speaker's remarks and discussion. Other items on the agenda of a Board of Education or other formal meeting are handled by simple sentences which indicate in the briefest possible form what took place. The following is typical:

> The marking system in effect at the junior high school was explained by a panel of teachers composed of Miss Alicia Jones, Mr. Claude Davis, and Mr. Harold Ott.

Recording differing points of view. Minutes of school faculty and committee meetings avoid naming persons who expressed certain or differing points of view. Whereas Board of Education minutes omit all reference to discussions leading to a motion, meetings of school faculty and committee meetings go to considerable lengths to list the points made. The reason for this difference is that a board of education is a legislative body established by state law. Their actions and motions are the important things; not the reasons why they took the action. Schools, on the other hand, are desirous of knowing or keeping a list of the reasons why certain procedures of policies were made. They want a record of the nature of the discussion, of the points pro and con, or the significant ideas presented by a speaker.

Recording of discussion in minutes. The following is an example of a discussion reported in the minutes of a school faculty meeting:

> A discussion of criteria of a good marking or grading system elicited the following points:
> 1. Teachers should agree upon standards for A's, B's, C's, etc.
> 2. Teachers should hold to their standards.
> 3. Teachers should explain their grading practices to the pupils.
> 4. Teachers who let pupils know throughout the entire term how each is progressing seldom have children who challenge the marks received.
> 5. Marks should tell the parent how his child is progressing.
> 6. Marks should indicate a pupil's strengths and weaknesses.
> 7. When a mark is entered on the pupil's school record, a teacher has no opportunity to explain it.

Recording verbatim reports. Verbatim reports are not necessary. Do not try to put everything down in full. Get the main ideas, the essential points. If you are uncertain, "shoot the principal an inquiring glance." He will give you the right nod.

Reporting of special instructions and procedures. Teachers often reach agreement without taking a formal vote. Teachers are interested in the steps to be followed and deadlines to be met. All minutes to be read by teachers should list, in chronological order, any procedures announced or agreed upon. It is a good practice to number these points and to start all statements uniformly with either verbs or nouns.

The following is a list of procedures appearing in the minutes of a faculty meeting. Note that each step begins with a verb.

The following steps are to be taken in preparing tests for scoring:
1. Arrange all tests alphabetically by pupil's last name.
2. Fill in the Test Data Sheet; alphabetically by pupil's last name; insert most recent index (IQ) and chronological age (years and months to nearest birth date).
3. Tie tests together with Test Data Sheet on top.
4. Deliver to office by Friday of this week.

Recording of dates and committee members. Dates for reports and other events should be noted in the minutes even if not mentioned in the meeting. Names of persons appointed to committees should be listed. A good set of school minutes will provide the teachers with all the facts and serve as a quick reference to deadlines, procedures, and points of discussion. If the chairman has had any experience, he will hold to the agenda. If he decides to make a change in the agenda, he will announce the change so that you and the members will know the revised order of business.

If there are unfinished items at the time of adjournment, these might well be listed in the minutes under a heading: "Agenda items not considered."

Securing pre-approval of minutes. If you have pre-read the agenda, you will have little difficulty in preparing minutes. If your meeting had a well-planned agenda, and you made a skeleton outline for recording the minutes, you practically write the minutes as the meeting goes along. The minutes, of course, are rough and have to be edited, but the minutes are ready for a first typing. They can even be submitted "as is" to the principal or chairman for editing.

If any person is quoted and the topic is at all controversial, it would be wise to submit a draft of the minutes to him for approval. It is easier to get prior approvals than to make corrections after the minutes are read at the next meeting. After a set of minutes has had preliminary approval from the persons most concerned, they should be typed in form for reading at the next meeting. If approved at the meeting, they can be signed, dated, and filed in the minute book. If corrections are extensive, the minutes may need to be retyped. If the changes are minor they may be made on the original copy, initialed by the chairman and the minutes inserted into the minute book.

Some groups may request that the approved minutes be duplicated and sent to each teacher or committee member. This is likely to be necessary in the case of teacher workshops and curriculum committees.

24

Preparing Mimeograph Stencils and Duplicating Mats

SCHOOLS MUST DUPLICATE a great many materials. Sometimes you may think that you spend most of your time stencilizing stencils or preparing spirit (fluid duplicating) masters. The duplicating method you use depends upon the equipment available and the number of copies needed. This chapter describes the method of preparing direct process master sets, mimeograph stencils, and direct image plates for offset presses.

PREPARING SPIRIT PROCESS MASTER SETS

Since most schools have rotary duplicating machines, direct process masters are in common use. Spirit duplicated material is the least expensive and perhaps the easiest to prepare when only two or three hundred copies are needed. However, when you attempt to print too many copies from one master copy, the final ones are often too light, difficult to read. A further disadvantage of this process is that the commonly used master set prints in purple. For very fine work, the contrast between purple and the white paper is not as good as the contrast produced by the mimeograph process. Furthermore, the purple color fades in time and is not as long lasting as mimeographed copies.

Ditto, Inc., Chicago 11, Illinois, and the A.B. Dick Company, Chicago 48, Illinois, publish excellent instructions on duplicating techniques and on the care and operation of duplicating equipment.

"Spirit or Fluid" process defined. When the fluid process is used, the master is prepared by typing, writing, or drawing on a sheet of master paper. The spirit carbon sheet behind the master paper releases a carbon deposit on the reverse side of the master paper wherever an image is made. A duplicating machine is used to bring this master and the moistened blank paper together to produce the printed copies. A liquid chemical dissolves a little of the dye from the master copy and deposits it on the paper brought into contact with it to make the copy.

Duplicating machines for spirit process work. These machines have several trade names. They may be called spirit duplicators, liquid process duplicators, ditto machines, or direct process duplicating machines. The technique of preparing the master copy is the same in each case. The master copy is placed on a drum which is turned by hand or an electric motor. The paper is fed through the machine to make the copy.

Another type of machine uses gelatin or a gelatin film. The process of preparing the master copy is again the same except that the carbon deposit is placed on the front of the master. In this process, however, the master is transferred to the gelatin, and the gelatin becomes the master. The paper for the copy is placed in contact with the gelatin, from which the paper picks up the image. Up to twenty clear copies can usually be made with this type of duplication. This is the simplest and least expensive type of spirit duplication which can be used.

Types of carbon. Spirit process carbon paper is available in five colors: purple, red, green, blue, and black. The commonly used master set duplicates in purple. It comes as an assembled unit and is easily placed in the typewriter without the necessity of assembling the carbon and the master paper. When the master copy is typed, it is detached from the set and placed on the duplicating machine.

Short run carbons are the least expensive and should be used for runs up to a hundred copies. For longer runs, you should use long-run carbons.

When colors are desired, the carbons and master papers are purchased separately and assembled for typing.

Types of paper. The best grade of paper is a twenty pound paper made especially for liquid duplicators. Other weights and types of paper can be used for some types of work, however. Inexpensive newsprint is sometimes used, but the contrast between the print and the paper is not as great as when regular duplicator paper is used. Newsprint absorbs too much fluid, thereby oversaturating the master and consequently spreading the image and causing copy deterioration.

Typing the master copy. The type faces should be cleaned. The typewriter touch control should be set at the stroke which provides the best reproduction of characters. This setting varies with your touch. Be sure that your typewriter is adjusted so that letters such as the "o" and the "c" do not cut holes in the master copy.

Insert the master paper and the carbon into the typewriter with the carbonized side of the carbon facing master with the master paper facing up. Be sure to remove the tissue, if any.

If you are using a master set (one in which the master is fastened to the carbon at one end and perforated, leaving the other end free), you will find it helpful to insert the master set into the typewriter so that the free end will form the top of your spirit master. This leaves the top of the master set separated so that you can easily make corrections. If you put the fastened edge in first, you would have to cut or separate the fastened edge—this is inconvenient at times.

A typewriter with a medium hard platen and clean sharp type produces the best results. If the platen roller is not in good condition or of the correct degree of hardness, place a backing sheet behind the carbon. This provides a uniform surface for the keys to strike on. Your touch determines the amount of carbon that is deposited on the master sheet. In general, a staccato uniform touch gives the best results.

Drawing on a spirit process master set. Fold the carbon under the master back out of the way or insert a sheet of paper between the carbon and the master. If separate carbons are being used, they should not be assembled at this time. It is a good idea to make a preliminary sketch drawing lightly with your pencil so that you avoid damaging the master. If a sheet has been inserted between the carbon, it is especially important to draw lightly so that the carbon won't be "used up" on the inserted sheet.

After the drawing has been sketched, fold the carbon back into place or remove the insert. Retrace the preliminary sketch with a hard pencil or ball-point pen, pressing firmly on the point. Work on a hard surface. If you write on the master, use the same method. Check the master occasionally to make sure that you are applying enough pressure. Light or broken lines indicate insufficient pressure.

Correcting errors on the master copy. Place an erasing shield over the error. These shields have several size openings to take care of one or more letters. Rub the error lightly with an ordinary pencil eraser or other handy eraser until the carbon is removed. Although the first strokes make a smudge, it will soon clear up. If you use the eraser too vigorously, the coating on the paper will be ruined.

Place an unused piece of carbon paper over the error and type or write the correction. If you have not typed corrections before, practice corrections to perfect your technique.

Gummed correction strips may be purchased which can be stuck on the master copy if an entire line needs to be corrected.

You can also use a razor blade to scrape the dye from the master, being careful not to break the surface of the paper. A small penknife can also be used. Retype the letter or word as explained above. Blow the scrapings into a waste basket or they will make purple smudges when rubbed on anything.

When words or lines are to be deleted (such as the last line on a page) you can place a piece of Scotch tape over them to prevent them from printing.

Remember that re-using a carbon does not make a clear master copy. Keep a supply of unused carbon papers on hand in a folder. Whenever you type a master copy, cut off and save any unused portions for future use.

PREPARING MIMEOGRAPH STENCILS

Directions for using stencils usually appear on the box in which they are packed. The major companies handling mimeograph supplies also publish instructions for their use. Some general principles which will help you in the preparation of your stencils are explained in the paragraphs which follow.

Selection of paper. Regular mimeograph paper of sixteen or more pounds weight is usually desirable. It has a fair degree of absorbency, is dull and slightly rough, and is free from lint. Lighter weight papers may be used if heavier sheets are interleaved between them. These paired sheets must then be hand fed through the machine. The lightweight sheet carries the image, and the "slip sheet" prevents the ink from transferring from one copy to the back of the next. Slip sheeting can be eliminated with the use of fast drying ink and a new, dual purpose mimeograph paper.

When lighter weight papers are used, the ink shows through the paper. Heavier weight papers, such as twenty-four-pound, should be used when both sides of a paper are to be mimeographed. Opaque twenty-pound papers give nearly as good results.

Colored papers are also available and will add interest when used for notices, invitations or programs. They can also be used for seasonal holiday work at Christmas time, Easter, or on Valentine's Day. Light colors are preferable to dark colors as they are cheery, suggest warmth, and the print shows up better. You should become familiar with the various kinds of paper which are available.

Needless to say, all paper should be stored flat and in a dry place. The paper should be kept squared up so that it will feed through the machine smoothly.

Selection of stencils. Several types of stencil are available. Select the one which best suits your needs. Some are more suitable for long runs; others, less expensive, are suitable for short runs. Certain types lend themselves to stylus work better than others. Various sizes are available so that you won't have to waste unused stencils when mimeographing small sheets. The smallest standard size stencil sheet is 8½ × 4 inches. Others come in letter and legal sizes.

Stencil films. Some stencil sheets come with the film attached. For others, the film is separate and must be placed on top of the stencil. These films should be used when broader letters are needed. The film pushes aside more of the stencil coating than the type alone does, thus permitting more ink to pass through the stencil. This extra ink also increases the drying time for the copies and increases the amount of "show through," particularly on lighter weight papers. When film is used, there is almost no chance of the type cutting out characters, particularly the "o." Films should not be used for medium or fine-line copy or if ink consumption is to be held to a minimum. Also keeps typewriter keys clean.

Cleaning the typewriter keys. Use a stiff brush and a liquid typecleaner to clean the typewriter keys before you cut a stencil. Take particular care to clean the "a," "e," "o," "m," and "w." For sharp clear copy quality, you should clean the type before cutting each new stencil.

Stencil guidemarks. You can determine the line at which you wish to start typing by placing a sheet of the paper you plan to use on top of the stencil with the top edge at the "Top Edge Guide" line. This placement of the paper automatically indicates a one-half inch top margin on the paper. Note that the line numbers at the side of the stencil are six lines to the inch. Typing on line one leaves a one-half inch top margin; line four leaves a one-inch margin; and so on.

The side margins on the stencil indicate an approximate five-eighths inch side margin on 8½ inch paper. For wider side margins, you should use the scales at the top and bottom of the stencil. Pica type sets ten characters to the inch; elite type sets twelve characters to the inch.

Mark the margins you desire on the guide paper, place it on top of the stencil and note the scale markings. Set the margin stops accordingly, and note the line at which to start typing. If you have an accurate layout, a very simple way to position it properly on the stencil is to place the original under the stencil sheet and put a dot of correction fluid at the beginning of each area to be typed. These dots will not affect the stencil in any way.

It is best to type three spaces inside the side guide lines for the best duplicating as some mimeograph machines do not print clearly when material is typed too close to the edge. The recommended last line on which typing should appear for 8½ × 11 inch paper is the sixtieth line.

Inserting the stencil in the typewriter. If there is an interleaving tissue between the stencil and the backing sheet, remove it, and insert in its place a tissue or whatever specially treated cushion sheet is supplied. Some of these inserts are a white wax type which improves visibility of stencil being prepared in typewriter and helps produce good sharp stencilization. If the cushion sheet is coated, be sure that the shiny side is placed next to the stencil sheet.

When inserting the stencil in the machine, be careful to line it up correctly as you would a sheet of paper. Be careful not to wrinkle the stencil by careless insertion.

Typing the stencil. Type at about three-fourths your regular typing speed, using a sharp, staccato touch. The stroke is too heavy if the center of the letter "o" falls out. The stroke should be uniform, except on punctuation marks such as , . ; :. Use a lighter touch on them. The larger letters (M, W) should get a slightly harder touch. Experiment with these and run a trial stencil so that you will get to know your typewriter before cutting a stencil for publication. Medium-hard platens are usually preferred to hard platens when stencils are being cut.

Different combinations of cushion sheets and typing films give different types of copy. Experiment with the use of tissue and white cushion sheets with and without films to determine the kind of copy you want to produce.

Making corrections. When the typewriter key strikes the stencil, it pushes aside part of the stencil coating, exposing the fibers through which the ink flows. Correction fluid is essentially a stencil coating in liquid form. When applied, it replaces the coating which was pushed aside by the type.

To correct an error, roll the platen five or six spaces upward to give yourself plenty of working space. If tissue cushion sheets are being used, gently rub the incorrect letter(s) with a paper clip to close the perforation. This burnishing is *not* necessary when a coated cushion sheet is used, as correction fluid will not stick to it.

Make corrections carefully; correct each letter separately. Apply a very thin coating of correction fluid with a brush, using vertical strokes. Be sure that the entire error is entirely covered. Do not use enough correction fluid to make a hump or the type will not cut a clear impression. Allow the fluid to dry for about thirty seconds before retyping.

Always use a lighter than normal touch when retyping over an error. If it is necessary to roll the platen back to make a correction, hold the stencil, the cushion sheet, and the backing firmly together to avoid wrinkling the stencil.

Be sure to keep the bottle of correction fluid tightly closed except when applying the fluid to a correction. This retards evaporation and keeps the fluid at the best consistency for further use.

Proofreading. Be sure to proofread the stencil before placing it on the mimeograph machine. If an error is found when the first copy is run, remove the stencil from the machine, clean it, and make the correction. The platen of the typewriter should be protected by covering it with a sheet of paper before putting a used stencil in it. Since this is a messy and time-consuming job, it behooves you to be careful with your proofreading.

Justifying lines. The method of typing which makes the right hand margin even ("justified") is particularly appropriate for school newspapers, news bulletins, and instruction sheets.

Signatures and handwriting. For this you need a roll-point stylus, which is similar to a ball-point pen, and a writing or signature plate. Remove the cushion sheet and insert the writing plate between the stencil and the backing. Place this assembly on a smooth surface, such as a desk top. Hold the stylus almost vertical and use considerable pressure so that a clear impression is made on the stencil. You may need to tell your principal how to do this, as he will sign most stencils.

Mimeographing cards. Since cards are fed into the mimeograph machine in a lengthwise position from the center of the feeding tray, type the stencil in the top center location. Most stencils have the card area indicated in the correct position by special guide lines.

If the copy is to run the narrow way of the card, place the stencil in the typewriter and type within the guide lines.

If the copy is to run the long way of the card, cut the stencil and backing sheet at line fifty. Insert the shortened stencil in the typewriter in a sideways position. Fold a piece of paper or the flap of an envelope over the side of the stencil (which becomes the top) so it can be inserted without wrinkling. Type the stencil lengthwise in the card area. Remove the typed stencil and take out the cushion sheet. Coat the top half-inch of the lower portion with mimeograph cement. Place the lower half-inch of the top section over this and rub the joint gently to bond it. Allow to dry. Mimeograph in the usual manner.

Never fold a stencil and try to type on it. It is far better to take enough time to prepare the stencil as explained.

Filing stencils for reruns. You should never destroy any stencil which has the slightest chance of needing to be rerun—unless you like to type stencils a second time.

When oil-base inks are used, remove the stencil from the machine and place it in an absorbent filing wrapper. This wrapper should be run through the machine before the stencil is removed so that the stencil can be identified or it can be placed over stencil on the mimeograph to transfer image. After the wrapper is closed, rub it firmly over the entire surface with hand to absorb all the surplus ink possible. Leave stencil in wrapper 5 to 60 minutes, then open wrapper to loosen stencil and turn it over. Close wrapper.

Hard-set inks should be washed off the stencil with soap and lukewarm water before filing it. You can wash stencils in plain water when using water base inks. Clean photochemical stencils with kerosene. If you read the instructions accompanying the stencils, you will have little difficulty.

Stencils can be filed flat in their wrappers with the identifying copy on top. You can also place an identifying code at the top of the stencils and hang them in a file cabinet made for the purpose.

Types of stylus. Many types of stylus are available, some with dual working ends. They are colored for easy identification. Styli are used for drawing, ruling, shading, tracing, handwriting, and lettering. They come in the following forms:

Broad, medium, and fine loops for heavy or fine lines.
Wheels for shading, tracing, or making dotted lines.
Needle points for detail work.
Screen plate styli for shading.
Roll-point styli for signatures.
Ball-point styli for tracing outlines and signatures.

Screen plates. Screen plates are used with certain styli for making shadings of various types such as diamond weaves, herringbone weaves, basket weaves, splatters, or half tones.

These plates are made of transparent plastic with raised patterns on one side. Place the plate under the stencil sheet with the pattern side up. Rub the area several times with the appropriate stylus, using a firm, even pressure to reproduce the pattern. Hold the stencil firmly in place with your left hand so the impression will be evenly made.

"Dummy" layouts. It is wise to make a "dummy" layout before tackling the actual typing of the stencil. Draw the margins on the dummy page. If thin paper, such as onion skin, is used, illustrations or other material can be placed under it and moved around to the visibly best location. You can either type the text and headings on the dummy sheet or outline the size of the space needed with a pencil or ink line.

When the dummy is completed, place it between the stencil and the backing to see where the material is to be cut on the stencil. Place small dots of correction fluid at the corners of paragraphs, illustrations, lettered areas, or boxes to mark off the areas. These dots serve as guide marks when cutting the actual stencil.

Self-mailers. When you prepare bulletins which are to be mailed, you can save time and money by making a self-mailer. Use the lower three and a half inches of the reverse side of the bulletin for the address. Mimeograph the return address in the upper left-hand corner. Type the address to which each is to be mailed on gummed paper and stick it in the proper place. If bulletins are being sent to the same people each time, use mimeographed addresses. The A. B. Dick Company makes a lined stencil sheet for just this purpose which holds thirty-three addresses. This may be used with gummed, perforated paper for printing the addresses. These addresses can be torn apart and used on the self-mailer. Use small gummed seals or a staple to seal the bulletin, which is folded into thirds. See Figure 28 for a diagram of a self-mailer.

Using the mimeoscope. The mimeoscope is an illuminated drawing board for use with stencils. It is a metal or plastic frame supporting a sheet of specially prepared glass which diffuses the light evenly. The light is located under the glass. The mimeoscope is a necessity and well

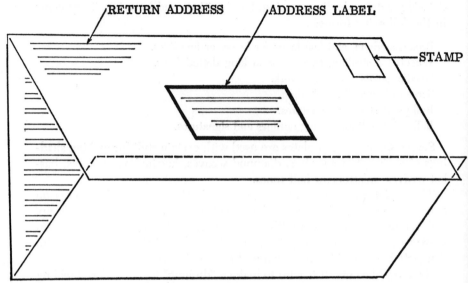

Figure 28. A self-mailer.

worth the expense if you do much drawing, lettering, illustrating, shading, or lining on stencils. You will need various styli, lettering guides, screen plates, and a T-square.

Instead of using a cushion sheet, use a plastic writing plate to provide a good working surface and to prevent tearing the stencil. Since it is translucent, the plate can be placed over anything which needs to be traced.

The dummy copy and its use. Place the stencil on the mimeoscope by lifting the backing (which you do not use) and feeding it through the opening at the top of the mimeoscope so it will be out of the way. On thin transparent paper, make a dummy copy which is the exact size of the layout to be used. Place this dummy copy on the mimeoscope glass so that the top edge is exactly under the line on the stencil which is labeled "Top Edge Guide." Line up the left edge of the dummy page with the left edge of the stencil. Be sure all parts of the layout are enclosed within the duplicating area of the stencil.

Place the writing plate between the dummy copy and the stencil. Illustrations or other similar items may then be placed under the dummy page in their exact position and fastened to the glass with transparent tape. The dummy should be removed if it is not needed. Place the stencil smoothly and firmly over the writing plate and fasten in position with the stencil clamps. Check the position of the dummy or the illustrations to see that they have not slipped. The stencil is then ready to be stencilized by drawing, lettering, or shading on it.

Lettering guides. Eye-catching headings and titles can be made by using lettering guides and lettering guide styli. These guides are made of plastic with openings in the shape of letters, numerals, or symbols. Instructions on the guide should list the correct stylus to use. This is important since the points of the stylus must fit exactly into the guide openings.

Place the stencil on the mimeoscope with the writing plate under the stencil. Locate the lettering guide over the starting point for the first letter. Place a T-square firmly against the side of the mimeoscope; rest the guide on the T-square. The stencil backing is not used.

Lettering on the stencil. To form a letter, draw the stylus gently through the opening, removing some of the stencil coating. Go over the stroke several times until all of the coating is removed and the line shows distinctly. Sometimes you must combine two sections of the guide to form a letter. For example to make a "B," draw the symbol "3." Then add the straight line from another part of the guide to complete the letter. Thus "1" and "3" will make "B" when carefully joined.

If it is necessary to join two lines, draw one line first. Lift the stylus and draw the second line toward its junction with the first line. This technique prevents the possibility of tearing the stencil or making ragged line joints. It is advantageous to practice with the lettering guide on an unwanted stencil before attempting a final job. Try out different styles of lettering so you can choose the one most suited to the material. Once you have become proficient, this experimental work will no longer be necessary. The company selling the machine will have a manual with examples of styles (also called fonts) of lettering guides.

Drawing and tracing on stencils. Instead of underlining words, headings, or sentences on the stencil with the typewriter, it is better to use a loop stylus and a ruler or T-square to make the underline. This is faster and makes a cleaner, better looking line. Use the mimeoscope for this work.

Using the loop and wheel styli. When a loop stylus is used, hold the loop parallel to the T-square. Draw along the square with enough pressure to make a clear white line in the stencil. Rest the fourth and fifth fingers on the T-square to help guide the stylus. Draw the border and vertical lines first followed by the horizontal lines. Be careful not to tear the stencil. If lines overlap at the corners, use correction fluid to block off the unwanted portion. Correct any errors with the fluid. Lift the stencil to apply the correction fluid. When dry, make the correction.

Wheel styli are used in much the same manner. Hold the wheel parallel and next to the T-square and in a vertical position. Do not lift stylus until the line is completed. Use heavy pressure to make a uniformly white line.

Drawings or tracings are made by selecting the correct loop or wheel styli for the job and tracing on the stencil the illustration or copy which is on the dummy or original illustration. When the outline is completed, add any shading by using the screen-plate method (page 293).

When all drawing is completed, remove the stencil from the mimeoscope, insert the cushion sheet, and add any necessary typing.

Making folds. You can add interest to your mimeographed bulletins, programs, or announcements by folding the copies. Stencils are available which are marked off with guide lines for four-page folders.

Two stencils are needed for a four-page folder. The cushion sheet should be inserted between the stencil and the backing. Cut all three sheets in half. Place a folder paper or an envelope over the lower half of the cut stencil to hold the assembly in position as you place it in the typewriter. The copy for page 1 should be typed in this position. Insert the top half of the stencil in the typewriter in the same manner and type the copy for page 4. When finished, remove the cushion sheet and cement the bottom half to the top half with a half inch overlap. When dry, the stencil is ready to be placed on the mimeograph machine.

Complete copy for pages 2 and 3 in the same manner, with page 3 at the bottom and page 2 at the top.

After the first stencil has been run, square up the printed copies and place them on the feed table, blank side up. Attach the second stencil to print pages 2 and 3. Page 2 should be printed on the back of page 1.

If other types of folds are desired or if booklets of more than four pages are needed, refer to special instructions which the major duplicating companies publish.

Mimeographing colored inks. Colored inks are easy to use and will enhance the appearance of your mimeographed material. Red, green, blue, yellow, purple, brown, and white inks are available. If long runs are to be made, it is better to buy extra ink cylinders and change them when you want a different color.

For shorter runs, prepare the stencil in the usual way. Then plan the color pattern you want to use. Run the regular black printed part first. Stack and re-run, using an overlay color pad to apply color to the heading or illustrations. This is easier than trying to ink a large area with the usual black and filling in the colored heading on the same pad.

Overlay ink pads. When you use only one cylinder and overlay ink pads, follow these steps with most mimeographs:

1. Place a protective cover over the black ink pad.
2. Attach a clean cloth ink pad over the protective cover.
3. Place the stencil face up on a flat surface.
4. Paint a light colored outline around the area to be printed in that color. If two or more colors are to be used, paint outlines in these other colors where they belong. Leave at least an inch between each colored area to prevent the mixing of the colors. Draw crayon marks between the

area for the two colors. This waxy substance prevent the colors from running. Paste inks from tubes are the easiest to use; they need no stirring.

5. Place the stencil over the mimeograph cylinder and rub the backing paper so that the colored outlines will be transferred to the cloth ink pad.
6. Raise the stencil and backing and lay them back out of the way.
7. Fill the outlined areas in with color. Work the ink thoroughly into the pad so it is saturated.
8. Lay the stencil over the cylinder and remove the backing.
9. Run the stencil. If the copies begin to run light, lift back the stencil and re-ink.

If it is necessary to overlap the colors or if they are too close to each other, use two or more stencils. After the first color is printed, re-stack the paper when dry and run through the machine again with the second color.

Insets. Insets are photochemically prepared mimeograph stencils which have been made by mimeograph companies. They are expertly drawn illustrations which come in sheets for various subject matter, ads, insignia, headings, or other such items.

Prepare your stencil in the usual manner but leave a space for the illustration which is to be inset. Leave a three-eighths inch margin between any typing or drawing and the space required for the inset.

With a sharp razor blade, cut the inset and its transparent wrapping out of its sheet. A half inch should be left for overlap when it is cemented. With the same blade, cut an opening in the stencil which you have prepared. This opening should be an eighth inch larger than the illustration.

Lay the stencil flat and face up. Place the inset, with the transparent wrapping side up, on top of the opening. Lift the overlapping edges and apply cement thinly. Press down tightly to cement and allow several minutes to dry. Be sure that there are no uncemented edges or the ink will leak through.

Apply a thin line of correction fluid to the overlapped edges on both sides of the stencil to permanently seal the inset to the original stencil. Be sure the fluid is dry before doing the second side. When completed, the stencil is ready to use.

Ink pad blockouts. For general use place a small piece of koroseal block-out material (about 6–9 inches long and 8½ inches wide) over the lower section of the ink pad. Position it so that one inch of the tail end of the stencil overlaps the blockout. This blockout makes it unnecessary to clamp the end of the stencil. The stencil is easier to attach and remove and is cleaner to handle, as it is free of ink at the tail end. When small stencils are used, it is necessary to cover the rest of the ink pad so that the ink won't get on the paper or the roller. Place a protective cover over the ink pad. Then place the small stencil on top. On the cover, mark with a pencil the limits of the typing or illustrations on the stencil. Lift off the stencil and with a knife cut an opening in the cover the size of the material to be printed, being careful not to damage the ink pad. Place the stencil on the machine and run the copies.

There are times when only part of the material on the stencil needs to appear on some copies. In such cases, run the number of copies of the entire stencil that you need. Then, block out the part that is not needed and run the rest of the copies.

If the blockout is to be temporary, place a strip of thin paper over the portion to be blocked out. If possible, fasten it under the top or bottom stencil clamps. If this can't be done, depend on the ink to hold the blockout paper in place. Run the copies slowly, watching to see that the blockout paper remains in place. If it falls off or becomes saturated with ink, replace it. When the blockout paper is removed, the entire stencil is again usable.

If the blockout is to be permanent, strips of gummed paper may be stuck over the unwanted portion, or a paper the size of the blockout can be stuck over the unwanted portion with gummed tape.

The A. B. Dick Company has the following booklets available at no charge when individual copies are requested: "Techniques of Mimeographing," "How to Plan and Publish a Mimeographed Newspaper," "Fluid Duplicator Supplies Selector," and "Mimeograph Supplies Selector."

DIRECT IMAGE PLATES FOR OFFSET PRESSES

Use of direct image plates such as Plastiplate or Colitho permits the reproduction of copy which has a superior appearance when compared with mimeographed or dittoed copies. Special equipment and materials are required. However, there is a trend toward the use of these newer processes in some schools.

Remington Rand publishes directions for the use of Plastiplate, which is the trade name for their masterplate. The ordinary non-plasticized paper master marketed by organizations such as Addressograph-Multigraph, Colitho, A. B. Dick Company and others is also commonly used. These companies publish specific instructions for its use in offset printing.

25

Copyreading, Proofreading, and Working with the Printer

THERE are occasions when a school secretary's responsibilities go beyond typing a manuscript, also called "copy," and extend to working with the printer, shepherding the publication through the various stages from hiring a printer to okaying the final page proofs.

Schools which have a journalism teacher or other faculty adviser familiar with printing processes (e.g., graduation, plays, awards programs) will seldom need to call upon the school secretary to help in the printing process. The secretary's duties quite likely will extend only to obtaining a printer, and perhaps typing the manuscript or reading the proofs.

Your school's duplicating facilities. Some schools are making use of their own duplicating facilities in the office or are asking the high school business education department to prepare such minor jobs as tickets, announcements, office forms, bulletins, and drama programs. This can be cheaper, but most school do-it-yourself jobs do not measure up to the standards of a professional printer, and there are occasions when a professional-looking job is necessary. Booklets, handbooks, class schedules, and programs for athletic events usually are too large for a school office to undertake.

Working with a commercial printer. Almost everything that needs to be printed for school use probably will be sent to a commercial printer. He can be counted upon to help you with many school printing problems.

Whatever the printing job, you will learn infinitely more about printing from practical experience in working with a printer than you can ever learn from reading thousands of words regarding printing. In any event, regardless of the type of job or who does the printing, the printer expects to be furnished with well-typed copy and complete instructions, or "specifications," for printing the job or booklet.

The printer and the school budget. In the initial planning stage, both you and the printer should be aware of the school budget for printing so that you both have an idea of how much money can be allowed for a particular printing job. Otherwise the printer may come up with some excellent ideas, the cost of which may be prohibitive. You will soon learn that short-run jobs (100 copies or less) are extremely expensive to print; multiple colors and artwork are beautiful but costly; the quality of paper affects the cost of the finished job.

Don't expect a printer to work miracles at rock-bottom prices. Always remember that per-copy printing costs decrease when a large number of copies are printed.

Basic stages in the printing process. There are four basic stages in the manufacturing or printing process with which you are intimately involved:

1. Preparing copy for the printer.
2. Designing or making the layout.
3. Ordering the printing.
4. Marking and approving proofs.

PREPARING COPY FOR THE PRINTER

Printers expect the manuscript to be free from all errors of capitalization, punctuation, spelling, and sentence structure. The process of ridding the manuscript of such errors is called copyediting. It is an essential step that must be done before the manuscript is given its final typing. In addition to well-edited manuscripts, printers expect the artwork also to be in correct form. Artwork includes pictures, charts, and photographs that illustrate and accompany the manuscript. Editing the manuscript is the responsibility of the author, whether he be the principal, a teacher, or a committee of teachers. Any experienced school secretary, though, will tell you that she has had to add many of the finishing touches. Most authors, it seems, are too close to the forest to see the trees. They know so well what they want to say that they fail to recognize that the reader may not find the meaning so clear. Too, the reader sees errors so elemental that they escape the author. You, then, become the stand-in reader who pretests the meaning of statements and detects errors that have escaped the author.

Your responsibility in editing. If you are an inexperienced school secretary, you will protest that you are neither trained nor qualified to question the accuracy of most statements in a manuscript. That is true. Your duty in this respect is discharged when you lightly pencil in a question mark in the margin which says, in effect, "I don't understand this—what does it really mean? Do you think your readers will understand it?" If your author is satisfied with what he has written, you have no further responsibility. But when it comes to old familiar errors in spelling, punctuation, and capitalization, you are in your domain; and you are expected to be alert to common manuscript errors.

What should you look for as you "edit" the manuscript? You should look for consistency! If *High School* is capitalized on one page, then it must be capitalized on all pages. If the comma is omitted before *and* in a series one place, it must be omitted throughout the entire manuscript. Chapter 26 is a guide to acceptable rules of grammar, capitalization, and punctuation, if the school has no rules of its own. Figure 24 shows a properly edited manuscript. Figure 25 shows how the manuscript looks after retyping.

Suggestions for editing. Here are the points a skilled school secretary will look for when she edits the manuscript:

1. Punctuation, particularly commas, quotation marks (especially the final pair), and dashes.
2. Capitalization (common nouns and proper nouns).
3. Spelling (check the dictionary if in doubt).
4. Abbreviations. Abbreviations should be avoided, but if they are used, check for consistency in use.
5. Paragraphs (especially if they are lengthy).
6. Headings (consistency in capitalization, underscoring, centering, and periods).
7. Lists of words, phrases, sentences (consistency throughout in starting with a verb, a noun, a question).
8. Deletions and insertions (typists sometimes fail to take out or put in something written in the margin or on a scrap of paper.
9. Split infinitives (wrong, *to quickly work;* correct, *to work quickly*).
10. "Jumps" (typists sometimes leave out the end of one sentence and beginning of the next by jumping one or two lines and picking up with an identical word or a line or two lower down in the copy).
11. Pronoun antecedents. (For every "he," "she," "it," "they," "then," in the manuscript, ask, "Who is *he?" "she?"* etc).
12. Transpositions of words and lines.
13. Margins. Check also for consistency in paragraph indentations and hanging indentations.
14. Continuity from page to page. Does the last word on a page read correctly to the top of the next page?
15. Page numbers (all sheets should be numbered consecutively.)

In making editing corrections, do so by crossing out the incorrect work and writing the correction above it—not in the margin. The margin is used for instructions to the printer. Make all the corrections between the lines of the typing. If the corrections arc lengthy, lightly draw a pencil line through each line of typing and retype a revised section on another sheet of paper. Then show clearly where the revision is to be inserted. Use copyeditor's (also called copyreader's) marks in correcting the manuscript. See Figure 29. After all corrections and insertions have been marked, the copy is ready for final typing. A final reading for typing errors, of course, is in order. The last typing operation is to number each page consecutively. Figure 30 shows edited manuscript with copyeditor's marks. Figure 31 shows the edited manuscript after retyping.

Preparing the artwork. An essential part of preparing manuscript for the printer is assembly and identification of the artwork.

Identifying the artwork. All artwork must be identified. The art can be numbered or labeled. If numbered, the art should be in the same order as the items will appear in the printed job. There are some precautions that must be observed in marking artwork, especially photographs.

Never write on photographs with a pen or pencil. This cuts the emulsion and the marks will show on the final printed copies. Never put paper clips on photographs, as they, too, leave marks. Type the identification on a sheet of paper and paste (tip) the sheet into the back side of the photograph, letting the sheet and photograph overlap by not more than three-sixteenths of an inch.

Indicate the size of the art. Most artwork is originally larger than it will appear when printed. Therefore the size of the print or photograph must be indicated. Write on the identification sheet the width of the pictures in inches as it is to be when printed. Sometimes the height should be indicated, too, but this is not often necessary.

Occasionally the entire picture is not to be printed. Use "crop marks" to indicate the horizontal and vertical boundaries of the picture to be printed. The crop marks can be tiny lines (about one-quarter inch) on the margins of the picture. Use a blue pencil. The photoengraver understands that any portion outside the crop marks is not to be printed.

Assemble and protect the artwork. A list of all the artwork should be typed with a simple description of each item. The list should be in the same order as the item will appear in the printed job. All valuable drawings should have kraft paper to cover the face. All artwork should be wrapped flat and placed in sturdy folders or envelopes so that they will be protected from damage. A cardboard somewhat larger than the artwork is sometimes used as a protective cover.

DESIGNING OR MAKING THE LAYOUT

Printing a booklet, program, or even a ticket is like building a house. A set of "blueprints" is necessary. The *printer's blueprint* is the layout or dummy. A *layout* is a hand-drawn "picture" of what the final printing will look like.

It is not often that a school has someone on the staff qualified to prepare a dummy or layout. A *"dummy"* consists of blank sheets of paper cut and folded to the size of the printed booklet. The placement of the type and pictures is indicated in pencil.

Figure 29. Marks for editing and proofreading.

Copyeditor's Marks	Meaning	Proofreader's Marks
	SIZE AND STYLE OF TYPE	
	(Wrong size or style of type) reset. *wf*	*wf*
l.c.	Use lower case letter.	*lc*
a	Use capital letter or SET IN capitals.	a
Quantity	Set in italic (or oblique) type.	ital
Bold	Set in bold face (black) type.	*bf*
	Use Roman (regular) type; not Italics or bold face.	*rom*
	PARAGRAPHING	
¶ L	Begin a paragraph.	¶
No ¶	No paragraph.	No ¶; run in.
	Run in or run together.	
hang indent	Use hanging indention. In this style the first line is flush (not indented) and all lines thereafter are indented.	
	INSERTION, DELETION, AND SPACING	
	Something has been left out; see copy.	OUT- S. C.
	Insert missing letters words.	missing
	Close up entirely.	Close up
	Omit the synonyms and words crossed out and bridged over.	
stet	Let it stand; disregard corrections.	stet

Figure 29 (*Continued*)

Copyeditor's Marks	Meaning	Proofreader's Marks
Thebook	Separate; insert space.	thebook
School	Take out (delete)	School

PUNCTUATION

⊙	Insert period.	⊙
⋏ :	Insert comma, colon.	⋏ ⊙ ⌒ :/
ꞌꞌ/ꞌꞌ	Insert quotation marks; ꞌꞌquotes.ꞌꞌ	ꞌꞌ ꞌꞌ
=	Insert hyphen.	/=/
/⸺/	Insert dash.	/⸺/

POSITIONING

	Move] to right.	⊐
	[Move to left.	⊏
(center) ⊐⊏	]Put in center of line of page.⊏	⊐ ⊏
	Line up.	//
∾	Transpose order of letters	lettres ⌒tr
⌒	Transpose or letters words.	⌒

MISCELLANEOUS

	(Upside down; reverse)	⊙
(Feb.)	Spell out; do not abbreviate.	(Feb.)
(February)	Abbreviate; do not spell out.	(February)
(16)	Spell out; do not use numerals.	(16)
(sixteen)	Use numbers; do not spell out.	(sixteen)

Examine the dummy to see whether every detail is the way you want it. If it isn't, correct it now. It won't cost any money to correct it at this point. You buy exactly what you see, and what the printer sees. Correcting oversights or altering the layout or dummy after it has been set in type can be very, very expensive.

Schools which have yearbook advisers or art instructors trained in commercial art and typographical design are fortunate. Such teachers usually can prepare an acceptable dummy or layout to guide the printer. Other schools may have to rely upon the printer's ability to make the printing look attractive.

ORDERING THE PRINTING

Ordering printing is as much buying a service as it is purchasing a product. No one can be absolutely certain of what the finished product will be like until it is done. Advertising agencies have solved this problem reasonably well, but schools are dependent upon the typographical skills and integrity of the printer.

Secure cost estimates. Most schools call upon one of the well-established commercial printers to help them with the specifications and to make a preliminary cost estimate. When the printing is likely to cost more than a specified amount, say $100, some schools must by law ask three printers to give a cost estimate or bid.

Prepare printing specifications. The list of printing specifications in Chapter 28 can be used as a guide in discussing with a printer what points are to be covered in his estimate or bid. These specifications are primarily for school booklets and similar publications. The points listed, with a few variations, are essentially the same for tickets, programs, invitations, and the like. You will find it helpful to follow this list in going over your copy or manuscript with the printer. It will remind him of the points to be agreed upon. He will add other specifications if your printing order calls for special handling.

Decide number of copies. A major expense in most printing is the cost of setting the type. So, whether there are to be 100 or 500 copies, the cost of typesetting is the same. The total printing cost, except when the most expensive papers are used, of a small job and a job of 1,000 copies is essentially the same. Only when additional quantities of 500 or 1,000 are added to the original order is a real savings to be made. The advice of any printer concerning this point will be reliable.

Place responsibility for proofreading. Where most schools experience difficulty, it is with the quality of the proofreading and the design of the printing. Many printers, especially small ones, dislike to accept responsibility for accurate proofreading. Schools must remain adamant that a printer submit error-free proofs, at least to the extent of typographical errors. Typographical errors are those due to so-called mechanical failures in the print shop or linotype machine and are not due to changes which the author—or the school—may make after the printer has set the type. Printers make an additional charge for correcting errors (*alterations*) in grammar, capitalization, even punctuation. Alterations are very expensive. It behooves every school to be sure that the original copy or manuscript is free from all errors.

Specify delivery and packaging. Indicate to the printer how the material is to be delivered—loose, banded, packaged, boxed, in rolls, or any other special instructions.

Set reasonable deadlines. Decide on a reasonable delivery date in planning the job with the printer; then make it a part of the contract. Most printers need a minimum of four to six weeks for a publication of any size. They can rush through simple jobs, such as tickets or programs, in a week but may charge extra for the fast service.

Remember that the more definite you can make the specifications, the more accurate the printer can be in his cost estimate or contract. This will result in a savings for your school.

MARKING AND APPROVING PROOFS

The printing specifications should provide that the printer is responsible for all typographical errors and for correcting them before submission of any proofs to the school. Be this as it may, unless the printer has a skilled proofreader on his staff, the school is quite likely to receive proofs in which the "typos" have not been eliminated. What can be done? There are three courses of action: (1) if more than one typographical error appears on the first proof or two, the entire set of proofs can be returned to the printer; (2) the school can go ahead and read the proofs for both typographical and other errors; (3) the school can refuse to let the printer have any further printing orders. There is likelihood that some printer will make no price adjustment for "typo" errors even if he doesn't quite live up to the terms of his contract in the matter of proofreading.

The school, and this often means "you," must be prepared to read proof. Proofs come in two forms, galleys proofs and page proofs.

Galley proofs. Galley proofs are sheets of paper about 5 or 6 inches wide and 20 to 24 inches long. They show the lines of type just as they were set on the linotype machine usually without headings or spacings, always without cuts. Galley proofs are always submitted when a booklet is to be printed. (For ordinary job printing, such as file cards and letterheads, only a proof of the job as it will look in final form is submitted.) Each galley is numbered, and the type is usually in the same sequence as in the manuscript.

Page proofs. Page proofs are sheets of paper somewhat larger than the final page size. They show exactly how the type on each printed page will look with all the headings, spacing, and cuts in place. There will be a page proof for each page in the printed book. Each page will carry the page number (sometimes called "folio") as it will appear in the final printing.

Revised proofs. If the number of errors runs more than five or six to a galley, or two or more to a page proof, it is wise to request revised proofs to check whether the corrections have been made properly. It is not uncommon for a new error to be made in the course of correcting an old error.

PROOFREADING

Up to recent years the practice was to use two persons in the proofreading process. One person, called the proofreader, silently read the galley proof and marked the errors. The other person, called the copyholder, read the manuscript aloud. The proofreader watched the lines of type as he listened to the sequence of words, punctuation, and capitalization read by the copyholder.

The trend is now toward having the proofreader read the galley proof against the manuscript. This eliminates the expense and time of one person, actually goes faster, and apparently results in as much accuracy as when the proofreader had to divide his attention between the lines of type and the copyholder's words. Figure 30 shows an uncorrected galley proof with proofreader's marks. Figure 31 shows a revised galley proof with errors corrected.

How to proofread galley proofs. When you receive the galley proofs, you should follow these steps:

1. Check the number of each galley proof received for sequence and omissions.
2. Check that the manuscript (copy) for every galley proof is also received.
3. Check the first and last words of each paragraph to see that no paragraphs have been omitted.
4. Check the last word on each galley proof with the first word of the next galley proof to see that they read together correctly and are in proper sequence.
5. Read each line of type with concentration, looking for inconsistencies and errors. Use a soft (No. 2) pencil to indicate errors.
6. Note each error in the margin and draw a horizontal line connecting the error in the type to the correction symbol in the margin.
7. Watch for incorrect word divisions. If in doubt, check the dictionary for location of the hyphen.
8. Compare all subheadings, center headings, and italicized type with the exact wording and capitalization shown in the manuscript.
9. Swing the eye from the galley proof to the manuscript to see that the correct words have been printed and that there are no word omissions or duplications.

10. If in doubt concerning what to do or if there seems to be something wrong, put a question mark in the margin with a circle around it and draw this to the author's attention *before* returning the proof to the printer.

11. At the end of each galley proof, write "OK" or "OK with corrections" and sign your name.

12. Return both the galley proofs and the manuscript to the printer. Avoid the temptation to rewrite what you read on the galley proof. Do not make changes from the original manuscript. Admittedly, this has to be done occasionally, but you'll have a real shock when the alteration charges come in for these apparently innocuous changes. And the business manager isn't going to like you if he has to pay more money!

How to proofread revised galley proofs. It is customary for first-class printers to submit revised galley proofs. Sometimes this step is omitted when the job is being rushed. In such event, checking of corrections must be done on the page proofs.

It is not necessary to re-read the entire galley proof when checking for revisions. Also, proofs of galleys with no errors may not be returned to the school. It is good practice, however, to insist upon a complete set of second (revised) proofs. The manuscript and the original galley proofs also should be returned to the school. Lay the revised proof alongside the original galley proof, starting with the first galley.

1. Read each line of type that had an error in it, checking that the error has been corrected.

2. Don't just look for the error alone, read the entire line. There may be a new error somewhere else in the line.

3. Check the line above and the line below the error line to be sure that the lines read together correctly. (Sometimes a printer takes out the wrong line or puts the new line in the wrong place.)

4. Check that the first and last lines of the revised galley proof are the same as on the original galley proof. (Sometimes a printer has to shift type from one galley to the next or he may drop a line or two.)

5. If errors have not been corrected, re-mark them as on the original galley proof.

6. At the end of each galley proof write, "OK" or "OK with corrections" and sign your name.

7. Return the original and revised galley proofs and manuscripts to the printer.

How to proofread page proofs. All errors marked on the galley proofs should have been corrected before the type was made up into pages. This is usually true when revised galley proofs have been proofread. When revised galley proofs have not been proofread, it is necessary to check each page proof against the original galley proof to be sure that every error has been corrected and that no additional errors have been made.

1. Check that all pages are complete and in proper sequence. (There should be a blank page even for pages with no printing on them.)

2. Systematically check the last word on each page proof with the first word of the next page to see that they read together correctly.

3. Systematically check that every paragraph is indented and that there is a period at the end of each.

4. Systematically check that all center heads and side heads have identical capitalization and bold face (if any). Check that they have the same amount of spacing (called "leading") above and below the line of type.

5. Check that there is the same amount of leading between every line. (Some indifferent printers are inclined to double-lead (double the spacing between lines) to avoid re-making pages.

6. Check that folios (page numbers) are in the correct position. Unless *all* folios are centered at the bottom of the page, odd page numbers should be on the right-hand side and even page numbers on the left-hand side.

7. Read every caption for errors. Check that the cut appears close to where it is mentioned in the manuscript.

8. Check the table of contents to be sure that the folios (page numbers) are the same as for each chapter in the page proofs. Repeat this procedure if there is a list of illustrations or figures.

9. Check and double check the spelling of proper names on the cover, title page, and acknowledgments page. Make one final and supreme effort to see that no name has been left out or misspelled. Even if you do have to pay an alterations charge, get people's names and titles absolutely correct.

10. At the end of each page proofed, write "OK" or "OK with corrections" and initial.

11. Return all galley proofs and manuscript with the page proofs. Insist upon revised page proofs if you have uncovered a lot of uncorrected errors or if you are beginning to have doubts about whether your printer is as meticulous in making corrections as he should be.

Do not be too concerned about margins. Printers usually are careful on this point, and page proofs seldom indicate the proper positioning of the type on the final page.

PREPARING THE ILLUSTRATIONS

In general, there are two ways of reproducing illustrations in a book—by line cut, or by halftone. Line cuts are illustrations (drawings, charts, graphs, pictographs) that consist only of lines or areas of solid black and white. Halftones must always be used to reproduce gradations of shading or tone, the grays between black and white, that are found in photographs, paintings, and wash drawings. Halftones, when examined closely, are composed of dots. These can be seen under a magnifying glass.

Pointers in preparing illustrations. Following are a few general rules which should help you in preparing line illustrations:

PREPARING THE ILLUSTRATIONS

¶ In general, there are two ways of ~~printing~~ *reproducing* illustrations in a book — by line cut or by halftone. Line cuts are made of these illustrations (drawings, charts, graphs, ~~and~~ pictographs) that consist only of lines and of areas of solid black and white.

Halftones must be used always to reproduce graduations of shading or tone between black and white found in photographs, paintings, and wash drawings.

¶ Here are a few general rules to follow:

1. make the original drawing at least (1 1/2) times but preferably no more than twice the size the illustration is to be in the book. This serves two purposes: (one) it is easier to achieve accuracy on a large drawing than on a small one, and (2) minor defects tend to disappear when the drawing is reduced.

2. Make the dimensions of the drawing in proportion to a type page 4 (ins.) wide by 7 inches deep, unless some other ~~size~~ size has been agreed upon in advance.

3. Use black drawing ink and make all lines, whatever their weight, densely black and sharp. In considering the weight of the various lines, keep the proposed reduction in mind and avoid making any so fine that they will be lost in reduction.

4. *Indicate* (Crosshatching or stippling) ~~should be indicated~~ on a tissue overlay. If you desire to apply the shading directly on the drawing, you may do it with ~~special~~ *a mechanical* shading ~~paper~~ *medium* such as Contak, ben Day, or zipatone, which can be purchased from any art *supply* store. Remember that the design of the shading will be reduced with the rest of the drawing; therefore

310

use a reducing glass to determine the effect of such reduction.

Typist out / See original / copy →

Be sure to submit a ~~first~~ *sample* drawing for approval *before proceeding*.

6. Do *the* lettering carefully and consistent*ly* in sans*-*serif (block)

letters, keeping their size after reduction constantly in mind.

LEROY lettering (a mechanical method involving the use of a

scriber and assorted templates) is prefer*r*ed to poor *by executed* free-hand

lettering.

Figure 30. Edited manuscript with copyeditor's marks. The figure shows manuscript copy properly edited with copyeditor's (copyreader's) marks. The typist retypes the edited manuscript before it is sent to the printer for typesetting. Copyeditor's marks are similar to proofreader's marks. Copyeditor's marks are inserted on the typing where the error occurs or where a change in wording is to be made.

PREPARING THE ILLUSTRATIONS

In general, there are two ways of reproducing illustrations in a book — by line cut or by halftone. Line cuts are made of those illustrations (drawings, charts, graphs, pictographs) that consist only of lines and of areas of solid black and white. Halftones must always be used to reproduce gradations of shading or tone between black and white found in photographs, paintings, and wash drawings.

Here are a few general rules to follow:

1. Make the original drawing at least one and one-half times but preferably no more than twice the size the illustration is to be in the book. This serves two purposes: (1) it is easier to achieve accuracy on a large drawing than on a small one; and (2) minor defects tend to disappear when the drawing is reduced.

2. Make the dimensions of the drawing in proportion to a type page

Figure 31 (*continues onto next page*)

4 inches wide by 7 inches deep, unless some other size has been agreed upon in advance.

3. Use black drawing ink and make all lines, whatever their weight, densely black and sharp. In considering the weight of the various lines, keep the proposed reduction in mind and avoid making any so fine that they will be lost in reduction.

4. Indicate crosshatching or stippling on a tissue overlay. If you desire to apply the shading directly on the drawing, you may do it with a mechanical shading medium such as Contak, Ben Day, or Zipatone, which can be purchased from any art-supply store. Remember that the design of the shading will be reduced with the rest of the drawing; therefore use a reducing glass to determine the effect of such reduction. Be sure to submit a sample drawing for approval before proceeding.

5. In plotting graphs, use a light-blue-lined paper if the grid is not to appear in the reproduction (light blue does not photograph); use black-, green-, or orange-lined paper if the grid should appear.

6. Do the lettering carefully and consistently in sans-serif (block) letters, keeping their size after reduction constantly in mind. LEROY lettering (a mechanical method involving the use of a scriber and assorted templates) is preferred to poorly executed free-hand lettering.

Figure 31. Edited manuscript after retyping. The figure shows the retyped manuscript after editing by the author. It is now ready to go to the printer for typesetting.

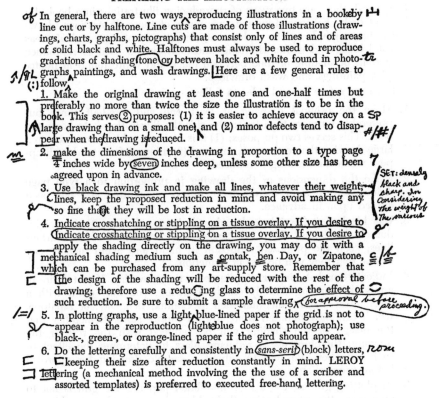

Figure 32. Uncorrected galley proof with proofreader's marks. The figure shows the original galley proof properly marked with proofreader's marks. The printer resets each line that contains an error. Proofmarks are placed in the margin of the galley proof nearest to the line containing the error. A line is drawn from the proofmark to the place in the line where the error occurs. The printer submits a revised galley proof to show that the error has been corrected.

PREPARING THE ILLUSTRATIONS

In general, there are two ways of reproducing illustrations in a book—by line cut or by halftone. Line cuts are made of those illustrations (drawings, charts, graphs, pictographs) that consist only of lines and of areas of solid black and white. Halftones must always be used to reproduce gradations of shading or tone between black and white found in photographs, paintings, and wash drawings.

Here are a few general rules to follow.

1. Make the original drawing at least one and one-half times but preferably no more than twice the size the illustration is to be in the book. This serves two purposes: (1) it is easier to achieve accuracy on a large drawing than on a small one; and (2) minor defects tend to disappear when the drawing is reduced.

2. Make the dimensions of the drawing in proportion to a type page 4 inches wide by 7 inches deep, unless some other size has been agreed upon in advance.

3. Use black drawing ink and make all lines, whatever their weight, densely black and sharp. In considering the weight of the various lines, keep the proposed reduction in mind and avoid making any so fine that they will be lost in reduction.

4. Indicate crosshatching or stippling on a tissue overlay. If you desire to apply the shading directly on the drawing, you may do it with a mechanical shading medium such as Contak, Ben Day, or Zipatone, which can be purchased from any art-supply store. Remember that the design of the shading will be reduced with the rest of the drawing; therefore use a reducing glass to determine the effect of such reduction. Be sure to submit a sample drawing for approval before proceeding.

5. In plotting graphs, use a light-blue-lined paper if the grid is not to appear in the reproduction (light blue does not photograph); use black-, green-, or orange-lined paper if the grid should appear.

6. Do the lettering carefully and consistently in sans-serif (block) letters, keeping their size after reduction constantly in mind. LEROY lettering (a mechanical method involving the use of a scriber and assorted templates) is preferred to poorly executed free-hand lettering.

Figure 33. Revised galley proof with errors corrected. The figure shows the revised galley proof with all the errors corrected. The printer can now proceed to make up the type into pages. Page proofs should be checked with similar care.

5

A Reference Shelf for
the School Secretary

26

A Guide to Punctuation, Capitalization, and Grammar

MANY TIMES you will play a major role in typing and editing letters and manuscripts. Writers—whether they are principals or teachers—often put their thoughts on paper rapidly and in rough form. Even though they know acceptable English style, they may not take the time to write carefully. Thus, to the school secretary, falls the job of editing the material.

Authorities often differ in their recommendations as to what is considered good usage. This chapter* explains some of the rules and principles regarding punctuation, capitalization, and grammar which are generally considered acceptable. For further information, consult a dictionary, a high school or college language book, or a manual which explains the preparation of manuscripts. You should also discuss with your principal or the writer the usage he wants you to use.

PUNCTUATION

The principal objective of punctuation is to make clear the meaning of the written word so that the reader knows and understands what is meant. Standard rules of grammar should be followed but, in any case, the punctuation should be consistent throughout the text.

Punctuation marks. The common marks of punctuation are indicated below. Their most important uses are explained in this chapter. Become familiar with them so that you can use them intelligently. Never forget that the principal object of punctuation is clarity.

[']	Apostrophe	[.]	Period
[,]	Comma	[?]	Question mark (interrogation.)
[:]	Colon	" "	Quotation marks
!	Exclamation point	;	Semicolon
-	Hyphen	. . .	Ellipsis
( )	Parentheses	_____	Underscore
[ ]	Brackets		

* This chapter is an adaptation from *Complete Secretary's Handbook*, by Lillian Doris and Besse May Miller (Englewood Cliffs, N.J.; Prentice-Hall, Inc., 1960).

Other punctuation marks which may be used on occasion are:

é	Accent, acute		(ö)	Diaresis
è	Accent, grave		‡	Double dagger
*	Asterisk		....	Leaders
{ or }	Braces		¶	Paragraph
ʌ	Caret		||	Parallels
(ç)	Cedilla		§	Section
ʌ	Circumflexion		~	Tilde
†	Dagger		/	Virgule

APOSTROPHES

POSSESSIVES. (1) Use the apostrophe and *s* to indicate the possessive case of singular nouns.

boy's hat   girl's dress

(2) Do not use the apostrophe to indicate possessive case of pronouns.

its (Note: it's is the contraction of it is.)

(3) Use the apostrophe and *'s* to form the possessive plural of nouns which do not end in *s*.

children's clothes

(4) Use the apostrophe only to form the possessive plural of nouns which end in *s*.

girls' hats

(5) By common usage the apostrophe can be omitted in names of many organizations where the possessive case is implied.

Teachers College
Veterans Administration
Blank Teachers Association

CONTRACTIONS. Use the apostrophe to denote a contraction or omission of letters. Place the apostrophe where the letter or letters are omitted.

it's for it is
haven't for have not
ass'n for association
class of '61

BUT omit the apostrophe in commonly used contractions.

phone for telephone
plane for airplane

LETTERS AND SYMBOLS. Use the apostrophe to form the plurals of letters and symbols.

a's and b's   7's   #'s   the 1930's

WORDS. Use an apostrophe to indicate the plural of a word referred to without regard to its meaning, but use the regularly formed plural if a meaning is attached to the word.

> There are three *but*'s in the sentence.
> There are six *fives* in thirty.

ABBREVIATIONS. Use an apostrophe to denote the plural or some other form of an abbreviation.

four OK's   OK'd   V.I.P's

COMMAS

APPOSITIVES. Use a comma to set off an appositive; that is, an expression that explains or gives additional information about a preceding expression.

The assistant superintendent, *Dr. Davis,* is in charge of the curriculum.

BUT do not separate two nouns, one of which identifies the other.

> The writer *Smith* is one of our principals.

CITIES AND STATES. Separate the name of a city from the name of a state; also, separate the name of the state from the rest of the sentence.

Baker Company of Chicago, *Illinois,* will supply the furniture for the new school.

COMPOUND PREDICATES. Compound predicates are not usually separated by commas.

The total number of residents in the school district is increasing *and* will probably continue to increase.

COMPOUND SENTENCES. Separate the independent clauses of a compound sentence by a comma, unless the thoughts expressed require a more emphatic separation than the comma. (See Semicolons.) The comma precedes the conjunction.

I would like to accept your invitation to the faculty breakfast, *but* I will be out of town at that time.

The comma may be omitted before *and* if the clauses are short and closely connected in thought.

We inspected the damage to the door *and* will repair it this Friday.

DASH AND COMMA. Do not use a dash and comma together.

DATES. Separate the day of the month from the year by a comma. If no day is given, separate the month from the year by a comma. The trend is to omit the comma after the year, unless the construction of the sentence requires punctuation.

> . . . payable May 16, 1961 to the business office.
> . . . as of July 6, 1961, the school board . . .

ELLIPSIS. Use a comma to indicate that one or more words, easily understood, have been omitted. (A construction of this type is known as an *ellipsis*.)

> The fourth grade tested 80 per cent; the fifth grade, 85 per cent.

ESSENTIAL AND NONESSENTIAL PHRASES AND CLAUSES. A restrictive phrase or clause is one that is essential to the meaning of the sentence and is not merely descriptive or parenthetical; it should not be set off by commas. A nonrestrictive phrase or clause is one that adds an additional thought to the sentence but is not essential to the meaning of the sentence; it should be set off by commas.

> The teacher *who spoke at the meeting* lives in this community.
> The school secretary, *who has been ill for the past week,* will return Tuesday.

INTRODUCTORY WORDS. Use a comma to separate an introductory word from the rest of the sentence.

> *Yes,* the graduation will be held as scheduled.

INSEPARABLES. Do not separate words that belong together and are interdependent, such as a verb from its subject or object or predicate nominative, or a limiting clause from its antecedent.

In the following examples the commas in brackets should be omitted.

> The increase in enrollment at the high school [,] is due to the opening of the new tract of homes. (*The comma separates the subject "increase" from its verb "is."*)
> The plans for changing the course of study add to the teacher's suggestions [,] the best ideas of the administrative staff. (*The comma separates the verb "add" from its object "ideas."*)
> The allowance made for depreciation in this appraisal, as in all others [,] where consideration is given to obsolescence, is a fair one. (*The "where" starts a limiting relative clause modifying "others."*)

NAMES. Do not use a comma between a name and *of* indicating place or position.

> Nash Company *of* El Paso, Texas.
> Mr. Jones *of* Norton & Co.

Place a comma between a name and *Inc., Sr.,* and the like.

> Lever Brothers, Ltd.   E. F. Smith, Sr.
> (*Some authorities say not to use the comma between the name and* Sr.)

NOUNS IN DIRECT ADDRESS. Separate a noun used in direct address with a comma.

> We want to thank you, Mrs. Jones, for your assistance.

NUMBERS. Use a comma when writing figures in thousands, BUT NOT in street, room, post office box, and telephone numbers.

$16,749.62	4,700	1432 Alondra Avenue
P.O. Box 5462		CLinton 6–3241

O, OH. Use a comma after *oh* if other words follow it, but do not use a comma after the vocative *O*.

> Oh, he reported on the meeting last week.
> O Shepherd, speak!

PARENTHESES AND COMMA. Use a comma after a closing parenthesis if the construction of the sentence requires a comma. Never use a comma before a parenthetical expression.

> The school building needs new lighting, a new heating system (preferably gas), and complete redecoration.

PARENTHETICAL WORDS AND PHRASES. Use commas to set off parenthetical words or phrases like *I believe, for example, however,* unless the connection is close and smooth enough not to call for a pause in reading.

> *Furthermore,* the boy may be suspended if he doesn't pay for the damage.
> The school system, *I believe,* is gradually improving.
> This type of program is interesting and *therefore* appeals to the children.

BUT distinguish between words used parenthetically and the same words used as adverbs.

> *However,* I shall be unable to meet you there. (*Parenthetical*)
> *However* carefully we prepare the school budget, changes must be made during the school year. (*Adverb*)
> *Thus* was a small incident built into a major issue. (*Adverb*)
> *Thus,* it is best to agree upon the type of guidance program we should have. (*Parenthetical*)

PARTICIPIAL PHRASES. Do not separate a participle from the noun it modifies when the noun is not the subject and the phrase itself is not closely connected with the rest of the sentence.

> The parents having agreed to the program, there was nothing further to discuss. (*There should be no comma between* parents *and* having.)

PHRASES WITH A COMMON ELEMENT. Place a comma before a word or words that are common to two or more phrases but are expressed only after the last phrase. In the following examples the commas in brackets are frequently *omitted in error*.

> The report was documented with references to many, if not all [,] of the research studies on spelling. (*The words "of the . . ." are common to "many" and to "all."*)

Mr. Green's reports are clearer, more concise, more accurate [,] than those of any other principal. (*The words "than those . . ." are common to "clearer," "more concise," and "more accurate."*)

NOTE: If the phrases are connected by a conjunction, the comma is not needed.

. . . are clearer, more concise [,] *and* more accurate than those . . .

QUOTATIONS. Set off direct quotations by commas.

Her answer was, "I enjoy teaching music to little children."
"I don't like class interruptions," he complained.

BUT if a question mark is needed at the end of the quotation, do not use a comma.

"Where is the class roll sheet?" he inquired.

QUOTATION MARKS AND COMMA. Place the comma on the *inside* of quotation marks.

When he spoke of a "teacher's teacher," it reminded me of old Mr. Hoskins.

SERIES. Separate words and phrases in a series by a comma. Use the comma before the conjunction connecting the last two members of a series. (See the use of a semicolon in a series, page 331.)

Our school is emphasizing the teaching of reading, spelling, *and* arithmetic this year.

Separate consecutive adjectives which modify the same noun, if the adjectives are coordinate in meaning.

He is a diligent, conscientious teacher.
He is a happy little child.

BUT do not use a comma between two parallel constructions joined by a conjunction.

The total test score includes (1) the language score and (2) the non-language score.
The teacher asked for a conference or at the least an explanation of our school safety rules.

SUBORDINATE CLAUSE. Set off a subordinate clause which precedes the main clause of a sentence by a comma.

When the textbooks arrive, we will deliver them to your classroom.

COLONS

INTRODUCTION TO LISTS, TABULATIONS. The most frequent use of the colon is after a word, phrase, or sentence that introduces lists, a series, tabulations, extracts, texts, and explanations that are in apposition to the introductory words. Words following a colon begin with a small letter unless using a proper name or typing a list.

The following is a summary of the test results: all children gained in reading, 80 per cent . . .
These problems must be met: cost of building maintenance, salaries, . . .

BUT do not use a colon to introduce a series of items that are the direct objects of a preposition or verb, or that follow a form of the verb *to be.*

Wrong: The secretary should get all information such *as:* name, address, birthdate, etc. (*Omit the colon.*)
Wrong: The winners of the spelling contest are: John, Mary, and Jimmy. (*Omit the colon.*)

NOTE: A colon may precede a formal tabulation even when the tabulated words or phrases are the objects of a preposition or verb or follow a form of the verb *to be.*

> Among the expense items are:
> maintenance and repair costs
> supplies and equipment
> salaries of personnel

QUOTATIONS. The colon is used before a long quotation.

TITLES OF BOOKS. The subtitle of a book is separated from the title by a colon.

A Brief Guide for Curriculum Committees: *Preparing a Curriculum Manuscript.*

SALUTATIONS. The colon is used after salutations of business letters.

Dear Mr. Roberts:

TIME. Use a colon to indicate clock time, unless the time indicated is on the hour.

5 A.M.   8:45 P.M.

FOOTNOTES. When reference is made to a publication in a footnote, use a colon to separate the name of the city of publication from the name of the publisher.

Arthur E. Traxler, *Techniques of Guidance* (New York: Harper & Brothers, Pubishers, 1945), p. 147.

BIBLE REFERENCES. Use a colon to separate the verse and chapter in Biblical references.

Matthew 10:4

DASH AND COLON. Do not use a dash with a colon.

DASHES

PRINCIPAL USE. The dash is used principally to set off explanatory clauses, to indicate abrupt changes in the continuity of expression, and to set off a thought that is repeated for emphasis.

SERIES. A dash may be used before or after a clause that summarizes a series of words or phrases, but a colon is more common *after* such a clause.

Guidance, counseling, schooling for the handicapped—these are a few of the services our school district offers.

Our school district overlaps three cities: Bellflower, Long Beach, and South Gate.

DASH AND OTHER PUNCTUATION MARKS. A dash may be used after an abbreviating period. If the material set off by dashes requires an interrogation or exclamation point, retain the punctuation before the second dash. Do not use a dash with a comma or semicolon. Do not use a dash and colon together before a list of items.

Minutes OK for P.T.A.—we made the correction.

The professor who wrote the article—is his name Benton or Stevenson?—stated that more science is now being taught in the schools.

EXCLAMATION POINTS

EXCLAMATORY SENTENCES. Place an exclamation point after a startling statement or a sentence expressing strong emotion.

How surprising that he failed the examination!

EXCLAMATORY WORDS. Place an exclamation point after exclamatory words.

Hurrah!

FOR EMPHASIS. If not used to excess, an exclamation point is a good device to lend emphasis or to drive home a point.

Teach well!
You are one in a million!

HYPHENS

DIVISIONS OF WORDS. Use a hyphen at the end of a line to show that a part of a word has been carried over to another line. See page 331 for the principles governing the division of words at the end of a line.

COMPOUND TERMS. A compound term refers to two or more short words written together or joined by a hyphen, or written separately but expressing a single idea. Thus, *editor-in-chief, businessman,* and *vice-princi-*

pal are all compounds. The authorities differ as to what compounds shall be written separately, hyphenated, or written as one word. Use a late edition of a standard dictionary as your guide.

Use the hyphen in compound words where its omission would cause confusion in meaning or pronunciation.

two-place table, head-on collision, double-period class

Hyphenate combinations of words used as single adjectives when preceding the nouns modified.

one-way street   up-to-date methods

Do not hyphenate these combinations when they are not used as adjectives preceding nouns.

Drive only one way on this street.
Our teaching methods are up to date.

SERIES OF HYPHENATED WORDS. In a series of hyphenated words having a common base, place a hyphen after the first element of each word and write the base after the last word only.

fourth-, fifth-, or sixth-floor offices

TIME. Use a hyphen to indicate a span of time.

1960–63

NUMBERS. Use a hyphen for all compound numbers from twenty-one through ninety-nine. Use hyphens in fractions when the numerator and denominator are one-word forms. (Some authorities do not recommend the use of a hyphen in such cases.)

one-third (1/3)   Two-fifths (2/5)

Omit the hyphen when either or both numerator and denominator already contain a hyphen.

three and three-fourths (3¾)

PREFIXES. The hyphen is usually omitted with the prefixes "in," "non," and "pre" except with proper nouns and adjectives.

inservice, prevocational, but pre-Roman

PARENTHESES AND BRACKETS

BRACKETS. If your typewriter has a bracket key, use brackets to enclose comments or explanations in quoted material, to rectify mistakes, and to enclose parentheses within parentheses; otherwise, use parentheses for these purposes. If necessary, brackets can be made by using the virgule and dash.

EXPLANATORY EXPRESSIONS. Use parentheses to enclose comments or explanatory expressions that are incidental to the meaning of the sentence. Parentheses indicate a stronger separation than do commas or dashes.

In Los Angeles, which has the largest city area in the the world (254 square miles), progress is being made toward solving the school housing problem.

FIGURES. Enclose a figure in parentheses when it follows an amount that has been written out in words, and when the American equivalent of foreign currency is given.

> Under the will he received £100,000 ($280,000).
> Six thousand three hundred (6,300) dollars
> Four thousand two hundred dollars ($4,200)

NOTE: If the figure is written before the word "dollars," do not use the dollar sign; if the figure is written after the word "dollars," use the dollar sign. This rule also applies to the per cent sign.

QUESTIONS AND ANSWERS. In question and answer material, use parentheses to enclose matter describing an action and, also, to indicate a person who has not previously taken part in the questions and answers.

Q. (By Mr. Jones, the principal) Will you identify this picture? (handing pupil the picture).

ENUMERATION. Enclose in parentheses letters or numbers in enumerations run into the text.

Building upkeep is concerned with two factors: (1) costs of repairs and (2) cost of maintenance.

SINGLE (CLOSING) PARENTHESES. Parentheses are usually used in pairs, but a single closing parentheses may be used instead of a period to follow a letter or small Roman numeral in outlines and in lettering and numbering paragraphs. See page 338.

PUNCTUATION IN PARENTHESES. Commas, periods, and similar punctuation marks belong within the parentheses if they belong to the parenthetical clause or phrase. They are outside the parentheses if they belong to the words of the rest of the sentence. See, also, periods and parentheses, page 327.

A 10-inch advertisement to appear in one column would be indicated as 140 × 1 (read "140 on 1," or "140 by 1," meaning a space of 140 agate lines deep by one column wide).

PERIODS

SENTENCES. Place a period at the end of a declarative or imperative sentence.

> The school board met last Wednesday. (*Declarative*)
> Keep the school grounds clean. (*Imperative*)

ENUMERATED LISTS. Omit the period after items in enumerated lists unless the items make complete sentences.

INITIALS AND ABBREVIATIONS. Place a period after initials and abbreviations. There are a few exceptions to this rule. Preferably, the periods are omitted between initials standing for Federal agencies.

Ph.D.   C.O.D.   *ibid.*   Chas.   Thos.   R.E. Smith   CAA

OUTLINES. Place a period after each letter or number in an outline or itemized list unless the letter or number is enclosed in parentheses. Do not use a period at the end of items in an outline when the phrase form is being used.

OMISSIONS. Omit the period after:

Contractions (ass'n, sec'y)
Roman numerals, except in an outline (Vol. IV, Henry VIII)
Sums of money in dollar denominations, unless cents are added ($30, $60.75)
Shortened forms of names and words in common use (Ed, Will, ad, memo, per cent, photo)
Letters identifying radio stations (KFI, CBS)

Do not use a period before a participial phrase, an appositive, or a subordinate clause which is rightfully the concluding part of a sentence.

Wrong: The report included the test summary for the school. Together with the results by grades.
Right: The report included the test summary for the school together with the results by grades.

PERIODS AND PARENTHESES. When an expression in parentheses comes at the end of a sentence and is part of the sentence, put the period outside the parentheses; if the expression is independent of the sentence and a period is necessary, place the period within the parentheses.

The cost of the inservice educational program is explained elsewhere in this report (see page 6).
The athletic field includes tennis courts, a football field, and three baseball diamonds. (Sketch here shows layout of play areas.)

BUT do not use a period when a complete declarative or imperative sentence is enclosed in parentheses *within a sentence.*

The business manager will not permit any duplicate keys to be made (all necessary keys will be furnished by the central office), but if more than two keys for any door-lock shall be desired, the principal must request them in writing.

PERIODS AND QUOTATION MARKS. Always place the period *inside* the quotation marks.

Ask the business manager for the definition of "capital outlay."

QUESTION MARKS (INTERROGATION POINTS)

INTERROGATIVE SENTENCES. Place a question mark after a direct question but not after an indirect question.

Did you understand what the principal said? (*Direct*)
Mrs. Allen asked me, "What grade will I teach next year?" (*Indirect*)

REQUESTS. Do not place a question mark after a question that is a request to which no answer is expected.

Will you please return the signed copy as soon as possible.

QUERIES. A question mark enclosed in parentheses may be used to query the accuracy of a fact or figure. Other punctuation is not affected by this use of the question mark.

The textbooks were delivered February 12(?), 1961.

SERIES OF QUESTIONS. A question mark is usually placed after each question in a series included within one sentence, and each question usually begins with a capital.

What attendance can we expect at our P.T.A. meetings? If afternoon meetings are held? If evening meetings are held?

BUT the question mark may be omitted in a series of questions in a construction like the one in the following example.

Who is responsible for (a) inspecting the school buildings, (b) keeping them in repair, (c) keeping them clean?

QUOTATION MARKS WITH QUESTION MARKS. See PLACEMENT OF QUOTATION MARKS, page 330.

QUOTATION MARKS

DIRECT QUOTATIONS. Enclose the exact words of a speaker or writer in quotation marks, but do not enclose words that are not quoted exactly. The quoted material may be a single or several paragraphs in length.

The principal told the parents, "We do everything we can to promote bicycle safety."
The principal told the parents that the school does everything it can to promote bicycle safety.
The principal stated that he was "vitally interested" in the bicycle safety program.

Interrupted quotations are punctuated as follows:

"I want to compliment you," the principal said, "on your outstanding art demonstration."

BUT do not use quotation marks when the name of the speaker or writer immediately precedes the quoted material or in question and answer material.

Mr. White: I know that children are taught phonics in our school.
Mr. Harris: Upon what do you base that opinion?

PARAGRAPHS. When quoted material is more than one paragraph in length, place quotation marks at the beginning of each paragraph but only at the close of the last paragraph.

DEFINITIONS. Use quotation marks to enclose a word or phrase that is accompanied by its definition; to denote a designation; to refer to a term.

The initials "A.D.A." refer to the average daily attendance. . . . (herein designated as the "First Party"), . . . Terms sometimes used are "extra-curricular," or "co-curricular."

UNUSUAL WORDS OR TRADE TERMS. Use quotation marks to enclose an unusual word or phrase or one used with a special trade meaning the first time the term is used. It is not necessary to use the quotation marks when the term is repeated.

In most American cities, industrial activities are segregated in areas "on the other side of the tracks."
Are the "no smoking" signs placed in positions where they will be seen?

TITLES AND NAMES. Use quotation marks to enclose the titles of:

Articles	Plays, motion pictures, sketches
Books, chapters or parts of books	Poems
Brochures, pamphlets	Songs
Operas	Stories in magazines
Paintings	

NOTE: In letters or advertising material, the title of a book may be capitalized for emphasis. In printed material the title of a book is usually italicized; therefore, in preparing material for the printer, underline the title of a book.

BUT do not use quotation marks with:

(1) Names of periodicals and well-known publications such as

Who's Who and dictionaries
The Bible or names of its books or other parts of it
Movements of a symphony, concerto, or other compositions, or names of numbered compositions

(2) Around names of characters in books and plays

Tom in *Tom Sawyer*

(3) With familiar nicknames unless used internally

> Skinny Jones
> Robert "Skinny" Jones

(4) With names of vessels, race horses, animals

> the Constitution
> Seabiscuit

SINGLE QUOTATION MARKS. Use single quotation marks to enclose a quotation within a quotation.

He stated, "I believe that the election of P.T.A. officers 'must be held during the first week in February.'"

PLACEMENT OF QUOTATION MARKS. Always place a period or comma inside quotation marks.

The bill was marked "paid," but the teacher never received a receipt.
The check was marked "canceled."

Always place colons and semicolons outside quotation marks.

Turn to the section entitled "The addition facts"; the reference is in the first paragraph.

Interrogation and exclamation points come before or after the quotation marks, depending upon the meaning of the text.

What school published the "Adventures in Kindergarten Bulletin"? (*The entire question is not quoted.*)
Remember the Chinese proverb: "One picture is worth 1,000 words!" (*The exclamation is part of the quotation.*)

SEMICOLONS

COMPOUND SENTENCES. A semicolon may be used to separate the parts of a compound sentence when the comma and conjunction are omitted.

Every child is different; there are no two exactly alike.

LONG, INVOLVED CLAUSES. Use a semicolon to separate long, involved clauses.

Recent years have seen the development of a wide variety of new floor materials; both hard and resilient floors, terrazzos and numerous forms of soft tiles and yard goods have all undergone developments that require specialized treatment.

PUNCTUATED CLAUSES. Use a semicolon to separate clauses that are punctuated by commas.

Action motivates us to realize that we have, and are still developing, a blended relationship between our educators and the general public; that is, more contacts are being made through joint meetings, cooperation with community organizations, and participation in policy development.

SERIES. In enumerations use semicolons to separate the items unless they are short and simple; also, to separate items that contain commas.

Supervision of instruction; administration of custodial services; interviewing, assigning, supervising, and evaluating the services of personnel—all are matters with which the principal must be concerned.

BEFORE A CONJUNCTIVE ADVERB. Use a semicolon before the conjunctive adverbs *accordingly, also, besides, consequently, furthermore, hence, however, indeed, likewise, moreover, nevertheless, otherwise, similarly, so, still, therefore, thus.*

He informed me that he did not plan to leave for the conference until next month; *therefore,* I did not consider it necessary to make his plane reservations until later.

QUOTATION MARKS AND SEMICOLON. Place the semicolon *outside* quotation marks.

PARENTHESES AND SEMICOLON. Use a semicolon after a closing parenthesis if the construction of the sentence requires a semicolon. Never use a comma or semicolon before a parenthesis or an expression enclosed in parentheses.

DIVISION OF WORDS

DIVISION OF WORDS AT THE END OF A LINE. To avoid a ragged right-hand margin, it is sometimes essential to divide a word at the end of a line, but divide *only* when necessary. Try not to have two successive lines with a divided word at the end, and *never* have more than two. Try not to divide the last word on the first line or the last word on a page. Try to avoid dividing the last word in a paragraph. In general, do not hyphenate words if the division leaves fewer than three letters on either line.

The correct division of a word depends first of all on the breakdown of the word into syllables. The American dictionaries syllabicate according to pronunciation, and not according to derivation. If you do not know the proper division into syllables for a word, look up the word in the dictionary. There are, however, a few simple rules in addition to the rule of syllables that govern the division of words.

Rules for the division of words at the end of a line:

1. Never divide words pronounced as one syllable.

through   deemed   gained

2. Never divide a four-letter word.

only   into   acid

3. Never separate one-letter syllables at the beginning of a word from the rest of the word.

enough   about

4. Divide a word with a one-letter syllable within the word after the one-letter syllable, except in the case of the suffixes -able or -ible.

busi-ness   sepa-rate   medi-cal   con-sider-able   reduc-ible

NOTE: There are many words ending in -*able* or -*ible* in which the *a* or *i* does not form a syllable by itself. These words are divided after the *a* or *i*.

pos-si-ble   char-i-ta-ble   ca-pa-ble

5. Do not carry over a two-letter syllable appearing at the end of a word.

caller   ended   over-looked   pur-chaser

6. Avoid separating two-letter syllables at the beginning of a word from the rest of the word.

eli-gi-ble   begin-ning   atten-tion

7. When the final consonant in a word is doubled before a suffix, the second consonant belongs with the letters following it.

run-ning   occur-ring

8. Do not carry over to the next line single or double consonants in the root word.

call-ing   forc-ing   divid-ing   fore-stall-ing

9. When two consonants occur within a word, divide the word between the consonants.

gram-mar   expres-sive   moun-tain   foun-da-tion

10. Words containing a prefix or suffix should usually be divided on the prefix or suffix unless the pronunciation would be contradicted.

dis-appear   south-ern   mal-adjusted

NOTE: The following suffixes are not divisible:

-cial	-sion	-ceous
-sial	-tion	-tious
-tial	-gion	-geous
-cion	-cious	-gious

11. Avoid dividing a compound hyphenated word except where the hyphen naturally falls.

father-in-law   self-discipline

12. Do not divide abbreviations.

Ph.D. Y.M.C.A. C.O.D.

13. Avoid dividing numbers. If it *is* necessary to divide, divide on a comma and retain the comma.

. . . 2,364,- 685

14. Divide dates between the day and the year, not between the month and the day. Avoid dividing dates, if possible.

. . . October 4,
1961 . . .

15. Do not separate the initials of a name. Avoid separating initials, titles, or degrees from the name.

D. L. Smith   Sir Winston Churchill   Edwin Dexter, Ph.D.

16. Avoid dividing proper names.

17. Do not carry over the -ed at the end of a word if it is pronounced as one syllable.

returned   passed   redeemed

18. Do not divide time or similar combinations.

7:15 P.M.

19. Divide after a vowel wherever possible.

physi-cal   sepa-rate   criti-cism

ELLIPSES

Use ellipses to indicate the omission of quoted material.

OMISSION OF WORDS. Use three dots alternating with spaces to indicate the omission of material less than a paragraph in length.

"This curriculum guide is not . . . the final authority for the language arts program in our school district."

OMISSION OF PARAGRAPHS. Use a single line of alternate dots and spaces to indicate the omission of a paragraph or more or a line or more of poetry.

"I saw you toss the kites on high
And blow the birds about the sky;

.   .   .   .

O wind, a-blowing all day long,
O wind, that sings so loud a song!"

ELLIPSES AND PERIODS. Use a period followed by the three dots when the omitted material follows the end of a sentence.

"When your child has been absent for any reason, he must bring a note signed by you giving the reason for the absence. . . . This information is required by law."

NOTE: When a new sentence follows an omission, a period and three dots should precede the sentence whether or not there was a period in the original material or not.

"We ask your fullest cooperation in seeing that your child attends school each day. . . . Absence from school works a hardship on both teacher and pupil." (*In the original there was no period after the word "day."*)

ELLIPSES AND QUOTATION MARKS. Periods should be placed within the quotation marks when they appear at the beginning or end of an ellipses.

"The school district makes every effort to interpret the educational program to parents and community through its guidance program. . . ."

UNDERSCORING OR ITALICS

Words that are underlined in a manuscript indicate to the printer that they are to be printed in italics.

1. Underline the titles of books, periodicals, plays, pamphlets, bulletins, and so forth if the *whole* title is given, whether in the text, in footnotes, or in the bibliography.

Kyte, George C. The Principal at Work. New York: Ginn and Company, 1952. 531 pp.

NOTE: Quotation marks should be used to enclose *parts* of titles, subdivisions or chapters of books, articles in periodicals, and so forth.

2. Underline all foreign words or phrases which appear in the text unless they are given in their entirety or are quoted.

By the time they arrived at the pension, they were tired enough to go to bed.

The superintendent said that the speaker read his speech "in toto."

NOTE: Foreign words which have become so generally used that they are considered part of the English language are not underlined.

| per se | per annum | ex officio |

3. Underline foreign and Latin abbreviations.

coup d'état (a bold seizure of government)
ibid. (the same reference)
op. cit. (in the work cited)

4. Underline to show emphasis.

You should never forward a report without checking it for accuracy.

5. In quoted material, the notation "italics mine" should be added if the writer desires to show by italicization emphasis which was not that way in the original material.

"It is an established fact that children who get proper nourishment tire less quickly, pay better attention in class, and are able to study better." (Italics mine.)

ABBREVIATIONS

It is considered good practice, whenever possible, to avoid all abbreviations in writing the text. Words should always be spelled out wherever there may be danger of confusion. The circumstances where abbreviations may or should be used are explained in the following paragraphs.

Abbreviate. Abbreviations should be used in the following cases:

1. Titles preceding a full name when the titles have an accepted abbreviation.

Rev. John Smith	Dr. Robert Jones
Prof. Richard Dunbar	Hon. Allan Brown
Mr. James Waller	Mrs. Helen Johnson

BUT: Spell out the titles when preceded by "the."

the Reverend Harry Carter

2. *Jr.* and *Sr.* when following a name.

Mr. John Olson, Jr.

3. Degrees after names. Use only the highest degree unless they are in different fields.

John Edwards, Ph.D.   Robert Trimble, M.D.

NOTE: Titles, such as Dr., are not used when the degree is given but another title may be used in combination with degree abbreviations.

Rev. Albert Morris, D.D., LL.D.

4. *No.* (for "number") when used before figures.

No. 41

5. The words "Saint" and "Mount" in proper names.

St. Joseph   Mt. Rushmore

6. In footnotes or bibliographies, certain abbreviations may be used which are not permissible in the text.

Chap. 20	Col. 4	*et al.* (for "and others")
2d ed.	Fig. 12	No. 8
p. 21	Pt. II	pp. 42–64
sec. 6	Vol. IV	

7. Symbols and abbreviations may be used in scientific and technical manuscripts even though they are not considered to be generally acceptable in other writing. Their use is so complicated that special instructions are generally prepared by editors to assist those preparing the manuscripts.

Do not abbreviate. Abbreviations should not be used in the following cases:

1. Names of months except in lists or where directed to do otherwise. Do not use numbers to indicate the month in writing manuscripts or letters.

January   October

2. Street, avenue, place, or boulevard in formal letters. Also, spell out the numerical names of streets.

Fourth Street   Alondra Boulevard
Kenter Avenue   St. James Place

3. Names of cities, states, territories, and possessions may be abbreviated although it is better practice not to do so.

Los Angeles, California, not L.A., Calif.
Honolulu, T.H. (Territory of Hawaii, before it became a state.)

4. Do not use *d, rd, st,* or *th* in writing dates.

July 4, not July 4th

5. *Fort* or *Mount* in proper names.

Fort Bragg   Mount Vernon

6. Business titles or positions even when they precede a name.

Secretary   President Kennedy

Mr., Mrs., or *Miss* precede the name, even when the business title is used.

Mr. George H. Peterson, manager

NOTE: The title following the name is not capitalized except when used in addresses in letters.

7. Christmas (Never use "Xmas.")

8. Railways.

Santa Fe Railway

9. Company, incorporated, manufacturing (unless abbreviated by the firm in its official signature).

Union Oil Company   Hydroponic Chemical Co., Inc.
Wagner Manufacturing Co.   Rival Mfg. Co.

10. Years, except in reference to school classes.

He graduated in 1959.   The class of '59

11. And. Do not use "&" unless used by a company as part of its legal name.

Jackson & Perkins Co.
Mr. Jones *and* Mr. Smith were late in arriving.

12. And so forth or and so on. Avoid the use of "etc." whenever possible, and never use "&tc."

Some boys prefer shop courses such as woodshop, metalshop, and so on.

13. Per cent or cents.

12 per cent (*not* 12%)   55 cents (*not* 55¢)

14. Names of classes.

senior (*not* sr.)   junior (*not* jr.)

15. Dimensions, weight, measure, distance.

height (*not* ht.)   pounds (*not* lb.)
weight (*not* wt.)   mile (*not* mi.)
feet (*not* ft.) (6 × 12 feet)

16. Chapter, page, column, line, volume, brother in the text.

Chapter 13   Page 315
Column 4   Line 11
Volume 22   He is my brother.

FIGURES

Secretaries should follow the generally accepted rules regarding the use of figures, or numbers as they are sometimes referred to. These rules help avoid confusion in the minds of the reader and make for a more uniform and consistent manuscript.

Enumerations. Use parentheses to enclose numbers which enumerate items within the text.

The health of a child is affected by: (1) diet, (2) amount of sleep, (3) rest, and (4) exercise.

Parentheses are not used for enumerations which begin a new line or paragraph.

Before leaving for the night, the custodian must:

1. Check all doors.
2. Turn out all lights.

In outline form, enumerations are used as follows:

I. Under the head of . . .
   A. Under . . .
      1. Under . . .
         a) Under . . .
            (1) Under . . .
   B. Under . . .
      1. Under . . .
II. Under . . .

Roman and Arabic numerals. Capital Roman numerals are used to indicate volume numbers and references to Parts, Divisions, or Acts. They are not used in references to classical or ancient works.

Vol. II   Part IV   Act I

Small Roman numerals are used to indicate references to chapters, introductory pages in a book, scenes in plays, and books in classical works.

Chapter vi   Page iv   Scene ii

However, Arabic numerals are used to indicate chapters in most cases.

Chapter 23

Footnote numbers. Arabic numbers, raised slightly above the line, are used in the text to refer to footnotes which carry the same number and which are also raised slightly. The number in the text should follow the passage to which it refers. If the passage is a quotation, the footnote number should follow the last word or the quotation marks.

> Doris advises the secretary, "Strive to have your employer's mail on his desk before he gets to the office."[1]

Footnote numbers should start with "1" and follow in numerical order throughout the chapter or the book, as the case may be.

Numbers not spelled out. It is permissible to use Arabic numbers without spelling them in the following instances:

1. Numbers of 100 or more
2. Numbers of size, whether under or over 100
   24 by 102 yards
3. Technical or statistical material which involves the use of many numbers
4. Financial or tabular matter
5. School grades

A-6   B-10

6. Election returns
7. Athletic records or sports references
8. Percentages. (The symbol % should not be used in the text.)

42 per cent

9. Sums of money. Use the dollar sign but not the cent sign.

$5   8 cents

10. Time of day

4 P.M.   3:35 P.M.

11. Latitude and longitude
12. Dates. Omit *rd, nd,* and *th.*

March 4, 1960   July 18

13. Dimensions, unless used as measures
14. Ages
15. Street and room numbers
16. Telephone numbers
17. Numbers combined with abbreviations

7 P.M.   No. 6

18. Fractions, if part of a number of three or more digits

327¼

19. Pages, except introductory pages
20. Columns, lines, tables, and figures

Column 4   Line 15   Table VI   Figure 21

21. Period of time. For two years, write 1945–6. For more than two years, write 1952–56. For a series of separate years, use commas. 1924, 1931, 1956
22. Numbers, both smaller and larger than 100 in the same series

Of the 624 children, 9 were considered outstanding, 94 superior, 128 good, and the rest average or lower.

Numbers spelled out. In the following instances, numbers should be spelled out:

1. Common fractions, unless part of larger numbers. Remember that some authorities do not recommend the use of the hyphen.

one-half   three-fourths

2. Numbers of less than 100

two, three, ten

3. Rounded numbers

About three thousand

4. At the beginning of sentences regardless of the size of the number

5. Ordinals

Ninth	fortieth	eighteenth

6. Time, when used with o'clock

Two o'clock or 2 P.M.

NOTE: If the same sentence contains two series of numbers, regardless of size, one series should be spelled out and the other written numerically.

When the test scores were tabulated, ten pupils had spelled all 50 words correctly, eighteen had spelled 45 or more correctly, and one hundred twenty-three had spelled 30 or more correctly.

Omissions. Omit all useless ciphers in time or money.

4 P.M. not 4:00 P.M.
$11, not $11.00

CAPITALIZATION

Many publishing houses and businesses have adopted rules and principles of capitalization which they believe are appropriate to their special fields or reader audiences. Because of this there is a wide divergence of opinion regarding the correct usages of capitalization. When you are in doubt, refer to a standard dictionary, high school or college textbook on grammar, or a manual of writing style. A trend is developing toward a more general use of lower case letters.

The principles and rules of capitalization which follow are generally recognized as good English usage.

Abbreviations.

COLLEGE DEGREES. Capitalize abbreviations of all college degrees. Do not space between letters.

B.A.	M.S.	Ed.D.	M.D.	D.D.S.

ONE LETTER. One-letter abbreviations are always capitalized.

72°F.	60°C.	12 M.

A.M. AND P.M. a.m. and p.m. may be lower case or upper case, BUT the trend is toward lower case (as below). Do not space between the initials. The abbreviation for *meridies* (noon) should be capitalized because it is one initial—M.

7:30 p.m.	4 a.m.	12 M.

FOR CAPITALIZED WORDS. Capitalize abbreviations when the words themselves would properly be capitalized.

John Smith, M.A. (Master of Arts)
P.T.A. (Parent-Teacher Association)

Acts, bills, codes, and laws.

OFFICIAL TITLE. Capitalize the official title of specific acts, bills, codes, and laws; also capitalize the accepted title by which the law is generally known.

National Defense Education Act
G.I. Bill of Rights
Smog Control Law

BUT lower case *bill* or *law* when used with the sponsor's name unless the formal title of the bill is given.

the Dilworth bill

GENERAL DESCRIPTIVE TERMS. Lower case *bill* and *act* when they are standing alone; also abbreviated titles and general descriptive terms designating them.

the school housing bill

Geographical terms.

POINTS OF COMPASS. Capitalize names of points of the compass when they refer to a section of the United States.

the South   the Northwest   the East

BUT lower case when they denote simple direction or compass points.

east   toward the north   northwest of Chicago

POPULAR NAMES. Capitalize popular names of definite localities.

Cotton Belt   West Side   the Delta
the Loop   the Continent   Mississippi Valley
(*but* valley of the Mississippi)

BUT lower case *ghetto, fatherland.*

He lived in the ghetto.   Norway is his fatherland.

REGIONAL TERMS. Capitalize regional terms that are part of a descriptive title and which identify definite localities such as cities, states or regions.

San Joaquin Valley   Gulf of Mexico
Nob Hill   the Lone Star State
the Bay Shore   South San Francisco

BUT lower case terms that are merely localizing adjectives.

western Arizona   northern Japan

COAST. Capitalize *coast* when it designates a specific locality or stands alone.

the Coast   Atlantic Coast   Gulf Coast

BUT lower case when it is used with geographic designations.

the coast of New England

DIVISIONS OF WORLD OR COUNTRY. Capitalize divisions of the world or of a country.

the Old World   Far East
Atlantic States   Orient, Occident
the Far West

BUT capitalize *oriental* and *occidental* only when they refer to a person.

He is an *Oriental* with *occidental* manners.

Governmental and political terms.

GOVERNMENT, ADMINISTRATION. Capitalize *government* and *administration* when they are applied to the government in power in a country and are used as a substitute title for a political party in power. These words are, in a sense, personifications when they are used in this way. Otherwise, lower case, except, of course, when they are part of a title.

Her Majesty's Government . . .
The Government announced that it is trying . . .
The Administration is pushing its program for . . .
The policies of a government that . . .
The government of Wisconsin is efficiently . . .

FEDERAL. Capitalize *federal* when it is part of a title or when it is used as an adjective referring to a *specific* government.

the Federal Housing Administration
the Federal Government
a Federal agency

BUT lower case when it is used as a general term.

the federal principle of government

NOTE: Many publications do not capitalize *federal* when it is used as an adjective, but the form given here is preferable for business letters and reports.

NATIONAL. Capitalize *national* when it precedes a capitalized word or when it is part of a title. Lower case when it is used as a general descriptive term. Also lower case *nationals,* meaning the citizens of a country, but capitalize if it refers to a political party.

the National Housing Act
national customs

STATE. 1. Capitalize *state* (or *commonwealth*) when it is part of a name.

Washington State   State of Iowa
Commonwealth of Massachusetts

2. Capitalize the noun *state* (or *commonwealth*) when it stands alone if it is applied to a specific state or states. Lower case when it is used in a general sense.

Our State is interested in its schools.
Some of the states east of the Mississippi River are . . .
The States east of the Mississippi River are . . .

3. Capitalize the adjective *state* when it describes something that is created, controlled, or administered by a specific state or states. Lower case when it is used in a general sense.

The heads of the city and State (*meaning California*) departments met in Sacramento.
The California school housing program will be financed from the sale of State bonds.
This State has too many state employees. (*Although the reference is to a specific state, the employees are not "created, controlled, or administered" by the state.*)

CITY. Capitalize *city* when it is part of a name.

New York City   Sioux City

BUT lower case when it is used as a general term or when standing alone.

city of Portland   The city is represented by . . .

COUNTY. Capitalize *county* when it is a part of a name.

Westchester County   Riverside County

BUT lower case when it is used in transposed form or when standing alone.

county of San Diego   The county is represented by . . .

DISTRICT. Capitalize district when it is part of a name.

Third Congressional District
Fifth Supervisorial District

BUT lower case when it is used as a general term or when standing alone, unless it is applied to the District of Columbia.

a Congressional district   the District (of Columbia)

WARD, PRECINCT. Capitalize *ward* and *precinct* when they are part of a name.

Fourth Ward	Ninth Precinct	Ward 6

BUT lower case when they stand alone.

this precinct	this ward

DEPARTMENTS, BOARDS, COMMITTEES, ETC. Capitalize the full title of governmental departments, boards, committees, commissions, bureaus, and so on.

School Board	Board of Education
Police Department	Local Draft Board
Veterans Administration	Foreign Affairs Committee
National Housing Authority	Office of Smog Control

BUT lower case *department, board, committee, commission, bureau,* and other similar words when they are used alone in place of the full name.

the department	the bureau
the council	the committee
the board	

NAMES OF LEGISLATIVE BODIES. Capitalize the names of legislative, administrative, and deliberative bodies, both domestic and foreign.

Congress	House of Commons
Senate	Parliament
House	Diet
the State Senate	Chamber of Deputies and Friends

POLITICAL PARTIES. Capitalize words referring to political parties.

Republican	Democrat
Democratic (*referring to the party*)	

Personal titles.

GENERAL RULE. The general rule is to capitalize all titles or designations preceding names.

Senator Thomas H. Kuchel
General George Washington
Superintendent James A. Kirby

BUT lower case titles following names or used instead of names except in the address of letters.

the secretary James A. Kirby, superintendent
Samuel Yorty, the mayor of Los Angeles
Richard A. Bell, Assistant Superintendent (*in a letter address*)

PRESIDENT. Always capitalize *president* when it refers to the President or Presidency of the United States or of a foreign government. Also capitalize other terms used to designate the President, such as Chief Executive.

the President
President Wilson appointed ex-President Taft to the Supreme Court.
The office of President is a high honor.
He was elected to the Presidency.
The Chief Executive said at his press conference . . .

NATIONAL GOVERNMENT OFFICIALS. Capitalize titles of cabinet members, heads of departments, and government dignitaries whether the titles stand alone or are used with names.

the Chief Justice	Ambassador
Acting Secretary of Defense	Under Secretary of State
Representative	Administrator
Speaker (of the House)	Congressman

STATE OR MUNICIPAL OFFICIALS. Capitalize the titles of governor, chief executive (of a state), lieutenant governor, mayor, borough president, president of any municipal body, and the like whether they are used with proper names or stand alone.

The Lieutenant Governor is acting in the absence of the Governor.
The Republicans nominated him for Mayor.
Mr. Hyde, President of the City Council . . .

BUT lower case these titles when they are used as general terms without reference to a specific office or official.

A governor must speak at many public functions.
Many things are discussed by councils.

Capitalize titles of heads of state and city departments, such as *Police Commissioner, Attorney General, Sheriff, Commissioner of Education, State Rent Administrator.* Also capitalize the shortened form of such titles.

the Commissioner the Comptroller

Lower case subordinate titles, such as *deputy sheriff, assistant attorney general,* except when they precede proper names.

The deputy sheriff handled the case.
Deputy Sheriff Smith

BUSINESS AND PROFESSIONAL TITLES. Capitalize business and professional titles when they precede a name.

Dr. Arthur Armstrong   Professor Edwards
President Dennis S. Holmes (of XYZ Company)

BUT lower case when they follow a name or when they are used instead of the name of a specific person except in the address of a letter.

the doctor
the professor
the president (of **XYZ** Company)
Bruce Roberts, secretary of XYZ Company (*except in an address where the word "secretary" is capitalized*)

In formal writings, such as contracts and minutes of meetings, titles referring to a specific officer of a specific company or organization may be lower or upper case, but in such writings you must capitalize *company, corporation,* and the like.

The personnel manager of the Corporation said . . .

HONOR OR NOBILITY. Capitalize titles of honor or nobility when they refer to specific persons and are used in place of proper names.

Queen Elizabeth   His Excellency
the Duke of York   your Grace
the Pope   (*in informal writings*)

ACTING, UNDER, ASSISTANT. Capitalize *acting* and *under* when they are part of a capitalized title. Titles that are subordinated by the word *assistant* are not capitalized, except when they precede names.

Acting Secretary of State   Under Secretary of State
assistant secretary of state

WORDS IN APPOSITION. When a common noun precedes a name but is separated from it by a comma, the noun does not have the force of a title and is not capitalized.

the secretary, John Smith

COMPOUND TITLES. Capitalize all parts of a compound title if any part is capitalized.

Attorney General

LISTS OF NAMES. In formal lists, titles and descriptive designations immediately following the names should be capitalized.

Other titles.

BOOKS, PLAYS, PROGRAMS, SONGS. Principal words in titles of books, plays, programs, songs, and so forth should be capitalized.

A Tale of Two Cities (book)
What's My Line (program)
My Wild Irish Rose (song)

Names. Capitalize all names in the following instances:

1. Months and days of the week.

Monday	August

2. Holidays or notable events.

Christmas	Labor Day
Mardi Gras	Hallowe'en
Festival of Lights	

3. Historic events.

Battle of the Bulge	Civil War
Declaration of Independence	

4. Specific schools, firms, societies, leagues, corporations, committees, buildings, and so forth.

Central High School	Bank of America
Annandale Golf Club	Statler Hotel
Phi Delta Kappa	American League
Salary Committee	

BUT do not capitalize names of classes or general schools.

freshman	senior
junior high school	university

5. School subjects which are proper nouns or proper adjectives or school departments.

English	French
Science Department	Latin

BUT do not capitalize names of general school subjects.

social studies	physical education
art	science

6. Streets, places, avenues, and boulevards.

First Street	Wilshire Boulevard
St. Andrew's Place	Fifth Avenue

7. Races and nationalities.

American	Caucasian
Negro	Spanish

8. Nicknames of athletic teams or organizations.

the Giants	the Yankees
the Browns	the Webfeet

9. Well-known clubs or organizations.

Boy Scouts	Woodcraft Rangers
Parent-Teacher Association	Elks

10. Buildings, places, depots, and hotels when referring to specific structures.

White House	Union Depot
Federal Building	Ambassador Hotel
Stork Club	Carlsbad Caverns

BUT do not capitalize such buildings, places, and so forth which are not specifically designated.

the prison	the hotel
the station	the caves

11. Trade names of manufactured products.

Arrow shirts	Admiral radios
Dodge cars	Maytag washers

NOTE: The name of the product is a common noun unless it has been legally adopted as part of the name by the company.

Nouns and adjectives. 1. Capitalize all proper nouns and adjectives derived from them.

Mary Jones	Los Angeles
France	French

2. Capitalize all nouns when followed by a number or letter.

Room 24	Area C
Page 36	Chapter 4
Section VII	

Family relationships. Words denoting family relationships when used with the name of a person or as a substitute for it should be capitalized.

Mary talked to Uncle John.
He wrote to Mother.

BUT words denoting family relationships when used with a possessive noun or pronoun are not capitalized.

my sister	his aunt	Mary's mother

Emphasis. Capitalize all letters in important words which are used for emphasis. Effectiveness is lost, however, when capital letters are overused.

The weather was hot and I do mean HOT.

Tabular material. Capitalize the first letters of first words in headings of columns in tabular material.

Number taking test

Outlines. Capitalize the first word of each outline division or subdivision or of a list.

1. Safety rules and regulations
   A. Playground safety
   B. Classroom safety
      1. Entering room
      2. Leaving room

The following list shows the factors which are considered in school guidance programs:

1. Academic proficiency
2. Social adjustment
3. Emotional stability

Punctuation. Capitalize the first word after a colon when it begins a complete sentence.

To conclude, I repeat: Education must be the concern of parents as well as teachers.

Enumerations. Capitalize the first word in each section of an enumeration that has been formally introduced by a sentence.

Two reasons were given for his failure: 1. He was absent too often. 2. He failed to turn in his assignments on time.

BUT do not capitalize brief items in enumerations when separated by commas.

The test consisted of three parts: (1) vocabulary, (2) grammar, and (3) spelling.

Quotations. Capitalize the first word of a direct quotation.

The teacher said, "The report cards will be given out tomorrow."

BUT do not capitalize continuation of quotations after interpolations of such words as "he said," "she asked."

"I was late," Jimmy explained, "because I forgot to set my alarm."

Capitals not used. Capitals are not used in the following instances:
1. Seasons of the year.

spring	winter	fall	summer

2. Units of measurement such as hour, minute, second, pound, yard, foot.

four inches	five pounds
fifty-yard dash	six hours

3. Initial definite articles unless part of the legal name of the organization or publication.

The New York Times	the University of Washington
the Second Man (a play)	the Hough Shade Corporation

SPELLING

Spelling is a means to an end. Its purpose is to communicate the written word clearly and precisely so that its meaning is understood. Written communication, to be socially acceptable, must be spelled in the manner which has been established by tradition or which has become conventional by current usage.

The public's impression of the kind of teaching which goes on in a school may be influenced by the spelling used in written communications. Parent's judgment of teachers and administrators will be affected by the accuracy of the spelling used. If the schools are teaching spelling—and this is often unfairly questioned—the school secretary must be particularly careful about her spelling. Through her typing and duplicating of letters and bulletins, she represents the school and education.

Every school secretary should have a standard dictionary close at hand. Whenever you have the slightest doubt about the spelling of a word, take the time to check the spelling. If you have difficulty with spelling, take the time to improve yourself. The following references may be found useful:

Horn, Ernest. A *Basic Writing Vocabulary of 10,000 Words Most Commonly Used in Writing*. Iowa City: State University of Iowa, 1926.

Thorndike, Edward L., and Irving Lorge, *The Teacher's Word Book of 30,000 Words*. New York: Bureau of Publications, Teachers College, Columbia University, 1939.

Another helpful source of spelling is a book listing common synonyms, antonyms, and homonyms.

Spelling clues. There are a number of spelling clues which may be of help. For example, *q* is always followed by *u* regardless of how the word is pronounced.

quick	bouquet	queue

Words ending in *s, x, z, ch*, and *sh* usually form their plurals by adding *es* to the singular.

buses	matches	pushes
fizzes	boxes	

Common exceptions to this rule are: *oxen, teeth.*
This rhyme may also be useful:

> *i* before *e*
> except after *c*
> or when sounded like *ā*
> as in *neighbor* and *weigh*

Exceptions to this rhyme are: *either, neither, weird, seize,* and *leisure.*
One-syllable words ending in a single consonant preceded by a single vowel. Double the final consonant when adding such endings as: *ed, ing, er,* and *est.*

running	swimmer	stopped
planning	planner	planned
reddest		

Similarly, words of more than one syllable which are accented on the last syllable and end in a single consonant preceded by a single vowel likewise double the final consonant before a suffix beginning with a vowel.

occurred	beginning	allotted

When the accent does not fall on the last syllable, the rule does not apply.

systematic	uttering	limited

When adding *ing* to a word ending in *e*, drop the *e*.

living	arriving	behaving

To form the plural of nouns ending in *y* add *s* if the *y* is preceded by a vowel.

says	plays	boys

Otherwise the *y* should be changed to *i* and *es* added.

babies	tries

Plurals of compound nouns are formed by adding the plural ending to the most important part.

runners-up	daughters-in-law
step-fathers	

Spelling rules. The following rules will serve as a guide.

1. Spell out dates when they precede the name of the month or when the month is not mentioned.

The fifth of March
The supplies will be delivered on the fourth.

2. Spell out all numbers, regardless of size, when used at the beginning of a sentence.

Fifteen hundred parents attended the concert.

3. Spell out figures to express time except when the abbreviations A.M. or P.M. are used.

The Parent-Teacher Association meeting will start at eight o'clock.

4. All quotations must be spelled exactly as in the original.
5. Simplified spelling such as "altho" for "although" should not be used.
6. For the spelling of possessives, see page 318 for the use of the apostrophe.
7. Refer to the best available authority to determine the spelling of proper names.

GRAMMAR

Writing is for the purpose of communicating ideas. The reader can only determine what the writer wants to communicate by use of the written word. Although you will not usually produce original written material, you may be able to suggest improvements which could be made in the text.

The ability to organize thought clearly and logically and to express ideas in words is difficult for some people. The writer may become so interested in translating his ideas to paper that acceptable grammatical construction may be overlooked. The good secretary will see that all grammatical errors and faulty composition are corrected or improved before any written material leaves the school office. As with spelling, the school and the educational program will be judged by the written communications which emanate from it.

It is impossible in this chapter to explain all the rules and principles which govern good grammatical construction. You should have a reference book on grammar or composition in your office. The high school or college textbooks on this subject are excellent sources of information.

General suggestions. These general suggestions may help you. Sentences should usually be short—twenty-five words or less. If longer, check them for clarity, coherence, and grammatical correctness. The writing should be "tightened" and all unnecessary words eliminated.

Everything written should be clear as the reader may not know what the writer (who may be all too familiar with his topic) has in mind.

Complete sentences should be used to express complete thoughts. A common fault is the use of phrases or clauses in place of a sentence.

Wrong: Running in the halls.
Right: Running in the halls can cause accidents.

The over-use of *and, then, well,* and similar words may be a problem. In case of doubt, eliminate the *and* and write two sentences.

Wrong: It might rain then we will have a rainy day session.
Right: We will have a rainy day session if it should rain.
Wrong: Well, he finally graded all the tests.
Right: He finally graded all the tests.
Wrong: The children had a good assembly program and they sang several beautiful numbers.
Right: The children had a good assembly program. They sang several beautiful numbers.

You should be familiar with the parts of speech and their use. You should know that sentences must contain a subject and predicate (noun or pronoun and verb) unless the subject is implied.

He will walk to the classroom.
Walk slowly (*You* [implied] walk slowly.)

Regular and irregular verbs may cause you some difficulty. Be sure to use the correct form. For example:

Regular	Irregular
I write	I am
You write	You are
He writes	He is

Adjectives and adverbs are often confused. Remember that adjectives modify nouns or pronouns and that adverbs modify verbs, adjectives, or other adverbs.

Other problems arise with case and number, the agreement of the verb with the noun or pronoun, the use of shall and will, gender, and split infinitives. If you are responsible for the final copy, make every effort to keep sentences simple and not too complex. Avoid dangling or incomplete constructions.

Person. Theses should be written in the third person. Avoid the use of personal pronouns such as *I, my, we, our, me,* and *us* in all formal writing whether or not in a thesis.

Tense. Theses should be written in past tense unless what is described is still taking place or will continue to be so in the future. In such cases, use the present and future tenses.

Proper names. Proper names should be written in the form generally used.

Richard Nixon, not Dick Nixon
George Bernard Shaw, not George B. Shaw

There should be no question on the part of the reader regarding the identity of the person named whether or not he is a specialist in the topic under discussion. Such names as Socrates, Plato, and Shakespeare are so well-known that they need no further identification.

If there is the chance of doubt, even with generally well-known names, write out the full name the first time it is mentioned.

> Bob Waterfield for Waterfield
> Warren Spahn for Spahn
> Greta Garbo for Garbo

Common courtesy also requires the use of the full name or the title and last name the first time a prominent name occurs in print.

President Kennedy	Kennedy
Sir Winston Churchill	Churchill
Adlai E. Stevenson	Stevenson

Nicknames. Nicknames of prominent people may be used when common acceptance over a period of time has made them well-known.

Casey Stengel	Connie Mack	Jimmy Stewart
Sugar Ray Robinson		

Language usage. STILTED OR TRITE PHRASES. Avoid the use of stilted or trite phrases. Use a book on synonyms to bring individuality to your writing.

1. Advise. *Say* or *tell* may be better words.

> We wish to *advise* . . .
> *Better:* We are pleased to *tell* you . . .

2. And oblige. Avoid the use of this phrase.
3. As per; per. "In *accordance with*" or "*According to*" are better terms.
4. At all times. *Always* may be a better choice.

> *Poor:* Be safety conscious *at all times*
> *Better: Always* be safety conscious.

5. At this time. *At present* or *now* are better words.
6. At your convenience; at an early date. Be more definite.

> *Indefinite:* Inform us *at an early date.*
> *Better:* Notify us *by return mail.*

7. Duly. Avoid the use of this word.
8. Enclosed please find. Use instead, *we are enclosing* or *we enclose.*
9. *Esteemed.* Avoid the use of this word.
10. Recent date. Be more definite and give the date.

> *Vague:* Your letter of *recent date* . . .
> *Better:* Your letter of *March 6* . . .

11. **State.** Use *say* or *tell* instead.

> *Poor:* We wish to *state* . . .
> *Better:* We are pleased to *tell* you . . .

12. **Take pleasure.** Use *are pleased, are happy,* or *are glad.*

> *Poor:* We *take pleasure* in telling . . .
> *Better:* We *are happy* to say . . .

13. **Thanking you in advance.** Avoid the use of this phrase.

> *Poor: Thanking you in advance* for the favor, I remain . . .
> *Better: I shall appreciate* any information you may have.

14. **Under separate cover.** Use a more definite explanation.

> *Poor:* We are sending you *under separate cover* . . .
> *Better:* We are pleased to send you *by parcel post* . . .

15. **Wish to say; wish to state; would say.** Omit these needless words.

> *Poor:* We *wish to say* that we cannot . . .
> *Better: We regret* our inability to . . .

SUMMARY

Eliminate unnecessary words and phrases. Some unnecessary words have been explained in the preceding section. It is a mistaken idea that padding lends emphasis to written material. If you write letters for your principal, eliminate all unnecessary words and strive to get to the point —"tighten up" your writing.

The italicized words in the following examples are unnecessary and should be eliminated:

It came *at a time* when we were busy.
During *the year of* 1958 . . .
The typewriter will cost *the sum of* $146.
We will send the bill *at a* later *date.*
The accident at *the hour of* noon . . .
In *the state of* Alabama . . .

Avoid duplications for emphasis. Two words should not be used for emphasis when one will suffice. One word in the following examples will do the job.

> sincere and good wishes
> the first and foremost
> unjust and unfair manner
> right and proper consideration

Avoid favorite words and expressions. Each writer tends to develop certain words or expressions which he uses too often. These should be avoided as much as possible. You may be able to help your principal in developing fresh and interesting approaches to his writing, particularly in letters.

Avoid use of big words. Simple, short words that express an idea and get to the heart of the matter are preferred to big words. A large vocabulary is an asset but the use of big words does not necessarily improve the idea which has been expressed.

Use words with various shades of meaning. For example, the *aroma* of a cigar, the *fragrance* of a flower, the *scent* of perfume are preferable to using the word *smell* in each of these phrases.

Avoid long sentences. Write simply and clearly in order to put across a point. Long, wordy sentences are often confusing and the entire point is missed.

Avoid words that antagonize. Words such as *failure, complaint, stupid, wrong,* and *mistake* should be avoided.

Poor: Did you *know* that you made a *mistake* in reporting the test results?

Use a positive approach and say: We would be glad to help you recheck the figures on your test score report.

27

A Filing System for Schools

THE FILING SYSTEM presented below is based upon that recommended by the National Association of Educational Secretaries in their publication *File It Right*. The headings are the major or basic subject classifications. Each school will wish to modify the list to fit its own needs.

Accreditation and School Evaluation
    Accredited schools
    Reports

Administration
    Bulletins, directives, handbooks, instructions, manuals
    Faculty and staff administration:
        Committees
        Meetings: agendas, minutes
        Members
    School organization and administration:
        County board of education
        District board of education
        State board of administration
        U.S. office of education
        Policies and procedures
        Reports

Associations and Organizations
    Business and industrial
    Charitable and welfare
    Civic
    International relations
    Labor
    Parents—P.T.A.
    Patriotic
    Professional, other than teacher
    Religious
    Social
    Teacher
    Youth

Athletics
    Accidents
    Contracts
    Eligibility
    Equipment
    Medical and physical
        examinations
    Policies
    Publicity

Radio and television
Records
Schedules

Sports and teams
Staff

Awards, Gifts, Honors, and Scholarships

Books and Publications

Articles
Bibliographies
Books: library
Bulletins and brochures
Catalogs (other than for
　purchasing)
Clippings

Magazines
Newspapers
Newspaper, student
Publishers
Textbooks, basic and supplemental
Workbooks
Yearbook, student

Buildings and Grounds

Blueprints and plans
Building codes
Housing
Inspection
Keys and locks
Lockers

Maintenance
Operation
Staff
Use of buildings, grounds, and
　property

Bulletins (other than instructional)

Business Affairs

Activity accounting:
　Board of education
　Student
　Trust
Agreements, bids, and contracts
Appraisals
Banking
Bonds
Bookkeeping
Bookstore
Budget:
　Accounts
　Appropriation
　Control
　Income
　Information Requests
Building programs:
　Additions, alterations,
　　new buildings
　Architects, plans, and
　　specifications
Cash receipts
Claims and aid
Equipment and supplies
Government finance and legal
　officers or staff

Insurance:
　Accident
　Athletic
　Automobile
　Bonding
　Building
　Equipment
　Fire
　Hospitalization
　Liability
　Life
　Medical
　Surgical
　Theft
Inventories
Legal matters and opinions
Payrolls:
　Time cards
　Time sheets
　Substitutes
Purchasing and requisitions:
　Bills and vouchers
　Catalogs
　Invoices
　Purchase orders

Receipts
Requisitions
Real estate, abstracts and
    deeds
Staff

Taxes:
    Amusement
    Assessment
    Levies
    Payroll withholding

Cafeterias See Food Services

Calendars and Schedules

Committees and Councils

Conventions

Correspondence

1. *File chronologically.*
2. *File by association, committee.*
3. *File by instructional area.*
4. *File by teacher or student.*

Curriculum (*See* Instruction)

Directories

Elections

Events and programs

Assemblies
Contests
Drives and collections

Holiday observances
Speakers and speeches
Special observances

Food Services

Cafeteria
Federal Aid (lunch and milk)

Menus
Staff

Forms (by form number or date of ordering)

Government (federal, state, county, local)

Civilian defense
Civil service
Flag

Laws and legislation
Military service
Postal regulations

In-Service, Staff

College courses
Institutes (*by date, subject,*
    grade)
Meetings (*by date, subject,*
    grade)

Regulations
Scholarship opportunities
Summer sessions
Travel opportunities
Workshops

Instruction (includes courses of study, materials, methods, school levels)

Adult education (includes
    evening schools)
Apprentice training
Art
Audio-Visual education
Business education (includes
    bookkeeping, typing, etc.)
Camps and camping

Child care
Correspondence schools
Driver education
Elementary education
English
First aid and safety
Foreign languages
Home making

Junior college
Junior high school
Kindergarten
Mathematics
Middle grades
Music
Physical education:
    Corrective
    Boys
    Girls

Primary education
Radio and television
Science
Senior high school
Social studies (includes
    geography, history)
State colleges
Veterans
University
Work-experience

Personnel (Individual Employee) Records

1. *File by certificated, non-certificated.*
2. *File by "active," "inactive."*
3. *File by name.*

Absence, leave of:
    Accident
    Illness
    Maternity
    Military
    Other
Accidents
Activities
Applications
Appointments and assignments:
    Extra-pay
Certification, credentials, licenses
Contracts and salary

Employment examinations
    and tests
Evaluations and ratings
Health records
Non-teaching employee lists
    (*by year, service*)
Recommendations
Student assistants, names of
    (*by year, subject or grade*)
Student practice teachers (cadets)
Substitutes
Transcripts of credit

Personnel (Employee) Services and Reports

Code of ethics
Employee lists:
    Administrator (*by year*)
    Teacher (*by year, school, grade or subject*)
    Non-teachers
Job specification
Pension and retirement
Personnel Reports (*by date of authorization or assignment*)
Placement agencies
Policies, regulations, procedures
Professional development
Salary schedules (*by year*)

Principal (personal)

Correspondence
Engagements
Speeches
Other

Public Relations

Advertising
Community contacts
Complaints and compliments
Direct mail
Newspapers
Photographs
Publicity
Radio and television
Telephone

Reports (Research, Statistics, Studies, Surveys)

1. *File by date.*
2. *File by subject.*

Schools and Institutions

Local (within own system or organization)
Outside (other than own system):
File correspondence by school name.

Special Services

Community resources:
   Citizens
   Libraries
   Museums
   Zoos
Exceptional children
Guidance
Health (exclusive of
   instructional units)
Libraries
Physically handicapped
   children
Religious education
Safety
Staff
Tours

Student Activities and Affairs (*See also Athletics, Awards*)

Activities
Alumni
Class gifts and histories
Clubs
Dance programs
Drama programs
Graduation programs
Schedules
Student body organization:
   Constitution, by-laws
   Officers, by year
Student property:
   Inventories
Recommendations
Tickets

Student Enrollment and Registration Services

File regulations, procedures, statistical reports, and lists.

Admission
Accident reports
Attendance
Census
Class lists
Corporal punishment reports
Driver-training assignments
Emergency referral
Enrollment and registration
   procedures
Graduation and
   promotion lists
Home-teacher assignments
Master schedule of classes
Non-residence permits
Student aid
Transfers, withdrawals
Vandalism reports
Work permits

Student (Individual) Records

1. *File by student name* (Use Cumulative Guidance Record).
2. *File by subject.*

Case studies:
  Reports of
  Requests for
Court or juvenile report
Cumulative Guidance Records
Discipline lists
Enrollment and registration
  records
Health cards

Personal behavior:
  Correspondence
Placement:
  Job requests, orders
  Job referrals
Program cards
Pupil personnel records
Scholastic progress
Student aid, welfare cases
Work-permits

Tests and Evaluations

Tests (samples or surplus)
1. *File by title.*
2. *File together manuals, scoring keys and stencils, norms, alternate forms, report forms pertaining to any one test.*

Aptitudes, separate
Arithmetic
English (other than reading)
Health
Intelligence
Interest Inventory
Personality
Reading
Science
Social Studies
Spelling

Test batteries:
  Achievement
  Aptitudes
  Other
Test catalogs
  File by publisher.
Test Results and Research Data
1. *File by grade, subject,*
    teacher.
2. *File by year.*
3. *File as "research."*

Transportation, Travel, and Trips

28

Checklist of Printing Specifications for School Publications

1. TITLE OR SUBJECT	Use exact title appearing on cover or title page.
2. PUBLICATION No.	List publication number, if any.
3. PUBLICATION DATE	List date, if any, to be printed on cover or title page. May be month and year, or year only.
4. METHOD OF REPRODUCTION	*Letterpress:* Most common form of printing. Suitable for line cuts. Best for halftones.

Offset: Considered less expensive than letterpress, especially if 5,000 or more copies. Photographs (halftones) less expensive to print but details are sometimes lost. Pictures, especially of people's faces, must be large. Contrasts must be strong. New offset papers and inks are resulting in improved reproduction of halftones. Ask printer to show samples of halftone work done by him. Typesetting is same as for letterpress.

If a letterpress job is to be re-run and the copy is clear and sharp, offset printing is considerably less expensive and usually acceptable. The saving is in the typesetting costs. Negatives must be made of each page to be reproduced.

Multilith: Especially suited for less than 5,000 copies. Process is same as offset only done on "office type" of offset press; photographs have same limitations as offset. Typewritten pages can be reproduced directly. Typesetting can be done by Varitype process, which is acceptable for most uses but lacks the aesthetic appeal of many letterpress types.

Most office offset presses cannot print pages larger than 6 × 9″ when folded.

5. NUMBER OF PAGES
   a. INSIDE PAGES

Specify: Number of printed pages exclusive of cover, division pages, or dividers. Pages are always in multiples of 4 (e.g., 4, 12, 16, 32, 64, 128, etc.). Allow for fly pages, if any, and for blank pages. (Number every sheet of copy.)

Most schools are not able to estimate the number of printed pages. Some school districts merely *specify:* "Printer to estimate number of pages." The weakness in this procedure is that printers may attempt to crowd pages and use narrow margins to reduce their bid.

Alternate: Specify: "Printer to estimate cost on basis of _____ printed pages and to state extra charge for each additional 8 pages." This procedure tends to cause bids to be more nearly alike.

   b. COVER, DIVISION
      PAGES OR
      DIVIDERS

Specify: "Plus cover and _____ (number of) division pages or dividers."

6. PAGE SIZE

Common page sizes are: 5 × 7, 6 × 9, 8½ × 11 inches.

7. COVER SIZE

Specify: Width and length in inches. Some schools prefer covers that overhang (are larger than) the inside pages. Then *specify:* "One-eighth inch overhang (top, bottom, one side)."

8. PAPER STOCK

Suggestion: Procure acceptable sample from a printer or paper dealer and *specify,* "As per attached sample or equivalent." (See pages 368 to 370 for description of available paper stocks.)

Specify, "Grain on all stock must run parallel to spine."

   a. COVER
      STOCK

Specify:
1. Color.
2. Substance.
3. Finish.

   b. DIVISION PAGES
      OR DIVIDERS

Specify:
1. Color (usually same as cover).
2. Substance (usually lighter in weight than cover; oftentimes same weight as inside pages).
3. Finish (usually same as cover).

Some schools use divider pages with file tabs. Consult a printer for help on such specifications.

c. INSIDE PAGES	*Inside pages* (book papers).
	Specify:
	1. Color (usually white).
	2. Substance (usually 60 or 70 lb., whichever is the same weight as cover or lighter).
	3. Finish:
	If no halftones or *only line cuts,* use antique or eggshell, machine finish or English finish.
	If halftones, use enamel or coated for screens of 120 or more. May use machine finish or English finish if screen is 110 or less. If *offset* process to be used, *specify* offset halftone stock.
9. MATCHING ENVELOPES	It may be desirable to have a matching envelope with printed corner card for some or all copies of a publication. A printer can advise.
10. INK	*Specify:* Colors for cover and division pages (usually black for inside pages).
11. TYPOGRAPHY OR FORMAT	If dummy is available, *specify:* "Follow style as per dummy or layout."
	Alternate: If sample or another publication is available, *may specify:* "Follow style as per accompanying publication (give exact title)."
	Recommendation: If a journalism teacher or school printing teacher is available to help, *can specify:* "Pasted-up dummy will be supplied for page make up."
12. MARGINS	*Specify:*

5 × 7" page size:

Inside (gutter):	½"
Top:	⅝"
Outside:	⅔"
Bottom:	1"
Line width:	3⅚" (23 picas)

6 × 9" page size:

Inside (gutter):	⅚"
Top:	⅞"
Outside:	1"
Bottom:	1¼"
Line Width:	4⅙" (25 picas)

8 × 11" page size:

Inside (gutter):	¾"
Top:	⅞"
Outside:	1¼"
Bottom:	1¾"
Line width:	7" (42 picas)
Two columns:	3⅓" (20 picas)

13. **TYPE SIZES AND FACES**

Specify: Printer is not to commence typesetting until type faces approved.

a. DISPLAY

Specify: Printer to submit samples of available type faces.

b. BODY

Specify: "Printer to submit samples of available type faces." In addition, type faces and sizes *should be* specified if bidding is likely to be close.

Recommendations:
5 × 7" page size:
  Type size: 8 pt. on 10 pt. body
6 × 9" page size:
  Type size: 10 pt. on 11 pt. body
8½ × 11" page size:
  Type size: 10 pt. on 12 pt. body.
  If publication to be used by elementary school children, suggest "Type size: 12 pt. on 14 pt. body."

14. **PROOFS AND PROOFREADING**

Specify: "Submit galley proofs in duplicate, one white and the second on pink paper, to (name, address)."

"Printer must proofread all proofs and submit galley proofs free from all typographical errors. Revised galley proofs may be requested."

and

"Printer to submit page proofs free from all typographical errors. Revised page proofs may be requested."

If *Varityping* is used, *specify:* "Varitypist to be responsible for all opaquing."

15. **PROOFREADING SCHEDULE**

Specify: "All galley proofs to be delivered within 2 (3, 4) weeks of approval of type face. Board of Education will return all galley proofs within one week of receipt."

16. **ART WORK**

Recommendation: Count and number each photograph and drawing. Be careful not to write on back of photographs, as sharp pencils can punch through photograph. Carefully type or clip sheet of typed instructions across bottom of picture. Suggest asking a printing teacher, commercial artist, or printer to help in indicating size of each piece of art work and screen to be used. If any cuts or halftones are to bleed (run off the margin), these must be specified.

Specify: "(Number) _____ of photographs and art work supplied. Sizes marked on each piece of copy."

For *letterpress* printing, *specify:* "All cuts and halftones to become the property of the Board of Education and must be returned within 60 days after final delivery of finished job unless notice given in writing that forms are to be held against possibility of re-run."

For *offset* printing, *specify:* "Negatives to become the property of the Board of Education and must be returned with all copy and art on final delivery."

17. BINDING

Specify: "Binding size and first bound copy must be submitted for approval."

Specify: "*Saddlestitched:* with 2 wire staples." (3 staples for 8½ × 11″ page.) This method is to be preferred to side stitching.

or

"Side-stitched: with 2 wire staples." (3 staples for 8½ × 11″ page.) This method is sturdier but pages do not open easily.

or

"Cerlox in _____ color with spine to be (or *not*) printed." (This is a plastic binding; pages lie flat. Publications do not stack well. Spine should be printed with name and number of publication.)

or

"Side-sewn, pre-bound books, three stitches per inch *with* an FF8 Myers thread. Nylon thread not acceptable." (Ordinarily side-sewing is not specified except for library and text-books.)

18. PACKAGING

Specify: "Wrap and label packages in quantities of _____ (10, 25, 50) copies."

Alternate: "Wrap and label packages in quantities not to exceed 16 inches in height."

19. COPY MAY BE SEEN

Specify: "Copy may be seen in Room _____, (address). Suggest printer call: (name of secretary, phone number) for appointment."

20. DELIVERY DATE

Specify: "Completed delivery must be on or before _____, to (name and address). All copy must be returned with final delivery."

> *Alternate:* "Partial delivery of first one-third of order may be on _____, second one-third by _____, and balance of completed job by not later than _____. Make all deliveries to (name, address). All copy must be returned with final delivery."

21. DEVIATIONS

> *Specify:* "There must be no deviation from the above specifications without the prior approval of _____ (name, title, address)."

22. PRINTER'S BID

1. _____ copies at $ _____ per copy. Total cost $ _____.
   a. Charge for _____ copies more
   b. Charge for _____ copies more
   c. Charge for _____ copies more
2. If number of printed pages specified,
   Charge for each: 4 pages more: $ _____
   8 pages more: $ _____
   12 pages more: $ _____
   16 pages more: $ _____
   above base bid of _____ copies.

PRINTING PAPERS

This is a guide to the selection of printing papers. Papers differ with the purpose and use of the publication and whether the printing is letterpress, offset, or multilith.

BOND PAPER

USE: For letters and other typewriting.

COLORS: White and variety of colors.

SUBSTANCE: Sulphite and unwatermarked suitable for ordinary use; 25% rag content suitable for erasing; 50% rag content suitable for permanent filing in archives.

BOOK PAPERS (letterpress)

USE: For pages of books and other school publications printed by letterpress process.

COLORS: Usually white, occasionally buff.

SUBSTANCE: 60 (120M) and 70 (140M) are satisfactory weights.

FINISHES:

> (1) If only line cuts or no halftones (photographs) to be used, specify:
>
> *Machine finish or English finish.* A smooth finish. Used when there are many pages or book is to be kept thin. Less expensive. Must be opaque if printed on both sides.
>
> *Antique or eggshell.* A plain finish. Used to give bulk when there are few pages. More expensive.

(2) If halftones (photographs) to be used, specify:

Machine finish or English finish. Suitable if halftone screen is 110 or less. May be used for additional colors of ink.

Enamel or coated. Appropriate if halftone screen is 120 or more. Bulkier, heavier, more expensive. Not suitable for additional colors of ink.

BOOK PAPERS (offset)

USE: For pages of books and other school publications printed by offset process. Bulkier than papers used in letterpress printing.

COLORS: Usually white.

SUBSTANCE: 60 (120M) and 70 (140M)

FINISHES: (1) *Vellum or wove offset.* Standard finish, uncoated.

(2) *Offset enamel or coated offset.* Has a gloss surface.

Either finish is suitable for halftones (photographs) regardless of screen; also suitable for additional colors of ink.

BRISTOL BOARD

USE: For file cards, tickets.

COLORS: White, buff, blue, canary, pink, salmon, green.

SUBSTANCE: 80 (160M), thin; 110 (220M), standard.

CHIPBOARD

USE: For backing tablets and other protective purposes.

COLORS: Gray.

SUBSTANCE: Usually varies between 51 and 81.

COVER PAPERS (letterpress)

USE: For covers and division or divider pages.

COLORS: Variety of colors available.

SUBSTANCE: Usually 60 (120M); 70 (140M); 80 (160M), sometimes called "single thick"; "double thick" is approximately 130 (260M) substance and, if used, must be scored for folding.

FINISHES: Usually *antique, eggshell, vellum, ripple,* or a *variety* of *embossed* patterns or grains.

If halftones (photographs) are to be printed, *enamel* finish must be specified.

COVER PAPERS (offset)

USE: For covers and division or divider pages.

COLORS: Usually white.

SUBSTANCE: Varies between 60 (120M) and 80 (160M).

FINISHES: Usually vellum or wove; also now available in enamel or coated. Either finish will print photographs.

DUPLICATOR PAPER

USE: For printing on liquid or gelatin process duplicating machines.

COLORS: White and some colors.

SUBSTANCE: 16-lb., standard; 20-lb. necessary if printing is on both sides.

LEDGER

USE: For bookkeeping, record forms, and other posting purposes; can be used as an offset book paper.

COLORS: White, buff, and others.

SUBSTANCE: 24-lb., thin; 28-lb., 32-lb., standard; 36-lb., heavy.

MIMEO PAPER

USE: For mimeographing; not suitable for pen and ink signatures.

COLORS: White and variety of colors.

SUBSTANCE: 16-lb., standard; 20-lb. necessary if printing is on both sides, 24-lb. preferred.

TAG BOARD

USE: For tags and file folders.

COLORS: Manila, white or ivory.

SUBSTANCE: 125, 150, 200

29

A Glossary of Educational Terms

Ability, Academic. The ability or aptitude necessary to do schoolwork.

Ability, Mechanical. Ability to deal with mechanisms and mechanical problems.

Absence. The failure of a pupil to be present at school.

Absence, Excused. Absence from school for any reason recognized as legitimate by the school.

Absence, Legal. Absence from school for reasons established by law, such as holidays and for religious ceremonies.

Absence, Unexcused. Absence from school for reasons that are not recognized by the school as legitimate.

Academic. Pertaining to the fields of English, foreign languages, history, economics, mathematics, and science.

Acceleration. Completion of school grades at a rate of more than one full grade each year.

Accounts Payable. Unpaid balances or invoices against an activity fund which are due and owing to private persons, firms, governmental units, or others.

Accounts Receivable. Amounts owed to an activity fund by private persons, firms, governmental units, or others.

Accredited High School. A secondary school whose graduates are accepted for admission to the university.

Accrediting Agency or Association. An organization that sets up criteria for judging the quality of educational institutions.

Achievement, Academic. The achievement of pupils in the so-called "academic" subjects, such as reading, arithmetic, and history, as contrasted with skills developed in such areas as industrial arts and physical education.

Achievement, Pupil. A pupil's status with reference to attained skills or knowledge, usually as compared with that of other pupils or with the scholastic standards of the school.

Action Research. Informal research a teacher does in connection with her teaching to study her pupils and her teaching methods.

Activities, Extracurricular. Programs and events, carrying no academic credit, sponsored and organized by pupils' organizations. Opposite of Cocurricular.

Activity. Any large learning situation which serves as a means toward reaching a worthwhile educational goal.

Activity, Curricular. Any student or teacher activity suggested in the course of study or provided for in the curriculum.

Activity Method. Any method of instruction that stresses the participation of pupils in learning activities; stresses doing instead of passive studying.

Adjustment, Pupil. The success the pupil has in getting along with himself, his classmates, his teachers, his school studies.

Administration. (1) The personnel who are responsible for the direction, control, and management of a school or the entire school system. (2) Those activities which have as their purpose the general regulation, direction, and control of the affairs of the school.

Administration, Educational. The direction, control, and management of those aspects of school administration most directly related to the instructional process, but not related to the business aspects of administration.

Administration of Supplies. The general supervision of materials necessary for the operation of schools for instruction.

Administrative Policy. A statement of procedure adopted by a board of education or administrative agency, stating the action to be followed with respect to specific matters under given conditions.

Administrative Unit, Local Basic. An administrative unit at the local level which exists primarily to operate schools or to contract for school services. (This term is used synonymously with the term "school district.")

Admission. Acceptance of a student's application for enrollment in a school.

Admission Requirements. Educational and personal qualifications established by a school, college, or university as requisites for admission.

Adult Education. Formal and informal instruction and aids to study for mature persons.

Adult Education, Public. Those organized public educational programs, other than regular full-time, which provide opportunity for adults and out-of-school youth to further their educational attainment.

Adviser. (1) One whom a person may consult with regard to his scholastic or vocational problems. (2) A member of the faculty to whom a student is assigned for advice and assistance with academic, vocational, and personal problems.

Age, Achievement. The age equivalent of a pupil's score on an achievement test.

Age, Admission. The minimum age for admission to the public school as established by ruling of the board of education.

Age, Chronological. (CA) The amount of time that has elapsed since an individual's birth.

Age, Entrance. The age at which children are permitted to enroll in school, quite generally fixed by the various states at 6 years.

Age, Mental. (MA) The level of a person's mental ability expressed in terms of the chronological age of persons having the same level of mental ability.

Age, Proof of. Any authentic evidence of the date of birth, often required before a child is admitted to the first grade.

Age, School-leaving. The earliest age, varying from state to state, at which pupils are no longer required by law to attend school.

Aggregate Days Absent. The sum of the number of days of absence for all pupils enrolled.

Aggregate Days Attended. The sum of the number of days attended by all pupils enrolled.

Aggregate Days Enrolled. The sum of the number of days of enrollment for all pupils.

Allotment. The portion of Federal or State education funds to which each state is entitled for each type of institutional school system.

All-year School. A school that is in session throughout the calendar year of twelve months.

Alumna. A female graduate. Plural—alumnae.

Alumnus. A male graduate. Plural—Alumni (covers both sexes).

Analysis, Item. A method used in test construction to determine whether a given question or item should be used in the test.

Analysis, Job. The determination of the skills and items of knowledge that a worker must possess in order to do a specific job.

Annual. An illustrated record of the school year usually in book form, written, edited, and published by a class or group of students.

Answer Key. A sheet of a series of strips on which are recorded the correct responses for a given test to facilitate objective scoring.

Answer Sheet. The separate sheet on which the examinee may record his responses for a test.

Application Blank for Admission. A record form for collecting educational and other personnel data on students seeking to be admitted to college from high school.

Appreciation, Art. A course designed to help the pupil understand aesthetic principles, artistic techniques and to recognize material of artistic worth.

Appreciation, Music. A course designed to help pupils obtain enjoyment of music.

Apprentice. A young person who has entered into an agreement under which the employer is to teach him a skilled trade or occupation.

Appropriation, Public School. Money received out of funds set aside periodically by the appropriating body (district meeting, city council, or other governmental bodies) for school purposes; which funds have not been specifically collected as school taxes.

Aptitude. Pronounced potential or innate capacity, the ability to learn a given school subject or vocation.

Articulation. (1) The degree of continuity, consistency, and interdependence in the offerings of the successive grades and divisions of the school system. (2) The extent to which the various school subjects or levels of the educational system are related to provide for continuous educational progress of pupils with a minimum of repetition and a maximum of efficiency.

Asocial. Indifferent to existing social customs, moral codes, or usual social relationships.

Assembly. A gathering of students, usually at a regular scheduled time and place and under the direction of adults, for the purpose of participating in concerts, social enjoyment, deliberations, etc. Examples of such assemblies include routine, daily or weekly assemblies; special assemblies for dramatic, music, or forensic activities; and student elections.

Assets. The entire property owned by a school activity organization.

Assignment. The work that has been allotted to the pupil or class.

Athletics, Interscholastic. Organized games and athletic activities engaged in by students specifically trained for such purposes with similarly trained students from other schools.

Athletics, Intramural. (1) Athletic contests and sports involving only students of the same institution. (2) Organized games and athletic activities engaged in by students of a school with other students from the same school. The intramural program may be an integral part of the physical education program or a distinctive program of its own; in either case, the program must be confined to a single school.

Attendance, Average Daily. *See* Average Daily Attendance.

Attendance Area. The territory from which children legally may attend a given school building or school center.

Attendance Clerk. A member of the school clerical staff who keeps the attendance records of the pupils.

Attendance Officer. A school employee empowered to compel school attendance and to investigate instances of nonattendance.

Attendance Teacher. The teacher who is responsible for keeping a record of or reporting on the attendance of the pupils of the entire school.

Attention Span. The extent or limit of the ability of a pupil to concentrate on something or on what he is reading without thinking of anything else.

Atypical. Differing to a marked degree in one or more characteristics from others of a given class or category.

Audiometer. An instrument for testing and measuring hearing.

Audit. The examination of records and documents and the securing of other evidence for one or more of the following purposes: (a) Determining the propriety of proposed or completed transactions; (b) ascertaining whether all transactions have been recorded; (c) determining whether transactions are accurately recorded in the accounts and in the statements drawn from the accounts.

Auditorium. A building or a room in a school building, usually equipped with a stage and arranged much like a theater, used for school assemblies and other meetings.

Average, Arithmetic. The sum of the items or scores divided by their number, or frequency.

Average, Class. The sum of the test scores of the pupils in a class divided by the number of pupils.

Average, Grade. A measure of central tendency, usually the mean, for a grade group of pupils on some test or measure; commonly used in determining the direction and degree of individual pupil deviation from the grade mean for assigning marks or for other purpose.

Average, Grade-point. A measure of average scholastic success in all school subjects taken by a student during a certain term or accumulated for several terms or semesters.

Average Daily Attendance, ADA. In a given school year, the average daily attendance for a given school is the aggregate days' attendance of the school divided by the number of days school was actually in session.

Baccalaureate Sermon. A sermon preached for a graduating class as a part of the graduation exercises.

Bachelor of Arts. The degree conferred by colleges for the completion of a four-year curriculum in liberal arts.

Balance Sheet. A statement, showing assets and other resources, liabilities, and other obligations (debits) and surplus (credits) of a fund.

Battery of Tests. A group of several tests intended to be given to the same pupil.

Bibliography. A list of books, maps, etc.; listing author, title, publisher, date and pages or size.

Bibliography, Annotated. A list of references accompanied by evaluations of each publication listed.

Bid. An offer, usually written, to furnish materials or services for a specified sum of money.

Bidding, Competitive. A system whereby a board of education invites bids or estimates from a number of contractors, dealers, or whole-salers for specified services or merchandise, with the understanding that the lowest bid may be accepted or all bids rejected.

Bilingual. The ability to speak two different languages, such as English and German.

Birth Rate. The number of children born during a given period of time per hundred or thousand of the total population.

Block. A large unit or division of instruction.

Block Building. An activity in which children learn to manipulate blocks of various types, sizes and shapes that express their ideas and experiences.

Block Method. A procedure for constructing high-school schedules of classes, the students being assigned to sections according to these blocks.

Board of Education, Public. The elected or appointed body which has been created according to State law and vested with responsibilities for educational activities in a given geographical area.

Board of Trustees. See Board of Education, **Public.**

Bond, School. A written promise to pay a specified sum of money at a fixed time in the future and carrying interest at a fixed rate, usually voted by taxpayers to raise money to pay for school buildings and similar purposes.

Bond Election. An election at which taxpayers vote on whether the board of education may sell bonds to raise money for school buildings or other stated purposes.

Book List. A list of books read or to be read, compiled by a pupil or class.

Borderline Case. Any instance that falls near but not exactly on a line of division or differentiation, for example, a pupil whose school achievement is such as to raise doubt about the desirability of his promotion.

Brain Damage. Injury to, or destruction of the tissue of the brain, which impairs some of the person's mental functions.

Broken Home. Any home where one or both parents are dead or where the parents are divorced or separated.

Budget. An estimate of proposed expenditures for a given period or purpose and the proposed means of financing them.

Budget Calendar. The time or date made and an estimate of the expenditures necessary to provide for the program of the school over a designated period of time.

Building Pass. A properly authorized form showing that the student holder is entitled to go to a room or part of a building in which he is not ordinarily expected to be at the time.

Building Specifications. A written or printed description of work to be done, the type and quality of material to be furnished, and the dimensions of the structure.

Bulletin Board. A board to which can be fastened notices or pictures of interest to teachers or pupils.

Business Manager. The officer of the school district directly responsible for its business affairs.

Busy Work. An expression, formerly respectable, that now means a waste of time, or doing something that lacks educational value.

Cadet Teacher. See Practice Teacher.

Calendar of Reports. A list by month and days showing when and where certain school reports are due.

Campus. The grounds of a university or college on which the buildings of the institution are situated. Sometimes used to refer to high school grounds.

Capacity of Classroom. The number of students that can be accommodated in a classroom.

Capital Outlay. (1) An expenditure for land or existing buildings, improvement of grounds, construction of buildings, additions to buildings, remodeling of buildings, or initial or additional equipment. (2) Any expenditure that results in the acquisition of buildings or other permanent facilities.

Card Punching. Recording data by punching holes into cards by means of a mechanical punch, a machine somewhat similar to a typewriter.

Card Sorter. A machine for sorting punch cards electrically or mechanically.

Case History. A summary of facts concerning a pupil's behavior, environment, family background, and personal history.

Cash. Currency, checks, postal and express money orders, and bankers' drafts on hand or on deposit with an official or agent designated as custodian of cash; and bank deposits. Any restriction of availability should be indicated.

Cash Discount. An allowance received or given if payment is completed within the stated period. The term is not to be confused with "trade discount."

Census, School. An enumeration to determine the number of children of certain ages resident in a given district, such as date of birth, names of parents, and occupation of parents.

Centile. See Percentile.

Certificate, Administrative. A certificate or license permitting a person who has met certain requirements to hold specified administrative positions in the schools.

Certificate, Physician's. The statement of a physician testifying to the health or illness of a child, used as a legal excuse for absence from school.

Certificate, Supervisory. A license stating that a teacher is qualified to oversee the instruction given in specified grades, subjects, or school units.

Certificate, Teacher's. A license stating that the holder is qualified to teach in a public school, usually with certain reservations as to the grade level and/or subjects in which the holder is qualified.

Certificate of Attendance. A form to certify to perfect attendance on the part of a pupil, or to the presence of the pupil at school on a given day or days.

Chart, Age Distribution. A sheet having various ages listed in one column and the number of pupils of these given ages shown in a second parallel column.

Chart, E. A chart for testing vision, lines of symbols similar to the letter E, drawn in various sizes according to the Snellen scale.

Chart, Profile. A chart on which a pupil's comparable scores on tests are shown graphically.

Child, Atypical. A child who deviates markedly above or below the norm of his group in respect to one or several mental, physical, or social traits.

Child, Exceptional. See Child, Atypical.

Child Accounting. The recording, classifying, and summarizing of data concerning the enrollment and attendance of pupils, including truancy, tardiness, exclusions from school, issuance of work permits, etc.

Child-centered School. A school that is organized around the needs, purposes, and interests of the children.

Civic Center. The school premises or plant when used by civic and other groups for legally authorized purposes.

Class, Adjustment. A special class providing remedial teaching for pupils who are handicapped in their school progress by specific disabilities, as in reading or arithmetic.

Class, Americanization. An organized class of persons, usually immigrants, preparing for naturalization as American citizens.

Class, Extension. A group of part-time students meeting in regular sessions once a week or oftener.

Class, Reimbursable. In vocational education, a class organized by a local school system so that a portion of its costs may be refunded by Federal funds made available through the state department of education.

Class, Sight-saving. A special class established for the education of children with vision so seriously defective that they cannot advantageously be taught with pupils of normal vision.

Class, Ungraded. A class so organized along lines of individualized instruction as to permit each pupil to work at his own rate, bright pupils being able to work more rapidly, dull pupils more slowly.

Class Book. A record book used by high school teachers to record the attendance and scholarship of students.

Class Norm. See teacher-pupil ratio.

Classes, Duplicate. Sections or groups of students receiving instruction in the same subject, at the same level, and doing approximately the same work.

Classification. (1) Placement of a pupil in his proper grade on the basis of test results and other data that seem to indicate that he is ready to do the work of that grade. (2) The process of grouping statistical data into categories or classes, on the basis of attributes or magnitudes.

Clerical Work. Activities of a routine, mechanical nature such as checking attendance and keeping records in order.

Clinic, Child-guidance. A place for the study and treatment of conduct and personality problems of children.

Clinic, Reading. A place where children with reading handicaps are examined, their difficulties analyzed, and remedial treatment prescribed.

Clock-and-Bell System. An electrically operated master clock that shows the time on dials installed in the various rooms of a building and regulates the ringing of electric bells at desired times or set intervals.

Closing Day. The last attendance day of the school term or year, when schoolwork for this period comes to an end.

Code of Ethics, Professional. A statement of ideals, principles, and standards of professional conduct.

Coding. A system of numbering, or otherwise designating, accounts, entries, invoices, vouchers, etc., in such a manner that the symbol used reveals quickly certain required information.

Coeducation. An educational practice whereby boys and girls attend the same classes.

Combination Classes or Grades. The merging, for instructional purposes, of the pupils of two or more classes or grades into a single group under one teacher.

Commencement. See Graduation.

Community Center. A meeting place in a city or rural community where people living near by come together to participate in social, recreational, and cultural activities.

Community College (Junior College, Technical Institute, etc.) A public school beginning with grade 12 which offers at least one but less than four years of work and does not grant the baccalaureate degree.

Community Coordinating Council. A council of representatives of civic, social, educational, service, and other agencies and organizations that correlates the services of those agencies and combines their efforts for a better constructive youth program.

Compulsory Attendance. The requirement under law that children between specified ages (in most states, 7 to 16), must attend school.

Concession. A concession is the granting to an individual or group the right to use portions of the school premises for some specific purpose. Usually, it is for the sale of confections, such as dairy products, sandwiches, peanuts, popcorn, and soft drinks sold at athletic games, plays, concerts, and similar events.

Conference, Case. A method of solving pupil difficulties in which those concerned with the individual (usually the school principal, adviser, school nurse, psychologist, teachers, and sometimes parents) consult together with a view to pooling and reviewing available data, and making recommendations as to the treatment to be used.

Conference, Parent. A meeting between a pupil's parent and his teacher to discuss the pupil's school progress.

Conference, Pupil. A meeting between a pupil and a teacher or counselor to discuss the pupil's educational, vocational, or emotional problems.

Conference, Supervisory. A conference among school workers to secure improvements in methods of teaching.

Consolidated School District. An enlarged school district formed by uniting two or more small school districts.

Consultant. A resource person who provides assistance to the regular personnel through conference, demonstration, research, or other means.

Continuation School. A public part-time school in which young workers may continue their education even though they are employed.

Contract, Bus. A written agreement between school authorities and an individual or corporation, providing transportation of pupils to and from school.

Contract, Teacher's. A formal agreement, entered into by a teacher and a board of education, stating the salary to be paid and the length of the term of the contract.

Controlling Account. An account usually kept in the general ledger in which the postings to a number of identical, similar, or related accounts are summarized so that the balance in the controlling account equals the sum of the balances of the detailed accounts. The controlling account serves as a check on the accuracy of the detailed account postings and summarizes the expenditures in relation to the budget estimates.

Cooperative Education. Alternation of study in school with off-campus jobs.

Coordinating Council. A group of representative community leaders and professional workers who study and plan ways of dealing with community problems, such as juvenile delinquency.

Coordinator. A general title frequently given to a teacher who has been assigned highly responsible school duties other than teaching.

Copy Reading. The act of revising manuscripts for the printer, usually involving editing, headline writing, and marking instructions to the printer.

Correlation. The act or process of ascertaining the degree of relationship of two or more statistical variables.

Cost. The amount of money or money's worth given for property or services.

Cost, Instructional. A financial accounting classification includes all items of expense directly concerned with teaching, teachers' salaries, supervisors' salaries and instructional supplies.

Cost, Pupil. The annual cost per pupil of operating the school.

Cost, Student-Clock-Hour. The average amount of money expended per student per *clock-hour* of instruction.

Cost Analysis. A study of the average cost of educating a single pupil, or of operating a single school or school activity for a semester, year, or other period of time.

Counselee. A student being assisted by means of counseling.

Counselor. One who assists pupils in life planning or in the solution of problems, especially as they relate to social, educational, and vocational situations.

Counselor, Class. One whose counseling is limited to the members of one class.

Counselor, Coordinator. A person who has the responsibility of bringing about a harmonious adjustment of the activities of the various counselors of a given system.

Counselor, Employment. A teacher who interviews and advises pupils applying for work.

Course. Organized subject matter in which instruction is offered within a given period of time, for which credit toward graduation or certification is usually given.

Course, Academic. At the elementary level, courses in the "3 R's"; at the secondary level, courses that prepare specifically for college entrance such as English, science, mathematics, foreign language, and social studies.

Course, Core. That course or group of subjects designed to provide all students with the minimum and basic essentials of living.

Course, Exploratory. A course affording students first-hand contacts and experiences in a variety of subject fields or occupational situations; designed to help students discover their interests and capacities.

Course, Extension. A course similar to adult education offered by a university; sometimes given by mail.

Course, Tryout. A course in which the pupil is given opportunity to try his ability to succeed in a given field of study or work before attempting more advanced courses.

Course, Vocational. A course consisting of practical work and instruction in some technical subject, preparing the student for employment.

Course of Study. Strictly, an official guide prepared for teachers stating the aims of the course, the expected outcomes, and the scope and nature of the materials to be studied, with suggestions as to suitable instructional aids, textbooks, supplementary reading, activities, teaching methods, and measurement of achievement. Sometimes loosely and incorrectly used as a synonym for *Curriculum.*

Course Content. The facts, methods, understandings, and appreciations to be taught in a course.

Credit. A unit for expressing the value of a course in relation to the total requirements for a degree or diploma.

Credit Union, Teachers'. An organization or association to accept funds from teachers for savings accounts and to make loans to teachers from these.

Cross-section Paper. Paper that is divided into small sections by means of horizontal and vertical lines. Also called *graph paper.*

Cumulative-Leave Plan. A plan whereby the unused days allowed for sick leave, with pay, are allowed to accumulate, sometimes for as long as 10 years and for as many as 100 days.

Cumulative Record, Pupil's. An individual record, usually permanent, that is kept continually up to date by a teacher or the school and that is an educational history about the pupil's school achievement, courses studied, attendance, health, and similar pertinent data.

Cumulative Record Folder. A folded form on which is recorded in orderly fashion a succession of pertinent data accumulating over a period.

Current Expense. Any expenditure except one for capital outlay or debt service. If any accounts are kept on the accrual basis, current expense includes total charges incurred, whether paid or unpaid. If accounts are kept on the cash basis, it includes only actual disbursements.

Curriculum. A systematic group of courses or sequence of subjects required for graduation.

Curriculum, Child-centered. A curriculum in which the selection and sequence of materials, activities, and experiences for any particular pupil are his needs, maturity, interests, and experiential background.

Curriculum, Community-centered. An educational program based on and adjusted to the life, culture, resources, needs, activities, and interests of the community in which it is offered.

Curriculum, Core. The areas of experience and learning required of all pupils or students prior to specialization; a center of interest and emphasis about which all other studies are oriented.

Custodian. The caretaker of a school building or the person in charge of all school housekeeping duties.

Daily-Lesson-Plan. A tentative plan of the activities of the class each day.

Daily Plan. A schedule or timetable indicating the sequence of educational activities for a particular school day.

Data (singular, Datum). Organized or systematically arranged information or facts (frequently numerical) reporting such matters of importance as pupil test scores, pupil attendance, cost of instruction, etc.

Day of Attendance. A day of attendance is one in which a pupil is present for the full day under the guidance and direction of a teacher while school is in session.

Day Nursery. An institution for the organized care of young children outside their homes.

Day in Session. A day on which the school is open and the pupils are under the guidance and direction of teachers in the teaching process.

Dean of Boys. A teacher whose primary function is the guidance of boys in their adjustments to their environment.

Dean of Girls. A teacher whose primary function is the guidance of girls in their adjustments to their environment.

Degree. A title bestowed by a college or university as official recognition for the completion of a course of study for a certain attainment.

Degree, Associate. A degree commonly conferred at the end of a two-year junior college course of study.

Degree, Master's. An academic degree of advanced character ranking above the bachelor's degree and below the Ph.D., Ed.D., or other equivalent doctor's degrees.

Demerit. A mark or unfavorable score given a pupil for misbehavior or for failure to meet an obligation.

Department. An administrative subdivision of a school or college giving instruction in a branch of study, as the *department of English.*

Department Chairman. A faculty member who, in addition to performing the usual duties of teaching in a department, has been designated to preside over staff meetings and to carry on certain administrative duties involved in managing the affairs of the department.

Deposit, Returnable. Money collected from students and held in a school fund for future return at a designated period for the purpose of covering losses or damages to school-owned supply and equipment items while being used by the students.

Detention. The act of confining or detaining a pupil after school in the detention hall or room for a limited period of time daily and for a specified number of days.

Diagnosis. The procedure by which the characteristics and problems of individual students being counseled are determined.

Diploma. A formal documentary credential given by an educational institution certifying the completion of a curriculum.

Director. A title sometimes given to the administrative head of a school, department, office, program or activity of a school system.

Director of Admission. A college or university officer who decides on the applications of new students for admission to the institution.

Discipline. The authoritative control of pupil behavior; the result of directing or subordinating immediate wishes, impulses, desires, or interests for the sake of dependable action.

Dismissal. The act of dropping a pupil's name from the roll, whether at the demand of the school authorities or as the result of the pupil's voluntary and legal withdrawal.

District, City School. A geographical area, frequently coterminous with a legally established municipality, designated as a local school unit by state authority, which also establishes its powers and duties.

Division. An administrative unit of a school usually consisting of more than one department.

Doctor of Education. A holder of the highest professional degree in education awarded by colleges or universities for the advanced study of educational problems.

Doctor of Philosophy. A holder of a doctor's degree conferred for mastery within a field of knowledge and for proved ability in original research.

Driver Education. Classroom instruction designed to develop proper habits, attitudes, skills, and background knowledge in motorists.

Driver Training. Road instruction behind the wheel of a motor vehicle.

Dropout. A pupil who leaves school before the completion of a grade or before graduation.

Dropping of Pupils. The act of removing pupils from the rolls of a school because of absences.

Eight-four Plan. An elementary school of eight years exclusive of kindergarten (grades 1 to 8) and a secondary school of four years (grades 9 to 12).

Elective. An optional course not required of all pupils.

Elementary Grades. Grades 1 to 8, and sometimes nursery school and kindergarten, or as ending with grade 6, where there is a junior high school.

Encumbrances. Obligations, in the form of purchase orders or contracts as yet unpaid, for which a part of the appropriation is reserved.

Enrollment. The number of pupils on the roll at any given date.

Enrollment, Average. An average of the monthly total enrollments in a class, grade, school, or school district.

Entry Notice. A form used to indicate that a pupil has been enrolled in the class or school.

Enumeration Sheet. A form used in taking a school census for the purpose of listing data about each child from birth to the age of eighteen.

Equalization. A plan for giving money to less wealthy school districts so that their educational program can be better.

Equipment. Articles such as furniture, machinery, and books that are used without being consumed. See supplies.

Error. A mistake or incorrect answer; also the degree of inaccuracy.

Evaluation. The process of judging the merits of the educational program.

Evening School. A school that offers courses at hours other than those commonly used for elementary- and secondary-school classes.

Ex Officio Member. A person who is a committee member by virtue of holding an elective or appointive office.

Examination, Final. A test given at the end of a course.

Examination Schedule. A timetable indicating day, time of day, and place for taking examinations.

Exceptional Child. See Child, Atypical.

Exchange Teacher. A teacher from another system who temporarily exchanges positions with a local teacher.

Exchanges. Copies of student publications from other schools.

Exclusion, Temporary. An order refusing a pupil the right to attend school for a limited period of time.

Excuse Slip. An administrative form used to explain a pupil's absence from his regular school assignment.

Expense, Travel. Expenses incurred by students and sponsors of a school activity in connection with travel related to the activity, other than those expenses directly chargeable to pupil transportation.

Experience, Work. Actual experience in an occupation before a student begins a full-time job.

Experimental School. An elementary or secondary school, in which new teaching methods are tried and tested.

Exploration. The taking of selected courses to try out and discover the pupil's interests and aptitudes and to give him an understanding of typical occupations, activities, and subjects.

Expulsion. The act of forcing a pupil to withdraw from school; particularly cases of extreme misbehavior.

Extended Day. The designation for that period of the day, usually 4 P.M. or later, when class instruction is held later than the normal day-school hours.

Extension, Trade. Designed to supplement or extend the trade knowledge or skill, or both, of employed workers in industry.

Faculty. The teachers of a school or college.

Faculty Sponsor. A teacher who is responsible for the leadership or supervision of a specified student activity.

Fade-out. A student, usually college, voluntarily withdraws without telling anyone. Contrast Dropout.

Family History. All available and pertinent data regarding all relatives of the pupil, present and past.

Federal Aid. Financial aid given by the Federal government to help carry out some aspect of the school program.

Fee, Incidental. A fee sometimes charged for school services other than tuition.

Fellowship. A position in a university held by a graduate student and paying a small stipend.

Fidelity Bond. A bond guaranteeing the school activities against losses resulting from the actions of the treasurer, employees, or other persons of the school.

Field Day. A day on which the pupils of one or more schools engage in organized outdoor sport and play activities.

Field Trip. An educational trip to a place away from school.

Film, Instructional. Any film planned and produced for use as an aid to teaching.

Film, Sound. Motion-picture film on which sound has been recorded.

Film Strip. A short length of film made of separate still pictures.

Financial Statement. A formal written presentation which sets forth information concerning the financial condition of a school activity fund.

Fiscal Year. A period of one year, at the end of which financial accounts are settled and reports made; usually ends on June 30 or December 31.

Fixed Charges. School expenses that cannot be put off, such as electric lights, taxes, and insurance.

Flash Card. A small card having on it letters, words, or numbers which the teacher holds up for the class to see for a brief interval.

Follow-up. A plan by which the experiences of young people who have left school are investigated.

Food Services. Those activities which have as their purpose the preparation and serving of regular and incidental meals, lunches, or snacks in connection with school activities.

Foods. A course dealing with the selection, buying, care, preparation, and serving of foods in the home.

Freedom, Academic. The right of teachers to "teach the truth as they see it," without interference.

Frequency List. A list of words or facts arranged according to the number of times they are used; (the arrangement may be alphabetical or in ascending or descending order of frequency of occurrence).

Fund. A sum of money or other resources set aside for specific activities of a school district.

Fund, Imprest. A petty cash fund.

Fund, Retirement. Money set aside for providing retirement allowances to teachers and other school employees.

Fundamentals. A common term used to indicate the 3 R's or other subjects considered essential to every pupil's education; also, the basic principles of any school subject.

General Education. A broad type of education aimed at developing attitudes, abilities, and behavior considered desirable by society.

General Ledger. A book, file, or other device in which accounts are kept to the degree of detail necessary, that summarizes the financial transactions of the school district.

Gift. Money received from a philanthropic foundation, private individual, or private organization for which no repayment or special service to the contributor is expected.

Goal. An aim or purpose of a course.

Grade, Primary. Any one of the first three grades of an elementary school.

Grade Placement. The assignment of a subject or test score to a specified grade, year, or level of schoolwork.

Grade-Point. A numerical value given to letter marks or grades, as 4 for an A, 3 for a B, 2 for a C, etc.

Grade Teacher. Any elementary school teacher.

Graduate Student. A student who has earned his bachelor's degree and is studying for a higher degree.

Graduation. The ceremony at which diplomas or degrees are conferred upon pupils or students who have completed the prescribed course of study.

Graduation Requirements. The qualifications necessary for the granting of a diploma.

Grammar School. An elementary school.

Grant. Money paid to a school activity by the school district for which no repayment is expected.

Graph. A diagram for presenting data, making comparisons, and depicting relationships.

Graph, Bar. A chart made up of a series of horizontal or vertical bars of differing lengths to show statistical facts.

Guidance. Assistance (aside from regular instructions) given to pupils to understand themselves, to recognize their basic needs and to take purposeful steps toward satisfying them.

Guidance, Vocational. Advice given a student regarding his vocational interests, aptitudes and employment opportunities in order to help him in selecting, preparing for, entering upon, and succeeding in an occupation.

Half Grade. A division or level of elementary school work requiring one-half a school year, or a semester, to complete.

Handbook. A booklet containing general information concerning school organization, marking system, attendance and tardiness regulations, etc.

Health Inspection. A brief inspection by a teacher of her pupils to ascertain whether hands, nails, faces, and clothing are clean and whether they have any signs of illness.

Home Call. A visit to a home by a pupil-personnel worker or an attendance officer.

Homework. School assignments to be completed out of regular school hours.

Homogeneous Grouping. A grouping of pupils so that those of similar qualifications or ability are placed in the same class.

Honor Society. An organization of students with outstanding scholarship.

Honor Student. A student who has an outstanding record for scholarship.

Honor System. A system under which students are on their honor not to cheat, steal, or disobey rules.

Honorary Society or Fraternity. A college organization of students having made outstanding records in scholarship in a subject field, in student activities, or both.

Humanities. Literature, language, art, philosophy, religion, and history.

I.Q. See Intelligence Quotient.

Illiteracy. Inability to read and write sufficiently well to meet the needs of adult life.

Induction. The instruction and aid given a new teacher or school employee so that he will become familiar with the school and his responsibilities.

Industrial Arts. High school courses giving the student an understanding of the work performed by employees in typical industrial occupations and trades.

Industrial Education. A term, broader in meaning than industrial arts, used to encompass all types of industrial training, including apprenticeship training.

Intelligence Quotient. The most well-known method of expressing mental development in relation to chronological age. A pupil's I.Q. is obtained by dividing his mental age (as measured by a general intelligence test) by his chronological age and then multiplying by 100.

Institute, Teachers'. A series of meetings for teachers to provide opportunities for discussion and study of teaching problems.

Instruction. The activities dealing directly with the teaching of students or improving the quality of teaching.

Instruction, Audio-visual. Instruction based on the use of visual materials with integral sound accompaniment, for example, sound motion pictures, sound slide films, etc.

Instructional Material. Anything used for teaching purposes, including textbooks, workbooks, and visual aids.

Instructor. In colleges and universities, a teacher holding a rank below that of any of the grades of professor.

Intelligence. Ability to make successful and rapid adaptation to new situations and to learn from experience.

Intelligence, Average. 100 I.Q. for the population as a whole; the average varies with each class, grade, and school.

Interest. The liking or preference a person has for an activity, subject, sport, or occupation.

Interfund Transfers. Money which is taken from one school activity fund and added to another activity fund. Interfund transfers are not receipts or expenditures of a school.

Intermediate Grade. Usually grades 4, 5, or 6 in an elementary school.

Intermediate School. A school offering only grades 7 and 8. COMPARE JUNIOR HIGH SCHOOL.

Interview, Exit. A regularly scheduled interview between pupil and counselor just before the former leaves school.

Inventory. A detailed list or record showing quantities, descriptions, values, and, frequently, units of measure and unit prices of property on hand at a given time.

Inventory, Equipment. A list of equipment assigned to a classroom.

Invoice. An itemized statement of merchandise shipped or sent to a purchaser, consignee, etc., with the quantity, value or prices, and charges annexed.

Item, Inventory. An article of school equipment or supply.

Item, Test. A single question or problem in a test.

Job Classification. A group of jobs having similar duties, wages, and employment qualifications.

Journal. Any form in which the financial transactions of the school district are formally recorded for the first time, such as the cash receipts book, check register, and journal voucher.

Journeyman. A worker who has learned the basic skills of his occupation or craft and is capable of performing his duties without close supervision or instruction.

Junior High School. A school for grades 7, 8, and 9. Sometimes applied to schools with only grades 7 and 8.

Juvenile Delinquent. A child who violates the law or whose behavior is so serious that he is considered a menace to himself or others.

Kindergarten. A school or class for small children, usually from 4 to 6 years of age.

Laboratory. A room equipped for scientific experimentation.

Language Arts. A group of school subjects including reading, composition, grammar, speech, spelling and literature.

Legal Residence. In the case of a child, the home of his parents or guardian.

Lesson Plan. A teaching outline of the important points of a lesson arranged in the order in which they are to be taught.

Liabilities. Debt or other legal obligations arising out of transactions in the past which are payable but not necessarily due. Encumbrances are not liabilities; they become liabilities when the services or materials for which the encumbrance was established have been rendered or received.

Liberal Arts. Courses taught in a university other than technical or professional education.

Load, Class. The sum total of the teacher's responsibilities for classroom instruction.

Load, Pupil. The number of pupils met daily for instruction by the teacher.

Lower Division. The freshman and sophomore years of a university.

Loyalty Oath. An oath in which the teacher swears he will support the Constitution of the United States and the state, and not teach certain theories of government that are in opposition to the government of the United States.

Lump-sum Appropriation. A sum of money allowed a school or department without specifying in detail the activities or uses for which it may be spent.

Mailable Letter. A typewritten letter that is suitable to send out when judged for accuracy of transcription and neatness and accuracy of typing.

Maintenance. The keeping of buildings and equipment in repair.

Maintenance of Plant. Those activities which are concerned with keeping the grounds, buildings, and equipment at their original condition of completeness or efficiency, either through repairs or by replacements of property. (Anything less than replacement of a total building.)

Major. The principal subject area studied by a student.

Malnutrition. A condition of imperfect nutrition resulting in retardation of healthy physical growth.

Manual. A booklet describing a test, book, or teaching method, indicating the use of the materials described and suggesting procedures to be followed.

Manuscript. An author's copy in typewriting or handwriting of an article, chapter, manual, or book to be put into printed form.

Mark. A rating of a pupil's achievement, such as A, B, C, D, or F.

Marking System. Any method or system of symbols used for recording the achievement of pupils in their studies at school.

Master Key. A key adapted to open several locks differing somewhat from each other.

Master List. The principal, most complete, or most authoritative listing of anything educational.

Master Teacher. A teacher who has exceptional ability in the art of teaching.

Matching Funds. Money that a school district must match or provide in order to receive money from other sources such as the state or federal government.

Mean. A synonym for arithmetic average or mean.

Median. The midway point in a list on either side of which is 50 per cent of the scores or items.

Mentally Retarded. A person with a mild degree of mental backwardness or dullness.

Merit System. Any plan for paying teachers on the basis of their efficiency.

Middle Grades. Grades 4, 5, and 6, or to any two of these grades, in an elementary school.

Mid-score. The middle score when an odd number of scores are arranged in ascending or descending order; if an even number of scores, the mean of the two middle scores.

Migrant Children. Children whose parents move periodically to and from certain sections of the country for the purpose of seasonal employment.

Minor. A field of study to which the student devotes less time than to the major.

Monitor. A pupil to whom is assigned the responsibility of performing some routine task.

Monograph. A treatise or research in the form of an enlarged bulletin or small book.

Month, Calendar. The conventional calendar of months, each month beginning with the first day of the new month. COMPARE MONTH, SCHOOL.

Month, School. The system of months, commencing with the opening day of school, in which a new month arbitrarily is started on a Monday at intervals of about four weeks.

Morale. Courage and faith maintained in the face of adversity.

Mother Goose. Old English rhymes, first compiled and published in London about 1760 by John Newbery.

Motivation. The use of incentives for the purpose of causing a pupil or student to excel in his school work.

Multiplication Tables. The arrangement of numbers, usually from 1 to 12, showing the value of each number when multiplied consecutively by the next higher number.

Multi-purpose Room. A room in an elementary school that can be used for several purposes, such as an auditorium or a cafeteria.

Net Expenditure of an Activity. The actual outlay of money by a school activity for some service or object after the deduction of any discounts, rebates, or reimbursements.

Norm. See Teacher-Pupil Ratio.

Norm, Class. The average number of pupils assigned to a class or teacher.

Nursery School. A beginning group or class that is organized to provide educational experiences for children for the year immediately preceding the kindergarten and conducted during the regular school year.

Operation of Plant. Those activities which are concerned with keeping the physical plant open and ready for use. It includes cleaning, disinfecting, heating, moving furniture, caring for grounds, operating telephone switchboards, and other such housekeeping activities which are repeated somewhat regularly: daily, weekly, monthly, or seasonally. It does not include repairing.

Overachiever. A pupil who does better in school than ordinarily expected for his ability.

Payroll. A list of individual employees entitled to pay, with the amounts due to each for personal services rendered.

Percentile. A point on a scale of test scores or other measures. This point is identified by the percentage of cases lying below it. Thus, 39 per cent of the measures fall below the 39th percentile and 61 per cent above it.

Personal and Contracted Services. Services rendered by personnel on a salary or contractual basis for the operation of an activity. It may include the full-time, part-time, and prorated portions of salaries paid out of a school activity fund for coaches, sponsors, trainers, and similar personnel, and for other contracted services such as fees for entertainment programs, producing publications, and photographing individuals and groups.

Petty Cash. A sum of money, either in the form of currency or a special bank deposit, set aside for the purpose of making change or immediate payments of comparatively small amount.

Petty Cash Voucher. A voucher used to support expenditures paid by cash.

Posting. The act of transferring to an account in a ledger the detailed or summarized data contained in the cash receipts book, check register, journal voucher, or similar books or documents of original entry.

Practice Teacher. An advanced student in a teacher-training institution who, as a part of his program, works in an elementary or secondary school for a period learning to perform many of the duties of a regular teacher. Sometimes called Cadet Teacher.

Principal. The administrative head of a school (not school district) to whom has been delegated the major responsibility for the coordination and supervision of the activities of the school.

Professional Education. Courses that stress preparation for a profession.

Prorating. The allocation of parts of a single expenditure to two or more different accounts in proportion to the benefits which the expenditure provides for the purpose or program area for which the accounts were established.

Purchase Order. A document which authorizes the delivery of specified merchandise or the rendering of certain services and the making of a charge for them.

Rebates. Abatements or refunds.

Receipts. Income to be used for the purpose of financing student activities and organizations.

Records. Written statements of information which are made by a person, unit, or organization for the use of that person, unit, or organization.

Refund. (1) An amount paid back or credit allowed because of an over-collection or on account of the return of an object sold; (2) to pay back or allow credit for an amount because of an over-collection or because of the return of an object sold; (3) to provide for the payment of a loan through cash or credit secured by a new loan.

Reimbursement. Cash or other assets received as a repayment of the cost of work or services performed, or of other expenditures made for or on behalf of another governmental unit or department, or for an individual, firm, or corporation.

Repairs. The restoration of a given piece of equipment, of a given building, or of grounds to original condition of completeness or efficiency from a worn, damaged, or deteriorated condition.

Replacement of Equipment. A complete unit of equipment purchased to take the place of another complete unit of equipment which is to be sold, scrapped, or written off the record, and serving the same purpose as the replaced unit in the same way.

Reports. Written statements of information which are made by a person, unit, or organization for the use of some other person, unit, or organization.

Requisition. A written demand or request, usually from one department to the purchasing officer or to another department, for specified articles or services.

Retirement Fund System. A plan whereby a fund of money, built up through contributions from participants and other sources, is used to make regular payments to those who retire from service in the educational system by reason of age, disability, or length of service.

Salary. The total amount regularly paid or stipulated to be paid to an individual, before deductions, for personal services rendered while on the payroll of the school activity.

Salary, Single. The practice of paying teachers the same salary regardless of whether teaching in an elementary school or a high school.

School, Accredited. A school that has been designated by a competent agency as meeting accepted standards or criteria of quality.

School, Junior High. A separately organized secondary school intermediate between elementary and senior high school.

School, Secondary. In this handbook a secondary school comprises any span of grades beginning with the next grade following the elementary school and ending with or below grade 12, including junior high schools, the different types of high schools, and vocational or trade high schools.

School, Senior High. A school offering the final years of high school work necessary for graduation; invariably preceded by a junior high school in the same system.

School, Vocational. A secondary school which is separately organized under a principal for the purpose of offering training in one or more skilled or semi-skilled trades or occupations.

School Bus. A vehicle with a manufacturer's rated seating capacity of 12 or more. (Seating capacity figured on the basis of at least 13 inches width of seat space per pupil.)

School Plant. The site, buildings, and equipment constituting the physical facilities used by a single school or by two or more schools sharing the use of common facilities.

School Publications. Newspapers, magazines, yearbooks, handbooks, or similar material produced by students for circulation among students and the public.

School Site. The land and all improvements to the site, other than structures, such as grading, drainage, drives, parking areas, walks, plantings, play courts, and playfields.

Secondary School. A high school, junior high school, or senior high school.

Senior High School. A school for grades 10, 11, and 12. If grade 9 is included the school is called *high school*.

Student-Body Activities. Direct and personal services for public school pupils, such as interscholastic athletics, entertainments, publications, clubs, band, and orchestra, that are managed or operated by the student body under the guidance and direction of adults, and are not part of the regular instructional program.

Student Organization, Club. An organized group of students with basically the same interests whose main objective is the furtherance of these interests. Included are social, hobby, instructional, recreational, athletic, honor, dramatic, musical, and similar clubs or societies which are managed and operated by the students under the direction and supervision of adults. All clubs must be approved by the proper school authorities.

Supervisors of Instruction. School personnel who have been delegated the responsibility of assisting teachers in improving the learning situation and instructional methods.

Supply. A material item of an expendable nature that is consumed, worn out, or deteriorated in use; or one that loses its identity through fabrication or incorporation into a different or more complex unit or substance.

Teacher-Pupil Ratio. The number of students divided by the number of instructors. Also called pupil-teacher ratio.

Technical Education. Courses that stress the use and appreciation of the course content.

Textbooks. Books obtained primarily for use in certain classes, grades, or other particular student groups rather than for general school use.

Times Tables. See multiplication tables.

Trade Discount. An allowance, usually varying in percentage with volume of transactions, made to those engaged in certain businesses and allowable irrespective of the time when the account is paid. The term should not be confused with "cash discount."

Trade School. A school offering trade instruction to prepare youths or adults for definite trades or occupations.

Underachiever. A pupil who does not do as well in school as his abilities indicate he can do.

Unified School District. A school district of the same boundaries having both elementary and secondary schools administered by a single board of education.

Vehicle, Privately Owned. A vehicle owned by the contractor; a vehicle partially owned by the contractor (for instance the contractor may own the chassis and the school own the body); or a car used by a parent who is paid from the activity funds to transport his own children and sometimes other children to school activities.

Voucher. A document which authorizes the payment of money and usually indicates the accounts to be charged.

Warrant. A written order drawn by the school board or its authorized officer directing the school district treasurer to pay a specified amount to a designated payee.

Work Order. A written order authorizing and directing the performance of a certain task, issued to the person who is to direct the work. Among the information shown on the order are the nature and location of the job, specifications of the work to be performed, and a job number which is referred to in reporting the amount of labor, materials, and equipment used.

Index